## Stephen Birnbaum Travel Guides

Acapulco
Bahamas, Turks & Caicos
Barcelona
Bermuda
Boston
Canada
Cancun, Cozumel, and Isla Mujeres
Caribbean
Chicago
Disneyland
Eastern Europe
Europe
Europe for Business Travelers
Florence
France
Great Britain
Hawaii
Ireland
Italy
Ixtapa & Zihuatanejo
London
Los Angeles
Mexico
Miami & Ft. Lauderdale
New York
Paris
Portugal
Rome
San Francisco
South America
Spain
United States
USA for Business Travelers
Venice
Walt Disney World
Western Europe

CONTRIBUTING EDITORS

Kathy Arnold
Anton Powell (Walks)
Melinda Tang
Gillian Thomas
Paul Wade

MAPS B. Andrew Mudryk, General Cartography Inc.
SYMBOLS Gloria McKeown

A Stephen Birnbaum Travel Guide

# Birnbaum's
# LONDON
# 1992

**Stephen Birnbaum**
**Alexandra Mayes Birnbaum**
EDITORS

**Lois Spritzer**
EXECUTIVE EDITOR

Laura L. Brengelman
*Managing Editor*

Mary Callahan
Ann-Rebecca Laschever
Beth Schlau
Dana Margaret Schwartz
*Associate Editors*

Gene Gold
*Assistant Editor*

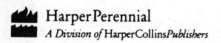 HarperPerennial
*A Division of* HarperCollins*Publishers*

*For Grace and Herbert Mayes, who set the standards and style.*

FIRST EDITION

ISSN: 0749-2561 (Stephen Birnbaum Travel Guides)
ISSN: 1056-4470 (London)
ISBN: 0-06-278033-6 (pbk.)

92 93 94 95 96 CC/MPC 10 9 8 7 6 5 4 3 2 1

# Contents

## WORDS TO THE WISE

## THE CITY

Thorough, qualitative guide to London. Each section offers a comprehensive report on the city's most compelling attractions and amenities, designed to be used on the spot.

## DIVERSIONS

A selective guide to more than a dozen active and/or cerebral theme vacations including the best places in London to pursue them.

## For the Body

## For the Mind

# DIRECTIONS

Eight of the most delightful walks through London.

# A Word from the Editor

This guide, and our guides to Great Britain and Ireland, are dedicated to Grace and Herbert Mayes, my in-laws. Though this dedication indicates the affection and regard in which we hold these two extraordinary people, it is also a recognition of the relationship they had with the British Isles in general, and London in particular.

To put it bluntly, my late father-in-law was an Anglophile of the most fanatic sort. I hardly consider it coincidental that his initials were HRM, his wife's name was Grace, and his two daughters were named Alexandra and Victoria. When he retired after long, successful reigns as editor-in-chief of *Good Housekeeping* and then *McCall's* magazines, he moved to London, where he occupied a flat just across the street from Hyde Park that someone once accurately described as "A wonderful place to get knighted." He loved London hard, and roamed every inch of it tirelessly.

His knowledge of the city was encyclopedic, and his enthusiasm for his adopted home was unflagging. The only problem was that he inflicted his zeal for arcane corners of the city on anyone and everyone who crossed his path. My poor, unsuspecting brother-in-law, for example, was once conned into a visit to the Roman Wall — believe me, it is the least impressive relic ever left behind by the Caesars — on what was probably the coldest, dampest day of that winter.

I remember being assaulted continually with the need to see the Reading Room in the *British Museum*. It didn't matter that I'd already seen it several times; I'd never had it shown to me by Herb Mayes! Well, in those days we had an office in Bloomsbury, and one afternoon after a staff lunch, my wife and I decided to walk back a ways toward central London. Our path took us past the *British Museum,* and as though we had made a specific date, there was her father pacing in front of the entrance. There was no choice but to capitulate when he suggested that this was a perfect time to visit the Reading Room.

If I told you the truth, I'd have to admit that seeing the Reading Room through his eyes made the experience special, only proving that you can visit the same place again and again and still not see it all. Learning how much is left to be learned is a sign of maturity in any undertaking, and traveling teaches this lesson as well as anything I know.

My own evolution as a traveler (which happily continues) is mirrored by the evolution of our guidebook series. When we began our series of contemporary travel guides, we logically began with "area" books, attempting to publish guides that would include the widest possible number of attractive destinations. When the public seemed to accept our new way of delivering travel data, we added titles covering only a single country, and when these became popular we began our newest expansion phase, which centers on a group of books that deal with only a single city. Now we can not only highlight our favorite urban destinations, but really describe how to get the very most out of a visit.

Such treatment in depth only mirrors an increasingly pervasive trend among travelers — the frequent return to a treasured foreign travel spot. Once upon a time, even the most dedicated travelers would visit distant parts of the world no more than once in a lifetime — usually as part of that fabled Grand Tour. But greater numbers of would-be sojourners are now availing themselves of the opportunity to visit a favored part of the world over and over again.

So where once it was routine to say that you'd "seen" a particular city after a very superficial, once-over-lightly encounter, the more perceptive travelers of today recognize that it's entirely possible to have only skimmed the surface of a specific travel destination even after having visited that place more than a dozen times. Similarly, repeated visits to a single site permit true exploration of special interests, whether they be sporting, artistic, or intellectual.

For those of us who spent several years working out the special system under which we present information in this series, the luxury of being able to devote nearly as much space as we like to just a single city is as close to paradise for guide writers and editors as any of us expects to come. But clearly this is not the first guide to the glories of London — one suspects that guides of one sort or another have existed at least since Arthur slipped his sword out of the stone. Guides to London have doubtless existed in one form or another for centuries, so a traveler might logically ask why a new one is suddenly necessary.

Our answer is that the nature of travel to London — and even of the travelers who now routinely make the trip — has changed dramatically of late. For the past 2,000 years or so, travel to any foreign address was an extremely elaborate undertaking, one that required extensive advance planning. Even as recently as the 1950s, a person who had actually been to London could dine out on his or her experiences for years, since such an adventure was quite extraordinary and usually the province of the privileged alone.

With the advent of jet air travel in the late 1950s, however, and of increased-capacity, wide-body aircraft during the 1960s, travel to and around once distant destinations became extremely common. In fact, in more than 2 decades of nearly unending inflation, airfares may be the only commodity in the world that have actually gone down in price.

Attitudes as well as costs have also changed significantly in the last couple of decades. Beginning with the so-called flower children of the 1960s, international travel lost much of its aura of mystery. Whereas their parents might have been happy with just a superficial sampling of London, these young people simply picked up and settled in various parts of Europe for an indefinite stay. While living as inexpensively as possible, they adapted to the local lifestyle, and generally immersed themselves in things European.

Thus began an explosion of travel. And over the years, the development of inexpensive charter flights and packages fueled and sharpened the new American interest in and appetite for more extensive exploration.

Now, in the 1990s, those same flower children who were in the forefront of the modern travel revolution have undeniably aged. While it may be impolite to point out that they are probably well into their untrustworthy thirties and forties, their original zeal for travel remains undiminished. For them, it's hardly news that the best way to get to *Covent Garden* is to make a left heading down the Strand. Such experienced and knowledgeable travelers have decided precisely where they want to go, and are more often searching for ideas and insights to expand their already sophisticated travel consciousnesses.

Obviously, any new guidebook to London must keep pace with and answer the real needs of today's travelers. That's why we've tried to create a guide that's specifically organized, written, and edited for this more demanding modern audience, travelers for whom qualitative information is infinitely more desirable than mere quantities of unappraised data. We think that this book and the other guides in our series represent a new generation of travel guides, one that is especially responsive to modern needs and interests.

For years, dating back as far as Herr Baedeker, travel guides have tended to be encyclopedic, seemingly much more concerned with demonstrating expertise in geography and history than with a real analysis of the sorts of things that actually concern a typical modern tourist. But today, when it is hardly necessary to tell a traveler where London is located (in some cases, the traveler has been there nearly as often as the guidebook editors), it becomes the responsibility of those editors to provide new perspectives and to suggest new directions in order to make the guide genuinely valuable.

That's exactly what we've tried to do in this series. I think you'll notice a different, more contemporary tone to the text, as well as an organization and focus that are distinctive and more functional. And even a random reading of what follows will demonstrate a substantial departure from the standard guidebook orientation, for we've not only attempted to provide information of a more compelling sort, but we also have tried to present it in a format that makes it particularly accessible.

Needless to say, it's difficult to decide precisely what to include in a guidebook of this size — and what to omit. Early on, we realized that giving up the encyclopedic approach precluded our listing of every single route and restaurant, a realization that helped define our overall editorial focus. Similarly, when we discussed the possibility of presenting certain information in other than strict geographic order, we found that the new format enabled us to arrange data in a way we feel best answers the questions travelers typically ask.

Large numbers of specific questions have provided the real editorial skeleton for this book. The volume of mail I regularly receive emphasizes that modern travelers want very precise information, so we've tried to organize our material in the most responsive way possible. Readers who want directions to the best pubs or the best places to have a suit made in London will have no trouble extracting that data from this guide.

Travel guides are, understandably, reflections of personal taste, and putting one's name on a title page obviously puts one's preferences on the line. But I think I ought to amplify just what "personal" means. I don't believe in the sort of personal guidebook that's a palpable misrepresentation on its face. It is, for example, hardly possible for any single travel writer to visit thousands of restaurants (and nearly as many hotels) in any given year and provide accurate appraisals of each. And even if it were physically possible for one human being to survive such an itinerary, it would of necessity have to be done at a dead sprint and the perceptions derived therefrom would probably be less valid than those of any other intelligent individual visiting the same establishments. It is, therefore, impossible (especially in a large, annually revised guidebook *series* such as we offer) to have only one person provide all the data on the entire world.

I also happen to think that such individual orientation is of substantially less value to readers. Visiting a single hotel for just one night, or eating one hasty meal in a random restaurant hardly equips anyone to provide appraisals that are of more than passing interest. No amount of doggedly alliterative or oppressively onomatopoeic text can camouflage a technique that is essentially specious. We have, therefore, chosen what I like to describe as the "thee and me" approach to restaurant and hotel evaluation and, to a somewhat more limited degree, to the sites and sights we have included in the other sections of our text. What this really reflects is a personal sampling tempered by intelligent counsel from informed local sources, and these additional friends-of-the-editors are almost always residents of the city and/or area about which they are consulted.

Despite the presence of several editors, writers, researchers, and local correspondents, very precise editing and tailoring keep our text fiercely subjective. So what follows is the gospel according to the Birnbaums, and represents as much of our own taste and instincts as we can manage. It is probable, therefore, that if you like your cities stylish and prefer small hotels with personality to huge high-rise anonymities, we're likely to have a long and meaningful relationship. Readers with dissimilar tastes may be less enraptured.

I also should point out something about the person to whom this guidebook is directed. Above all, he or she is a "visitor." This means that such elements as restaurants have been specifically picked to provide the visitor with a representative, enlightening, stimulating, and above all, pleasant experience. Since so many extraneous considerations can affect the reception and service accorded a regular restaurant patron, our choices can in no way be construed as an exhaustive guide to resident dining. We think we've listed all the best places, in various price ranges, but they were chosen with a visitor's enjoyment in mind.

Other evidence of how we've tried to tailor our text to reflect modern travel habits is most apparent in the section we call DIVERSIONS. Where once it was common for travelers to spend a foreign visit in a determinedly passive state, the emphasis is far more active today. So we've organized every activity we could reasonably evaluate and presented the material in a way that is especially accessible to activists of either athletic or cerebral bent. It is no longer necessary, therefore, to wade through a pound or two of superfluous prose just to find the very best crafts shop or the quaintest country inn within a reasonable distance of the city.

If there is a single thing that best characterizes the revolution in and evolution of current holiday habits, it is that most travelers now consider travel a right rather than a privilege. No longer is a trip to the far corners of the globe necessarily a once-in-a-lifetime thing; nor is the idea of visiting exotic, faraway places in the least worrisome. Travel today translates as the enthusiastic desire to sample all of the world's opportunities, to find that elusive quality of experience that is not only enriching but comfortable. For that reason, we've tried to make what follows not only helpful and enlightening but the sort of welcome companion of which every traveler dreams.

Finally, I also should point out that every good travel guide is a living enterprise; that is, no part of this text is carved in stone. In our annual revisions, we refine, expand, and further hone all our material to serve your travel needs better. To this end, no contribution is of greater value to us than your personal reaction to what we have written, as well as information reflecting your own experiences while using the book. We earnestly and enthusiastically solicit your comments about this book *and* your opinions and perceptions about places you have recently visited. In this way, we will be able to provide the most current information — including the actual experiences of recent travelers — and to make those experiences more readily available to others. So please write to us at 60 E. 42nd St., New York, NY 10165.

We sincerely hope to hear from you.

STEPHEN BIRNBAUM

# How to Use This Guide

A great deal of care has gone into the organization of this guide-book, and we believe it represents a real breakthrough in the presentation of travel material. Our aim is to create a new, more modern generation of travel books and to make this guide the most useful and practical travel tool available today.

Our text is divided into five basic sections in order to present information in the best way on every possible aspect of a London vacation. This organization itself should alert you to the vast and varied opportunities available, as well as indicate all the specific data necessary to plan a successful trip. You won't find much of the conventional "swaying palms and shimmering sand" text here; we've chosen instead to deliver more useful and practical information. Prospective itineraries tend to speak for themselves, and with so many diverse travel opportunities, we feel our main job is to highlight what's where and to provide basic information — how, when, where, how much, and what's best — to assist you in making the most intelligent choices possible.

Here is a brief summary of the five basic sections and what you can expect to find in each. We believe that you will find both your travel planning and en-route enjoyment enhanced by having this book at your side.

## GETTING READY TO GO

This mini-encyclopedia of practical travel facts is a sort of know-it-all companion with all the precise information necessary to create a successful trip to London. There are entries on more than 2 dozen separate topics, including how to get where you're going, what preparations to make before leaving, what your trip is likely to cost, and how to avoid prospective problems. The individual entries are specific, realistic, and where appropriate, cost-oriented.

We expect you to use this section most in the course of planning your trip, for its ideas and suggestions are intended to simplify this often confusing period. Entries are intentionally concise, in an effort to get to the meat of the matter with the least extraneous prose. These entries are augmented by extensive lists of specific sources from which to obtain even more specialized data, plus some suggestions for obtaining travel information on your own.

### Words to the Wise

The English, of course, speak English — but their use of words isn't always the same ours (our boot is something to be worn on the foot; in Great Britain, it's the trunk of the car). This collection of often-used words and phrases will help you order a meal or a drink, shop, and get around.

## THE CITY

Our individual report on London has been created with the assistance of researchers, contributors, professional journalists, and experts who live in the city. Although useful at the planning stage, THE CITY is really designed to be taken along and used on the spot. The report offers a short-stay guide, including an essay introducing the city as a historic entity and as a contemporary place to visit. *At-a-Glance* material is actually a site-by-site survey of the most important, interesting (and sometimes most eclectic) sights to see and things to do. *Sources and Resources* is a concise listing of pertinent information meant to answer a range of potentially pressing questions as they arise — simple things such as the address of the local tourist office, how to get around, which sightseeing tours to take, when special events occur, where to find the best nightspot or hail a taxi, which are the best places to shop, and where the best museums and theaters are to be found. *Best in Town* is our collection of cost-and-quality choices of the best places to eat and sleep on a variety of budgets.

## DIVERSIONS

This section is designed to help travelers find the best places in which to pursue a wide range of physical and cerebral activities, without having to wade through endless pages of unrelated text. This very selective guide lists the broadest possible range of activities, including all the best places to pursue them.

We start with the places, activities, and moments that make up the quintessential London, followed by a list of possible places to stay, eat, drink, and shop, and move to those that require some perspiration — sports preferences and other rigorous pursuits — and go on to report on a number of more cerebral and spiritual vacation opportunities. In every case, our suggestion of a particular location — and often our recommendation of a specific hotel — is intended to guide you to that special place where the quality of experience is likely to be the highest. Whether you seek a romantic hostelry or an inspiring cooking school, each category is the equivalent of a comprehensive checklist of the absolute best in London.

## DIRECTIONS

Here are 8 walks that cover the city, along its main thoroughfares and side streets, past its most spectacular landmarks and magnificent parks. DIRECTIONS is the only section of this book that is organized geographically; itineraries can be "connected" for longer sojourns or used individually for short, intensive explorations.

Although each of the book's sections has a distinct format and a special function, they have all been designed to be used together to provide a complete inventory of travel information. To use this book to full advantage, take a few minutes to read the table of contents and random entries in each section to get a firsthand feel of how it all fits together.

Pick and choose needed information. Assume, for example, that you have always wanted to take that typically British vacation, a culture-rich tour of the city's wealth of museums (with some wonderful dining experiences thrown in for good measure) — but you never really knew how to organize it or where to go. Choose specific museums and restaurants from the selections offered in London, THE CITY, in each walking tour in DIRECTIONS, and in the roundups of the best in the city called *London's Best Restaurants* and *Marvelous Museums* in the DIVERSIONS section.

In other words, the sections of this book are building blocks designed to help you put together the best possible trip. Use them selectively as a tool, a source of ideas, a reference work for accurate facts, and a guidebook to the best buys, the most exciting sights, the most pleasant accommodations, the tastiest food — *the best travel experience* that you can possibly have in London.

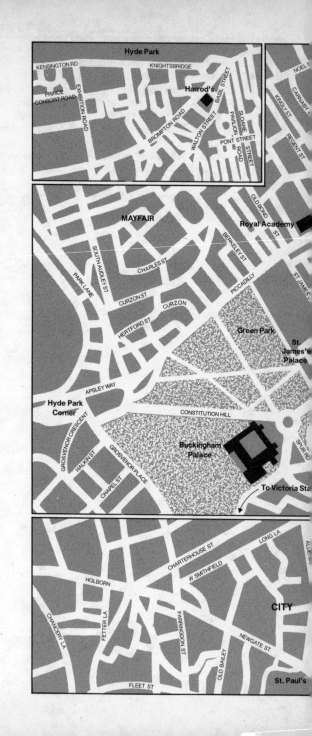

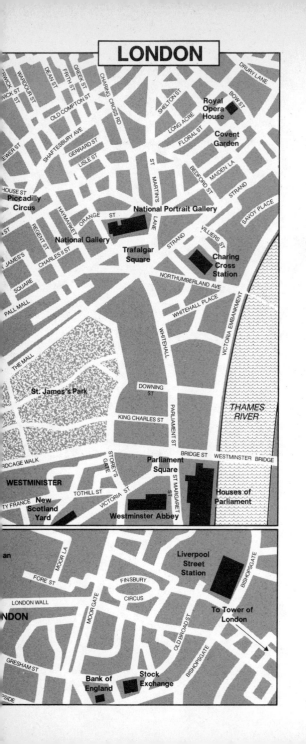

# LONDON

# GETTING READY
# TO GO

# When and How to Go

## What's Where

For a city steeped in tradition and history, London also abounds with the hustle and bustle you would find in any other major metropolis. The center of British economic, political, and cultural life, London has attracted people from all over the world. With 6.8 million people, it is rich, diverse, and commercial. It is filled with art and other treasures that are unique to this city. People come here to explore its intriguing history, made even more mysterious by Sherlock Holmes and Jack the Ripper. Literary buffs come here to retrace the neighborhoods immortalized by Charles Dickens. A mosaic of museums and centuries-old churches and buildings are yours to discover. Its notorious traffic jams, fast-paced city life, and wide choices of nighttime entertainment, all create a city that is totally mesmerizing.

## When to Go

There really isn't a "best" time to visit London. For North Americans, as well as Europeans, the period from April to mid-September has long been — and remains — the peak travel period, traditionally the most popular vacation time.

It is important to emphasize that London, like the rest of Great Britain, is hardly a single-season destination; more and more vacationers who have a choice are enjoying the substantial advantages of off-season travel. Though some tourist attractions may close during the off-season — roughly November to March — the major ones remain open and tend to be less crowded. During the off-season, people relax and British life proceeds at a more leisurely pace. What's more, travel generally is less expensive.

For some, the most convincing argument in favor of off-season travel is the economic one. Getting there and staying there are less expensive during less popular travel periods, as airfares, hotel rooms, and car rental rates go down and less expensive package tours become available; the independent traveler can go farther on less, too.

A definite bonus to visiting during the off-season is that even the most basic services are performed more efficiently. In theory, off-season service is identical to that offered during high season, but the fact is that the absence of demanding crowds inevitably begets much more thoughtful and personal attention.

Even during the off-season, high-season rates may prevail because of an important local event. Particularly in the larger cities, and London is a major commercial city, special events and major trade shows or conferences held at the time of your visit are sure to affect not only the availability of discounts on accommodations, but the basic availability of a place to stay.

It also should be noted that the months immediately before and after the peak summer months — what the travel industry refers to as shoulder seasons — often are sought out because they offer fair weather and somewhat smaller crowds.

In short, like many other popular places, in Great Britain and elsewhere, London's vacation appeal has become multi-seasonal. But the noted exceptions notwithstanding, most travel destinations are decidedly less heavily trafficked and less expensive during the winter.

**CLIMATE:** London maintains fairly moderate temperatures year-round. However, London's temperature can fluctuate widely in a short period of time. For example, the average temperature range is 30–57F (−1–14C) in January, 41–77F (5–24C) in April, 60–86F (10–31C) in July, and 41–68F (5–20C) in October. The London skyline is constantly covered by fog, which can be heavy sometimes, and drizzle and showers can be a daily occurrence. Rain gear is an absolute necessity in this town.

Travelers can get current readings and 3-day Accu-Weather forecasts through *American Express Travel Related Services*' Worldwide Weather Report number. By dialing 900-WEATHER and punching in the access code for numerous travel destinations worldwide, an up-to-date recording will provide current temperature, sky conditions, wind speed and direction, heat index, relative humidity, local time, highway reports, and beach and boating reports or ski conditions (where appropriate). For the weather in London, punch in LON. This 24-hour service can be accessed from any touch-tone phone in the US or Canada and costs 95¢ per minute. The charge will show up on your phone bill. For a free list of the areas covered, send a self-addressed, stamped envelope to *1-900-WEATHER*, 261 Central Ave., Farmingdale, NY 11735.

**SPECIAL EVENTS:** London abounds with cultural events, from opera to rock concerts, ballet to modern dance, Shakespearean plays to experimental theater — there is always something happening for everybody. London is home to two opera companies: The *English National Opera*'s season starts in August and lasts until May, with performances held at the *London Coliseum;* the world-famous *Royal Opera* performs throughout the year at the *Royal Opera House.* The *Royal Ballet* also performs at the *Royal Opera House.* For ticket information, call the box office at 71-240-1066/1911. Events information and schedules are also available by writing to Mailing List, *Royal Opera House,* Covent Garden, London WC2E 9DD (phone: 71-240-1200). Overseas subscription rate is £15.

London is the capital of theater, with over 40 plays showing on any one night. Long-running shows include classics like *Macbeth, A Midsummer Night's Dream,* and *The Mousetrap;* blockbuster hits like *Miss Saigon, Les Misérables,* and *Phantom of the Opera;* and the ever-popular *Cats* and *Me and My Girl.* More recent productions have included *Shirley Valentine* and a revival of Tennessee Williams's *The Rose Tattoo.* In addition, the *Royal Shakespeare Company* performs regularly at *Barbican Centre.*

Classical music lovers would certainly be kept busy in London. Performance venues include the *Royal Albert Hall, Barbican Centre, Queen Elizabeth Hall, Purcell Room,* and the *Royal Festival Hall.* The *BBC Symphony Orchestra, London Symphony Orchestra, National Symphony Orchestra,* the *Royal Philharmonic Orchestra,* and a wide range of international guest artists and musical groups perform regularly at these world-famous concert halls.

The *London International Festival of Theatre* invites theater companies from all over the world to perform in the month of July. The popular *BBC Henry Wood Promenade Concerts,* known as "the *Proms,"* is held every year from July to September in *Royal Albert Hall.* Performances range from Bach and Mozart to jazz and pop music.

For other special events, see *Sources and Resources* in THE CITY.

# Traveling by Plane

Flying is the most efficient way to get to London, and it is the quickest, most convenient means of travel between different parts of Great Britain once you are there.

The air space between North America and Europe is the most heavily trafficked in the world. It is served by dozens of airlines, almost all of which sell seats at a variety of prices under a vast spectrum of requirements and restrictions. You probably will spend more for your airfare than for any other single item in your travel budget, so try to take advantage of the lowest fares offered by either scheduled airlines or charter companies. You should know what kinds of flights are available, the rules under which air travel operates, and all the special package options.

**GATEWAYS:** At present, nonstop flights to London leave from Anchorage, Atlanta, Boston, Chicago, Dallas/Ft. Worth, Detroit, Houston, Los Angeles, Miami, Newark, New York, Orlando, Philadelphia, Pittsburgh, San Francisco, Seattle, Tampa, and Washington, DC. Additional connecting flights depart from some of the above cities and a few others as well.

**SCHEDULED FLIGHTS:** US airlines offering regularly scheduled flights to London are *American, Continental, Delta* (nonstop from Atlanta and Cincinnati), *Northwest* (nonstop from Boston and Minneapolis), *TWA, United,* and *USAir* (nonstop only from Charlotte). *British Airways* operates nonstop flights to London from all of the above cities.

A number of other European carriers serve London from the US with connecting flights through their main hubs: *Air France* via Paris's Charles de Gaulle Airport; *Iberia* from Los Angeles, Miami, and New York via Barcelona and Madrid; *KLM* from Atlanta, Baltimore, Chicago, Houston, Los Angeles, and New York, via Amsterdam; and *TAP Air Portugal* from Boston, Newark, and New York by way of Lisbon. However, all these routes extend the flight time and would not be worth it unless you are planning to stop at the connecting city.

**Tickets** – When traveling on one of the many regularly scheduled flights, a full-fare ticket provides maximum travel flexibility (although at considerable expense) because there are no advance booking requirements. A prospective passenger can buy a ticket for a flight right up to the minute of takeoff — if a seat is available. If your ticket is for a round trip, you can make the return reservation whenever you wish — months before you leave or the day before you return. Assuming foreign immigration requirements are met, you can stay at your destination for as long as you like. (Tickets generally are good for a year and can be renewed if not used.) You also can cancel your flight at any time without penalty. However, while it is true that this category of ticket can be purchased at the last minute, it is advisable to reserve well in advance during popular vacation periods and around holiday times.

**Fares** – Airfares continue to change so rapidly that even experts find it difficult to keep up with them. This ever-changing situation is due to a number of factors, including airline deregulation, volatile labor relations, increasing fuel costs, and vastly increased competition.

Perhaps the most common misconception about fares on scheduled airlines is that the cost of the ticket determines how much service will be provided on the flight. This is true only to a certain extent. A far more realistic rule of thumb is that the less you pay for your ticket, the more restrictions and qualifications are likely to come into play *before* you board the plane (as well as after you get off). These qualifying aspects relate to the months (and the days of the week) during which you must travel, how far in advance you must purchase your ticket, the minimum and maximum amount of time you may or must remain away, your willingness to decide on a return date at the time of booking — and your ability to stick to that decision. It is not uncommon for passengers sitting side by side on the same wide-body jet to have paid fares varying by hundreds of dollars, and all too often the traveler paying more would have been equally willing (and able) to accept the terms of the far less expensive ticket.

In general, the great variety of fares between the US and London can be reduced to four basic categories — first class, business class, coach (also called economy or tourist class), and excursion or discount fares. In addition, Advance Purchase Excursion (APEX) fares offer savings under certain conditions.

In a class by itself is the *Concorde,* the supersonic jet developed jointly by France and Great Britain that cruises at speeds of 1,350 miles per hour (almost twice the speed of sound) and makes transatlantic crossings in half the time (3¾ hours from New York to London) of conventional, subsonic jets. *British Airways* flies from Miami, Washington, DC, and New York to London; *Air France* offers *Concorde* service to Paris from New York. Service is "single" class (with champagne and caviar all the way), and the fare is expensive, about 20% more than a first class ticket on a subsonic aircraft. Some discounts have been offered, but time is the real gift of the *Concorde.* For travelers to European destinations other than Paris or London, this "gift" may be more or less valuable as compared to a direct flight when taking connecting flights into account.

A **first class** ticket admits you to the special section of the aircraft with larger seats, more legroom, better (or more elaborately served) food, free drinks and headsets for movies and music channels, and above all, personal attention. First class fares are about twice those of full-fare (often called "regular") economy.

Behind first class often lies **business class**, usually a separate cabin or cabins. While standards of comfort and service are not as high as in first class, they represent a considerable improvement over conditions in the rear of the plane, with roomier seats, more leg and shoulder space between passengers, and fewer seats abreast. Free liquor and headsets, a choice of meal entrées, and a separate counter for speedier check-in are other inducements. Note that airlines often have their own names for their business class service — such as Le Club on *Air France,* Medallion Class on *Delta,* and Ambassador Class on *TWA.*

The terms of the **coach** or **economy** fare may vary slightly from airline to airline; from time to time airlines may be selling more than one type of economy fare. Coach or economy passengers sit more snugly, as many as 10 in a single row on a wide-body jet, behind the first class and business class sections. Normally, alcoholic drinks are not free, nor are the headsets.

In first, business, and economy class, passengers are entitled to reserve seats and are sold tickets on an open reservation system, with tickets sold up to the last minute if seats are available. The passengers may travel on any scheduled flight they wish, buy a one-way or round-trip ticket, and have the ticket remain valid for a year. There are no requirements for a minimum or maximum stay or for advance booking and no cancellation penalties. The first class and business tickets also allow free stopover privileges; limited free stopovers often are permitted in some economy fares, while with others a surcharge may apply. The cost of economy and business class tickets between the US and London does not vary much in the course of the year.

**Excursion** and other **discount** fares are the airlines' equivalent of a special sale and usually apply to round-trip bookings only. These fares generally differ according to the season and the number of travel days permitted. They are only a bit less flexible than full-fare economy tickets, and are, therefore, often useful for both business and holiday travelers. Most round-trip excursion tickets include strict minimum and maximum stay requirements and can be changed only within prescribed time limits. So don't count on extending a ticket beyond the specified time of return or staying less time than required. Different airlines may have different regulations concerning the number of stopovers permitted, and sometimes excursion fares are less expensive during midweek. The availability of these reduced-rate seats is most limited at busy times such as holidays. Discount or excursion fare ticket holders sit with the coach passengers and, for all intents and purposes, are indistinguishable from them. They receive all the same basic services, even though they may have paid anywhere between 30% and 55% less for the trip. Obviously, it's wise to make plans early enough to qualify for this less expensive transportation if possible.

These discount or excursion fares may masquerade under a variety of names and invariably have strings attached. A common requirement is that the ticket be purchased a certain number of days — usually no fewer than 7 or 14 days — in advance of departure, though it may be booked weeks or months in advance (it has to be "ticketed," or paid for, shortly after booking, however). The return reservation usually has to be made at the time of the original ticketing and cannot be changed later than a certain number of days (again, usually 7 or 14) before the return flight. If events force a passenger to change the return reservation after the date allowed, the difference between the round-trip excursion rate and the round-trip coach rate probably will have to be paid, though most airlines allow passengers to use their discounted fares by standing by for an empty seat, even if the carrier doesn't otherwise have standby fares. Another common condition is the minimum and maximum stay requirement; for example, 1 to 6 days or 6 to 14 days (but including a Saturday night). Last, cancellation penalties of up to 50% of the full price of the ticket have been assessed — check the specific penalty in effect when you purchase your discount/excursion ticket — so careful planning is imperative.

Of even greater risk — and bearing the lowest price of all the current discount fares — is the ticket where no change at all in departure and/or return flights is permitted, and where the ticket price is totally nonrefundable. If you do buy a nonrefundable ticket, you should be aware of a new policy followed by many airlines that may make it easier to change your plans if necessary. For a fee — set by each airline and payable at the airport when checking in — you *may* be able to change the time or date of a return flight on a nonrefundable ticket. However, if the nonrefundable ticket price for the replacement flight is higher than that of the original (as often is the case when trading in a weekday for a weekend flight), you also will have to pay the difference. Any such change must be made a certain number of days in advance — in some cases as little as 2 days — of either the original or the replacement flight, whichever is earlier; restrictions are set by the individual carrier. (Travelers holding a nonrefundable or other restricted ticket who must change their plans due to a family emergency should know that some carriers may make special allowances in such situations; see *Medical and Legal Aid and Consular Services,* in this section.)

One excursion fare available for travel between the US and London comes unencumbered by advance booking requirements and cancellation penalties, permits one stopover (for a fee) in each direction, and has "open jaws," meaning that you can fly to one city and depart from another, arranging and paying for your own transportation between the two. The ticket costs about a third less than economy — during the off-season. High-season prices may be less attractive. The ticket currently is good for a minimum of 7 days and a maximum of 6 months abroad.

There also is a newer, often less expensive, type of excursion fare, the **APEX**, or **Advanced Purchase Excursion**, fare. (In the case of flights to Europe, this type of fare also may be called a "Eurosaver" fare.) As with traditional excursion fares, passengers paying an APEX fare sit with and receive the same basic services as any other coach or economy passengers, even though they may have paid up to 50% less for their seats.

In return, they are subject to certain restrictions. In the case of flights to London, the ticket usually is good for a minimum of 7 days abroad and a maximum, currently, of 2 months (depending on the airline and the destination); and as its name implies, it must be "ticketed," or paid for in its entirety, a certain period of time before departure — usually 21 days, although in the case of London it may be as little as 14 days.

The drawback to an APEX fare is that it penalizes travelers who change their minds — and travel plans. The return reservation must be made at the time of the original ticketing, and if for some reason you change your schedule, you will have to pay a penalty of $100 or 10% of the ticket value, whichever is greater, as long as you travel within the validity period of your ticket. But if you change your return to a date less than the minimum stay or more than the maximum stay, the difference between the round-trip APEX fare and the full round-trip coach rate will have to be paid. There also is a penalty of anywhere from $75 to $125 or more for canceling or changing a reservation *before* travel begins — check the specific penalty in effect when you purchase your ticket. No stopovers are allowed on an APEX ticket, but it is possible to create an open-jaw effect by buying an APEX on a split ticket basis; for example, flying to London and returning from Edinburgh. The total price would be half the price of an APEX to London plus half the price of an APEX to Edinburgh. APEX tickets to Great Britain are sold at basic and peak rates (peak season is around May through September) and may include surcharges for weekend flights.

There also is a Winter or Super APEX, which may go under different names for different carriers. Similar to the regular APEX fare, it costs slightly less but is more restrictive. Depending on the airline and destination, it usually is available only for off-peak winter travel and is limited to a stay of between 7 and 21 days. Advance purchase still is required (currently, 30 days prior to travel), and ticketing must be completed within 48 hours of reservation. The fare is nonrefundable, except in cases of hospitalization or death.

Another type of fare that sometimes is available is the youth fare. At present, most US airlines and *British Airways* are using a form of APEX fare as a youth fare for those age 12 through 24. The maximum stay is extended to a year. Seats can be reserved no more than 3 days before departure, and tickets must be purchased when the reservation is made. The return is booked at time of reservation, or it can be left open. There is no cancellation penalty, but the fare is subject to availability, so it may be difficult to book a return during peak travel periods, and as with the regular APEX fare, it may not even be available for travel to or from Great Britain during high season, especially if you have a strict traveling schedule.

The major airlines serving London from the US also may offer individual excursion fares in conjunction with ground accommodation packages. Previously called ITX, and sometimes referred to as individual tour-basing fares, these fares generally are offered as part of "air/hotel/car/transfer packages," and can reduce the cost of an economy fare by more than a third. The packages are booked for a specific length of time, with return dates specified; rescheduling and cancellation restrictions and penalties vary from carrier to carrier. At the time of this writing, airlines that offer this type of fare to London include *British Airways, KLM,* and major US airlines. Note that their offerings may or may not represent substantial savings over standard economy fares, so check at the time you plan to travel. (For further information on package options, see *Package Tours,* in this section.)

Travelers looking for the least expensive possible airfares should, finally, scan the travel pages of their hometown newspapers (especially the Sunday travel sections) for announcements of special promotional fares. Most airlines traditionally have offered their most attractive special fares to encourage travel during slow seasons, and to inaugurate and publicize new routes. Even if none of these factors apply, prospective passengers can be fairly sure that the number of discount seats per flight at the lowest price is strictly limited, or that the fare offering includes a set expiration date — which means it's absolutely necessary to move fast to enjoy the lowest possible price.

It's always wise to ask about discount or promotional fares and about any conditions that might restrict booking, payment, cancellation, and changes in plans. Check the prices from other neighboring cities. A special rate may be offered in a nearby city but not in yours, and it may be enough of a bargain to warrant your leaving from that city. Ask if there is a difference in price for midweek versus weekend travel, or if there is a further discount for traveling early in the morning or late at night. Also be sure to investigate package deals, which are offered by virtually every airline. These may include a car rental, accommodations, and dining and/or sightseeing features in addition to the basic airfare, and the combined cost of packaged elements usually is considerably less than the cost of the exact same elements when purchased separately.

If in the course of your research you come across a deal that seems too good to be true, keep in mind that logic may not be a component of deeply discounted airfares — there's not always any sane relationship between miles to be flown and the price to get there. More often than not, the level of competition on a given route dictates the degree of discount, and don't be dissuaded from accepting an offer that sounds irresistible just because it also sounds illogical. Better to buy that inexpensive fare while it's being offered and worry about the sense — or absence thereof — while you're flying to your desired destination.

When you're satisfied that you've found the lowest possible price for which you can conveniently qualify, make your booking. You may have to call the airline more than once, because different airline reservations clerks have been known to quote different prices, and different fares will be available at different times for the same flight because of a relatively new computerized airline practice called yield management, which adds or subtracts low-fare seats to a given flight depending on how well it is selling.

To protect yourself against fare increases, purchase and pay for your ticket as soon as possible after you've received a confirmed reservation. Airlines generally will honor their tickets, even if the operative price at the time of your flight is higher than the price you paid; if fares go up between the time you *reserve* a flight and the time you *pay* for it, you likely will be out of luck. Finally, with excursion or discount fares, it is important to remember that when a reservation clerk says that you must purchase a ticket by a specific date, this is an absolute deadline. Miss it and the airline may automatically cancel your reservation without telling you.

**Frequent Flyers** – The leading carriers serving London — including *American, British Airways, Continental, Delta, Northwest, TWA,* and *United* — offer a bonus system to frequent travelers. After the first 10,000 miles, for example, a passenger might be eligible for a first class seat for the coach fare; after another 10,000 miles, he or she might receive a discount on his or her next ticket purchase. The value of the bonuses continues to increase as more miles are logged.

Bonus miles also may be earned by patronizing affiliated car rental companies or hotel chains, or by using one of the credit cards that now offers this reward. In deciding whether to accept such a credit card from one of the issuing organizations that tempt you with frequent flyer mileage bonuses on a specific airline, first determine whether the interest rate charged on the unpaid balance is the same as (or less than) possible alternate credit cards, and whether the annual "membership" fee also is equal or lower. If these charges are slightly higher than those of competing cards, weigh the difference against the potential value in airfare savings. Also ask about any bonus miles awarded just for signing up — 1,000 is common, 5,000 generally the maximum.

For the most up-to-date information on frequent flyer bonus options, you may want to send for the monthly newsletter *Frequent.* Issued by Frequent Publications, it provides current information about frequent flyer plans in general, as well as specific data about promotions, awards, and combination deals to help you keep track of the profusion — and confusion — of current and upcoming availabilities. For a year's subscription, send $33 to Frequent Publications, 4715-C Town Center Dr., Colorado Springs, CO 80916 (phone: 800-333-5937).

There also is a monthly magazine called *Frequent Flyer,* but unlike the newsletter mentioned above, its focus is primarily on newsy articles of interest to business travelers and other frequent flyers. Published by Official Airline Guides (PO Box 58543, Boulder, CO 80322-8543; phone: 800-323-3537), *Frequent Flyer* is available for $24 for a 1-year subscription.

**Low-Fare Airlines** – Increasingly, the stimulus for special fares is the appearance of airlines associated with bargain rates. On these airlines, all seats on any given flight generally sell for the same price, which is somewhat below the lowest discount fare offered by the larger, more established airlines. It is important to note that tickets offered by the smaller airlines specializing in low-cost travel frequently are not subject to the same restrictions as the lowest-priced ticket offered by the more established carriers. They may not require advance purchase or minimum and maximum stays, may involve no cancellation penalties, and may be available one way or round trip. A disadvantage to low-fare airlines, however, is that when something goes wrong, such as delayed baggage or a flight cancellation due to equipment breakdown, their smaller fleets and fewer flights mean that passengers may have to wait longer for a solution than they would on one of the equipment-rich major carriers.

At press time, one of the few airlines offering a consistently low fare to Europe was *Virgin Atlantic* (phone: 800-862-8621 or 212-242-1330), which flies daily from New York (Newark) to London's Gatwick Airport. The airline sells tickets in several categories, including business or "upper" class, economy, APEX, and nonrefundable variations on standby. Fares from New York to London include Late Saver fares — which must be purchased not less than 7 days prior to travel — and Late Late Saver fares — which are purchased no later than 1 day prior to travel.

In a class by itself is *Icelandair,* which always has been a scheduled airline but long has been known as a good source of low-cost flights to Europe. *Icelandair* flies from Baltimore/Washington, DC, New York, and Orlando to Copenhagen (Denmark), Glasgow and London (Great Britain), Gothenburg and Stockholm (Sweden), Helsinki (Finland), Luxembourg (in the country of the same name), Oslo (Norway), Paris (France), and Reykjavik (Iceland). In addition, the airline increases the options for its passengers by offering "thru-fares" on connecting flights to other European cities. (The price of the intra-European flights — aboard Luxembourg's *Luxair* — is included in the price *Icelandair* quotes for the transatlantic portion of the travel to these additional destinations.)

*Icelandair* sells tickets in a variety of categories, from unrestricted economy fares to a sort of standby "3-days-before" fare (which functions just like the youth fares described above but has no age requirement). For reservations and tickets, contact a travel agent or *Icelandair* (phone: 800-223-5500 or 212-967-8888).

**Intra-European Fares** – The cost of the round trip across the Atlantic is not the only expense to consider, for flights between European cities can be quite expensive. But discounts have recently been introduced on routes between some European cities, and other discounts do exist.

Recent Common Market moves toward airline deregulation are expected to lead gradually to a greater number of budget fares. In the meantime, however, the high cost of fares between most European cities can be avoided by careful use of stopover rights on the higher-priced transatlantic tickets — first class, business class, and full-fare economy. If your ticket doesn't allow stopovers, ask about excursion fares such as PEX and Super PEX, APEX, and other excursion fares for one-way trips. If you are able to comply with applicable restrictions (which are similar to those of transatlantic APEX fares) and can use them, you may save as much as 35% to 50% off full-fare economy. Note that these tickets, which once could be bought only after arrival in Europe, now are sold in the US and can be bought before departure.

**Taxes and Other Fees** – Travelers who have shopped for the best possible flight at the lowest possible price should be warned that a number of extras will be added to that price and collected by the airline or travel agent who issues the ticket. These taxes *usually* (but not always) are included in the prices quoted by airline reservations clerks.

The $6 International Air Transportation Tax is a departure tax paid by all passengers flying from the US to a foreign destination. A $10 US Federal Inspection Fee is levied on all air and cruise passengers who arrive in the US from outside North America. Still another fee is charged by some airlines to cover more stringent security procedures, prompted by recent terrorist incidents. The 8% federal US Transportation Tax applies to travel within the US or US territories, as well as to passengers flying between US cities en route to a foreign destination if the trip includes a stopover of more than 12 hours at a US point. Someone flying from Los Angeles to New York and stopping in New York for more than 12 hours before boarding a flight to London, for instance, would pay the 8% tax on the domestic portion of the trip.

**Reservations** – For those who don't have the time or patience to investigate personally all possible air departures and connections for a proposed trip, a travel agent can be of inestimable help. A good agent should have all the information on which flights go where and when, and which categories of tickets are available on each. Most have computerized reservation links with the major carriers, so that a seat can be reserved and confirmed in minutes. An increasing number of agents also possess fare-comparison computer programs, so they often are very reliable sources of detailed competitive price data. (For more information, see *How to Use a Travel Agent,* in this section.)

When making reservations through a travel agent, ask the agent to give the airline your home phone number, as well as your daytime business phone number. All too often the agent uses the agency number as the official contact for changes in flight plans. Especially during the winter, weather conditions hundreds or even thousands of miles away can wreak havoc with flight schedules. Aircraft are constantly in use, and a plane delayed in the Orient or on the West Coast can miss its scheduled flight from the East Coast the next morning. The airlines are fairly reliable about getting this sort of information to passengers if they can reach them; diligence does little good at 10 PM if the airline has only the agency's or an office number.

Reconfirmation is strongly recommended for all international flights, and in the case of flights to London, it is a good idea to confirm your round-trip reservations — especially the return leg — as well as any point-to-point flights within Europe. Some (though increasingly fewer) reservations to and from international destinations are automatically canceled after a required reconfirmation period (typically 72 hours) has passed — even if you have a confirmed, fully paid ticket in hand. It always is wise to call ahead to make sure that the airline did not slip up in entering your original reservation, or in registering any changes you may have made since, and that it has your seat reservation and/or special meal request in the computer. If you look at the printed information on the ticket, you'll see the airline's reconfirmation policy stated explicitly. Don't be lulled into a false sense of security by the "OK" on your ticket next to the number and time of the return flight. This only means that a reservation has been entered; a reconfirmation still may be necessary. If in doubt — call.

If you plan not to take a flight on which you hold a confirmed reservation, by all means inform the airline. Because the problem of "no-shows" is a constant expense for airlines, they are allowed to overbook flights, a practice that often contributes to the threat of denied boarding for a certain number of passengers (see "Getting Bumped," below).

**Seating** – For most types of tickets, airline seats usually are assigned on a first-come, first-served basis at check-in, although some airlines make it possible to reserve a seat at the time of ticket purchase. Always check in early for your flight, even with advance seat assignments. A good rule of thumb for international flights is to arrive at the airport *at least* 2 hours before the scheduled departure to give yourself plenty of time in case there are long lines.

Most airlines furnish seating charts, which make choosing a seat much easier, but there are a few basics to consider. You must decide whether you prefer a window, aisle, or middle seat. On flights where smoking is permitted, you also should specify if you prefer the smoking or nonsmoking section. There is a useful quarterly publication called the *Airline Seating Guide* that publishes seating charts for most major US airlines and many foreign carriers as well. Your travel agent should have a copy, or you can buy the US edition for $39.95 per year and the international edition for $44.95. Order from Carlson Publishing Co., Box 888, Los Alamitos, CA 90720 (phone: 800-728-4877 or 213-493-4877).

Simply reserving an airline seat in advance, however, actually may guarantee very little. Most airlines require that passengers arrive at the departure gate at least 45 minutes (sometimes more) ahead of time to hold a seat reservation. Some US airlines may cancel seat assignments and may not honor reservations of passengers not "checked in" 45 minutes before the scheduled departure time, and they *ask* travelers to check in at least 2 hours before all international flights. It pays to read the fine print on your ticket carefully and plan ahead.

A far better strategy is to visit an airline ticket office (or one of a select group of travel agents) to secure an actual boarding pass for your specific flight. Once this has been issued, airline computers show you as checked in, and you effectively own the seat you have selected (although some carriers may not honor boarding passes of passengers arriving at the gate less than 10 minutes before departure). This also is good — but not foolproof — insurance against getting bumped from an overbooked flight and is, therefore, an especially valuable tactic at peak travel times.

**Smoking –** For information on airline smoking regulations, there is a wallet-size guide that notes in detail the rights of smokers and nonsmokers according to current US regulations. It is available by sending a self-addressed, stamped envelope to ASH (Action on Smoking and Health), Airline Card, 2013 H St. NW, Washington, DC 20006 (phone: 202-659-4310).

**Meals –** If you have specific diet requirements, be sure to let the airline know well before departure time. The available meals include vegetarian, seafood, kosher, Muslim, Hindu, high-protein, low-calorie, low-cholesterol, low-fat, low-sodium, diabetic, bland, and children's menus. There is no extra charge for this option. It usually is necessary to request special meals when you make your reservations — check-in time is too late. It's also wise to reconfirm that your request for a special meal has made its way into the airline's computer — the time to do this is 24 hours before departure. (Note that special meals generally are not available on intra-European flights on small local carriers. If this poses a problem, try to eat before you board, or bring a snack with you.)

**Baggage –** When you fly on a US airline or on a major international carrier such as *British Airways,* US baggage regulations will be in effect. Though airline baggage allowances vary slightly, in general all passengers are allowed to carry on board, without charge, one piece of luggage that will fit easily under a seat of the plane or in an overhead bin and whose combined dimensions (length, width, and depth) do not exceed 45 inches. A reasonable amount of reading material, camera equipment, and a handbag also are allowed. In addition, all passengers are allowed to check two bags in the cargo hold: one usually not to exceed 62 inches when length, width, and depth are combined, the other not to exceed 55 inches in combined dimensions. Generally no single bag may weigh more than 70 pounds.

**Airline Clubs –** US carriers often have clubs for travelers who pay for membership. These clubs are not solely for first class passengers, although a first class ticket *may* entitle a passenger to lounge privileges. Membership (which, by law, requires a fee) entitles the traveler to use the private lounges at airports along their route, to refreshments served in these lounges, and to check-cashing privileges at most of their counters. Extras include special telephone numbers for individual reservations, embossed luggage tags, and a membership card for identification. Airlines serving London that offer membership in such clubs include the following:

> *American:* The *Admiral's Club.* Single yearly membership $175 for the first year; $125 yearly thereafter; spouse an additional $70 per year.
>
> *Continental:* The *President's Club.* Single yearly membership $140 for the first year; $90 yearly thereafter; spouse an additional $25 per year.
>
> *Delta:* The *Crown Club.* Single yearly membership $150; spouse an additional $50 per year.
>
> *Northwest:* The *World Club.* Single yearly membership $150 (plus a onetime $25 initiation fee); spouse an additional $45 per year; 3-year and lifetime memberships also available.
>
> *TWA:* The *Ambassador Club.* Single yearly membership $150, spouse an additional $25; lifetime memberships also available.
>
> *United:* The *Red Carpet Club.* Single yearly membership $200 for the first year; $100 yearly thereafter; spouse an additional $50 per year; 3-year and lifetime memberships also available.

Note that such companies do not have club facilities in all airports. Other airlines also offer a variety of special services in many airports.

**CHARTER FLIGHTS:** By booking a block of seats on a specially arranged flight, charter operators offer travelers air transportation for a substantial reduction over the full coach or economy fare. These operators may offer air-only charters (selling transportation alone) or charter packages (the flight plus a combination of land arrangements such as accommodations, meals, tours, or car rentals). Charters are especially attractive to people living in smaller cities or out-of-the-way places, because they frequently leave from nearby airports, saving travelers the inconvenience and expense of getting to a major gateway.

From the consumer's standpoint, charters differ from scheduled airlines in two main respects: You generally need to book and pay in advance, and you can't change the itinerary or the departure and return dates once you've booked the flight. In practice, however, these restrictions don't always apply. Today, although most charter flights still require advance reservations, some permit last-minute bookings (when there are unsold seats available), and some even offer seats on a standby basis.

Though charters almost always are round-trip, and it is unlikely that you would be sold a one-way seat on a round-trip flight, on rare occasions one-way tickets on charters are offered. Although it may be possible to book a one-way charter in the US, giving you more flexibility in scheduling your return, note that US regulations pertaining to charters may be more permissive than the charter laws of other countries. For example, if you want to book a one-way foreign charter back to the US, you may find advance booking rules in force.

Some things to keep in mind about charter travel:

1. It cannot be repeated often enough that if you are forced to cancel your trip, you can lose much (and possibly all) of your money unless you have cancellation insurance, which is a *must* (see *Insurance,* in this section). Frequently, if the cancellation occurs far enough in advance (often 6 weeks or more), you may forfeit only a $25 or $50 penalty. If you cancel only 2 or 3 weeks before the flight, there

may be no refund at all unless you or the operator can provide a substitute passenger.

2. Charter flights may be canceled by the operator up to 10 days before departure for any reason, usually underbooking. Your money is returned in this event, but there may be too little time for you to make new arrangements.

3. Most charters have little of the flexibility of regularly scheduled flights regarding refunds and the changing of flight dates; if you book a return flight, you must be on it or lose your money.

4. Charter operators are permitted to assess a surcharge, if fuel or other costs warrant it, of up to 10% of the airfare up to 10 days before departure.

5. Because of the economics of charter flights, your plane almost always will be full, so you will be crowded, though not necessarily uncomfortable. (There is, however, a new movement among charter airlines to provide flight accommodations that are more comfort-oriented, so this situation may change in the near future.)

To avoid problems, *always* choose charter flights with care. When you consider a charter, ask your travel agent who runs it and carefully check the company. The Better Business Bureau in the company's home city can report on how many complaints, if any, have been lodged against it in the past. Protect yourself with trip cancellation and interruption insurance, which can help safeguard your investment if you or a traveling companion is unable to make the trip and must cancel too late to receive a full refund from the company providing your travel services. (This is advisable whether you're buying a charter flight alone or a tour package for which the airfare is provided by charter or scheduled flight.)

**Bookings –** If you do take a charter, read the contract's fine print carefully and pay particular attention to the following:

**Instructions concerning the payment of the deposit and its balance and to whom the check is to be made payable.** Ordinarily, checks are made out to an escrow account, which means the charter company can't spend your money until your flight has safely returned. This provides some protection for you. To ensure the safe handling of your money, make out your check to the escrow account, the number of which must appear by law on the brochure, though all too often it is on the back in fine print. Write the details of the charter, including the destination and dates, on the face of the check; on the back, print "For Deposit Only." Your travel agent may prefer that you make out your check to the agency, saying that it will then pay the tour operator the fee minus commission. It is perfectly legal to write the check as we suggest, however, and if your agent objects too vociferously (he or she should trust the tour operator to send the proper commission), consider taking your business elsewhere. If you don't make your check out to the escrow account, you lose the protection of that escrow should the trip be canceled. Furthermore, recent bankruptcies in the travel industry have served to point out that even the protection of escrow may not be enough to safeguard a traveler's investment. More and more, insurance is becoming a necessity. The charter company should be bonded (usually by an insurance company), and if you want to file a claim against it, the claim should be sent to the bonding agent. The contract will set a time limit within which a claim must be filed.

**Specific stipulations and penalties for cancellations.** Most charters allow you to cancel up to 45 days in advance without major penalty, but some cancellation dates are 50 to 60 days before departure.

**Stipulations regarding cancellation and major changes made by the charterer.** US rules say that charter flights may not be canceled within 10 days of departure except when circumstances — such as natural disasters or political upheavals — make it impossible to fly. Charterers may make "major changes," however, such as in the date or place of departure or return, but you are entitled to cancel and receive a full refund if you don't wish to accept these changes. A price increase of more than 10% at any time up to 10 days before departure is considered a major change; no price increase at all is allowed during the last 10 days immediately before departure.

At the time of this writing, the following companies regularly offered charter flights to London. Check with these companies at the time you plan to travel for possible connecting flights from your departure city. As indicated, one of these companies sells charter flights directly to clients, while the others are wholesalers and must be contacted through a travel agent.

> *Amber Tours* (7337 W. Washington St., Indianapolis, IN 46251; phone: 800-225-9920). Retails to the general public.
>
> *American Trans Air* (PO Box 51609, Indianapolis, IN 46251; phone: 317-243-4150). This agent is a wholesaler, so use a travel agent.
>
> *GWV International* (300 First Ave., Needham, MA 02194; phone: 800-225-5498). This agency is a wholesaler, so use a travel agent.
>
> *Travel Charter* (1120 E. Longlake Rd., Detroit, MI 48098; phone: 313-528-3570). This agency is a wholesaler, so use a travel agent.

For the full range of possibilities at the time you plan to travel, you may want to subscribe to the travel newsletter *Jax Fax,* which regularly features a list of charter companies and packagers offering seats on charter flights and may be a source for other charter flights to London. For a year's subscription, send a check or money order for $12 to *Jax Fax* (397 Post Rd., Darien, CT 06820; phone: 203-655-8746).

**DISCOUNTS ON SCHEDULED FLIGHTS:** Promotional fares often are called discount fares because they cost less than what used to be the standard airline fare — full-fare economy. Nevertheless, they cost the traveler the same whether they are bought through a travel agent or directly from the airline. Tickets that cost less if bought from some outlet other than the airline do exist, however. While it is likely that the vast majority of travelers flying to London in the near future will be doing so on a promotional fare or charter rather than on a "discount" air ticket of this sort, it still is a good idea for cost-conscious consumers to be aware of the latest developments in the budget airfare scene. Note that the following discussion makes clear-cut distinctions among the types of discounts available based on how they reach the consumer; in actual practice, the distinctions are not nearly so precise.

**Net Fare Sources –** The newest notion for reducing the costs of travel services comes from travel agents who offer individual travelers "net" fares. Defined simply, a net fare is the bare minimum amount at which an airline or tour operator will carry a prospective traveler. It doesn't include the amount that normally would be paid to the travel agent as a commission. Traditionally, such commissions amount to about 10% on domestic fares and from 10% to 20% on international fares — not counting significant additions to these commission levels that are paid retroactively when agents sell more than a specific volume of tickets or trips for a single supplier. At press time, at least one travel agency in the US was offering travelers the opportunity to purchase tickets and/or tours for a net price. Instead of making its income from individual commissions, this agency assesses a fixed fee that may or may not provide a bargain for travelers; it requires a little arithmetic to determine whether to use the services of a net travel agent or those of one who accepts conventional commissions. One of the potential drawbacks of buying from agencies selling travel services at net fares is that some airlines refuse to do business with them, thus possibly limiting your flight options.

*Travel Avenue* is a fee-based agency that rebates its ordinary agency commission to the customer. For domestic flights, they will find the lowest retail fare, then rebate 7% to 10% (depending on the airline selected) of that price minus a $10 ticket-writing charge. The rebate percentage for international flights varies from 5% to 16% (again depending on the airline), and the ticket-writing fee is $25. The ticket-writing charge is imposed per ticket; if the ticket includes more than eight separate flights, an additional $10 or $25 fee is charged. Customers using free flight coupons pay the ticket-writing charge, plus an additional $5 coupon processing fee.

*Travel Avenue* will rebate its commissions on all tickets, including heavily discounted fares and senior citizen passes. Available 7 days a week, reservations should be made far enough in advance to allow the tickets to be sent by first class mail, since extra charges accrue for special handling. It's possible to economize further by making your own airline reservation, then asking *Travel Avenue* only to write/issue your ticket. For travelers outside the Chicago area, business may be transacted by phone and purchases charged to a credit card. For further information, contact *Travel Avenue* at 641 W. Lake St., Suite 201, Chicago, IL 60606-1012 (phone: 312-876-1116 in Illinois; 800-333-3335 elsewhere in the US).

**Consolidators and Bucket Shops –** Other vendors of travel services can afford to sell tickets to their customers at an even greater discount because the airline has sold the tickets to them at a substantial discount (usually accomplished by sharply increasing commissions to that vendor), a practice in which many airlines indulge, albeit discreetly, preferring that the general public not know they are undercutting their own "list" prices. Airlines anticipating a slow period on a particular route sometimes sell off a certain portion of their capacity to a wholesaler or consolidator. The wholesaler sometimes is a charter operator who resells the seats to the public as though they were charter seats, which is why prospective travelers perusing the brochures of charter operators with large programs frequently see a number of flights designated as "scheduled service." As often as not, however, the consolidator, in turn, sells the seats to a travel agency specializing in discounting. Airlines also can sell seats directly to such an agency, which thus acts as its own consolidator. The airline offers the seats either at a net wholesale price, but without the volume-purchase requirement that would be difficult for a modest retail travel agency to fulfill, or at the standard price, but with a commission override large enough (as high as 50%) to allow both a profit and a price reduction to the public.

Travel agencies specializing in discounting sometimes are called "bucket shops," a term fraught with connotations of unreliability in this country. But in today's highly competitive travel marketplace, more and more conventional travel agencies are selling consolidator-supplied tickets, and the old bucket shops' image is becoming respectable. Agencies that specialize in discounted tickets exist in most large cities, and usually can be found by studying the smaller ads in the travel sections of Sunday newspapers.

Before buying a discounted ticket, whether from a bucket shop or a conventional, full-service travel agency, keep the following considerations in mind: To be in a position to judge how much you'll be saving, first find out the "list" prices of tickets to your destination. Then, do some comparison shopping among agencies. Also bear in mind that a ticket that may not differ much in price from one available directly from the airline may, however, allow the circumvention of such things as the advance purchase requirement. If your plans are less than final, be sure to find out about any other restrictions, such as penalties for canceling a flight or changing a reservation. Most discount tickets are non-endorsable, meaning that they can be used only on the airline that issued them, and they usually are marked "nonrefundable" to prevent their being cashed for a list price refund.

A great many bucket shops are small businesses operating on a thin margin, so it's a good idea to check the local Better Business Bureau for any complaints registered against the one with which you're dealing — before parting with any money. If you still do not feel reassured, consider buying discounted tickets only through a conventional travel agency, which can be expected to have found its own reliable source of consolidator tickets — some of the largest consolidators, in fact, sell only to travel agencies.

A few bucket shops require payment in cash or by certified check or money order, but if credit cards are accepted, use that option. Note, however, if buying from a charter operator selling seats for both scheduled and charter flights, that the scheduled seats are not protected by the regulations — including the use of escrow accounts — governing the charter seats. Well-established charter operators, nevertheless, may extend the same protections to their scheduled flights, and when this is the case, consumers should be sure that the payment option selected directs their money into the escrow account.

Among the numerous consolidators offering discount fares to London are the following:

*Bargain Air* (655 Deep Valley Dr., Suite 355, Rolling Hills, CA 90274; phone: 800-347-2345 or 213-377-2919).

*Maharaja/Consumer Wholesale* (393 Fifth Ave., 2nd Floor, New York, NY 10016; phone: 212-213-2020 in New York; 800-223-6862 elsewhere in the US).

*TFI Tours International* (34 W. 37th St., 12th Floor, New York, NY 10001; phone: 212-736-1140).

*Travac Tours and Charters* (989 Sixth Ave., New York, NY 10018; phone: 212-563-3303).

*25 West Tours* (2490 Coral Way, Miami, FL 33145; phone: 305-856-0810; 800-423-6954 in Florida; 800-252-5052 elsewhere in the US).

*Unitravel* 1177 N. Warson Rd., St. Louis, MO 63132; phone: 314-569-0900 in Missouri; 800-325-2222 elsewhere in the US).

The newsletter *Jax Fax* (see "Charter Flights," above) is also a good source of information on consolidators.

■**Note:** Although rebating and discounting are becoming increasingly common, there is some legal ambiguity concerning them. Strictly speaking, it is legal to discount domestic tickets, but not international tickets. On the other hand, the law that prohibits discounting, the Federal Aviation Act of 1958, is ignored consistently these days, in part because consumers benefit from the practice and in part because many illegal arrangements are indistinguishable from legal ones. Since the line separating the two is so fine that even the authorities can't always tell the difference, it is unlikely that most consumers would be able to do so, and in fact it is not illegal to *buy* a discounted ticket. If the issue of legality bothers you, ask the agency whether any ticket you're about to buy would be permissible under the above-mentioned act.

**OTHER DISCOUNT TRAVEL SOURCES:** An excellent source of information on economical travel opportunities is the *Consumer Reports Travel Letter,* published monthly by Consumers Union. It keeps abreast of the scene on a wide variety of fronts, including package tours, rental cars, insurance, and more, but it is especially helpful for its comprehensive coverage of airfares, offering guidance on all the options from scheduled flights on major or low-fare airlines to charters and discount sources. For a year's subscription, send $37 ($57 for 2 years) to *Consumer Reports Travel Letter* (PO Box 53629, Boulder, CO 80322-3629; phone: 800-999-7959). For information on other travel newsletters, see *Sources and Resources,* in this section.

**Last-Minute Travel Clubs** – Still another way to take advantage of bargain airfares is open to those who have a flexible schedule. A number of organizations, usually set up as last-minute travel clubs and functioning on a membership basis, routinely keep in touch with travel suppliers to help them dispose of unsold inventory at discounts of between 15% and 60%. A great deal of the inventory consists of complete tour packages and cruises, but some clubs offer air-only charter seats and, occasionally, seats on scheduled flights.

Members generally pay an annual fee and receive a toll-free hotline number to call for information on imminent trips. In some cases, they also receive periodic mailings with information on bargain travel opportunities for which there is more advance notice. Despite the suggestive names of the clubs providing these services, last-minute travel does not necessarily mean that you cannot make plans until literally the last minute. Trips can be announced as little as a few days or as much as 2 months before departure, but the average is from 1 to 4 weeks' notice.

Among the organizations regularly offering such discounted travel opportunities to Europe, including Great Britain, are the following:

*Discount Club of America*, 61-33 Woodhaven Blvd., Rego Park, NY 11374 (phone: 800-321-9587 or 718-335-9612). Annual fee: $39 per family.

*Encore Short Notice*, 4501 Forbes Blvd., Lanham, MD 20706 (phone: 800-242-9913). Annual fee: $48 per family.

*Last-Minute Travel Club*, 132 Brookline Ave., Boston, MA 02215 (phone: 800-LAST-MIN or 617-267-9800). As of this year, no fee.

*Moment's Notice*, 425 Madison Ave., New York, NY 10017 (phone: 212-486-0503). Annual fee: $45 per family.

*Spur-of-the-Moment Tours and Cruises*, 10780 Jefferson Blvd., Culver City, CA 90230 (phone: 213-839-2418 in California; 800-343-1991 elsewhere in the US). No fee.

*Traveler's Advantage*, 3033 S. Parker Rd., Suite 1000, Aurora, CO 80014 (phone: 800-548-1116). Annual fee: $49 per family.

*Worldwide Discount Travel Club*, 1674 Meridian Ave., Miami Beach, FL 33139 (phone: 305-534-2082). Annual fee: $40 per person; $50 per family.

**Generic Air Travel** – Organizations that apply the same flexible-schedule idea to air travel only and sell tickets at literally the last minute also exist. The service they provide sometimes is known as "generic" air travel, and it operates somewhat like an ordinary airline standby service, except that the organizations running it offer seats on not one but several scheduled and charter airlines.

One pioneer of generic flights is *Airhitch* (2790 Broadway, Suite 100, New York, NY 10025; phone: 212-864-2000), which arranges flights to London from various US gateways. Prospective travelers register by paying a fee (applicable toward the fare) and stipulate a range of acceptable departure dates and their desired destination, along with alternate choices. The week before the date range begins, they are notified of at least two flights that will be available during the time period, agree on one, and remit the balance of the fare to the company. If they do not accept any of the suggested flights, they lose their deposit; if, through no fault of their own, they do not ultimately get on any agreed-on flight, all of their money is refunded. Return flights are arranged the same way.

**Bartered Travel Sources** – Suppose a hotel buys advertising space in a newspaper. As payment, the hotel gives the publishing company the use of a number of hotel rooms in lieu of cash. This is barter, a common means of exchange among hotels, airlines, car rental companies, cruise lines, tour operators, restaurants, and other travel service companies. When a bartering company finds itself with empty airline seats (or excess hotel rooms, or cruise ship cabin space, and so on) and offers them to the public, considerable savings can be enjoyed.

Bartered-travel clubs often offer discounts of up to 50% to members who pay an annual fee (approximately $50 at press time) which entitles them to select from the flights, cruises, hotel rooms, or other travel services that the club obtained by barter. Members usually present a voucher, club credit card, or scrip (a dollar-denomination voucher negotiable only for the bartered product) to the hotel, which in turn subtracts the dollar amount from the bartering company's account.

Selling bartered travel is a perfectly legitimate means of retailing. One advantage to club members is that they don't have to wait until the last minute to obtain flight or room reservations.

Among the companies specializing in bartered travel, several that frequently offer members travel services to London are the following:

*IGT (In Good Taste) Services* (1111 Lincoln Rd., 4th Floor, Miami Beach, FL 33139; phone: 800-444-8872 or 305-534-7900). Annual fee: $48 per family.

*Travel Guide* (18210 Redmond Way, Redmond, WA 98052; phone: 206-885-1213). Annual fee: $48 per family.

*Travel World Leisure Club* (225 W. 34th St., Suite 2203, New York, NY 10122; phone: 800-444-TWLC or 212-239-4855). Annual fee: $50 per family.

# On Arrival

 **FROM THE AIRPORT TO THE CITY:** London now has four airports. The two main airports are Heathrow (phone: 81-759-4321) and Gatwick (phone: 293-28822), both of which handle international and domestic traffic. Heathrow is 15 miles and about 50 minutes from downtown; a taxi into town will cost about $30 to $40 unless you share — two passengers to the West Central district, for example, pay about $15; three pay $12 each; four, $11 each; and five (the maximum), $10 each. (When sharing, the cab meter is turned off and passengers agree beforehand on the order of destinations. There's a shared-cab rank at Terminal 1, and they're also available at London's 200 taxi stands.) If you aren't carrying heavy luggage, the trip downtown can be made easily on the London underground (subway) from two stations at Heathrow: One serves terminals 1, 2, and 3; the other serves Terminal 4. *Piccadilly Line* trains leave every 4 to 10 minutes and operate between 5 AM (6:45 AM on Sundays) and 11:30 PM; the trip takes about 1 hour. Stops are convenient to most of London's main hotel areas, and the line feeds into the rest of the London underground network. *Airbus A1* runs between Heathrow and Victoria Station (one of the city's main and most central railway terminals); *Airbus* A2 goes from the airport to Euston Station. Both stop at major airport hotels en route. Get a pamphlet at any airport London Transport Information Desk. Facilities for the disabled are available; US currency accepted (phone: 81-995-8092).

Gatwick Airport is 27 miles and 1½ hours from downtown. Express buses leave every 15 minutes and cost about $5. Gatwick is not connected to the underground system, but it does have its own rail station, with express trains leaving for Victoria Station every 15 minutes from 6 AM to 10 PM during the day and hourly through the rest of the night; the cost is about $11. The journey takes about 30 minutes and is by far the best transportation alternative between airport and town. A taxi into the city will cost about $70 and up! *Green Line* bus No. 777 travels between Gatwick Airport and Victoria Station (phone: 81-668-7261 for information) and costs about $5.50 for the 70-minute trip.

London's newest air terminal is the upgraded Stanstead Airport, 30 miles northeast of the city. A shuttle train connects it to Liverpool Street Rail Station (45 minutes). Connections to Scotland and to major cities in Belgium, France, and Holland are relieving pressure on the other London airports.

The London "City" airport is 4 miles from downtown; the 15-minute taxi ride to the airport costs about $16. Riverboat service from either Chelsea Harbour or Charing Cross costs about $4.

**CAR RENTAL:** While cars are useful for day trips outside London, they are usually more trouble than they are worth for touring within the city. The visitor to London and the rest of Great Britain needs to know, however, how to drive in the country and how to rent a car; there are differences from what you are used to at home.

Although there are other options, such as leasing or outright purchase, most travelers who want to drive in Europe simply rent a car. Travelers to London can rent a car through a travel agent or international rental firm before leaving home, or from a local company once they are there.

Renting a car in London is not inexpensive, but it is possible to economize by determining your own needs and then shopping around among the car rental companies until you find the best deal. As you comparison shop, keep in mind that rates vary considerably from location to location. For instance, it might be less expensive to rent a car in the center of London rather than at the airport. Ask about special rates or promotional deals, such as weekend or weekly rates, bonus coupons for airline tickets, or 24-hour rates that include gas and unlimited mileage.

Rental car companies operating in Europe can be divided into three basic categories: large international companies; national or regional companies; and smaller local companies. Because of aggressive local competition, the cost of renting a car can be less expensive once a traveler arrives in Europe, compared to the prices quoted in advance from the US. Local companies usually are less expensive than the international giants.

Given this situation, it's tempting to wait until arriving to scout out the lowest-priced rental from the company located the farthest from the airport high-rent district and offering no pick-up services. But if your arrival coincides with a holiday or a peak travel period, you may be disappointed to find that even the most expensive car in town was spoken for months ago. Whenever possible, it is best to reserve in advance, anywhere from a few days in slack periods to a month or more during the busier seasons.

**Renting from the US** – Travel agents can arrange foreign rentals for clients, but it is just as easy to call and rent a car yourself. Listed below are some of the major international rental companies that have representation in London and have information and reservations numbers that can be dialed toll-free from the US:

*Avis* (phone: 800-331-1084). Has representatives at Heathrow Airport and 8 other city locations.

*Budget* (phone: 800-527-0700). Has representatives at Gatwick and Heathrow airports, and 12 other city locations.

*Dollar Rent-a-Car* (known in Europe as *Eurodollar;* phone: 800-800-6000). Has representatives at Gatwick and Heathrow airports.

*Hertz* (phone: 800-654-3001). Has representatives at Gatwick and Heathrow airports, and 19 other city locations.

*National* (known in Europe as *Europcar;* phone: 800-CAR-EUROPE). Has representatives at Gatwick and Heathrow airports, and 13 other city locations.

It also is possible to rent a car before you go by contacting any number of smaller or less well known US companies that do not operate worldwide. These organizations specialize in European auto travel, including leasing and car purchase in addition to car rental, or actually are tour operators with well-established European car rental programs. These firms, whose names and addresses are listed below, act as agents for a variety of European suppliers, offer unlimited mileage almost exclusively, and frequently manage to undersell their larger competitors by a significant margin.

There are legitimate bargains in car rentals if you shop for them. Call all the familiar car rental names whose toll-free numbers are given above (don't forget to ask about their special discount plans), and then call the smaller companies listed below, all of which offer rentals in London. In the recent past, the latter have tended to offer significantly lower rates, but it always pays to compare. Begin your comparison shopping early, because the best deals may be booked to capacity quickly and may require payment 14 to 21 days or more before picking up the car.

*Auto Europe* (PO Box 1097, Camden, ME 04843; phone: 207-236-8235; 800-223-5555 throughout the US; 800-458-9503 in Canada).

*Europe by Car* (One Rockefeller Plaza, New York, NY 10020; phone: 212-581-3040 in New York State; 800-223-1516 elsewhere in the US; and 9000 Sunset Blvd., Los Angeles, CA 90069; phone: 800-252-9401 or 213-272-0424).

*European Car Reservations* (349 W. Commercial St., Suite 2950, East Rochester, NY 14445; phone: 800-535-3303).

*Foremost Euro-Car* (5430 Van Nuys Blvd., Suite 306, Van Nuys, CA 91401; phone: 818-786-1960 or 800-272-3299 in California; 800-423-3111 elsewhere in the US).

*Kemwel Group* (106 Calvert St., Harrison, NY 10528; phone: 800-678-0678 or 914-835-5555).

*Meier's World Travel* (6033 W. Century Blvd., Suite 1080, Los Angeles, CA 90045; phone: 800-937-0700). In conjunction with major car rental companies, arranges economical rentals throughout Europe, including London.

One of the ways to keep the cost of car rentals down is to deal with a car rental consolidator, such as *Connex International* (23 N. Division St., Peekskill, NY 10566; phone: 800-333-3949 or 914-739-0066). *Connex*'s main business is negotiating with virtually all of the major car rental agencies for the lowest possible prices for its customers. This company arranges rentals throughout Europe, including London.

**Local Rentals** – It long has been common wisdom that the least expensive way to rent a car is to make arrangements in Europe. This is less true today than it used to be. Many medium to large European car rental companies have become the overseas suppliers of stateside companies such as those mentioned previously, and often the stateside agency, by dint of sheer volume, has been able to negotiate more favorable rates for its US customers than the European firm offers its own. Still lower rates may be found by searching out small, strictly local rental companies overseas, whether at less than prime addresses in major cities or in more remote areas. But to find them you must be willing to invest a sufficient amount of vacation time comparing prices on the scene. You also must be prepared to return the car to the location that rented it; drop-off possibilities are likely to be limited.

There is not a wide choice of small local car rental companies in London; however, the local branch of the British Tourist Authority might be able to supply the names of some British car rental companies. The local yellow pages is another good place to begin.

If you are in the mood to splurge on something luxurious, you can hire a chauffeur-driven Rolls-Royce from *Hugh Damien,* located at Heathrow Airport (801 Bath Rd., Cranford, Middlesex TW5 9UJ; phone: 81-897-0555); or call *Avis Luxury Car Services* (220 Norwood Crescent, Hounslow; phone: 81-897-2621) for a chauffeur-driven Rolls-Royce, Daimler, Mercedes, or limousine.

**Requirements** – Whether you decide to rent a car in advance from a large international rental company with European branches or wait to rent from a local company, you should know that renting a car is rarely as simple as signing on the dotted line and roaring off into the night. To drive in London, you need only a valid US driver's license; however, if you plan to rent from a local company, you probably will be asked for an International Driving Permit (IDP; see below), and will have to convince the renting agency that (1) you are personally creditworthy, and (2) you will bring the car back at the stated time. This will be easy if you have a major credit card; most rental companies accept credit cards in lieu of a cash deposit, as well as for payment of your final bill. If you prefer to pay in cash, leave your credit card imprint as a "deposit," then pay your bill in cash when you return the car.

If you are planning to rent a car once you're in London, *Avis, Budget, Hertz,* and other US rental companies usually *will* rent to travelers paying in cash and leaving either a credit card imprint or a substantial amount of cash as a deposit. This is not necessarily standard policy, however, as other international chains, and a number of local and regional European companies will *not* rent to an individual who doesn't have a valid credit card. In this case, you may have to call around to find a company that accepts cash.

Also keep in mind that although the minimum age to drive a car in Great Britain is 17, the minimum age to rent a car is set by the rental company. (Restrictions vary from company to company, as well as at different locations.) Many firms have a minimum age requirement of 21, some raise that to 23 or 25, and for some models of cars it rises to 30. The upper age limit at many companies is between 69 and 75; others have no upper limit or may make drivers above a certain age subject to special conditions.

Don't forget that all car rentals are subject to value added tax. This tax rarely is included in the rental price that's advertised or quoted, but it always must be paid — whether you pay in advance in the US or pay it when you drop off the car. In Great Britain, the VAT rate on car rentals is 17.5%.

Finally, currency fluctuation is another factor to consider. Most brochures quote rental prices in US dollars, but these dollar amounts frequently are only guides; that is, they represent the prevailing rate of exchange at the time the brochure was printed. The rate may be very different when you call to make a reservation, and different again when the time comes to pay the bill (when the amount owed may be paid in cash in foreign currency or as a charge to a credit card, which is recalculated at a still later date's rate of exchange). Some companies guarantee rates in dollars (often for a slight surcharge), but this is an advantage only when the value of the dollar is steadily declining overseas. If the dollar is growing stronger in Great Britain, you may be better off with rates guaranteed in British pounds.

**Driving documents –** A valid driver's license from his or her own state of residence is required for a US citizen to drive in Great Britain. In addition, an International Driving Permit (IDP), which is a translation of the US license in 9 languages, may be required if you plan to rent a car from a local firm.

You can obtain your IDP, before you leave, from most branches of the *American Automobile Association (AAA)*. Applicants must be at least 18 years old, and the application must be accompanied by two passport-size photos (some *AAA* branches have a photo machine available), a valid US driver's license, and a fee of $10. The IDP is good for 1 year and must be accompanied by your US license to be valid.

Proof of liability insurance also is required and is a standard part of any car rental contract. (To be sure of having the appropriate coverage, let the rental staff know in advance about any national borders you plan to cross.) Car rental companies also make provisions for breakdowns, emergency service, and assistance; ask for a number to call when you pick up the vehicle.

**Rules of the road –** Contrary to first impressions, British drivers generally are prudent and efficent on the road. Driving in Great Britain is on the left side of the road. Passing is on the right; the right turn signal must be flashing before and while passing, and the left indicator must be used when pulling back to the right. In most larger cities, such as London, honking is forbidden (except to avoid accidents) at night between 11 PM and 7:30 AM in residential areas; flash your headlights instead. Also, don't be intimidated by tailgaters — everyone does it.

Note that cars coming from the left at intersections do not automatically have the right of way; however, pedestrians, provided they are in marked crosswalks, have priority over all vehicles. In many areas, signposting is meager, and traffic at intersections converges from all directions, resulting in a proceed-at-your-own-risk flow.

In the city, speed limits usually are 30 mph (about 48 kph). Outside the city, the speed limit is 70 mph (about 112 kph) on major motorways, 60 mph (about 96 kph) on secondary motorways, and 50 mph (about 80 kph) on country roads.

■**Note:** Finding a parking spot in London can be a major hassle. There are controlled parking zones in all the major thoroughfares in the city, and drivers who park in those areas risk having their cars clamped or towed away, and getting a heavy fine of up to £60.

**Gasoline –** Called "petrol" in Great Britain, gasoline is sold either by the liter (which is slightly more than 1 quart; approximately 3.8 liters equal 1 US gallon) or by the British or "imperial" gallon, which is 20% larger than the American gallon (1 imperial gallon equals about 1.2 US gallons). Both leaded (regular) and unleaded gas are available (as is diesel fuel) in a variety of grades. Unleaded gas is common in London but still a rarity in some parts of Great Britain, so at least until all gas stations sell unleaded, your safest bet if you're planning to drive outside the city is to rent a car that takes leaded gasoline.

Gas prices everywhere rise and fall depending on the world supply of oil, and an American traveling overseas is further affected by the prevailing rate of exchange, so it is difficult to say exactly how much fuel will cost when you travel. It is not difficult to predict, however, that gas prices will be much higher in Great Britain than you are accustomed to paying in the US.

# Package Tours

If the mere thought of buying a package for visiting London conjures up visions of a march through the city in lockstep with a horde of frazzled fellow travelers, remember that packages have come a long way. For one thing, not all packages necessarily are escorted tours, and the one you buy does not have to include any organized touring at all — nor will it necessarily include traveling companions. If it does, however, you'll find that people of all sorts — many just like yourself — are taking advantage of packages today because they are economical and convenient, save you an immense amount of planning time, and exist in such variety that it's virtually impossible not to find one that suits at least the majority of your travel preferences. Given the high cost of travel these days, packages have emerged as a particularly wise buy.

In essence, a package is just an amalgam of travel services that can be purchased in a single transaction. A London package (tour or otherwise) may include any or all of the following: round-trip transatlantic transportation, transfers between the airport and the hotel, local transportation (and/or car rentals), accommodations, some or all meals, sightseeing, entertainment, taxes, tips, escort service, and a variety of incidental features that might be offered as options at additional cost. Its principal advantage is that it saves money: The cost of the combined arrangements invariably is well below the price of all of the same elements if bought separately, and, particularly if transportation is provided by charter or discount flight, the whole package could cost less than just a round-trip economy airline ticket on a regularly scheduled flight. A package provides more than economy and convenience: It releases the traveler from having to make individual arrangements for each separate element of a trip.

Tour programs generally can be divided into two categories — "escorted" (or locally hosted) and "independent." An escorted tour means that a guide will accompany the group from the beginning of the tour through to the return flight; a locally hosted tour means that the group will be met upon arrival at each location by a different local host. On independent tours (which are the ones generally available for visiting cities, such as London), there usually is a choice of hotels, meal plans, and sightseeing trips in each city, as well as a variety of special excursions. The independent plan is for travelers who do not want a totally set itinerary, but who do prefer confirmed hotel reservations. Always bring along complete contact information for your tour operator in case a problem arises, although US tour operators often have European affiliates who can give additional assistance or make other arrangements on the spot.

To determine whether a package — or, more specifically, *which* package — fits your travel plans, start by evaluating your interests and needs, deciding how much and what you want to spend, see, and do. Gather whatever package tour information is available for your schedule. Be sure that you take the time to read the brochure *carefully* to determine precisely what is included. Keep in mind that travel brochures are written to entice you into signing up for a package tour. Often the language is deceptive and devious. For example, a brochure may quote the lowest prices for a package tour based on facilities that are unavailable during the off-season, undesirable at any season, or just plain nonexistent. Information such as "breakfast included" (as it often is in packages to Great Britain) or "plus tax" (which can add up) should be taken into account. Note, too, that the prices quoted in brochures almost always are based on double occupancy: The rate listed is for each of two people sharing a double room, and if you travel alone, the supplement for single accommodations can raise the price considerably (see *Hints for Single Travelers,* in this section).

In this age of erratic airfares, the brochure most often will *not* include the price of an airline ticket in the price of the package, though sample fares from various gateway cities usually will be listed separately, to be added to the price of the ground arrangements. Before figuring your actual cost, check the latest fares with the airlines, because the samples invariably are out of date by the time you read them. If the brochure gives more than one category of sample fares per gateway city — such as an individual tour-basing fare, a group fare, an excursion, APEX, or other discount ticket — your travel agent or airline tour desk will be able to tell you which one applies to the package you choose, depending on when you travel, how far in advance you book, and other factors. (An individual tour-basing fare is a fare computed as part of a package that includes land arrangements, thereby entitling a carrier to reduce the air portion almost to the absolute minimum. Though it always represents a savings over full-fare coach or economy, lately the individual tour-basing fare has not been as inexpensive as the excursion and other discount fares that also are available to individuals. The group fare usually is the least expensive fare, and it is the tour operator, not you, who makes up the group.) When the brochure does include round-trip transportation in the package price, don't forget to add the cost of round-trip transportation from your home to the departure city to come up with the total cost of the package.

Finally, read the general information regarding terms and conditions and the responsibility clause (usually in fine print at the end of the descriptive literature) to determine the precise elements for which the tour operator is — and is not — liable. Here the tour operator frequently expresses the right to change services or schedules as long as equivalent arrangements are offered. This clause also absolves the operator of responsibility for circumstances beyond human control, such as floods, or injury to you or your property. While reading, ask the following questions:

1. Does the tour include airfare or other transportation, sightseeing, meals, transfers, taxes, baggage handling, tips, or any other services? Do you want all these services?
2. If the brochure indicates that "some meals" are included, does this mean a welcoming and farewell dinner, two breakfasts, or every evening meal?
3. What classes of hotels are offered? If you will be traveling alone, what is the single supplement?
4. Does the tour itinerary or price vary according to the season?

5. Are the prices guaranteed; that is, if costs increase between the time you book and the time you depart, can surcharges unilaterally be added?
6. Do you get a full refund if you cancel? If not, be sure to obtain cancellation insurance.
7. Can the operator cancel if too few people join? At what point?

One of the consumer's biggest problems is finding enough information to judge the reliability of a tour packager, since individual travelers seldom have direct contact with the firm putting the package together. Usually, a retail travel agent is interposed between customer and tour operator, and much depends on his or her candor and cooperation. So ask a number of questions about the tour you are considering. For example:

● Has the travel agent ever used a package provided by this tour operator?
● How long has the tour operator been in business? Check the Better Business Bureau in the area where the tour operator is based to see if any complaints have been filed against it.
● Is the tour operator a member of the *United States Tour Operators Association* (*USTOA;* 211 E. 51st St., Suite 12B, New York, NY 10022; phone: 212-944-5727)? *USTOA* will provide a list of its members upon request; it also offers a useful brochure, *How to Select a Package Tour.*
● How many and which companies are involved in the package?
● If air travel is by charter flight, is there an escrow account in which deposits will be held; if so, what is the name of the bank?

This last question is very important. US law requires that tour operators place every charter passenger's deposit and subsequent payment in a proper escrow account (see "Charter Flights," above).

■**A word of advice:** Purchasers of vacation packages who feel they're not getting their money's worth are more likely to get a refund if they complain in writing to the operator — and bail out of the whole package immediately. Alert the tour operator or resort manager to the fact that you are dissatisfied, that you will be leaving for home as soon as transportation can be arranged, and that you expect a refund. They may have forms to fill out detailing your complaint; otherwise, state your case in a letter. Even if difficulty in arranging immediate transportation home detains you, your dated, written complaint should help in procuring a refund from the operator.

**SAMPLE PACKAGES:** Generally speaking, escorted tours cover whole countries or sections of countries. For stays that feature London only, you would be looking at an independent city package, sometimes known at a "stay-put" program. Basically the city package includes round-trip transfer between airport and hotel, a choice of hotel accommodations (usually including breakfast) in several price ranges, plus any number of other features you may not need or want but would lose valuable time arranging if you did. Common package features are 1 or 2 half-day guided tours of the city; a boat cruise; passes for unlimited local travel by bus or train; discount cards for shops, museums, and restaurants; temporary membership in and admission to clubs, disco-theques, or other nightspots; and car rental for some or all of your stay. Other features may include anything from a souvenir travel bag to a tasting of local wines, dinner, and a show. The packages usually are a week long — although 4-day and 14-day packages also are available, and most packages can be extended by extra days — and often are hosted; that is, a representative of the tour company may be available at a local office or even in the hotel to answer questions, handle problems, and assist in arranging activities and option excursions.

Among companies offering package tours in Great Britain are the following:

*Abercrombie & Kent* (1520 Kensington Rd., Suite 212, Oak Brook, IL 60521; phone: 708-954-2944 in Illinois; 800-323-7308 elsewhere in the US). Offers escorted tours, as well as independent self-drive packages.

*Abreu Tours* (317 E. 34th St., New York, NY 10016; phone: 800-223-1580 or 212-661-0555). Offers 3- to 6-night packages in London.

*American Express Travel Related Services* (offices throughout the US; phone: 800-241-1700 for information and local branch offices). Offers 4- to 7-night packages in London and Edinburgh.

*California Parlor Car Tours* (1101 Van Ness Ave., San Francisco, CA 94109; phone: 800-331-9259). The US representative of Frames Tours in London, a 100-year-old company that specializes in tours of Great Britain, it offers a wide range of programs including London and other British cities.

*Cavalcade Tours* (450 Harmon Meadow Blvd., Secaucus, NJ 07094; phone: 800-356-2405). Offers 7-night packages in London. As this tour operator is a wholesaler, bookings must be made through a travel agent.

*Collette Tours* (124 Broad St., Pawtucket, RI 02860; phone: 800-752-2655 in New England, New Jersey and New York or 800-832-4656 elsewhere in the US). Offers a number of different itineraries in London.

*Contiki Holidays* (1432 E. Katella Ave., Anaheim, CA 92805; phone: 714-937-0611 or 800-624-0611 in California; 800-626-0611 elsewhere in the US). This agency specializes in travel for the younger set. It offers 11- to 37-day motorcoach tours in Europe that include excursions in London.

*Dailey-Thorp Travel* (315 W. 57th St., New York, NY 10019; phone: 212-307-1555). This music and opera specialist regularly offers cultural tours in London, such as a London Cultural Week package, with tickets to a top West End production, the *Royal Opera,* and the *Royal Shakespeare Company.*

*Edwards & Edwards* (1 Times Sq. Plaza, 20th Floor, New York, NY 10036; phone: 212-944-0290 in New York State; 800-223-6108 elsewhere in the US). Packages 3- and 5-night London show tours. Their 7-night Week on the British Aisle includes 3 evenings of London theater, to which can be added an overnight theater tour to Stratford-upon-Avon and/or a 2-night tour to Edinburgh.

*Globus-Gateway and Cosmos* (95-25 Queens Blvd., Rego Park, NY 11374; phone: 800-221-0090; or 150 S. Los Robles Ave., Pasadena, CA 91101; phone: 818-449-2019 or 800-556-5454). These affiliated agencies offer 8- to 28-day escorted tours in Great Britain and Europe that include excursions in London. If you prefer to travel on your own, there is a 7-day independent city package in London. Note that bookings must be made through a travel agent.

*Insight International Tours* (745 Atlantic Ave., Suite 720, Boston, MA 02111; phone: 800-582-8380 or 617-426-6666). It offers 4- to 38-day escorted tours in Great Britain and other European countries, all of which include 1- or 2-day excursions in London. It also can arrange independent programs.

*Jet Vacations* (1775 Broadway, New York, NY 10019; phone: 212-247-0999 or 800-JET-0999). Offers London city packages with a wide range of hotel choices.

*Keith Prowse & Co. Ltd.* (234 W. 44th St., Suite 902, New York, NY 10036; phone: 800-669-7469 or 212-398-1430). Offers several Star-Studded London packages, including tickets to the hottest shows in town.

*Marsans International* (19 W. 34th St., Suite 302, New York, NY 10001; phone: 212-239-3880 in New York State; 800-777-9110 elsewhere in the US). Offers 4- to 7-night packages in London.

*Maupintour* (PO Box 807, Lawrence, KA 66044; phone: 800-255-4266). Offers a variety of packages in Great Britain, including a 14-day English Countryside tour that begins and ends in London.

*Mill-Run Tours* (20 E. 49th St., New York, NY 10017; phone: 212-486-9840 in New York State; 800-MILL-RUN elsewhere). Offers 3-night packages in London.

*Petrabax Tours* (97-45 Queens Blvd., Suite 505, Rego Park, NY 11374; phone: 718-897-7272 in New York State; 800-367-6611 elsewhere). Offers 6-night city packages in London.

*Saga Holidays* (120 Boylston St., Boston, MA 02116-9719; phone: 617-451-6808 or 800-343-0273). This company specializes in older travelers. It offers an 18-day package, visiting London, Brussels, Heidelberg, and Paris, among other cities, as well as a 23-day tour of Great Britain that includes London and cities in Ireland and Scotland.

*SuperCities* (7855 Haskell Ave., Van Nuys, CA 91406; phone: 818-988-7844 or 800-633-3000). Offers 2- and 3-night packages. This tour operator is a wholesaler, so use a travel agent.

*Thomas Cook* (*In London:* 45 Berkeley St., Piccadilly, London W1A 1EB, England; phone: 71-499-4000. Also has offices throughout the US.) The best known British tour operator, *Cook*'s tours span the world. Among the packages centered in Great Britain is a 17-day Best of Britain tour that visits London, as well as Cambridge, Cardiff, and Edinburgh. Although this company is a wholesaler, you can book a tour directly through any of its offices in major cities in North America or through travel agents.

*Travcoa* (PO Box 2630, Newport Beach, CA 92658; phone: 800-992-2004 or 714-476-2800 in California; 800-992-2003 elsewhere in the US). This deluxe tour operator offers various escorted tours throughout Great Britain, including excursions to London.

*Travel Bound* (599 Broadway, Penthouse, New York, NY 10012; phone: 212-334-1350 or 800-456-8656). Offers flexible city packages, depending on arrangements desired. This tour operator is a wholesaler, so use a travel agent.

*Trophy Tours* (1810 Glenville Rd., Suite 124, Richardson, TX 75081; phone: 800-527-2473). An associate of *Gray Line,* it offers a wide range of half- and one-day sightseeing trips in and around London.

And for the golfer — there are a number of courses surrounding the city — *ITC Golf Tours* (Box 5144, Long Beach, CA 90805; phone: 213-595-6905 or 800-257-4981) can arrange custom golf packages anywhere and any way you want it, including in and around London.

There also are packages focused around — and guaranteeing entrance in — London's spring marathon, one of the the world's largest. Both *Keith Prowse & Co. Ltd.* (address above) and *Marathon Tours* (108 Main St., Boston, MA 02129; phone: 617-242-7845) offer these.

Among sports-oriented packages for spectators are the seven *Wimbledon* tennis packages run by *Keith Prowse & Co. Ltd.* (234 W. 44th St., Suite 902, New York, NY 10036; phone: 800-669-7469 or 212-398-1430). The most popular packages include seats for 4 days of play on the Centre and No. 1 courts and tickets to either the men's final and ladies' semifinals or the ladies' final and men's semifinals. For the horsey set are the *Keith Prowse & Co.* packages to the *Derby* at *Epsom Downs* and to *Royal Ascot.*

Many of the major air carriers maintain their own tour departments or subsidiaries to stimulate vacation travel to the cities they serve. In all cases, the arrangements may be booked through a travel agent or directly with the company.

*American Airlines FlyAAway Vacations* (Southern Reservation Center, Mail Drop 1000, Box 619619, Dallas/Fort Worth Airport, TX 75261-9619; phone: 800-321-2121).

*British Airways Holidays* (65-70 Astoria Blvd., Jackson Heights, NY 11370; phone: 800-AIRWAYS).

*Delta's Dream Vacations* (PO Box 1525, Fort Lauderdale, FL 33302; phone: 800-872-7786).

*KLM's Vacation Center* (3755 W. Alabama St., Suite 750, Houston, TX 77098; phone: 800-777-1668).

*Northwest WorldVacations* (5130 Highway 101, Minnetonka, MN; phone: 800-727-1400).

*TWA Getaway* (10 E. Stow Rd., Marlton, NJ 08053; phone: 800-GETAWAY).

■ **Note:** Frequently, the best city packages are offered by the hotels, which are trying to attract guests during the weekends, when business travel drops off, and during other off periods. These packages are often advertised in the local newspapers and sometimes in the travel sections of big metropolitan papers, such as *The New York Times.* It's worth asking about packages, especially family and special-occasion offerings, when you call to make a hotel reservation. Calling several hotels can garner you a variety of options from which to choose.

# Preparing

## How to Use a Travel Agent

 A reliable travel agent remains the best source of service and information for planning a trip abroad, whether you have a specific itinerary and require an agent only to make reservations or you need extensive help in sorting through the maze of airfares, tour offerings, hotel packages, and the scores of other arrangements that may be involved in a trip to London.

**Know what you want from a travel agent so that you can evaluate what you are getting.** It is perfectly reasonable to expect your agent to be a thoroughly knowledgeable travel specialist, with information about your destination and, even more crucial, a command of current airfares, ground arrangements, and other wrinkles in the travel scene.

**Most travel agents work through computer reservations systems (CRS).** These are used to assess the availability and cost of flights, hotels, and car rentals, and through them they can book reservations. Despite reports of "computer bias," in which a computer may favor one airline over another, the CRS should provide agents with the entire spectrum of flights available to a given destination, as well as the complete range of fares, in considerably less time than it takes to telephone the airlines individually — and at no extra charge to the client.

**Make the most intelligent use of a travel agent's time and expertise; understand the economics of the industry.** As a client, traditionally you pay nothing for the agent's services; with few exceptions, it's all free, from hotel bookings to advice on package tours. Any money the travel agent makes on the time spent arranging your itinerary — booking hotels or flights, or suggesting activities — comes from commissions paid by the suppliers of these services — the airlines, hotels, and so on. These commissions generally run from 10% to 15% of the total cost of the service, although suppliers often reward agencies that sell their services in volume with an increased commission, called an override. In most instances, you'll find that travel agents make their time and experience available to you at no cost, and you do not pay more for an airline ticket, package tour, or other product bought from a travel agent than you would for the same product bought directly from the supplier.

**Exceptions to the general rule of free service by a travel agent are the agencies beginning to practice net pricing.** In essence, such agencies return their commissions and overrides to their customers and make their income by charging a flat fee per transaction instead (thus adding a charge after a reduction for the commissions has been made). Net fares and fees are a growing practice, though hardly widespread.

**Even a conventional travel agent sometimes may charge a fee for special services.** These chargeable items may include long-distance telephone or cable costs incurred in making a booking, for reserving a room in a place that does not pay a commission (such as a small, out-of-the-way hotel), or for special attention such as planning a highly personalized itinerary. A fee also may be assessed in instances of deeply discounted airfares.

**Choose a travel agent with the same care with which you would choose a doctor or lawyer.** You will be spending a good deal of money on the basis of the agent's judgment, so you have a right to expect that judgment to be mature, informed, and interested. At the moment, unfortunately, there aren't many standards within the travel agent industry to help you gauge competence, and the quality of individual agents varies enormously.

**At present, only nine states have registration, licensing, or other forms of travel agent–related legislation on their books.** Rhode Island licenses travel agents; Florida, Hawaii, Iowa, and Ohio register them; and California, Illinois, Oregon, and Washington have laws governing the sale of transportation or related services. While state licensing of agents cannot absolutely guarantee competence, it can at least ensure that an agent has met some minimum requirements.

Perhaps the best way to find a travel agent is by word of mouth. If the agent (or agency) has done a good job for your friends over a period of time, it probably indicates a certain level of commitment and competence. Always ask for the name of the company *and* for the name of the specific agent with whom your friends dealt, for it is that individual who will serve you, and quality can vary widely within a single agency. There are some superb travel agents in the business, and they can facilitate vacation or business arrangements.

# Entry Requirements and Documents

A valid US passport is the only document a US citizen needs to enter Great Britain, and then to reenter the US. As a general rule, a US passport entitles the bearer to remain in Great Britain for up to 6 months as a tourist. A resident alien of the US should inquire at the nearest British consulate (see *The British Embassy and Consulates in the US,* in this section, for addresses) to find out what documents are needed to enter Great Britain; similarly, a US citizen intending to work, study, or reside in Great Britain should also get in touch with the consulate, because a visa will then be required.

Vaccination certificates are required only if the traveler is entering from an area of contagion — which the US is not — as defined by the World Health Organization.

**DUTY AND CUSTOMS:** As a general rule, the requirements for bringing the majority of items *into Great Britain* is that they must be in quantities small enough not to imply commercial import. Among the items that may be taken into the country duty-free are 200 cigarettes, 2 bottles of wine, and 1 bottle of liquor. Personal effects and sports equipment appropriate for a pleasure trip also are allowed.

If you are bringing along a computer, camera, or other electronic equipment for your own use that you will be taking back to the US, you should register the item with the US Customs Service in order to avoid paying duty both entering and returning from Great Britain. (Also see *Customs and Returning to the US,* in this section.) For information on this procedure, as well as for a variety of pamphlets on US customs regulations, contact the local office of the US Customs Service or the central office, PO Box 7407, Washington, DC 20044 (phone: 202-566-8195).

Additional information regarding British customs regulations is available from the British Tourist Authority. See *Tourist Information Offices,* in this section, for addresses of offices in the US.

■ **One rule to follow:** When passing through customs, it is illegal not to declare dutiable items; penalties range from stiff fines and seizure of the goods to prison terms. So don't try to sneak anything through — it just isn't worth it.

# Insurance

It is unfortunate that most decisions to buy travel insurance are impulsive and usually are made without any real consideration of the traveler's existing policies. Therefore, the first person with whom you should discuss travel insurance is your own insurance broker, not a travel agent or the clerk behind the airport insurance counter.

**TYPES OF INSURANCE:** To make insurance decisions intelligently, however, you first should understand the basic categories of travel insurance and what they cover. There are seven basic categories of travel insurance:

1. Baggage and personal effects insurance
2. Personal accident and sickness insurance
3. Trip cancellation and interruption insurance
4. Default and/or bankruptcy insurance
5. Flight insurance (to cover injury or death)
6. Automobile insurance (for driving your own or a rented car)
7. Combination policies

**Baggage and Personal Effects Insurance** – Ask your insurance agent if baggage and personal effects are included in your current homeowner's policy, or if you will need a special floater to cover you for the duration of a trip. The object is to protect your bags and their contents in case of damage or theft anytime during your travels, not just while you're in flight and covered by the airline's policy. Furthermore, only limited protection is provided by the airline, and baggage liability varies from carrier to carrier. For most international flights, including domestic portions of international flights, the airline's liability limit is approximately $9.07 per pound or $20 per kilo (which comes to about $360 per 40-pound suitcase) for checked baggage and up to $400 per passenger for unchecked baggage. These limits should be specified on your airline ticket, but to be awarded any amount, you'll have to provide an itemized list of lost property, and if you're including new and/or expensive items, be prepared for a request that you back up your claim with sales receipts or other proof of purchase.

If you are carrying goods worth more than the maximum protection offered by the airline, consider excess value insurance. Additional coverage is available from airlines at an average, currently, of $1 to $2 per $100 worth of coverage, up to a maximum of $5,000. This insurance can be purchased at the airline counter when you check in, though you should arrive early enough to fill out the necessary forms and to avoid holding up other passengers.

Major credit card companies also provide coverage for lost or delayed baggage — and this coverage often is over and above what the airline will pay. The basic coverage usually is automatic for all cardholders who use the credit card to purchase tickets, but to qualify for additional coverage, cardholders generally must enroll.

Additional baggage and personal effects insurance also is included in certain of the combination travel insurance policies discussed below.

■ **A note of warning:** Be sure to read the fine print of any excess value insurance policy; there often are specific exclusions, such as cash, tickets, furs, gold and silver objects, art, and antiques. Insurance companies ordinarily will pay only the depreciated value of the goods rather than their replacement value. The best way to protect your property is to take photos of your valuables, and keep a record of the serial numbers of such items as cameras, typewriters, laptop computers, radios, and so on. If an airline loses your luggage, you will be asked to fill out a Property Irregularity Report before you leave the airport. Also report the loss to the police (since the insurance company will check with the police when processing your claim).

**Personal Accident and Sickness Insurance** – This covers you in case of illness during your trip or death in an accident. Most policies insure you for hospital and doctor's expenses, lost income, and so on. In most cases, it is a standard part of existing health insurance policies, though you should check with your broker to be sure that your policy will pay for any medical expenses incurred abroad. If not, take out a separate vacation accident policy or an entire vacation insurance policy that includes health and life coverage.

Two examples of such comprehensive health and life insurance coverage are the travel insurance packages offered by *Wallach & Co:*

*HealthCare Global:* This insurance package, which can be purchased for periods of 10 to 180 days, is offered for two age groups: Men and women up to age 75 receive $25,000 medical insurance and $50,000 accidental injury or death benefit; those from ages 76 to 84 are eligible for $12,500 medical insurance and $25,000 injury or death benefit. For either policy, the cost for a 10-day period is $25.

*HealthCare Abroad:* This program is available to individuals up to age 75. For $3 per day (minimum 10 days, maximum 90 days), policy holders receive $100,000 medical insurance and $25,000 accidental injury or death benefit.

Both of these basic programs also may be bought in combination with trip cancellation and baggage insurance at extra cost. For further information, write to *Wallach & Co.,* 243 Church St. NW, Suite 100-D, Vienna, VA 22180 (phone: 703-281-9500 in Virginia; 800-237-6615 elsewhere in the US).

**Trip Cancellation and Interruption Insurance** – Most charter and package tour passengers pay for their travel well before departure. The disappointment of having to miss a vacation because of illness or any other reason pales before the awful prospect that not all (and sometimes none) of the money paid in advance might be returned. So cancellation insurance for any package tour is a must.

Although cancellation penalties vary (they are listed in the fine print of every tour brochure, and before you purchase a package tour you should know exactly what they are), rarely will a passenger get more than 50% of this money back if forced to cancel within a few weeks of scheduled departure. Therefore, if you book a package tour or charter flight, you should have trip cancellation insurance to guarantee full reimbursement or refund should you, a traveling companion, or a member of your immediate family get sick, forcing you to cancel your trip or *return home early.*

The key here is *not* to buy just enough insurance to guarantee full reimbursement for the cost of the package or charter in case of cancellation. The proper amount of coverage should be sufficient to reimburse you for the cost of having to catch up with a tour after its departure or having to travel home at the full economy airfare if you have to forgo the return flight of your charter. There usually is quite a discrepancy between a charter fare and the amount charged to travel the same distance on a regularly scheduled flight at full economy fare.

Trip cancellation insurance is available from travel agents and tour operators in two forms: as part of a short-term, all-purpose travel insurance package (sold by the travel agent); or as specific cancellation insurance designed by the tour operator for a specific charter tour. Generally, tour operators' policies are less expensive, but also less inclusive. Cancellation insurance also is available directly from insurance companies or their agents as part of a short-term, all-inclusive travel insurance policy.

Before you decide on a policy, read each one carefully. (Either type can be purchased from a travel agent when you book the charter or package tour.) Be certain that your policy includes enough coverage to pay your fare from the farthest destination on your itinerary should you have to miss the charter flight. Also, be sure to check the fine print for stipulations concerning "family members" and "pre-existing medical conditions," as well as allowances for living expenses if you must delay your return due to bodily injury or illness.

**Default and/or Bankruptcy Insurance** – Although trip cancellation insurance usually protects you if *you* are unable to complete — or begin — your trip, a fairly recent innovation is coverage in the event of default and/or bankruptcy on the part of the tour operator, airline, or other travel supplier. In some travel insurance packages, this contingency is included in the trip cancellation portion of the coverage; in others, it is a separate feature. Either way, it is becoming increasingly important. Whereas sophisticated travelers long have known to beware of the possibility of default or bankruptcy when buying a charter flight or tour package, in recent years more than a few respected airlines unexpectedly have revealed their shaky financial condition, sometimes leaving hordes of stranded ticket holders in their wake. Moreover, the value of escrow protection of a charter passenger's funds lately has been unreliable. While default/bankruptcy insurance will not ordinarily result in reimbursement in time to pay for new arrangements, it can ensure that you will get your money back, and even independent travelers buying no more than an airplane ticket may want to consider it.

**Flight Insurance** – Airlines have carefully established limits of liability for injury to or the death of passengers on international flights. For all international flights to, from, or with a stopover in the US, all carriers are liable for up to $75,000 per passenger. For all other international flights, the liability is based on where you purchase the ticket: If booked in advance in the US, the maximum liability is $75,000; if arrangements are made abroad, the liability is $10,000. But remember, these liabilities are not the same thing as insurance policies; every penny that an airline eventually pays in the case of injury or death may be subject to a legal battle.

But before you buy last-minute flight insurance from an airport vending machine, consider the purchase in light of your total existing insurance coverage. A careful review of your current policies may reveal that you already are amply covered for accidental death. Be aware that airport insurance, the kind typically bought at a counter or from a vending machine, is among the most expensive forms of life insurance coverage, and that even within a single airport, rates for approximately the same coverage vary widely.

If you buy your plane ticket with a major credit card, you generally receive automatic insurance coverage at no extra cost. Additional coverage usually can be obtained at extremely reasonable prices, but a cardholder must sign up for it in advance.

**Automobile Insurance** – Public liability and property damage (third-party) insurance is compulsory in Europe, and whether you drive your own or a rental car you must carry insurance. Car rentals in Great Britain usually include public liability, property damage, fire, and theft coverage and, sometimes (depending on the car rental company), collision damage coverage with a deductible.

In your car rental contract, you'll see that for about $11 to $13 a day, you may buy optional collision damage waiver (CDW) protection. (If partial coverage with a deductible is included in the rental contract, the CDW will cover the deductible in the event of an accident, and can cost as much as $25 per day.) If you do not accept the CDW coverage, you may be liable for as much as the full retail value of the rental car if it is damaged or stolen; by paying for the CDW, you are relieved of all responsibility for any damage to the car. Before agreeing to this coverage, however, check with your own broker about your existing personal auto insurance policy. It very well may cover your entire liability exposure without any additional cost, or you automatically may be covered by the credit card company to which you are charging the cost of your rental. To find out the amount of rental car insurance provided by major credit cards, contact the issuing institutions.

You also should know that an increasing number of the major international car rental companies automatically are including the cost of the CDW in their basic rates. Car rental prices have increased to include this coverage, although rental company ad campaigns may promote this as a new, improved rental package "benefit." The disadvantage of this inclusion is that you may not have the option to turn down the CDW — even if you already are adequately covered by your own insurance policy or through a credit card company.

Your rental contract (with the appropriate insurance box checked off), as well as proof of your personal insurance policy, if applicable, are required as proof of insurance. If you will be driving your own car in Great Britain, you must carry an International Insurance Certificate, available through insurance brokers in the US.

**Combination Policies** – Short-term insurance policies, which may include a combination of any or all of the types of insurance discussed above, are available through retail insurance agencies, automobile clubs, and many travel agents. These combination policies are designed to cover you for the duration of a single trip.

Companies offering policies of this type include the following:

*Access America International* (600 Third Ave., PO Box 807, New York, NY 10163; phone: 800-284-8300 or 212-490-5345).

*Carefree Travel Insurance* (Arm Coverage, PO Box 310, Mineola, NY 11501; phone: 800-645-2424 or 516-294-0220).

*NEAR Services* (450 Prairie Ave., Suite 101, Calumet City, IL 60409; phone: 708-868-6700 in the Chicago area; 800-654-6700 elsewhere in the US and Canada).

*Tele-Trip Co.* (PO Box 31685, 3201 Farnam St., Omaha, NE 68131; phone: 402-345-2400 in Nebraska; 800-228-9792 elsewhere in the US).

*Travel Assistance International* (1333 15th St. NW, Suite 400, Washington, DC 20005; phone: 202-331-1609 in Washington, DC; 800-821-2828 elsewhere in the US).

*Travel Guard International* (1145 Clark St., Stevens Point, WI 54481; phone: 715-345-0505 in Wisconsin; 800-826-1300 elsewhere in the US).

*Travel Insurance PAK* c/o *The Travelers Companies* (One Tower Sq., Hartford, CT 06183-5040; phone: 203-277-2319 in Connecticut; 800-243-3174 elsewhere in the US).

*WorldCare Travel Assistance Association* (605 Market St., Suite 1300, San Francisco, CA 94105; phone: 800-666-4993 or 415-541-4991).

# Hints for Handicapped Travelers

From 40 to 50 million people in the US have some sort of disability, and over half this number are physically handicapped. Like everyone else today, they — and the uncounted disabled millions around the world — are on the move. More than ever before, they are demanding facilities they can use comfortably, and they are being heard.

Great Britain has been comparatively slow in developing access for the handicapped. Even though most of the modern hotels and restaurants are accessible to a person in a wheelchair, it would be quite an ordeal to try to travel within the city by public transportation, since most of the underground (subway) and train stations are inaccessible to wheelchair passengers, and some underground routes even prohibit wheelchair passengers for safety reasons. However, the London Transport Service publishes a booklet, *Access to the Underground,* detailing which stations are accessible to wheelchairs (even though there aren't many); it is available for £1 from Unit for Disabled Passengers, Regional Transport Service, 55 Broadway, London, SW1H 0BD (phone: 71-918-3312). The London Transport Service also runs a special bus service, called Carelink, for disabled passengers. It is an hourly service and runs among all the major underground and train stations in the city. Generally, unless you are on a special tour for the handicapped, you will need to rely mostly on taxis for transportation. Nevertheless, with ingenuity and the help of an able-bodied traveling companion, you can get around London well enough to thoroughly enjoy its varied delights. What the British lack in facilities for the handicapped, they more than make up for in willingness to help.

**PLANNING:** Collect as much information as you can about facilities for travelers with your sort of disability in London. Make your travel arrangements well in advance and specify to all services involved the exact nature of your condition or restricted mobility. The best way to find out is to write or call the local tourist authority or hotel and ask specific questions. If you require a corridor of a certain width to maneuver a wheelchair or if you need handles on the bathroom walls for support, ask the hotel manager. A travel agent or the local chapter or national office of the organization that deals with your particular disability will supply the most up-to-date information on the subject. The following organizations offer general information on access:

*ACCENT on Living* (PO Box 700, Bloomington, IL 61702; phone: 309-378-2961). This information service for persons with disabilities provides a free list of travel agencies specializing in arranging trips for the disabled; for a copy send a self-addressed, stamped envelope. It also offers a wide range of publications, including a quarterly magazine ($8 per year; $14 for 2 years) for persons with disabilities.

*Mobility International USA (MIUSA;* PO Box 3551, Eugene, OR 97403; phone: 503-343-1284; both voice and TDD). This US branch of *Mobility International,* a nonprofit British organization with affiliates worldwide, offers members advice and assistance — including information on accommodations and other travel services, and publications applicable to the traveler's disability. It also offers a quarterly newsletter and a comprehensive sourcebook, *A World of Options for the 90s: A Guide to International Education Exchange, Community Service and Travel for Persons with Disabilities* ($14 for members; $16 for non-members). Membership includes the newsletter and is $20 a year; subscription to the newsletter alone is $10 annually.

*National Rehabilitation Information Center* (8455 Colesville Rd., Suite 935, Silver Spring, MD 20910; phone: 301-588-9284). A general information, resource, research, and referral service.

*Paralyzed Veterans of America (PVA;* PVA/ATTS Program, 801 18th St. NW, Washington, DC 20006; phone: 202-416-7708 in Washington, DC; 800-424-8200 elsewhere in the US). The members of this national service organization all are veterans who have suffered spinal cord injuries, but it offers advocacy services and information to all persons with a disability. *PVA* also sponsors *Access to the Skies (ATTS),* a program that coordinates the efforts of the national and international air travel industry in providing airport and airplane access for the disabled. Members receive several helpful publications, as well as regular notification of conferences on subjects of interest to the disabled traveler.

*Royal Association for Disability and Rehabilitation (RADAR;* 25 Mortimer St., London W1N 8AB, England; phone: 44-71-637-5400). Offers a number of publications for the handicapped. Their comprehensive guide, *Holidays and Travel*

*Abroad 1991/92 — A Guide for Disabled People,* focuses on international travel. This publication can be ordered by sending payment in British pounds to *RADAR.* As we went to press, it cost just over £6; call for current pricing before ordering.

**Society for the Advancement of Travel for the Handicapped** (*SATH;* 26 Court St., Penthouse, Brooklyn, NY 11242; phone: 718-858-5483). To keep abreast of developments in travel for the handicapped as they occur, you may want to join *SATH,* a nonprofit organization whose members include consumers, as well as travel service professionals who have experience (or an interest) in travel for the handicapped. For an annual fee of $45 ($25 for students and travelers who are 65 and older), members receive a quarterly newsletter and have access to extensive information and referral services. *SATH* also offers a useful publication, *Travel Tips for the Handicapped* (a series of informative fact sheets); to order, send a self-addressed, #10 envelope and $1.

**Travel Information Service** (Moss Rehabilitation Hospital, 1200 W. Tabor Rd., Philadelphia, PA 19141-3099; phone: 215-456-9600 for voice; 215-456-9602 for TDD). This service assists physically handicapped people in planning trips and supplies detailed information on accessibility for a nominal fee.

Blind travelers should contact the *American Foundation for the Blind* (15 W. 16th St., New York, NY 10011; phone: 212-620-2147 in New York State; 800-232-5463 elsewhere in the US) and *The Seeing Eye* (Box 375, Morristown, NJ 07963-0375; phone: 201-539-4425); both provide useful information on resources for the visually impaired. *Note:* All animals imported into Great Britain must go through a 6-month quarantine, including Seeing Eye Dogs. *The American Society for the Prevention of Cruelty to Animals* (*ASPCA,* Education Dept., 441 E. 92 St., New York, NY 10128; phone: 212-876-7700) offers a useful booklet, *Traveling With Your Pet,* which lists inoculation and other requirements by country. It is available for $5 (including postage and handling).

In addition, there are a number of publications — from travel guides to magazines — of interest to handicapped travelers. Among these are the following:

*Access to the World,* by Louise Weiss, offers sound tips for the disabled traveler. Published by Facts on File (460 Park Ave. S., New York, NY 10016; phone: 212-683-2244 in New York State; 800-322-8755 elsewhere in the US; 800-443-8323 in Canada), it costs $16.95. Check with your local bookstore; it also can be ordered by phone with a credit card.

*The Diabetic Traveler* (PO Box 8223 RW, Stamford, CT 06905; phone: 203-327-5832) is a useful quarterly newsletter. Each issue highlights a single destination or type of travel and includes information on general resources and hints for diabetics. A 1-year subscription costs $15. When subscribing, ask for the free fact sheet including an index of special articles; back issues are available for $4 each.

*Guide to Traveling with Arthritis,* a free brochure available by writing to the Upjohn Company (PO Box 307-B, Coventry, CT 06238), provides lots of good, commonsense tips on planning your trip and how to be as comfortable as possible when traveling by car, bus, train, cruise ship, or plane.

*Handicapped Travel Newsletter* is regarded as one of the best sources of information for the disabled traveler. It is edited by wheelchair-bound Vietnam veteran Michael Quigley, who has traveled to 93 countries around the world. Issued every 2 months (plus special issues), a subscription is $10 per year. Write to *Handicapped Travel Newsletter,* PO Box 269, Athens, TX 75751 (phone: 214-677-1260).

*Handi-Travel: A Resource Book for Disabled and Elderly Travellers,* by Cinnie

Noble, is a comprehensive travel guide full of practical tips for those with disabilities affecting mobility, hearing, or sight. To order this book, send $12.95, plus shipping and handling, to the *Canadian Rehabilitation Council for the Disabled,* 45 Sheppard Ave. E., Suite 801, Toronto, Ontario M2N 5W9, Canada (phone: 416-250-7490; both voice and TDD).

*The Itinerary* (PO Box 2012, Bayonne, NJ 07002-2012; phone: 201-858-3400). This bimonthly travel magazine for people with disabilities includes information on accessibility, listings of tours, news of adaptive devices, travel aids, and special services, as well as numerous general travel hints. A subscription costs $10 a year.

*The Physically Disabled Traveler's Guide,* by Rod W. Durgin and Norene Lindsay, rates accessibility of a number of travel services and includes a list of organizations specializing in travel for the disabled. It is available for $9.95, plus shipping and handling, from Resource Directories, 3361 Executive Pkwy., Suite 302, Toledo, OH 43606 (phone: 419-536-5353 in the Toledo area; 800-274-8515 elsewhere in the US).

*Ticket to Safe Travel* offers useful information for travelers with diabetes. A reprint of this article is available free from local chapters of the *American Diabetes Association.* For the nearest branch, contact the central office at 505 Eighth Ave., 21st Floor, New York, NY 10018 (phone: 212-947-9707 in New York State; 800-232-3472 elsewhere in the US).

*Travel for the Patient with Chronic Obstructive Pulmonary Disease,* a publication of the George Washington University Medical Center, provides some sound practical suggestions for those with emphysema, chronic bronchitis, asthma, or other lung ailments. To order, send $2 to Dr. Harold Silver, 1601 18th St. NW, Washington, DC 20009 (phone: 202-667-0134).

*Traveling Like Everybody Else: A Practical Guide for Disabled Travelers*, by Jacqueline Freedman and Susan Gersten, offers the disabled tips on traveling by car, cruise ship, and plane, as well as lists of accessible accommodations, tour operators specializing in tours for disabled travelers, and other resources. It is available for $11.95, plus postage and handling, from Modan Publishing, PO Box 1202, Bellmore, NY 11710 (phone: 516-679-1380).

*Travel Tips for Hearing-Impaired People,* a free pamphlet for deaf and hearing-impaired travelers, is available from the *American Academy of Otolaryngology* (One Prince St., Alexandria, VA 22314; phone: 703-836-4444). For a copy, send a self-addressed, stamped, business-size envelope to the academy.

*Travel Tips for People with Arthritis,* a free 31-page booklet published by the *Arthritis Foundation,* provides helpful information regarding travel by car, bus, train, cruise ship, or plane, planning your trip and medical considerations, and includes listings of helpful resources, such as associations and travel agencies that operate tours for disabled travelers. For a copy, contact your local *Arthritis Foundation* chapter, or write to the national office, PO Box 19000, Atlanta, GA 30326 (phone: 404-872-7100).

A few more basic resources to look for are *Travel for the Disabled,* by Helen Hecker ($9.95), and by the same author, *Directory of Travel Agencies for the Disabled* ($19.95). *Wheelchair Vagabond,* by John G. Nelson, is another useful guide for travelers confined to a wheelchair (hardcover, $14.95; paperback, $9.95). All three are published by Twin Peaks Press, PO Box 129, Vancouver, WA 98666 (phone: 800-637-CALM or 206-694-2462).

Another good source of information is the British Tourist Authority. The US offices provide an information pamphlet about disabled travelers in Great Britain. They can also provide information about accessibility of certain hotels and tourist areas. (For the addresses of this agency's US branches, see *Tourist Information Offices,* in this section.)

Two organizations based in Great Britain offer information for handicapped persons traveling throughout Europe, including London. *Tripscope* (63 Esmond Rd., London W4 1JE, UK; phone: 44-81-994-9294) is a telephone-based information and referral service (not a booking agent) that can help with transportation options for journeys throughout Europe. It may, for instance, be able to recommend outlets leasing small family vehicles adapted to accommodate wheelchairs. *Tripscope* also provides information on cassettes for blind or visually impaired travelers, and accepts written requests for information from those with speech impediments. And for general information, there's *Holiday Care Service* (2 Old Bank Chambers, Station Rd., Horley, Surrey RH6 9HW, UK; phone: 44-293-774535), a first-rate, free advisory service on accommodations, transportation, and holiday packages throughout Europe for disabled visitors.

Regularly revised hotel and restaurant guides use the symbol of access (a person in a wheelchair; see the symbol at the beginning of this section) to point out accommodations suitable for wheelchair-bound guests. The red *Michelin Guide to Great Britain* (Michelin; $19.95), found in general and travel bookstores, is one such publication.

**PLANE:** The US Department of Transportation (DOT) has ruled that US airlines must accept all passengers with disabilities. As a matter of course, US airlines were pretty good about accommodating handicapped passengers even before the ruling, although each airline has somewhat different procedures. Foreign airlines also generally are good about accommodating the disabled traveler, but again, policies vary from carrier to carrier. Ask for specifics when you book your flight.

Disabled passengers always should make reservations well in advance and should provide the airline with all relevant details of their conditions. These details include information on mobility and equipment that you will need the airline to supply — such as a wheelchair for boarding or portable oxygen for in-flight use. Be sure that the person to whom you speak fully understands the degree of your disability — the more details provided, the more effective help the airline can give you.

On the day before the flight, call back to make sure that all arrangements have been prepared, and arrive early on the day of the flight so that you can board before the rest of the passengers. It's a good idea to bring a medical certificate with you, stating your specific disability or the need to carry particular medicine.

Because most airports have jetways (corridors connecting the terminal with the door of the plane), a disabled passenger usually can be taken as far as the plane, and sometimes right onto it, in a wheelchair. If not, a narrow boarding chair may be used to take you to your seat. Your own wheelchair, which will be folded and put in the baggage compartment, should be tagged as escort luggage to assure that it's available at planeside upon landing rather than in the baggage claim area. Travel is not quite as simple if your wheelchair is battery-operated: Unless it has non-spillable batteries, it might not be accepted on board, and you will have to check with the airline ahead of time to find out how the batteries and the chair should be packaged for the flight. Usually people in wheelchairs are asked to wait until other passengers have disembarked. If you are making a tight connection, be sure to tell the attendant.

Passengers who use oxygen may not use their personal supply in the cabin, though it may be carried on the plane as cargo when properly packed and labeled. If you will need oxygen during the flight, the airline will supply it to you (there is a charge) provided you have given advance notice — 24 hours to a few days, depending on the carrier.

Useful information on every stage of air travel, from planning to arrival, is provided in the booklet *Incapacitated Passengers Air Travel Guide.* To receive a free copy, write to the *International Air Transport Association* (Publications Sales Department, 2000 Peel St., Montreal, Quebec H3A 2R4, Canada; phone: 514-844-6311). Another helpful publication is *Air Transportation of Handicapped Persons,* which explains the general guidelines that govern air carrier policies. For a copy of this free booklet, write to the US Department of Transportation (Distribution Unit, Publications Section, M-443-2, Washington, DC 20590) and ask for "Free Advisory Circular #AC-120-32." *Access Travel: A Guide to the Accessibility of Airport Terminals,* a free publication of the *Airport Operators Council International,* provides information on more than 500 airports worldwide — including major airports throughout Europe — and offers ratings of 70 features, such as accessibility to bathrooms, corridor width, and parking spaces. For a copy, contact the Consumer Information Center (Dept. 563W, Pueblo, CO 81009; phone: 719-948-3334).

Among the major carriers serving Great Britain, the following airlines have TDD toll-free lines in the US for the hearing-impaired:

>*American:* 800-582-1573 in Ohio; 800-543-1586 elsewhere in the US.
>*Continental:* 800-343-9195.
>*Delta:* 800-831-4488.
>*Northwest:* 800-242-1713.
>*TWA:* 800-252-0622 in California; 800-421-8480 elsewhere in the US.
>*United:* 800-942-8819 in Illinois; 800-323-0170 elsewhere in the US.
>*USAir:* 800-242-1713 in Pennsylvania; 800-245-2966 elsewhere in the US.

**GROUND TRANSPORTATION:** Perhaps the simplest solution to getting around is to travel with an able-bodied companion who can drive. Another alternative in Great Britain is to hire a driver with a car. The organizations listed above may be able to help you make arrangements — another source is your hotel concierge.

If you are accustomed to driving your own hand-controlled car and are determined to rent one, you may have to do some extensive research, as in Great Britain it is difficult to find rental cars fitted with hand controls. If agencies do provide hand-controlled cars, they are apt to be offered only on a limited basis in major metropolitan areas, such as London, and usually are very much in demand. The best course is to contact the major car rental agencies listed in "Car Rental" in *Traveling by Plane,* in this section, well before your departure (at least 7 days, much earlier preferably); but be forewarned, you still may be out of luck. Other sources for information on vehicles adapted for the handicapped are the organizations discussed above.

The *American Automobile Association (AAA)* publishes a useful booklet, *The Handicapped Driver's Mobility Guide.* Contact the central office of your local *AAA* club for availability and pricing, which may vary at different branch offices.

**TOURS:** Programs designed for the physically impaired are run by specialists, and the following travel agencies and tour operators specialize in making group and individual arrangements for travelers with physical or other disabilities:

>*Access: The Foundation for Accessibility by the Disabled* (PO Box 356, Malverne, NY 11565; phone: 516-887-5798). A travelers' referral service that acts as an intermediary with tour operators and agents worldwide, and provides information on accessibility at various locations.
>*Accessible Tours/Directions Unlimited* (720 N. Bedford Rd., Bedford Hills, NY 10507; phone: 914-241-1700 in New York State; 800-533-5343 elsewhere in the continental US). Arranges group or individual tours for disabled persons traveling in the company of able-bodied friends or family members. Accepts the unaccompanied traveler if completely self-sufficient.
>*Evergreen Travel Service* (4114 198th St. SW, Suite 13, Lynnwood, WA 98036-6742; phone: 206-776-1184 or 800-435-2288 throughout the continental US and Canada). It offers worldwide tours for the disabled (Wings on Wheels Tours) and the sight-impaired/blind (White Cane Tours).
>*Flying Wheels Travel* (143 W. Bridge St., Box 382, Owatonna, MN 55060; phone:

507-451-5005 or 800-535-6790). Handles both tours and individual arrangements.

*Guided Tour* (613 W. Cheltenham Ave., Suite 200, Melrose Park, PA 19126-2414; phone: 215-782-1370). Arranges tours for people with developmental and learning disabilities and sponsors separate tours for members of the same population who also are physically disabled or who simply need a slower pace.

*Handi-Travel* (First National Travel Ltd., Thornhill Sq., 300 John St., Suite 405, Thornhill, Ontario L3T 5W4, Canada; phone: 416-731-4714). Handles individual arrangements.

*USTS Travel* (11 E. 44th St., New York, NY 10017; phone: 800-487-8787 or 212-687-5121). Travel agent and registered nurse Mary Ann Hamm designs trips for individual travelers requiring all types of kidney dialysis and handles arrangements for the dialysis.

*Whole Person Tours* (PO Box 1084, Bayonne, NJ 07002-1084; phone: 201-858-3400). Handicapped owner Bob Zywicki travels the world with his wheelchair and offers a lineup of escorted tours (many conducted by him) for the disabled. Call for current itinerary at the time you plan to travel. *Whole Person Tours* also publishes *The Itinerary,* a bimonthly newsletter for disabled travelers (see the publication source list above).

Travelers who would benefit from being accompanied by a nurse or physical therapist also can hire a companion through *Traveling Nurses' Network,* a service provided by Twin Peaks Press (PO Box 129, Vancouver, WA 98666; phone: 800-637-CALM or 206-694-2462). For a $10 fee, clients receive the names of three nurses, whom they can then contact directly; for a $125 fee, the agency will make all the hiring arrangements for the client. Travel arrangements also may be made in some cases — the fee for this further service is determined on an individual basis.

A similar service is offered by *MedEscort International* (ABE International Airport, PO Box 8766, Allentown, PA 18105; phone: 800-255-7182 in the continental US; elsewhere, call 215-791-3111). The service arranges for clients to be accompanied by a nurse, paramedic, respiratory therapist, or physician. The fees are based on the disabled traveler's needs. *MedEscort* also can assist in making travel arrangements.

# Hints for Single Travelers

Just about the last trip in human history on which the participants were neatly paired was the voyage of Noah's Ark. Ever since, passenger lists and tour groups have reflected the same kind of asymmetry that occurs in real life, as countless individuals set forth to see the world unaccompanied (or unencumbered, depending on your outlook) by spouse, lover, friend, companion, or relative.

The truth is that the travel industry is not very fair to people who vacation by themselves. People traveling alone almost invariably end up paying more than individuals traveling in pairs. Most travel bargains, including package tours, accommodations, resort packages, and cruises, are based on *double-occupancy* rates. The single traveler will have to pay a surcharge, called a single supplement, for exactly the same package. In extreme cases, this can add as much as 30% to 55% to the basic per-person rate.

The obvious, most effective alternative is to find a traveling companion. Even special "singles' tours" that promise no supplements usually are based on people sharing double rooms. Perhaps the most recent innovation along these lines is the creation of organizations that "introduce" the single traveler to other single travelers. Some charge fees, while others are free, but the basic service offered is the same: to match an unattached person with a compatible travel mate, often as part of the company's own package tours. Among such organizations are the following:

*Jane's International* (2603 Bath Ave., Brooklyn, NY 11214; phone: 718-266-2045). This service puts potential traveling companions in touch with one another. No age limit, no fee.

*Odyssey Network* (118 Cedar St., Wellesley, MA 02181; phone: 617-237-2400). Originally founded to match single women travelers, this company now includes men in its enrollment. *Odyssey* offers a quarterly newsletter for members who are seeking a travel companion, and occasionally organizes small group tours. A newsletter subscription is $50.

*Partners-in-Travel* (PO Box 491145, Los Angeles, CA 90049; phone: 213-476-4869). Members receive a list of singles seeking traveling companions; prospective companions make contact through the agency. The membership fee is $40 per year and includes a chatty newsletter (6 issues per year).

*Travel Companion Exchange* (PO Box 833, Amityville, NY 11701; phone: 516-454-0880). This group publishes a newsletter for singles and a directory of individuals looking for travel companions. On joining, members fill out a lengthy questionnaire and write a small listing (much like an ad in a personal column). Based on these listings, members can request copies of profiles and contact prospective traveling companions. It is wise to join well in advance of your planned vacation so that there's enough time to determine compatibility and plan a joint trip. Membership fees, including the newsletter, are $36 for 6 months or $60 a year for a single-sex listing; $66 and $120, respectively, for a complete listing. Subscription to the newsletter alone costs $24 for 6 months or $36 per year.

In addition, a number of tour packagers cater to single travelers. These companies offer packages designed for individuals interested in vacationing with a group of single travelers or in being matched with a traveling companion. Among these agencies are the following:

*Singles in Motion* (545 W. 236th St., Suite 1D, Riverdale, NY 10463; phone: 212-884-4464). Recent itineraries include an 8-day London and Paris city package.

*Singleworld* (401 Theodore Fremd Ave., Rye, NY 10580; phone: 914-967-3334 or 800-223-6490 in the continental US). It offers its own package tours for singles, with departures categorized by age group — 35 or younger — or for all ages. Recent offers include a 14-day escorted tour of England, France, and Italy, with a stay in London.

*Student Travel International* (*STI;* 8619 Reseda Blvd., Suite 103, Northridge, CA 91324; phone: 800-525-0525). Specializes in travel for 18- to 30-year-olds. Recent itineraries include a 1-week London theater program.

A good book for single travelers is *Traveling On Your Own,* by Eleanor Berman, which offers tips on traveling solo and includes information on trips for singles, ranging from outdoor adventures to educational programs. Available in bookstores, it also can be ordered by sending $12.95, plus postage and handling, to Random House, Order Dept., 400 Hahn Rd., Westminster, MD 21157 (phone: 800-733-3000).

Single travelers also may want to subscribe to *Going Solo,* a newsletter that offers helpful information on going on your own. Issued eight times a year, a subscription costs $36. Contact Doerfer Communications, PO Box 1035, Cambridge, MA 02238 (phone: 617-876-2764).

An attractive alternative for the single traveler who is particularly interested in meeting the British are home stay programs. See our discussion of accommodations in *Best in Town,* THE CITY, for information on these and other accommodations alternatives suitable for single travelers.

**WOMEN AND STUDENTS:** Two specific groups of single travelers deserve special mention: women and students. Countless women travel by themselves in London, and such an adventure need not be feared. One lingering inhibition many female travelers still harbor is that of eating alone in public places. The trick here is to relax and enjoy your meal and surroundings; while you may run across the occasional unenlightened waiter, a woman dining solo is no longer uncommon.

**Studying Abroad** – A large number of single travelers are students. Travel *is* education. Travel broadens a person's knowledge and deepens his or her perception of the world in a way no media or "armchair" experience ever could. In addition, to study a country's language, art, culture, or history in one of its own schools is to enjoy the most productive method of learning.

By "student" we do not necessarily mean a person who wishes to matriculate at a foreign university to earn a degree. Nor do we necessarily mean a younger person. A student is anyone who wishes to include some sort of educational program in a trip to London.

There are many benefits for students abroad, and the way to begin to discover them is to consult the *Council on International Educational Exchange (CIEE),* the US sponsor of the International Student Identity Card (ISIC), which permits reductions on airfare, other transportation, and entry fees to most museums and other exhibitions. The organization also is the source of the Federation of International Youth Travel Organizations (FIYTO) card, which provides many of the same benefits. For further information and applications, write to *CIEE* at one of the following addresses: 205 E. 42nd St., New York, NY 10017 (phone: 212-661-1414); 312 Sutter St., Suite 407, San Francisco, CA 94108 (phone: 415-421-3473); and 919 Irving St., Suite 102, San Francisco, CA 94122 (phone: 415-566-6222). Mark the letter "Attn. Student ID."

*CIEE* also offers a free, informative, annual, 64-page *Student Travel Catalog,* which covers all aspects of youth travel abroad for vacation trips, jobs, or study programs, and also includes a list of other helpful publications. It also sells *Work, Study, Travel Abroad: The Whole World Handbook,* an informative, chatty guide on study programs, work opportunities, and travel hints, with a particularly good section on Great Britain. It is available for $10.95, plus shipping and handling. The publications are available from the Information and Student Services Department at the New York address given above.

*CIEE* also sponsors charter flights to Europe that are open to students and non-students of any age. For example, flights between New York and London and other British cities (with budget-priced add-ons available from Chicago, Cleveland, Miami, Minneapolis, Phoenix, Portland, Salt Lake City, San Diego, Seattle, and Spokane) arrive and depart at least three times a week from Kennedy (JFK) Airport during the high season.

Students and singles in general should keep in mind that youth hostels exist throughout Great Britain. They always are inexpensive, generally clean and well situated, and they are a sure place to meet other people traveling alone. Hostels are run by the hosteling associations of 68 countries that make up the *International Youth Hostel Federation (IYHF);* membership in one of the national associations affords access to the hostels of the rest. To join the American affiliate, *American Youth Hostels (AYH),* contact the national office (PO Box 37613, Washington, DC 20013-7613; phone: 202-783-6161), or the local *AYH* council nearest you.

Those who go abroad without an *AYH* card may purchase a youth hostel International Guest Card (for the equivalent of about $18), and obtain information on local youth hostels by contacting the *Youth Hostel Association* (14 Southampton St., *Covent*

*Garden,* London WC2E 7HY; phone: 71-836-8541). This association also provides information on hostels throughout Great Britain.

*Student Travel International (STI;* address above) specializes in European travel for students.

Opportunities for study range from summer or academic-year courses in the language and civilization of Great Britain, designed specifically for foreigners (including those whose school days are well behind them), to long-term university attendance by those intending to take a degree.

Complete details on more than 3,000 courses available abroad (including at British universities) and suggestions on how to apply are contained in two books published by the *Institute of International Education* (IIE Books, 809 UN Plaza, New York, NY 10017; phone 212-883-8200): *Vacation Study Abroad* ($24.95, plus shipping and handling) and *Academic Year Abroad* ($31.95, plus shipping and handling). IIE Books also offers a free pamphlet called *Basic Facts on Study Abroad.*

The *National Registration Center for Study Abroad* (*NRCSA;* PO Box 1393, Milwaukee, WI 53201; phone: 414-278-0631) also offers a publication called *Worldwide Classroom: Study Abroad and Learning Vacations in 40 Countries: 1991–1992,* available for $8, which includes information on over 160 schools and cultural centers, including in London, that offer courses for Americans, with the primary focus on foreign language and culture.

Those who are interested in a "learning vacation" abroad also may be interested in *Travel and Learn* by Evelyn Kaye. This guide to educational travel discusses a wide range of opportunities — everything from archaeology to whale watching — and provides information on organizations that offer programs in these areas of interest. The book is available in bookstores for $23.95; or you can send $26 (which includes shipping charges) to Blue Penguin Publications (147 Sylvan Ave., Leonia, NJ 07605; phone: 800-800-8147 or 201-461-6918). *Learning Vacations* by Gerson G. Eisenberg also provides extensive information on seminars, workshops, courses, and so on — in a wide variety of subjects. Available in bookstores, it also can be ordered from Peterson's Guides (PO Box 2123, Princeton, NJ 08543-2123; phone: 609-243-9111) for $11.95, plus shipping and handling.

# Hints for Older Travelers

Special discounts and more free time are just two factors that have given Americans over age 65 a chance to see the world at affordable prices. Senior citizens make up an ever-growing segment of the travel population, and the trend among them is to travel more frequently and for longer periods of time.

**PLANNING:** When planning a vacation, prepare your itinerary with one eye on your own physical condition and the other on your interests. One important factor to keep in mind is not to overdo anything and to be aware of the effects that the weather may have on your capabilities.

Older travelers may find the following publications of interest:

*Discount Guide for Travelers Over 55,* by Caroline and Walter Weintz, is an excellent book for budget-conscious older travelers. It is available by sending $7.95, plus shipping and handling, to Penguin USA (Att. Cash Sales, 120 Woodbine St., Bergenfield, NJ 07621); when ordering, specify the ISBN number: 0-525-48358-6.

*Going Abroad: 101 Tips for the Mature Traveler* offers tips on preparing for your trip, commonsense precautions en route, and some basic travel terminology.

This concise, free booklet is available from *Grand Circle Travel,* 347 Congress St., Boston, MA 02210 (phone: 800-221-2610 or 617-350-7500).

*International Health Guide for Senior Citizen Travelers,* by Dr. W. Robert Lange, covers such topics as trip preparations, food and water precautions, adjusting to weather and climate conditions, finding a doctor, motion sickness, jet lag, and so on. Also includes a list of resource organizations that provide medical assistance for travelers. It is available for $4.95 postpaid from Pilot Books, 103 Cooper St., Babylon, NY 11702 (phone: 516-422-2225).

*Mature Traveler* is a monthly newsletter that provides information on travel discounts, places of interest, useful tips, and other topics of interest for travelers 49 and up. To subscribe, send $21.95 to GEM Publishing Group, PO Box 50820, Reno, NV 89513 (phone: 702-786-7419).

*Travel Easy: The Practical Guide for People Over 50,* by Rosalind Massow, discusses a wide range of subjects — from trip planning, transportation options, and preparing for departure to avoiding and handling medical problems en route. It's available for $6.50 to members of the *American Association of Retired Persons (AARP),* and for $8.95 to non-members; call about current charges for postage and handling. Order from *AARP* Books, c/o Customer Service, Scott, Foresman & Company, 1900 E. Lake Ave., Glenview, IL 60025 (phone: 708-729-3000).

*Travel Tips for Older Americans* is a useful booklet that provides good, basic advice. This US State Department publication (stock number: 044-000-02270-2) can be ordered by sending a check or money order for $1 to the Superintendent of Documents (US Government Printing Office, Washington, DC 20402) or by calling 202-783-3238 and charging the order to a credit card.

*Unbelievably Good Deals & Great Adventures That You Absolutely Can't Get Unless You're Over 50,* by Joan Rattner Heilman, offers travel tips for older travelers, including discounts on accommodations and transportation, as well as a list of organizations for seniors. It is available for $7.95, plus shipping and handling, from Contemporary Books, 180 N. Michigan Ave., Chicago, 1L 60601 (phone: 312-782-9181).

**DISCOUNTS AND PACKAGES:** Many hotel chains, airlines, cruise lines, bus companies, car rental companies, and other travel suppliers offer discounts to older travelers. For instance, *TWA* offers those age 62 and over (and one traveling companion per qualifying senior citizen) discounts on flights from the US to London. Other airlines also offer discounts for passengers age 60 (or 62) and over, which also may apply to one traveling companion. For information on current prices and applicable restrictions, contact the individual carriers.

Some discounts, however, are extended only to bona fide members of certain senior citizens organizations. Because the same organizations frequently offer package tours to both domestic and international destinations, the benefits of membership are twofold: Those who join can take advantage of discounts as individual travelers and also reap the savings that group travel affords. In addition, because the age requirements for some of these organizations are quite low (or nonexistent), the benefits can begin to accrue early. In order to take advantage of these discounts, you should carry proof of your age (or eligibility). A driver's license, membership card in a recognized senior citizens organization, or a Medicare card should be adequate. Among the organizations dedicated to helping older travelers see the world are the following:

*American Association of Retired Persons (AARP;* 1909 K St. NW, Washington, DC 20049; phone: 202-872-4700). The largest and best known of these organizations. Membership is open to anyone 50 or over, whether retired or not; dues are $5 a year, $12.50 for 3 years, or $35 for 10 years, and include spouse. The

*AARP* Travel Experience Worldwide program, available through *American Express Travel Related Services,* offers members travel programs worldwide designed exclusively for older travelers. Call for their current itineraries at your time of travel. Members can book these services by calling *American Express* at 800-927-0111 for land and air travel.

*Mature Outlook* (Customer Service Center, 6001 N. Clark St., Chicago, IL 60660; phone: 800-336-6330). Through its *TravelAlert,* vacation packages are available to members at special savings. Hotel and car rental discounts and travel accident insurance also are available. Membership is open to anyone 50 years of age or older, costs $9.95 a year, and includes a bimonthly newsletter and magazine, as well as information on package tours.

*National Council of Senior Citizens* (1331 F St., Washington, DC 20005; phone: 202-347-8800). Here, too, the emphasis is on keeping costs low. This nonprofit organization offers members a different roster of package tours each year, as well as individual arrangements through its affiliated travel agency *(Vantage Travel Service).* Although most members are over 50, membership is open to anyone (regardless of age) for an annual fee of $12 per person or couple. Lifetime membership costs $150.

Many travel agencies, particularly the larger ones, are delighted to make presentations to help a group of senior citizens select destinations. A local chamber of commerce should be able to provide the names of such agencies. Once a time and place are determined, an organization member or travel agent can obtain group quotations for transportation, accommodations, meal plans, and sightseeing. Larger groups usually get the best breaks.

Another choice open to older travelers is a trip that includes an educational element. *Elderhostel,* a nonprofit organization, offers programs at educational institutions worldwide, including London. The foreign programs generally last about 2 weeks, and include double occupancy accommodations in hotels or student residence halls and all meals. Travel to the programs usually is by designated scheduled flights, and participants can arrange to extend their stay at the end of the program. Elderhostelers must be at least 60 years old (younger if a spouse or companion qualifies), in good health, and not in need of a special diet. For a free catalogue describing the program and current offerings, write to *Elderhostel* (75 Federal St., Boston, MA 02110; phone: 617-426-7788). Those interested in the program also can borrow slides at no charge or purchase an informational videotape for $5.

# Hints for Traveling with Children

 What better way to encounter the world's variety than in the company of the young, wide-eyed members of your family? Their presence does not have to be a burden or an excessive expense. The current generation of discounts for children and family package deals can make a trip together quite reasonable.

**PLANNING:** Here are several hints for making a trip with children easy and fun:

1. Children, like everyone else, will derive more pleasure from a trip if they know something about their destination before they arrive. Begin their education about a month before you leave. Using maps, travel magazines, and books, give children a clear idea of where you are going and how far away it is.

2. Children should help to plan the itinerary, and where you go and what you do

should reflect some of their ideas. If they already know something about the sites they'll visit, they will have the excitement of recognition when they arrive.

3. Familiarize your children with pounds, shillings, and pence. Give them an allowance for the trip, and be sure they understand just how far it will or won't go.

4. Give children specific responsibilities: The job of carrying their own flight bags and looking after their personal things, along with some other light chores, will give them a stake in the journey.

5. Give each child a diary or scrapbook to take along.

And for parents, *Travel With Your Children* (*TWYCH;* 80 Eighth Ave., New York, NY 10011; phone: 212-206-0688) publishes a newsletter, *Family Travel Times,* that focuses on families with young travelers and offers helpful hints. An annual subscription (10 issues) is $35 and includes a copy of the "Airline Guide" issue (updated every other year), which focuses on the subject of flying with children. This special issue is available separately for $10.

Another newsletter devoted to family travel is *Getaways.* This quarterly publication provides reviews of family-oriented literature, activities, and useful travel tips. To subscribe, send $25 to *Getaways,* Att. Ms. Brooke Kane, PO Box 11511, Washington, DC 20008 (phone: 703-534-8747).

Also of interest to parents traveling with their children is *How to Take Great Trips With Your Kids,* by psychologist Sanford Portnoy and his wife, Joan Flynn Portnoy. The book includes helpful tips from fellow family travelers, tips on economical accommodations and touring by car, recreational vehicle, and train, as well as over 50 games to play with your children en route. It is available for $8.95, plus shipping and handling, from Harvard Common Press, 535 Albany St., Boston, MA 02118 (phone: 617-423-5803).

Another book on family travel, *Travel with Children* by Maureen Wheeler, offers a wide range of practical tips on traveling with children, and includes accounts of the author's family travel experiences. It is available for $10.95, plus shipping and handling, from Lonely Planet Publications, Embarcadero West, 112 Linden St., Oakland, CA 94607 (phone: 510-893-8555).

Also look for the London volume of the "Kidding Around" series, published by John Muir Publications. This book starts with an overview of the city, along with some interesting background information, and then is divided into areas, with descriptions of the various attractions in the general order in which you might encounter them. It can be ordered directly from the publisher by sending $9.95, plus shipping, to John Muir Publications, PO Box 613, Santa Fe, NM 87504, or by calling 800-888-7504 or 505-982-4087.

Finally, parents arranging a trip with their children may want to deal with an agency specializing in family travel such as *Let's Take the Kids* (1268 Devon Ave., Los Angeles, CA 90024; phone: 213-274-7088 or 800-726-4349). In addition to arranging and booking trips for individual families, this group occassionally organizes trips for single-parent families traveling together. They also offer a parent travel network, whereby parents who have been to a particular destination can evaluate it for others.

**PLANE:** Begin early to investigate all available family discounts and charter flights, as well as any package deals and special rates offered by the major airlines. When you make your reservations, tell the airline that you are traveling with a child. Children ages 2 through 11 generally travel at about a 20% to 30% discount off regular full-fare adult ticket prices on domestic flights. This children's fare, however, usually is much higher than the excursion fare, which may be used by any traveler, regardless of age. An infant under 2 years of age usually can travel free if it sits on an adult's lap. A second infant without a second adult would pay the fare applicable to children ages 2 through 11.

Although some airlines will, on request, supply bassinets for infants, most carriers encourage parents to bring their own safety seat on board, which then is strapped into the airline seat with a regular seat belt. This is much safer — and certainly more comfortable — than holding the child in your lap. If you do not purchase a seat for your baby, you have the option of bringing the infant restraint along on the off-chance that there might be an empty seat next to yours — in which case some airlines will let you use that seat at no charge for your baby and infant seat. However, if there is no empty seat available, the infant seat no doubt will have to be checked as baggage (and you may have to pay an additional charge), since it generally does not fit under the seat or in the overhead racks.

The safest bet is to pay for a seat — this usually will be the same as fares applicable to children ages 2 through 11. It usually is less expensive to pay for an adult excursion rate than the discounted children's fare.

Be forewarned: Some safety seats designed primarily for use in cars do not fit into plane seats properly. Although nearly all seats manufactured since 1985 carry labels indicating whether they meet federal standards for use aboard planes, actual seat sizes may vary from carrier to carrier. At the time of this writing, the FAA was in the process of reviewing and revising the federal regulations regarding infant travel and safety devices — it was still to be determined if children should be *required* to sit in safety seats and whether the airlines will have to provide them.

If using one of these infant restraints, you should try to get bulkhead seats, which will provide extra room to care for your child during the flight. You also should request a bulkhead seat when using a bassinet — again, this is not as safe as strapping the child in. On some planes bassinets hook into a bulkhead wall; on others it is placed on the floor in front of you. (Note that bulkhead seats often are reserved for families traveling with small children.) As a general rule, babies should be held during takeoff and landing.

Request seats on the aisle if you have a toddler or if you think you will need to use the bathroom frequently. Carry onto the plane all you will need to care for and occupy your children during the flight — formula, diapers, a sweater, books, favorite stuffed animals, and so on. Dress your baby simply, with a minimum of buttons and snaps, because the only place you may have to change a diaper is at your seat or in a small lavatory.

On US carriers, you also can ask for a hot dog or hamburger instead of the airline's regular dinner if you give at least 24 hours' notice. Some, but not all, airlines have baby food aboard, and the flight attendant can warm a bottle for you. While you should bring along toys from home, also ask about children's diversions. Some carriers have terrific free packages of games, coloring books, and puzzles.

When the plane takes off and lands, make sure your baby is nursing or has a bottle, pacifier, or thumb in its mouth. This sucking will make the child swallow and help to clear stopped ears. A piece of hard candy will do the same thing for an older child.

Parents traveling by plane with toddlers, children, or teenagers may want to consult *When Kids Fly,* a free booklet published by Massport (Public Affairs Department, 10 Park Plaza, Boston, MA 02116-3971; phone: 617-973-5600), which includes helpful information on airfares for children, infant seats, what to do in the event of overbooked or canceled flights, and so on.

■**Note:** Newborn babies, whose lungs may not be able to adjust to the altitude, should not be taken aboard an airplane. And some airlines may refuse to allow a pregnant woman in her 8th or 9th month to fly. Check with the airline ahead of time, and carry a letter from your doctor stating that you are fit to travel — and indicating the estimated date of birth.

**ACCOMMODATIONS AND MEALS:** Often a cot for a child will be placed in a hotel room at little or no extra charge. If you wish to sleep in separate rooms, special rates sometimes are available for families; some places do not charge for children under a certain age. In many of the larger chain hotels, the staffs are more used to children. These hotels also are likely to have swimming pools or gamerooms — both popular with most youngsters. Apartments, condominiums, and other rental options offer families privacy, flexibility, some kitchen facilities, and often lower costs.

Most better hotels will try to arrange for a sitter for the times you will want to be without the children — for an evening's entertainment or a particularly rigorous stint of sightseeing.

At mealtime, don't deny yourself or your children the delights of a new style of cooking. Children like to know what kind of food to expect, so the family can have the pleasure of looking up traditional British dishes before leaving. Encourage your children to try new things, although you can find American-style food in London — even *McDonald's*.

### Things to Remember
1. Pace the days with children in mind. Break the touring time into half-day segments, with running around or "doing" time built in.
2. Don't forget that a child's attention span is far shorter than an adult's. Children don't have to see every sight or all of any sight to learn something from their trip; watching, playing with, and talking to other children can be equally enlightening.
3. Let your children lead the way sometimes; their perspective is different from yours, and they may lead you to things you would never have noticed on your own.
4. Remember the places that children love to visit: aquariums, zoos, amusement parks, beaches, and so on. Among the activities that may pique their interest are bicycling, snorkeling, boat trips, horseback riding, visiting children's museums, and viewing natural habitat exhibits. The children's favorites in London include the *London Zoo*, with an aquarium and petting zoo; the Changing of the Guard, at Buckingham Palace; the *Rock Circus* and the *Guinness World of Records*, in the London Pavilion, Piccadilly Circus; the *Bethnal Green Museum of Childhood*, with more than 4,000 toys; and the *London Toy and Model Museum*, which contains an extensive collection dating back to the 1800s.

# Staying Healthy

The surest way to return home in good health is to be prepared for medical problems that might occur while on vacation. Below, we've outlined some things about which you need to think before you go.

Older travelers or anyone suffering from a chronic medical condition, such as diabetes, high blood pressure, cardiopulmonary disease, asthma, or ear, eye, or sinus trouble, should consult a physician before leaving home. Those with conditions requiring special consideration when traveling should think about seeing, in addition to their regular physician, a specialist in travel medicine. For a referral in a particular community, contact the nearest medical school or ask a local doctor to recommend such a specialist. Dr. Leonard Marcus, a member of the *American Committee on Clinical Tropical Medicine and Travelers' Health*, provides a directory of more than 100 travel doctors across the country. For a copy, send a 9-by-12-inch self-addressed, stamped envelope to Dr. Marcus at 148 Highland Ave., Newton, MA 02165 (phone: 617-527-4003).

**FIRST AID:** Put together a compact, personal medical kit including Band-Aids, first-aid cream, antiseptic, nose drops, insect repellent, aspirin, an extra pair of prescription glasses or contact lenses (and a copy of your prescription for glasses or contact lenses), sunglasses, over-the-counter remedies for diarrhea, indigestion, and motion sickness, a thermometer, and a supply of those prescription medicines you take regularly.

In a corner of your kit, keep a list of all the drugs you have brought and their purpose, as well as duplicate copies of your doctor's prescriptions (or a note from your doctor). As brand names may vary in different countries, it's a good idea to ask your doctor for the generic name of any drugs you use so that you can ask for their equivalent should you need a refill.

It also is a good idea to ask your doctor to prepare a medical identification card that includes such information as your blood type, your social security number, any allergies or chronic health problems you have, and your medical insurance information. Considering the essential contents of your medical kit, keep it with you, rather than in your checked luggage.

**HELPFUL PUBLICATIONS:** Practically every phase of health care — before, during, and after a trip — is covered in *The New Traveler's Health Guide,* by Drs. Patrick J. Doyle and James E. Banta. It is available for $4.95, plus postage and handling, from Acropolis Books Ltd., 13950 Park Center Rd., Herndon, VA 22071 (phone: 800-451-7771 or 703-709-0006).

The *Traveling Healthy Newsletter,* which is published six times a year, also is brimming with health-related travel tips. For a year's subscription, which costs $24, contact Dr. Karl Neumann (108-48 70th Rd., Forest Hills, NY 11375; phone: 718-268-7290). Dr. Neumann also is the editor of the useful free booklet *Traveling Healthy,* which is available by writing to the *Travel Healthy Program* (PO Box 10208, New Brunswick, NJ 08906-9910; phone: 215-732-4100).

For more information regarding preventive health care for travelers, contact the *International Association for Medical Assistance to Travelers* (*IAMAT;* 417 Center St., Lewiston, NY 14092; phone: 716-754-4883). The Centers for Disease Control also publishes an interesting booklet, *Health Information for International Travel.* To order send a check or money order for $5 to the Superintendent of Documents (US Government Printing Office, Washington, DC 20402), or charge it to your credit card by calling 202-783-3238. For information on vaccination requirements, disease outbreaks, and other health information pertaining to traveling abroad, you also can call the Centers for Disease Control's 24-hour International Health Requirements and Recommendations Information Hotline: 404-332-4559.

# On the Road

## Credit and Currency

 It may seem hard to believe, but one of the greatest (and least understood) costs of travel is money itself. So your one single objective in relation to the care and retention of travel funds is to make them stretch as far as possible. Herewith, a primer on making money go as far as possible overseas.

**CURRENCY:** The basic unit of British currency is the pound (abbreviated £). This is distributed in coin denominations of 1, 2, 5, 10, 20, and 50 pence (there are 100 pence to a pound), and 1 pound. Paper money is issued in bills of 5, 10, 20, and 50 pounds. The value of British currency in relation to the US dollar fluctuates daily, affected by a wide variety of phenomena.

There is no limit to the amount of US currency that can be brought into Great Britain. To avoid problems anywhere along the line, it's advisable to fill out any customs forms provided when leaving the US on which you can declare all money you are taking with you — cash, traveler's checks, and so on. US law requires that anyone taking more than $10,000 into or out of the US must report this fact on customs form No. 4790, which is available from US Customs. If taking over $10,000 out of the US, you must report this *before* leaving the US; if returning with such an amount, you should include this information on your customs declaration. Although travelers usually are not questioned by customs officials about currency when entering or leaving, the sensible course is to observe all regulations just to be on the safe side.

In London, as in the rest of Great Britain, you will find the official rate of exchange posted in banks, airports, money exchange houses, and some shops. As a general rule, expect to get more local currency for your US dollar at banks than at any other commercial establishment. Exchange rates do change from day to day, and most banks offer the same (or very similar) exchange rates. (In a pinch, the convenience of cashing money in your hotel — sometimes on a 24-hour basis — *may* make up for the difference in the exchange rate.) Don't try to bargain in banks or hotels — no one will alter the rates for you.

Money exchange houses (called *bureau de change*) are financial institutions that charge a fee for the service of exchanging dollars into local currency. When considering alternatives, be aware that although the rate varies among these establishments, the rates of exchange offered are bound to be slightly less favorable than the terms offered at nearby banks — again, don't be surprised if you get fewer pence for your dollar than the rate published in the papers.

That said, however, the following rules of thumb are worth remembering:

**Rule number one: Never (repeat: *never*) exchange dollars for foreign currency at hotels, restaurants, or retail shops.** If you do, you are sure to lose a significant amount of your US dollar's buying power. If you do come across a storefront exchange counter offering what appears to be an incredible bargain, there's too much counterfeit specie in circulation to take the chance. (see Rule number three, below.)

**Rule number two: Estimate your needs carefully; if you overbuy you lose twice —**

**buying and selling back.** Every time you exchange money, someone is making a profit, and rest assured it isn't you. Use up foreign notes before leaving, saving just enough for last-minute incidentals, and tips.

**Rule number three: Don't buy money on the black market.** The exchange rate may be better, but it is a common practice to pass off counterfeit bills to unsuspecting foreigners who aren't familiar with the local currency. It's usually a sucker's game, and you almost always are the sucker; it also can land you in jail.

**Rule number four: Learn the local currency quickly and keep abreast of daily fluctuations in the exchange rate.** These are listed in the English-language *International Herald Tribune* daily for the preceding day, as well as in every major newspaper in Europe. Rates change to some degree every day. For rough calculations, it is quick and safe to use round figures, but for purchases and actual currency exchanges, carry a small pocket calculator to help you compute the exact rate. Inexpensive calculators specifically designed to convert currency amounts quickly for travelers are widely available.

When changing money, don't be afraid to ask how much commission you're being charged, and the exact amount of the prevailing exchange rate. In fact, in any exchange of money for goods or services, you should work out the rate before making any payment.

**TRAVELER'S CHECKS:** It's wise to carry traveler's checks instead of (or in addition to) cash, since it's possible to replace them if they are stolen or lost. Issued in various denominations and available in both US dollars and British pounds, with adequate proof of identification (credit cards, driver's license, passport), traveler's checks are as good as cash in most hotels, restaurants, stores, and banks. Don't assume, however, that restaurants, small shops, and other establishments are going to be able to change checks of large denominations.

Although traveler's checks are available in foreign currencies such as British pounds, the exchange rates offered by the issuing companies in the US generally are far less favorable than those available from banks both in the US and abroad. Therefore, it usually is better to carry the bulk of your travel funds abroad in US dollar–denomination traveler's checks.

Every type of traveler's check is legal tender in banks around the world and each company guarantees full replacement if checks are lost or stolen. After that the similarity ends. Some charge a fee for purchase, while others are free; you can buy traveler's checks at almost any bank, and some are available by mail. Most important, each traveler's check issuer differs slightly in its refund policy — the amount refunded immediately, the accessibility of refund locations, the availability of a 24-hour refund service, and the time it will take for you to receive replacement checks. For instance, *American Express* guarantees replacement of lost or stolen traveler's checks in under 3 hours at any *American Express* office — other companies may not be as prompt. In London, two of the *American Express* offices are located at 6 Haymarket St. (phone: 71-920-4411) and 52 Cannon St. (phone: 71-248-2671). Travelers should keep in mind that *American Express*'s 3-hour policy is based on the traveler being able to provide the serial numbers of the lost checks. Without these numbers, refunds can take much longer.

We cannot overemphasize the importance of knowing how to replace lost or stolen checks. All of the traveler's check companies have agents around the world, both in their own name and at associated agencies (usually, but not necessarily, banks), where refunds can be obtained during business hours. Most of them also have 24-hour toll-free telephone lines, and some will even provide emergency funds to tide you over on a Sunday.

Be sure to make a photocopy of the refund instructions that will be given you at the time of purchase. To avoid complications should you need to replace lost checks (and to speed up the process), keep the purchase receipt and an accurate list, by serial number, of the checks that have been spent or cashed. Always keep these records separate from the checks and the original records themselves (you may want to give them to a traveling companion to hold).

Following is a list of the major companies issuing traveler's checks and the numbers to call in the event that loss or theft makes replacement necessary:

*American Express:* The company advises travelers in London to call 273-571600 (in Brighton), collect, or 800-521313. Another (slower) option is to call 801-968-8300 (in the US), collect, or contact the nearest *American Express* office (see above for the London address).

*Bank of America:* In Great Britain and elsewhere worldwide, call 415-624-5400 or 415-622-3800, collect.

*Citicorp:* In Great Britain and elsewhere worldwide, call 813-623-1709 or 813-626-4444, collect.

*MasterCard:* In Great Britain, call the New York office at 212-974-5696, collect.

*Thomas Cook MasterCard:* In Great Britain, call 733-502995, or 609-987-7300 (in the US), collect, and they will direct you to the nearest branch of Thomas Cook or *Wagons-Lits,* their European agent.

*Visa:* In Great Britain, call 415-574-7111, collect.

**CREDIT CARDS:** Some establishments you encounter during the course of your travels may not honor any credit cards and some may not honor all cards, so there is a practical reason to carry more than one. Most US credit cards, including the principal bank cards, are honored in Spain; however, keep in mind that some cards may be issued under different names in Europe. For example, *MasterCard* may go under the name *Access* or *Eurocard,* and *Visa* often is called *Carte Bleue* — wherever these equivalents are accepted, *MasterCard* and *Visa* may be used. The following is a list of credit cards that enjoy wide international acceptance:

*American Express:* For information call 800-528-4800 in the US; to report a lost or stolen *American Express* card in London, contact the local *American Express* office (see address above) or call 212-477-5700, collect.

*Carte Blanche:* For medical, legal, and travel assistance in Great Britain, call 214-680-6480, collect. For information call 800-525-9135 in the US; to report a lost or stolen *Carte Blanche* card in Great Britain, call 303-790-2433, collect.

*Diners Club:* For medical, legal, and travel assistance in Great Britain, call 214-680-6480, collect. For information call 800-525-9135 in the US; to report a lost or stolen *Diners Club* card in Great Britain, call 303-790-2433, collect.

*Discover Card:* For information call 800-DISCOVER in the US; to report a lost or stolen *Discover* card in Great Britain, call 302-323-7652, collect.

*MasterCard:* For 24-hour emergency lost card service, call 314-275-6690, collect.

*Visa:* For 24-hour emergency lost card service, call 415-574-7700, collect.

**SENDING MONEY ABROAD:** If you have used up your traveler's checks, cashed as many emergency personal checks as your credit card allows, drawn on your cash advance line to the fullest extent, and still need money, have it sent to you via one of the following services:

*American Express* (phone: 800-543-4080). Offers a service called "Moneygram," completing money transfers in anywhere from 15 minutes to 5 days. The sender can go to any *American Express* office in the US and transfer money by presenting cash, a personal check, money order, or credit card — *Discover, MasterCard, Visa,* or *American Express Optima Card* (no other *American Express* or other credit cards are accepted). *American Express Optima* cardholders also can arrange for this transfer over the phone. To collect at the other end, the receiver must show identification (passport, driver's license, or other picture ID) at the *American Express* office in London and present a passport as identification. For further information on this service, call 800-543-4080.

*Western Union Telegraph Company* (phone: 800-325-4176 throughout the US). A friend or relative can go, cash in hand, to any *Western Union* office in the US, where, for a *minimum* charge of $13 (it rises with the amount of the transaction), the funds will be transferred to one of the numerous associate companies of *Western Union* in London. When the money arrives, you will not be notified — you must go to the bank to inquire. Transfers generally take anywhere from 15 minutes to 3 days. The funds will be turned over in local currency, based on the rate of exchange in effect on the day of receipt. For a higher fee, the US party to this transaction may call *Western Union* with a *MasterCard* or *Visa* number to send up to $2,000.

If you are literally down to your last pound, the nearest US consulate (see *Medical and Legal Aid and Consular Services,* in this section) will let you call home to set these matters in motion.

**CASH MACHINES:** Automatic teller machines (ATMs) are increasingly common throughout the world. If your bank participates in one of the international ATM networks (most do), the bank will issue you a "cash card" along with a personal identification code or number (also called a PIC or PIN). You can use this card at any ATM in the same electronic network to withdraw cash instantly. Network ATMs generally are located in banks, commercial and transportation centers, and near major tourist attractions.

Some financial institutions offer exclusive automatic teller machines for their own customers only at bank branches. At the time of this writing, ATMs that *are* connected generally belong to one of the following two international networks:

*Cirrus:* Has over 55,000 ATMs in more than 22 countries, including about 150 in London. *MasterCard* holders also may use their cards to draw cash against their credit lines. For a free booklet listing the locations of these machines and further information on the *Cirrus* network, call 800-4-CIRRUS.

*Plus System:* Has over 30,000 automatic teller machines worldwide, including over 30 in London. *MasterCard* and *Visa* cardholders also may use their cards to draw cash against their credit lines. For a free directory listing the locations of these machines and further information on the *Plus System* network, call 800-THE-PLUS.

Information about these networks also may be available at member bank branches. A recent agreement between these two companies permits banking institutions to join both networks, allowing users of either system to withdraw funds from participating *Cirrus* or *Plus System* ATMs.

# Accommodations

London has no shortage of expensive, deluxe 4-star hotels; however, those watching their wallets will be pleased to find that if a little effort is put into researching more affordable accommodations, they will not be disappointed. At the lower end of the price scale, you will not necessarily have to forgo charm. While a fair number of inexpensive establishments are simply no-frills, "generic" places to spend the night, even the sparest room may have the cachet of once having been the nightly retreat of a monk or nun. And some of the most delightful places to stay are the smaller, less expensive, often family-run small inns or bed and breakfast establishments.

And in London, you'd not only enjoy all the modern amenities many Americans had become accustomed to, but also a sense of charm coming from the unique history and long-running tradition peculiar to the British people. For more information, see *Best in Town* in THE CITY.

# Time Zones, Business Hours, and Public Holidays

**TIME ZONES:** The countries of Europe fall into three time zones. Greenwich Mean Time — the time in Greenwich, England, at longitude 0°0′ — is the base from which all other time zones are measured. Areas in zones west of Greenwich have earlier times and are called Greenwich Minus; those to the east have later times and are called Greenwich Plus. For example, New York City — which falls into the Greenwich Minus 5 time zone — is 5 hours earlier than Greenwich, England.

The entire territory of Great Britain, including London, is in the Greenwich time zone (or Central European Time). Since New York is in the Greenwich Minus 5 time zone, it means when it is noon in London, it is 7AM in New York.

As do most Western European nations, Great Britain moves its clocks ahead an hour in late spring and an hour back in the fall, although the date of the change tends to be about a week earlier (in spring) and a week later (in fall) than the dates we have adopted in the US. For about 2 weeks a year, then, the time difference between the US and Great Britain is 1 hour more or less than usual.

European timetables often use a 24-hour clock to denote arrival and departure times, which means that hours are expressed sequentially from 1 AM. By this method, 9 AM is recorded as 0900, noon as 1200, 1 PM as 1300, 6 PM as 1800, midnight as 2400, and so on. For example, the departure of a train at 7 AM will be announced as "0700"; one leaving at 7 PM will be noted as "1900." However, both systems are generally used in Great Britain.

**BUSINESS HOURS:** In London, as throughout Great Britain, most businesses are open Mondays through Fridays from 9 AM to 5 PM. Stores are open Mondays through Saturdays from 9 AM to 5:30 PM. Shops in the West End and Kensington areas stay open until 9 PM on Thursdays, and those in the Knightsbridge and Chelsea areas are open late on Wednesdays.

Weekday banking hours in London are from 9:30 AM to 5:30 PM. Some of the major banks are open on Saturday mornings. Most banks are closed on Sundays and public holidays. There are banks at Gatwick and Heathrow airports; both are open 24 hours a day.

Restaurant hours are similar to those in the US. Most restaurants are open all week during the high season and close 1 day each week during the off-season — the day varies from restaurant to restaurant.

**PUBLIC HOLIDAYS:** In London, as in the rest of England (Scotland and Northern Ireland may have some different holidays), the public holidays (and their dates this year) are as follows:

*New Year's Day* (January 1)
*Good Friday* (April 17)
*Easter Monday* (April 20)

*May Day* (May 4)
*Spring Bank Holiday* (May 25)
*Summer Bank Holiday* (August 31)
*Christmas Day* (December 25)
*Boxing Day* (December 26)

# Mail and Electricity

 **MAIL:** The main post office (London Chief Office, King Edward Building, King Edward St., EC1; phone: 71-239-2000) is open Mondays through Fridays from 8:30 AM to 6:30 PM. A centrally located branch, off Trafalgar Square (24 William IV St., WC2; phone: 71-930-9580), is open Mondays through Saturdays from 8 AM to 8 PM. Most other post offices are open Mondays through Fridays from 9AM to 6 PM, and Saturdays from 9 AM to 1 PM. Postal rates change frequently; stamps can be bought at the post office or a few authorized shops. Mailing a letter or package, however, is not as straightforward as in the US. Post offices have different windows for each step in the procedure (one window to buy stamps, another to weigh a package, and so on).

Be advised that delivery from Great Britain usually takes at least 1 week (postcards often are given lowest priority, so don't use them for important messages). Send your correspondence via air mail if it's going any distance.

If your correspondence is important, you may want to send it via a special courier service; *DHL International*'s main office in London is at Orbital Park, 178-188 Great Southwest Rd., Hounslow, Middlesex (phone: 81-890-9000); *Federal Express*'s main office is at 9 Elms Lane, Unit 4 (phone: 71-622-3933; for pickup, 800-123800). The cost is considerably higher than sending something via the postal services, but the assurance of its timely arrival may be worth it.

If you're mailing to an address within Great Britain, a good way to ensure or speed delivery is to use the postal code. And since small towns in Great Britain may have similar names, the postal code always should be specified — delivery of a letter may depend on it. If you do not know the correct postal code, call the British Tourist Authority (see *Tourist Information Offices,* in this section, for telephone numbers) — they should be able to look it up for you.

There are several places that will receive and hold mail for travelers in Great Britain. Mail sent to you at a hotel and clearly marked "Guest Mail, Hold for Arrival" is one safe approach. British post offices, including the main London office, also will extend this service to you if the mail is addressed to the equivalent of US general delivery — called *poste restante* in London. It should be addressed to Poste restante, London Chief Office, King Edward Building, King Edward St., London EC1. Don't forget to take your passport with you when you go to collect it. Most British post offices require formal identification before they will release anything; there also may be a small charge for picking up your mail.

If you are an *American Express* customer (a cardholder, a carrier of *American Express* traveler's checks, or traveling on an *American Express Travel Service* tour) you can have mail sent to its office in London. Letters are held free of charge — registered mail and packages are not accepted. You must be able to show an *American Express* card, traveler's checks, or a voucher proving you are on one of the company's tours to avoid paying for mail privileges. Those who aren't clients must pay a nominal charge each time they inquire if they have received mail, whether or not they actually have a letter. Mail should be addressed to you, care of *American Express,* and should be marked "Client Mail Service."

While US embassies and consulates abroad will not under ordinary circumstances accept mail for tourists, they *may* hold mail for US citizens in an emergency situation, especially if the papers sent are important. It is best to inform them either by separate letter or cable, or by phone (particularly if you are in the country already), that you will be using their address for this purpose.

**ELECTRICITY:** The US runs on 110-volt, 60-cycle alternating current; London (and the rest of Great Britain; however, there may be some exceptions in small villages) runs on 220- or 240-volt, 50-cycle alternating current. (Some large tourist hotels also *may* offer 110-volt currency or a converter for your convenience — but don't count on it.) The difference between US and British voltage means that, without a converter, at 220 volts the motor of a US appliance used overseas would run at twice the speed at which it's meant to operate and would quickly burn out.

# Medical and Legal Aid and Consular Services

**MEDICAL AID ABROAD:** Nothing ruins a vacation or business trip more effectively than sudden injury or illness. The level of medical care in Great Britain, especially in the larger cities like London, generally is very good, providing the same basic specialties and services that are available in the US.

Before you go, be sure to check with your insurance company about the applicability of your hospitalization and major medical policies while you're abroad; many policies do not apply, and others are not accepted in Great Britain. Older travelers should know that Medicare does not make payments outside the US.

If a bona fide emergency occurs, the fastest way to get attention may be to take a taxi to the emergency room of the nearest hospital. In London, go to *St. Bartholomew's Hospital* (West Smithfield, EC1; phone: 71-601-8888), *University College Hospital* (Gower St., WC1; phone: 71-387-9300), or *Middlesex Hospital* (Mortimer St., W1; phone: 71-636-8333). An alternative is to dial the free national "emergency" number used to summon the police, fire trucks, and ambulances — 999 in Great Britain.

Great Britain has socialized medicine and there are two types of hospitals: public and private. The public hospitals are government hospitals, which provide low-cost medical care; the private hospitals usually charge much more for their services.

If a doctor is needed for something less than an emergency, there are several ways to find one. If you are staying in a hotel or at a resort, ask for help in reaching a doctor or other emergency services, or for the house physician, who may visit you in your room or ask you to visit an office.

Dialing the nationwide emergency number (999) also may be of help in locating a physician. It also usually is possible to obtain a referral through a US consulate (see addresses and phone numbers below) or directly through a hospital, especially if it is an emergency.

There are no 24-hour drugstores (chemists) in London. However, it should not be difficult to find one in central London that is open until 10 PM.

Bring along a copy of any prescription you may have from your doctor in case you should need a refill. In the case of minor complaints, British pharmacists may do some prescribing and *may* fill a foreign prescription; however, do not count on this. In most cases, you will need a local doctor to rewrite the prescription. Even in an emergency, a traveler will more than likely be given only enough of a drug to last until a local prescription can be obtained.

Emergency assistance also is available from the various medical programs designed for travelers who have chronic ailments or whose illness requires them to return home:

*International Association for Medical Assistance to Travelers* (*IAMAT;* 417 Center St., Lewiston, NY 14092; phone: 716-754-4883). Entitles members to the services of participating doctors around the world, as well as clinics and hospitals in various locations. Participating physicians agree to adhere to a basic charge of around $40 to see a patient referred by *IAMAT.* To join, simply write to *IAMAT;* in about 3 weeks you will receive a membership card, the booklet of members, and an inoculation chart. A nonprofit organization, *IAMAT* appreciates donations; with a donation of $25 or more, you will receive a set of worldwide climate charts detailing weather and sanitary conditions. (Delivery can take up to 5 weeks, so plan ahead.)

*International SOS Assistance* (PO Box 11568, Philadelphia, PA 19116; phone: 800-523-8930 or 215-244-1500). Subscribers are provided with telephone access — 24 hours a day, 365 days a year — to a worldwide, monitored, multilingual network of medical centers. A phone call brings assistance ranging from a telephone consultation to transportation home by ambulance or aircraft, or, in some cases, transportation of a family member to wherever you are hospitalized. Individual rates are $35 for 2 weeks of coverage ($3.50 for each additional day), $70 for 1 month, or $240 for 1 year; couple and family rates also are available.

*Medic Alert Foundation* (2323 N. Colorado, Turlock, CA 95380; phone: 800-ID-ALERT or 209-668-3333). If you have a health condition that may not be readily perceptible to the casual observer — one that might result in a tragic error in an emergency situation — this organization offers identification emblems specifying such conditions. The foundation also maintains a computerized central file from which your complete medical history is available 24 hours a day by phone (the telephone number is clearly inscribed on the emblem). The onetime membership fee (between $25 and $45) is based on the type of metal from which the emblem is made — the choices range from stainless steel to 10K gold-filled.

*TravMed* (PO Box 10623, Baltimore, MD 21204; phone: 800-732-5309 or 301-296-5225). For $3 per day, subscribers receive comprehensive medical assistance while abroad. Major medical expenses are covered up to $100,000, and special transportation home or of a family member to wherever you are hospitalized is provided at no additional cost.

---

■ **Note:** Those who are unable to take a reserved flight due to personal illness or who must fly home unexpectedly due to a family emergency should be aware that airlines may offer a discounted airfare (or arrange a partial refund) if the traveler can demonstrate that his or her situation is indeed a legitimate emergency. Your inability to fly or the illness or death of an immediate family member usually must be substantiated by a doctor's note or the name, relationship, and funeral home from which the deceased will be buried. In such cases, airlines often will waive certain advance purchase restrictions or you may receive a refund check or voucher for future travel at a later date. Be aware, however, that this bereavement fare may not necessarily be the least expensive fare available and, if possible, it is best to have a travel agent check all possible flights through a computer reservations system (CRS).

---

 **LEGAL AID AND CONSULAR SERVICES:** There is one crucial place to keep in mind when outside the US, namely, the American Embassy, which is located at 24-31 Grosvenor Sq. W., London W1A 1AE (phone: 71-499-9000).

If you are injured or become seriously ill, or if you encounter legal difficulties, the consulate is the first place to turn, although its powers and capabilities are limited. It will direct you to medical assistance and notify your relatives if you are ill; it can advise you of your rights and provide a list of lawyers if you are arrested, but it cannot interfere with the local legal process.

For questions about US citizens arrested abroad, how to get money to them, and other useful information, call the *Citizens' Emergency Center* of the Office of Special Consular Services in Washington, DC, at 202-647-5225. (For further information about this invaluable hotline, see below.)

A consulate exists to aid US citizens in serious matters, such as illness, destitution, and the above legal difficulties. It is not there to aid in trivial situations, such as canceled reservations or lost baggage, no matter how important these matters may seem to the victimized tourist. If you should get sick, the US consul can provide names of doctors, dentists, local hospitals, and clinics; the consul also will contact family members in the US and help arrange special ambulance service for a flight home. In a situation involving "legitimate and proven poverty" of an US citizen stranded abroad without funds, the consul will contact sources of money (such as family or friends in the US), apply for aid to agencies in foreign countries, and in the last resort — which is *rarely* — arrange for repatriation at government expense, although this is a loan that must be repaid. And in case of natural disasters or civil unrest, consulates around the world handle the evacuation of US citizens if it becomes necessary.

As mentioned above, the US State Department operates a *Citizens' Emergency Center,* which offers a number of services to US citizens abroad and their families at home. In addition to giving callers up-to-date information on trouble spots, the center will contact authorities abroad in an attempt to locate a traveler or deliver an urgent message. In case of illness, death, arrest, destitution, or repatriation of an US citizen on foreign soil, it will relay information to relatives at home if the consulate is unable to do so. Travel advisory information is available 24 hours a day to people with touch-tone phones (phone: 202-647-5225). Callers with rotary phones can get information at this number from 8:15 AM to 10 PM (eastern standard time) on weekdays; 9 AM to 3 PM Saturdays. In the event of an emergency, this number also may be called during these hours. For emergency calls only, at all other times, call 202-634-3600 and ask for the duty officer.

# Drinking and Drugs

 **DRINKING:** It is more than likely that some of the warmest memories of a trip to London will be moments of conviviality shared over a drink in a neighborhood pub or sunlit café. Visitors will find that liquor, wine, and brandies in Great Britain are distilled to the same proof and often are the same labels as those found at home.

You'll want to try the country's specialties. English beer is among the favorites in pubs and cafés. English beer usually has at least three varieties: regular, light, and dark. Most English pubs and cafés serve beer in bottles and on tap. Besides Fuller's, a local London brew, Watney's and Charrington's are popular national brands.

British pubs are open Mondays through Saturdays from 11 AM to 11 PM, although some pubs don't serve liquor until noon. On Sundays, pubs are open from noon to 3 PM and 7 to 11:30 PM. In Great Britain, the legal drinking age is 18.

As in the US, national taxes on alcohol affect the prices of liquor in Great Britain, and as a general rule, mixed drinks — especially imported liquors such as whiskey and gin — are more expensive than at home. If you like a drop before dinner, a good way to save money is to buy a bottle of your favorite brand at the airport before leaving the US and enjoy it in your hotel before setting forth.

Visitors to Great Britain may bring in 2 bottles of wine and 1 bottle of liquor per person duty-free. If you are buying any quantity of alcohol (such as a case of wine) in Great Britain and traveling through other European countries on your route back to the US, you will have to pass through customs and pay duty at each border crossing, so you might want to arrange to have it shipped home. Whether bringing it with you or shipping, you will have to pay US import duties on any quantity over the allowed 1 liter (see *Customs and Returning to the US,* in this section).

**DRUGS:** Illegal narcotics are as prevalent in Great Britain as in the US, but the moderate legal penalties and vague social acceptance that marijuana has gained in the US have no equivalents in Great Britain. Due to the international war on drugs, enforcement of drug laws is becoming increasingly strict throughout the world. Local European narcotics officers and customs officials are renowned for their absence of understanding and lack of a sense of humor — especially where foreigners are involved.

Opiates and barbiturates, and other increasingly popular drugs — "white powder" substances like heroin, cocaine, and "crack" (the cocaine derivative) — continue to be of major concern to narcotics officials. Most European countries — including Great Britain — have toughened laws regarding illegal drugs and narcotics, and it is important to bear in mind that the type or quantity of drugs involved is of minor importance. Particularly for foreigners, the maximum penalties may be imposed for possessing even *traces* of illegal drugs. There is a high conviction rate in these cases, and bail for foreigners is rare. Persons arrested are subject to the laws of the country they are visiting, and there isn't much that the US consulate can do for drug offenders beyond providing a list of lawyers. The best advice we can offer is this: Don't carry, use, buy, or sell illegal drugs.

Those who carry medicines that contain a controlled drug should be sure to have a current doctor's prescription with them. Ironically, travelers can get into almost as much trouble coming through US customs with over-the-counter drugs picked up abroad that contain substances that are controlled in the US. Cold medicines, pain relievers, and the like often have codeine or codeine derivatives that are illegal, except by prescription, in the US. Throw them out before leaving for home.

■ **Be forewarned:** US narcotics agents warn travelers of the increasingly common ploy of drug dealers asking travelers to transport a "gift" or other packages back to the US. Don't be fooled into thinking that the protection of US law applies abroad — accused of illegal drug trafficking, you will be considered guilty until you prove your innocence. In other words, do not, under any circumstances, agree to take anything across the border for a stranger.

# Tipping

In London, as throughout Great Britain and most of the rest of Europe, you will find the custom of including some kind of service charge on the bill for a meal more common than in North America. This can confuse Americans unfamiliar with the custom. On the one hand, many a traveler, unaware of this policy, has left many a superfluous tip. On the other hand, travelers aware of this policy may make the mistake of assuming that it takes care of everything. It doesn't. While "service included" in theory eliminates any question about how much and whom to tip, in practice there still are occasions when on-the-spot tips are appropriate. Among these are tips to show appreciation for special services, as well as tips meant to say "thank you" for services rendered. So keep a pocketful of 50 pence or £1 bills (or coins) ready, and hand these out like dollar bills.

In London restaurants, the service charge is usually calculated as part of the prices listed; if not, it will be added to the final bill (the more expensive restaurants tend to follow the latter practice). In either instance, the establishments are required to state clearly on the menu that its patrons will automatically be billed a service charge. For the most part, if you see a notation at the bottom of the menu without a percentage figure, the charge should be included in the prices; if a percentage figure is indicated, the service charge had not previously been added. To further confuse the issue, not every restaurant notes what its policy is. If you are at all unsure, ask a waiter.

This service charge generally range between 10% and 15%. In the rare instance where it isn't added, a 15% tip to the waiter — just as in the US — usually is a safe figure, although one should never hesitate to penalize poor service or reward excellent and efficient attention by leaving less or more. If the tip has been added, no further gratuity is expected — though it's a common practice in Europe to leave a few extra coins on the table. The emphasis is on *few,* and the current equivalent of $1 usually is quite adequate.

Although it's not necessary to tip the maître d' of most restaurants — unless he has been especially helpful in arranging a special party or providing a table (slipping him something in a crowded restaurant *may* get you seated sooner or procure a preferred table) — when tipping is desirable or appropriate, the least amount should be the local equivalent of $5. In the finest restaurants, where a multiplicity of servers are present, plan to tip 5% to the captain. The sommelier (wine waiter) is entitled to a gratuity of approximately 10% of the price of the bottle.

As in restaurants, visitors may find a service charge of 10% to 15% included in their final bill at some London hotels, although not all hotels do. And if there is a service charge, it may again appear in two forms: either included in the room rate or added to the final bill. No additional gratuities are required — or expected — if the service charge is already billed. It is unlikely that a service charge will be added to bills in small family-run guesthouses or other modest establishments. In these cases, guests should let their instincts be their guide; no tipping is expected by members of the family who own the establishment, but it is a nice gesture to leave something for others — such as a dining room waiter or a maid — who may have been helpful. A gratuity of around $1 per night is adequate in most cases.

If a hotel does not automatically add a service charge, it is perfectly proper for guests to ask to have an extra 10% to 15% added to their bill, to be distributed among those who served them. This may be an especially convenient solution in a large hotel, where it's difficult to determine just who out of a horde of attendants actually performed particular services.

For those who prefer to distribute tips themselves, a chambermaid generally is tipped at the rate of approximately $1 per day. Tip the concierge or hall porter for specific services only, with the amount of such gratuities dependent on the level of service provided. For any special service you receive in a hotel, a tip is expected — the current equivalent of $1 being the minimum for a small service.

Bellhops, doormen, and porters at hotels and transportation centers generally are tipped at the rate of $1 per piece of luggage, along with a small additional amount if a doorman helps with a cab or car. Once upon a time, taxi drivers in Europe would give you a rather odd look if presented with a tip for a fare, but times have changed, and 10% of the amount on the meter is now a standard gratuity.

**Miscellaneous tips:** Tipping ushers in a movie house, theater, or concert hall used to be the rule, but is becoming less common — the best policy is to check what other patrons are doing and follow suit. Most of the time, the program is not free, and in lieu of a tip it is common practice to purchase a program from the person who seats you. Sightseeing tour guides also should be tipped. If you are traveling in a group, decide together what you want to give the guide and present it from the group at the end of the tour. If you have been individually escorted, the amount paid should depend on the degree of your satisfaction, but it should not be less than 10% of the total tour price. Museum and monument guides also usually are tipped, and it is a nice touch to tip a caretaker who unlocks a small church or turns on the lights in a chapel.

In barbershops and beauty salons, tip as you would at home, keeping in mind that the percentages vary according to the type of establishment — 10% in the most expensive salons; 15% to 20% in less expensive establishments. (As a general rule, the person who washes your hair should get an additional small tip.) The washroom attendants in these places, or wherever you see one, should get a small tip — they usually set out a little plate with a coin already on it indicating the suggested denomination.

Tipping always is a matter of personal preference. In the situations covered above, as well as in any others that arise where you feel a tip is expected or due, feel free to express your pleasure or displeasure. Again, never hesitate to reward excellent and efficient attention and to penalize poor service. Give an extra gratuity and a word of thanks when someone has gone out of his or her way for you. Either way, the more personal the act of tipping, the more appropriate it seems. And if you didn't like the service — or the attitude — don't tip.

# Duty-Free Shopping and Value Added Tax

**DUTY-FREE SHOPS:** Note that at the time of this writing, because of the newly integrated European economy, there was some question as to the fate and number of duty-free shops that would be maintained at international airports in member countries of the European Economic Community (EEC). It appears, however, that those traveling between EEC countries and any country *not* a member of the Common Market will still be entitled to buy duty-free items. Since the United States is not a Common Market member, duty-free purchases by US travelers will, presumably, remain as they have been even after the end of 1992.

If common sense says that it always is less expensive to buy goods in an airport duty-free shop than to buy them at home or in the streets of a foreign city, travelers should be aware of some basic facts. Duty-free, first of all, does not mean that the goods travelers buy will be free of duty when they return to the US. Rather, it means that the shop has paid no import tax in acquiring goods of foreign make, because the goods are not to be used in the country where the shop is located. This is why duty-free goods are available only in the restricted, passengers-only area of international airports or are delivered to departing passengers on the plane. In a duty-free store, travelers save money only on goods of foreign make because they are the only items on which an import tax would be charged in any other store. There usually is no saving on locally made items, although in countries such as Great Britain that impose value added taxes (see below) that are refundable to foreigners, the prices in airport duty-free shops are minus this tax, sparing travelers the often cumbersome procedures they otherwise have to follow to obtain a VAT refund.

Beyond this, there is little reason to delay buying locally made merchandise and/or souvenirs until reaching the airport. In fact, because airport duty-free shops usually pay high rents, the locally made goods they sell may well be more expensive than they would be in downtown stores. The real bargains are foreign goods, but — let the buyer beware — not all foreign goods automatically are less expensive in an airport duty-free shop. You can get a good deal on even small amounts of perfume, costing less than the usually required minimum purchase, tax-free. Other fairly standard bargains include spirits, smoking materials, cameras, clothing, watches, chocolates, and other food and luxury items — but first be sure to know what these items cost elsewhere. Terrific savings do exist (they are the reason for such shops, after all), but so do overpriced items that an unwary shopper might find equally tempting. In addition, if you wait to do your shopping at airport duty-free shops, you will be taking the chance that the desired item is out of stock or unavailable.

Duty-free shops are located in most major international airports throughout Europe, including London.

**VALUE ADDED TAX:** Commonly abbreviated as VAT, this is a tax levied by various European countries, including Great Britain, and added to the purchase price of most goods and services. The VAT on most items is 17.5%.

The tax is intended for residents (and already is included in the price tag), but visitors are also required to pay it unless they have purchases shipped by the store directly to an address abroad. If visitors pay the tax and take purchases with them, they generally are entitled to a refund under a retail export scheme that has been in operation for several years. However, retail stores participate in this refund scheme on a voluntary basis; there is no legislation requiring them to do so. If you make purchases at a store that does not participate in the refund scheme, you will not be able to get the VAT refund. To further complicate matters, each store sets its own minimum amount of purchase for which a refund can be granted. But most stores require you to spend at least £50 to £75 at one store before you can get a refund. If you are planning any major purchase, make sure the store that you are shopping at participates in the refund scheme, and inquire about the required minimum amount of purchase.

In most cases, stores will provide the appropriate refund forms on request. If the store does not have this form, it can be obtained at the refund office at the airport, which also can provide information on the procedure for submitting the paperwork to obtain the refund. Visitors leaving Great Britain must have all of their receipts for purchases and refund vouchers stamped by customs; as customs officials may well ask to see the merchandise, it's a good idea not to pack it in the bottom of your suitcase. A copy of the stamped form has to be mailed to the store (there's always a mailbox nearby the customs desk), and you can arrange with the store owner whether you wish to have the refund credited to your credit card or have a check sent to you. In the past, returning travelers have complained of delays in receiving the refunds, however, the situation has improved somewhat, and you can generally expect a check or credit card refund in about a month.

Note that at London's Heathrow Airport you can receive an on-the-spot cash VAT refund (for any amount up to £500) at various desks near customs and passport control (any British customs official can direct you). For further information, or to trace a delayed refund, write to Tourist Tax Free Shopping, Europa House, 266 Upper Richmond Rd., London SW15 6TQ, England (phone: 81-785-3277).

A VAT refund by dollar check or by credit to a credit card account is relatively hassle-free. If it arrives in the form of a foreign currency check and if the refund is less than a significant amount, charges imposed by US banks for converting foreign currency refund checks — which can run as high as $15 or more — could make the whole exercise hardly worth your while.

Far less costly is sending your foreign currency check (after endorsing it) to *Ruesch International,* which will covert it to a check in US dollars for a $2 fee (deducted from the dollar check). Other services include commission-free traveler's checks and foreign currency, which can be ordered by mail. Contact *Ruesch International* at one of the following address: 191 Peachtree St., Atlanta, GA 30303 (phone: 404-222-9300); 3 First National Plaza, Suite 2020, Chicago, IL 60602 (phone: 312-332-5900); 1925 Century Park E., Suite 240, Los Angeles, CA 90067 (phone: 213-277-7800); 608 Fifth Ave., "Swiss Center," New York, NY 10020 (phone: 212-977-2700); and 1350 Eye St. NW, 10th Floor and street level, Washington, DC 20005 (phone: 800-424-2923 or 202-408-1200).

■ **Buyer Beware:** You may come across shops *not* at airports that call themselves duty-free shops. These require shoppers to show a foreign passport but are subject to the same rules as other stores, including paying import duty on foreign items. What "tax-free" means in the case of these establishments is something of an advertising strategy: They are announcing loud and clear that they do, indeed, offer the VAT refund service — sometimes on the spot (minus a fee for higher overhead). Prices may be no better at these stores, and could be even higher due to this service.

# Customs and Returning to the US

 Whether you return to the United States by air or sea, you must declare to the US Customs official at the point of entry everything you have bought or acquired while in Europe. The customs check can go smoothly, lasting only a few minutes, or can take hours, depending on the officer's instinct. To speed up the process, keep all your receipts handy and try to pack your purchases together in an accessible part of your suitcase. It might save you from unpacking all your belongings.

**DUTY-FREE ARTICLES:** In general, the duty-free allowance for US citizens returning from abroad is $400. This duty-free limit covers purchases that accompany you and are for personal use. This limit includes items used or worn while abroad, souvenirs for friends, and gifts received during the trip. A flat 10% duty based on the "fair retail value in country of acquisition" is assessed on the next $1,000 worth of merchandise brought in for personal use or gifts. Amounts above those two levels are dutiable at a variety of rates. The average rate for typical tourist purchases is about 12%, but you can find out about specific items by consulting *Tariff Schedules of the United States* in a library or at any US Customs Service office.

Families traveling together may make a joint declaration to customs, which permits one member to exceed his or her duty-free exemption to the extent that another falls short. Families also may pool purchases dutiable under the flat rate. A family of three, for example, would be eligible for up to a total of $3,000 at the 10% flat duty rate (after each member had used up his or her $400 duty-free exemption) rather than three separate $1,000 allowances. This grouping of purchases is extremely useful when considering the duty on a high-tariff item, such as jewelry or a fur coat.

Personal exemptions can be used once every 30 days; in order to be eligible, an individual must have been out of the country for more than 48 hours. If any portion of the exemption has been used once within any 30-day period or if your trip is less than 48 hours long, the duty-free allowance is cut to $25.

There are certain articles, however, that are duty-free only up to certain limits. The $25 allowance includes the following: 10 cigars (not Cuban), 60 cigarettes, and 4 ounces of perfume. Individuals eligible for the full $400 duty-free limit are allowed 1 carton of cigarettes (200), 100 cigars, and 1 liter of liquor or wine if the traveler is over 21.

Alcohol above this allowance is liable for both duty and an Internal Revenue tax. Antiques, if they are 100 or more years old and you have proof from the seller of that fact, are duty-free, as are paintings and drawings if done entirely by hand.

To avoid paying duty twice, register the serial numbers of foreign-made watches and electronic equipment with the nearest US Customs bureau before departure; receipts of insurance policies also should be carried for other foreign-made items. (Also see the note at the end of *Entry Requirements and Documents,* in this section.)

Gold, gold medals, bullion, and up to $10,000 in currency or negotiable instruments may be brought into the US without being declared. Sums over $10,000 must be declared in writing.

The allotment for individual "unsolicited" gifts mailed from abroad (no more than one per day per recipient) is $50 retail value per gift. These gifts do not have to be declared and are not included in your duty-free exemption (see below). Although you should include a receipt for the purchases with each package, the examiner is empowered to impose a duty based on his or her assessment of the value of the goods. The duty owed is collected by the US Postal Service when the package is delivered (also see below). More information on mailing packages home from abroad is contained in the US Customs Service pamphlet *Buyer Beware, International Mail Imports* (see below for where to write for this and other useful brochures).

**CLEARING CUSTOMS:** This is a simple procedure. Forms are distributed by airline or ship personnel before arrival. (Note that a $5-per-person service charge — called a user fee — is collected by airlines to help cover the cost of customs checks, but this is included in the ticket price.) If your purchases total no more than the $400 duty-free limit, you need only fill out the identification part of the form and make an oral declaration to the customs inspector. If entering with more than $400 worth of goods, you must submit a written declaration.

Customs agents are businesslike, efficient, and not unkind. During the peak season, clearance can take time, generally because of the strain imposed by a number of jumbo jets simultaneously discharging their passengers, not because of unwarranted zealousness on the part of the customs people.

Efforts to streamline procedures used to include the so-called Citizens' Bypass Program, which allowed US citizens whose purchases were within their duty-free allowance to go to the "green line," where they simply showed their passports to the customs inspector. Although at the time of this writing this procedure still is being followed at some international airports in the US, most airports have returned to an earlier system. US citizens arriving from overseas now have to go through a passport check by the Immigration & Naturalization Service (INS) before recovering their baggage and proceeding to customs. (This additional wait will delay clearance on re-entry into the US, although citizens will not be on the same line as foreign visitors.) Although all passengers have to go through this passport inspection, those entering with purchases within the duty-free limit may be spared a thorough customs inspection. Inspectors still retain the right to search any luggage they choose, however, so don't do anything foolish.

It is illegal not to declare dutiable items; not to do so, in fact, constitutes smuggling, and the penalty can be anything from stiff fines and seizure of the goods to prison sentences. It simply isn't worth doing. Nor should you go along with the suggestions of foreign merchants who offer to help you secure a bargain by deceiving customs officials in any way. Such transactions frequently are a setup, using the foreign merchant as an agent of US customs. Another agent of US customs is TECS, the Treasury Enforcement Communications System, a computer that stores all kinds of pertinent information on returning citizens. There is a basic rule to buying goods abroad, and it should never be broken: *If you can't afford the duty on something, don't buy it.* Your list or verbal declaration should include all items purchased abroad, as well as gifts received abroad, purchases made at the behest of others, the value of repairs, and anything brought in for resale in the US.

Do not include in the list items that do not accompany you, i.e., purchases that you have mailed or had shipped home. These are dutiable in any case, even if for your own use and even if the items that accompany your return from the same trip do not exhaust your duty-free exemption. It is a good idea, if you have accumulated too much while abroad, to mail home any personal effects (made and bought in the US) that you no longer need rather than your foreign purchases. These personal effects pass through US Customs as "American goods returned" and are not subject to duty.

If you cannot avoid shipping home your foreign purchases, however, the US Customs Service suggests that the package be clearly marked "Not for Sale," and that a copy of the bill of sale be included. The US Customs examiner usually will accept this as indicative of the article's fair retail value, but if he or she believes it to be falsified or feels the goods have been seriously undervalued, a higher retail value may be assigned.

**FORBIDDEN ITEMS:** Narcotics, plants, and many types of food are not allowed into the US. Drugs are totally illegal, with the exception of medication prescribed by a physician. It's a good idea not to travel with too large a quantity of any given prescription drug (although, in the event that a pharmacy is not open when you need it, bring along several extra doses) and to have the prescription on hand in case any question arises either abroad or when re-entering the US.

Any sculpture that is part of an architectural structure, any authentic archaeological find, or other artifacts that may be of national interest may not be exported from Great Britain without the authorization of the Department of Trade and Industry; for information on items that might fall into this category, contact the Department of Trade and Industry (Export Licensing Division, Kingsgate House, 66/74 Victoria St., London SW1E 6SW; phone: 71-215-8029). If you do not obtain prior permission of the proper regulatory agencies, such items will be confiscated at the border, and you will run the risk of being fined or imprisoned.

Tourists have long been forbidden to bring into the US foreign-made, US-trademarked articles purchased abroad (if the trademark is recorded with customs) without written permission. It's now permissible to enter with one such item in your possession as long as it's for personal use.

The US Customs Service implements the rigorous Department of Agriculture regulations concerning the importation of vegetable matter, seeds, bulbs, and the like. Living vegetable matter may not be imported without a permit, and everything must be inspected, permit or not. Approved items (which do not require a permit) include dried bamboo and woven items made of straw; beads made of most seeds (but not jequirity beans — the poisonous scarlet and black seed of the rosary pea); cones of pine and other trees; roasted coffee beans; most flower bulbs; flowers (without roots); dried or canned fruits, jellies, or jams; polished rice, dried beans and teas; herb plants (not witchweed); nuts (but not acorns, chestnuts, or nuts with outer husks); dried lichens, mushrooms, truffles, shamrocks, and seaweed; and most dried spices.

Other processed foods and baked goods usually are okay. Regulations on meat products generally depend on the country of origin and manner of processing. As a rule, commercially canned meat, hermetically sealed and cooked in the can so that it can be stored without refrigeration, is permitted, but not all canned meat fulfills this requirement. Be careful when buying European-made pâté, for instance. Goose liver pâté in itself is acceptable, but the pork fat that often is part of it, either as an ingredient or a rind, may not be. Even canned pâtés may not be admitted for this reason. (The imported ones you see in US stores have been prepared and packaged according to US regulations.) So before stocking up on a newfound favorite, it pays to check in advance — otherwise you might have to leave it behind.

The US Customs Service also enforces federal laws that prohibit the entry of articles made from the furs or hides of animals on the endangered species list. Beware of shoes, bags, and belts made of crocodile and certain kinds of lizard, and anything made from tortoiseshell; this also applies to preserved crocodiles, lizards, and turtles sometimes sold in gift shops. And if you're shopping for big-ticket items, beware of fur coats made from the skins of spotted cats. They are sold in Europe, but they will be confiscated upon your return to the US, and there will be no refund. For information about other animals on the endangered species list, contact the Department of the Interior, US Fish and Wildlife Service (Publications Unit, 4401 N. Fairfax Dr., Room 130, Arlington, VA 22203; phone: 703-358-1711), and ask for the free publication *Facts About Federal Wildlife Laws.*

Also note that some foreign governments prohibit the export of items made from certain species of wildlife, and the US honors any such restrictions. Before you go shopping in any foreign country, check with the US Department of Agriculture (G110 Federal Bldg., Hyattsville, MD 20782; phone: 301-436-8413) and find out what items are prohibited by the country you will be visiting.

The US Customs Service publishes a series of free pamphlets with customs information. It includes *Know Before You Go,* a basic discussion of customs requirements pertaining to all travelers; *Buyer Beware, International Mail Imports; Travelers' Tips on Bringing Food, Plant, and Animal Products into the United States; Importing a Car; GSP and the Traveler; Pocket Hints; Currency Reporting; Pets, Wildlife, US Customs; Customs Hints for Visitors (Nonresidents);* and *Trademark Information for Travelers.* For the entire series or individual pamphlets, write to the US Customs Service (PO Box 7407, Washington, DC 20044) or contact any of the seven regional offices — in Boston, Chicago, Houston, Long Beach (California), Miami, New Orleans, and New York. The US Customs Service has a tape-recorded message whereby callers using touch-tone phones can get more information on various topics; the number is 202-566-8195. These pamphlets provide great briefing material, but if you still have questions when you're in Europe, contact the nearest US consulate.

# Sources and Resources

## Tourist Information Offices

North American branches of the British Tourist Authority generally are the best sources of travel information, and most of their many, varied publications are free for the asking. For the best results, request general information on specific counties or cities, as well as publications relating to your particular areas of interest: accommodations, restaurants, special events, sports, guided tours, and facilities for specific sports. There is no need to send a self-addressed, stamped envelope with your request, unless specified. Following are the tourist information offices located in the US:

**Atlanta:** 2580 Cumberland Pkwy., Suite 470, Atlanta, GA 30339 (phone: 404-432-9635).

**Chicago:** 625 N. Michigan Ave., Suite 1510, Chicago, IL 60611 (phone: 312-787-0490).

**Los Angeles:** World Trade Center, 350 S. Figueroa St., Suite 450, Los Angeles, CA 90071 (phone: 213-628-3525).

**New York:** 40 W. 57th St., Suite 320, New York, NY 10019 (phone: 212-581-4700).

## The British Embassy and Consulates in the US

The British government maintains an embassy and a number of consulates in the US. One of their primary functions is to provide visas for certain resident aliens (depending on their country of origin) and for Americans planning to visit for longer than 6 months, or to study, reside, or work in Great Britain. Consulates also are empowered to sign official documents and to notarize copies or translations of US documents, which may be necessary for those papers to be considered legal abroad.

The British Embassy is located at 3100 Massachusetts Ave. NW, Washington, DC 20008 (phone: 202-462-1340). Listed below are the British consulates in the US. In general, these offices are open 9 AM to 1 PM, Mondays through Fridays — call ahead to be sure.

### British Consulates in the US

**Anchorage:** Honorary British Consulate, University of Alaska, Anchorage, 3211 Providence Dr., Anchorage, AK 99508 (phone: 907-786-4848).

**Atlanta:** British Consulate-General, Suite 2700, Marquis I Tower, 245 Peachtree Center Ave., Atlanta, GA 30303 (phone: 404-524-5856).

**Boston:** British Consulate-General, Federal Reserve Plaza, 600 Atlantic Ave., 25th Floor, Boston, MA 02210 (phone: 617-248-9555).

**Chicago:** British Consulate-General, 33 N. Dearborn St., Chicago, IL 60602 (phone: 312-346-1810).

**Cleveland:** British Consulate, 55 Public Sq., Suite 1650, Cleveland, OH 44113-1963 (phone: 216-621-7674).

**Dallas:** British Consulate, 813 Stemmons Tower W., 2730 Stemmons Fwy., Dallas, TX 75207 (phone: 214-637-3600).

**Houston:** British Consulate-General, Suite 2250, Dresser Tower, 601 Jefferson, Houston, TX 77002 (phone: 713-659-6270).

**Los Angeles:** British Consulate-General, Suite 312, 3701 Wilshire Blvd., Los Angeles, CA 90010 (phone 213-385-7381).

**Miami:** British Consulate, Suite 2110, Brickell Bay Office Tower, 1001 S. Bayshore Dr., Miami, FL 33131 (phone: 305-374-1522).

**New Orleans:** Honorary British Consulate, 321 St. Charles Ave., 10th Floor, New Orleans, LA 70130 (phone: 504-586-8300).

**New York City:** British Consulate-General, 845 Third Ave., New York, NY 10022 (phone: 212-745-0200).

**Philadelphia:** Honorary British Consulate, c/o Mather & Co., 226 Walnut St., Philadelphia, PA 19106 (phone: 215-925-0118).

**Portland (Oregon):** British Consulate, 3515 SW Council Crest Dr., Portland, OR 97201 (phone: 503-227-5669).

**St. Louis:** Honorary British Consulate, 14904 Manor La., St. Louis, MO 63017 (phone: 314-227-1334).

**San Francisco:** British Consulate-General, 1 Sansome St., Suite 850, San Francisco, CA 94104 (phone: 415-981-3030).

**Seattle:** British Consulate, 820 First Interstate Center, 999 Third Ave., Seattle, WA 98104 (phone: 206-622-9255).

# Theater and Special Event Tickets

As you read this book, you will learn about events that spark your interest — everything from music festivals and special theater seasons to sporting championships — along with telephone numbers and addresses to which to write for descriptive brochures, reservations, or tickets. The British Tourist Authority can supply information on these and other special events and festivals that take place in London and the rest of Great Britain, though they cannot in all cases provide the actual program or detailed information on ticket prices.

Since many of these occasions often are fully booked well in advance, think about having your reservation in hand before you go. In some cases, tickets may be reserved over the phone and charged to a credit card, or you can send an international money order or foreign draft. If you do write, remember that any request from the US should be accompanied by an International Reply Coupon to ensure a response (send two of them for an airmail response). These international coupons, money orders, and drafts are available at US post offices.

For further information, write for the *European Travel Commission*'s extensive list of events scheduled for the entire year for its 24 member countries (including Great Britain). For a free copy, send a self-addressed, stamped, business-size (4 x 9½) envelope to "European Events," *European Travel Commission,* PO Box 1754, New York, NY 10185.

# Books, Newspapers, Magazines, and Newsletters

**BOOKS:** Throughout GETTING READY TO GO, numerous books and brochures have been recommended as good sources of further information on a variety of topics.

    **Suggested Reading** – The list below is made up of books we have seen and think worthwhile; it is by no means complete — but meant merely to start you on your way. These titles include some informative guides to special interests, solid fictional tales, and books that call your attention to things you might not notice otherwise.

## Travel

*The Best of Britain Guide: Heritage, Culture and Fine Hotels,* edited by Susan Grossman (published by American Express Europe; $29.95).

*Birnbaum's Great Britain 1992,* edited by Stephen Birnbaum and Alexandra Mayes Birnbaum (HarperCollins; $10).

*Blue Guide Wales,* by John Tomes (W. W. Norton & Company; $19.95).

*Egon Ronay's Guide to Hotels and Restaurants of Great Britain* (St. Martin's Press; $19.95).

*Gardens of England and Wales* (The National Gardens Scheme Charitable Trust; $6.95).

*Guide to Golf Courses in Britain* (published by Britain's *Automobile Association;* $15.95).

*Guide to National Trust Properties in Britain,* edited by Richard Powell (published by Britain's *Automobile Association;* $15.95).

*Nicholson's London Night Life Guide* (published jointly by Britain's *Automobile Association* and Ordnance Survey; $34.95).

*Ordnance Survey Guide to Historic Houses in Britain* (Hamlyn Publishing Group; $14.95).

*The Usborne Book of London,* by Moira Butterfield (Usborne Publishing; $11.95).

*Wales: Castles and Historic Places,* by David M. Robinson and Roger S. Thomas (Wales Tourist Board; $14.95).

## History, Biography, and Culture

*Ancient Britain,* by Timothy Darvill (published by Britain's *Automobile Association;* $9.95).

*Harbrace History of England,* by John Morton-Blum. A four-volume series (Harcourt Brace Jovanovich; $9.50 each).

*Henry VIII,* by G. D. Palmer (Longman; $9.48).

*Henry VIII and the English Nobility,* by Helen Miller (Basil Blackwell; $16.95).

*London: The Biography of a City,* by Christopher Hibbert (Viking Penguin; $16.95).

*Matriarch: Queen Mary and the House of Windsor,* by Anne Edwards (Morrow; $15.45).

*Understanding the United Kingdom: A Short Guide to British Culture, Politics, Geography, Economics and History,* by Henry G. Weisser (Hippocrene Books; $11.95).

## Literature

*The Adventures of Sherlock Holmes,* by Sir Arthur Conan Doyle (Avon; $12.95).

*Brideshead Revisited,* by Evelyn Waugh (Little, Brown & Co.; $7.95).

*The Canterbury Tales,* by Geoffrey Chaucer (Penguin, $3.50; Random House, $8.95; and Macmillan, $12.19).

*A Christmas Carol and Other Victorian Fairy Tales,* by Charles Dickens (Bantam; $2.95).

*Complete Works of William Shakespeare* (Doubleday; $22.95).

*Great Expectations,* by Charles Dickens (Berkley; $3.75).

*Jane Eyre,* by Emily Brontë (Penguin; $2.95).

*London Crimes,* by Charles Dickens (Rowan Tree; $7.95).

*Oliver Twist,* by Charles Dickens (Silver Burdett Press; $4.95).

*The Portable Milton,* works of John Milton (Viking Penguin; $8.95).

*The Portable Oscar Wilde* (Viking Penguin; $8.95).

## Food

*British Cookery,* edited by Lizzie Boyd (British Tourist Authority; $30.95).

*Egon Ronay's Good Food and Pub Guide* (St. Martin's Press; $13.95).

*Let's Stop for Tea* (published jointly by Britain's *Automobile Association* and Ordnance Survey; $34.95).

*Nicholson's London Pub Guide,* by Judy Allen (Robert Nicholson; $7.95).

## Shopping

*Born to Shop London,* by Suzy Gershman and Judith Thomas (Bantam Books; $8.95).

*Guide to the Antique Shops of Britain 1991,* compiled by Carol Adams (Antique Collector's Club, Ltd.; $29.50).

*The Serious Shopper's Guide to London,* by Beth Reiber (Prentice Hall Press; $15.95).

In addition, *Culturgrams* is a handy series of pamphlets that provide a good sampling of information on the people, cultures, sights, and bargains to be found in over 90 countries around the world. Each four-page, newsletter-size leaflet covers one country, and Great Britain is included in the series. The topics included range from customs and courtesies to lifestyles and demographics. These fact-filled pamphlets are published by the David M. Kennedy Center for International Studies at Brigham Young University; for an order form, contact the group c/o Publication Services (280 HRCB, Provo, UT 84602; phone: 801-378-6528). When ordering from 1 to 5 *Culturgrams,* the price is $1 each; 6 to 49 pamphlets cost 50¢ each; and for larger quantities, the price per copy goes down proportionately.

Another source of cultural information is *Do's and Taboos Around the World,* compiled by the Parker Pen Company and edited by Roger E. Axtell. It focuses on protocol, customs, etiquette, hand gestures and body language, gift giving, the dangers of using US jargon, and so on, and can be fun to read even if you're not going anyplace. It's available for $10.95 in bookstores or through John Wiley & Sons, 1 Wiley Dr., Somerset, NJ 08875 (phone: 908-469-4400).

**NEWSPAPERS AND MAGAZINES:** A subscription to the *International Herald Tribune* is a good idea for dedicated travelers. This English-language newspaper is written and edited mostly in Paris and is *the* newspaper read most regularly and avidly by Americans abroad to keep up with world news, US news, sports, the stock market (US and foreign), fluctuations in the exchange rate, and an assortment of help-wanted ads, real estate listings, and personals, global in scope. Published 6 days a week (no Sunday paper), it is available at newsstands throughout the US and in cities worldwide. You should be able to find it in most of the newsstands on the streets and in hotels. A 1-year subscription in the US costs $349. To subscribe, write or call the Subscription Manager, *International Herald Tribune,* 850 Third Ave., 10th Floor, New York, NY 10022 (phone: 800-882-2884 or 212-752-3890).

Among the major US publications that can be bought (generally a day or two after distribution in the US) in many of the larger cities, such as London, at hotels, airports, and newsstands, are the *Los Angeles Times, The New York Times, USA Today,* and the *Wall Street Journal.* As with other imports, expect these and other US publications to cost considerably more in London than in the US.

**NEWSLETTERS:** Throughout GETTING READY TO GO we have mentioned specific newsletters that our readers may be interested in consulting for further information. One of the very best sources of detailed travel information is *Consumer Reports Travel Letter.* Published monthly by Consumers Union (PO Box 53629, Boulder, CO 80322-3629; phone: 800-999-7959), it offers comprehensive coverage of the travel scene on a wide variety of fronts. A year's subscription costs $37; 2 years, $57.

In addition, the following travel newsletters provide useful up-to-date information on travel services and bargains:

> *Entree* (PO Box 5148, Santa Barbara, CA 93150; phone: 805-969-5848). This newsletter caters to a sophisticated, discriminating traveler with the means to explore the places mentioned. Subscribers have access to a 24-hour hotline providing information on restaurants and accommodations around the world. Monthly; a year's subscription costs $59.
>
> *Travel Smart* (Communications House, 40 Beechdale Rd., Dobbs Ferry, NY 10522; phone: 914-693-8300 in New York; 800-327-3633 elsewhere in the US). This monthly covers a wide variety of trips and travel discounts. A year's subscription costs $37.

---

■ **Computer Services:** Anyone who owns a personal computer and a modem can subscribe to a database service providing everything from airline schedules and fares to restaurant listings. Two such services of particular use to travelers are *CompuServe* (5000 Arlington Center Blvd., Columbus, OH 43220; phone: 800-848-8199 or 614-457-8600; $39.95 to join, plus usage fees of $6 to $12.50 per hour) and *Prodigy Services* (445 Hamilton Ave., White Plains, 10601; phone: 800-822-6922 or 914-993-8000; $12.95 per month's subscription, plus variable usage fees). Before using any computer bulletin-board services, be sure to take precautions to prevent downloading of a computer "virus." First install one of the programs designed to screen out such nuisances.

---

# Weights and Measures

When traveling in Great Britain, you'll find that many quantities, whether length, weight, or capacity, are expressed in unfamilar terms. In fact, this is true for travel almost everywhere in the world, since the US is one of the last countries to make its way to the metric system. Your trip to London may serve to familiarize you with what one day may be the weights and measures at your local grocery store. Although the British are in the process of adopting the continental standards, the British *also* still use the pre–Common Market system, which is more familiar to US travelers. There are, however, a few quirks to British measurements that correspond to neither system.

There are some specific things to keep in mind during your trip. Fruits and vegetables at a market are recorded in pounds and ounces, but your luggage at the airport and your body weight may be measured in kilos (kilograms). This latter is particularly pleasing to people of significant size, who, instead of weighing 220 pounds, hit the scales at a mere 100 kilos. (A kilo equals 2.2 pounds, and 1 pound is .45 kilos.) The British more often discuss body weight in their own measurement, stones (1 stone equals 14 pounds); again, those who weigh 220 pounds will be pleased with the equivalent of approximately 16 stone.

Body temperature is measured in degrees centigrade or Celsius as well as on the more familiar Fahrenheit scale, so that a normal body temperature may be expressed as either 37C or 98.6F, and freezing is either 0 degrees C or 32F. Highway signs are written in several styles: in black and white for miles; in green and white for kilometers; or in miles and kilometers (1 mile equals 1.6 kilometers; 1 kilometer equals .62 mile). Gasoline is sold either by the liter (approximately 3.8 to 1 gallon) or by the gallon; and remember that a British or "imperial" gallon (another measurement unique to the British) is 20% larger than an American gallon.

The tables and conversion factors listed below should give you all the information you will need to understand any transaction, road sign, or map you encounter during your travels.

| APPROXIMATE EQUIVALENTS | | |
|---|---|---|
| **Metric Unit** | **Abbreviation** | **US Equivalent** |
| LENGTH | | |
| meter | m | 39.37 inches |
| kilometer | km | .62 mile |
| millimeter | mm | .04 inch |
| CAPACITY | | |
| liter | l | 1.057 quarts |
| WEIGHT | | |
| gram | g | .035 ounce |
| kilogram | kg | 2.2 pounds |
| metric ton | MT | 1.1 tons |
| ENERGY | | |
| kilowatt | kw | 1.34 horsepower |

## CONVERSION TABLES
## METRIC TO US MEASUREMENTS

| Multiply: | by: | to convert to: |
|---|---|---|
| **LENGTH** | | |
| millimeters | .04 | inches |
| meters | 3.3 | feet |
| meters | 1.1 | yards |
| kilometers | .6 | miles |
| | | |
| **CAPACITY** | | |
| liters | 2.11 | pints (liquid) |
| liters | 1.06 | quarts (liquid) |
| liters | .26 | gallons (liquid) |
| | | |
| **WEIGHT** | | |
| grams | .04 | ounces (avoir.) |
| kilograms | 2.2 | pounds (avoir.) |

## US TO METRIC MEASUREMENTS

| | | |
|---|---|---|
| **LENGTH** | | |
| inches | 25.0 | millimeters |
| feet | .3 | meters |
| yards | .9 | meters |
| miles | 1.6 | kilometers |
| | | |
| **CAPACITY** | | |
| pints | .47 | liters |
| quarts | .95 | liters |
| gallons | 3.8 | liters |
| | | |
| **WEIGHT** | | |
| ounces | 28.0 | grams |
| pounds | .45 | kilograms |

**TEMPERATURE**

$$°F = (°C \times 9/5) + 32 \qquad °C = (°F - 32) \times 5/9$$

# WORDS TO THE WISE

# Words to the Wise

**?** "Two people divided by the same language" is how Oscar Wilde described the transatlantic relationship between Britain and the US. He had a point. Below are some common British terms followed by their standard American translations. For definitions of terms that do not necessarily have American equivalents — such as "bubble and squeak" (a dish of leftover cabbage and potatoes) and "royal duke" (a duke who, as a member of the royal family, is also a prince) — consult the *Dictionary of Britain: An A to Z of the British Way of Life,* by Adrian Room (Oxford University Press; $29.95). It can also take the mystery out of the local newspapers by supplying the meanings of all sorts of British acronyms, from CAMRA (Campaign for Real Ale) to USDAW (Union of Shop, Distributive, and Allied Workers).

The following words and phrases should help you:

| | |
|---|---|
| *anorak* | parka |
| *aubergine* | eggplant |
| *bank holiday* | any legal holiday |
| *basin* | any bowl |
| *bathroom* | for baths, not a toilet |
| *beer* | Always order a type of beer, never just "beer." |
| *bitter* | a dark, dry beer |
| *lager* | American-style beer |
| *light ale* | sweet lager |
| *pale ale* | light-colored ale |
| *shandy* | beer mixed with a soft drink |
| *stout* | a dark, sweetish beer |
| *bespoke* | custom-tailored |
| *bill* | check |
| *billion* | a million millions |
| *Biro* | ballpoint pen |
| *biscuit* | cookie or cracker |
| *block (of flats)* | apartment house |
| *bonnet (car)* | hood |
| *boot (car)* | trunk |
| *bowler* | usually refers to the hat, not a player |
| *braces* | suspenders |
| *brolly or bumbershoot* | umbrella |
| *busker* | street musician |
| *café (pronounced "caff")* | cheap restaurant, greasy spoon |
| *candy floss* | cotton candy |
| *car park* | parking lot |
| *caravan* | RV, mobile home |
| *carriage* | rail car |
| *charabanc* | long-distance sightseeing bus |
| *chemist's* | pharmacy |
| *chips* | French fries |
| *Christian name* | first name |
| *City, the (in London)* | equivalent to American Wall Street |

| | |
|---|---|
| *clotted cream* | very thick sweet cream |
| *coach* | long-distance bus |
| *cold (drinks)* | cool, not iced |
| *corn* | any edible grain |
| *cot* | baby's crib |
| *cotton* | thread |
| *cotton wool* | absorbent cotton |
| *crisps* | potato chips |
| *crumpet* | English muffin; female sex partner |
| *cul-de-sac* | dead end |
| *cupboard* | closet |
| *double cream* | very heavy sweet cream |
| *dual carriageway* | divided highway |
| *dynamo (car)* | generator |
| *egg flip* | eggnog |
| *face flannel* | washcloth |
| *first floor* | second floor |
| *flat* | apartment |
| *flyover* | overpass |
| *fortnight* | 2 weeks |
| *gallon (British)* | about 1.2 US gallons |
| *galoshes* | short rubber boots |
| *gammon* | ham |
| *garden* | yard |
| *gear lever* | gearshift |
| *Geordie* | northeasterner |
| *grammar school* | selective middle school |
| *guinea* | one pound plus one shilling |
| *hat trick* | three successive wins |
| *high tea* | tea plus light supper |
| *hire purchase* | installment plan |
| *hoarding* | billboard |
| *hogmanay* | Scottish *New Year* |
| *hood (car)* | soft top of a convertible |
| *hoot* | a laugh, a riot |
| *hoover* | vacuum cleaner |
| *hump* | carry something heavy |
| *ice* | ice cream |
| *ironmonger* | hardware store |
| *jelly* | gelatin dessert (Jell-O) |
| *joint (meat)* | roast |
| *jumper (or jersey)* | sweater |
| *kettle* | teakettle |
| *knickers* | panties |
| *knock up* | wake up |
| *ladder* | a run in pantyhose |
| *left luggage office* | baggage room |
| *lemon squash* | what Americans call lemonade |
| *lemonade* | general term for soda |
| *lift* | elevator |
| *loo, lavatory, WC* | toilet |
| *lorry* | truck |
| *mackintosh, mac* | raincoat |

| | |
|---|---|
| *marrow* | zucchini |
| *mince, minced meat* | hamburger |
| *mod cons* | modern conveniences |
| *nappy* | diaper |
| *neat (liquor)* | straight up |
| *newsagents* | newsstands |
| *nipple* | *not* of a baby's bottle (anatomical reference only); |
|   see *teat* | |
| *noggin* | drink of beer or ale |
| *nosh* | hasty meal, not a snack |
| *off licence/wine merchant* | liquor store |
| *on special offer* | on sale |
| *overtake* | pass while driving |
| *pantomime* | song-and-dance show |
| *pants* | underpants (never trousers) |
| *petrol* | gasoline |
| *plimsolls* | sneakers |
| *pram* | baby carriage |
| *public school* | private school |
| *queue* | line of people |
| *queue up* | to stand in line |
| *quid* | pound (currency) |
| *rasher* | slice of bacon |
| *reception* | front desk |
| *return ticket* | round-trip ticket |
| *ring* | to telephone |
| *roundabout* | traffic circle |
| *rubber* | eraser |
| *saloon bar* | upper class pub |
| *schooner* | ordinary beer mug |
| *serviette* | napkin |
| *shepherd's pie* | mashed potato and ground meat pie |
| *shop* | small store |
| *sick* | nauseous (not ill in general) |
| *silencer (car)* | muffler |
| *single ticket* | one-way ticket |
| *stalls (theater)* | orchestra seats |
| *starkers* | naked |
| *starters* | hors d'oeuvres |
| *stone* | measure of weight equal to 14 pounds |
| *store* | department store |
| *surgery* | doctor's or dentist's office |
| *sweet* | dessert |
| *ta* | thanks |
| *ta-ta* | good-bye |
| *take-away* | take-out |
| *teat* | baby-bottle nipple |
| *telly* | television |
| *tights* | pantyhose |
| *to let* | to rent |
| *trainers* | sneakers |
| *trousers* | never called pants |
| *trunk call* | long-distance call |

| | |
|---|---|
| *underground, tube* | subway |
| *VAT* | value added tax (sales tax) |
| *vest* | man's undershirt |
| *wally* | a fool |
| *wellingtons or wellies* | rubber boots |
| *whisky* | Scotch whisky only |
| *wireless* | radio |
| *yard* | paved area |
| *zebra crossing* | pedestrian crosswalk |
| *Z* | pronounced "zed" |

# THE CITY

# LONDON

British author and journalist V. S. Pritchett noted that the essence of London is contained in the very sound of its name: Lon-don, a weighty word, solid, monumental, dignified, even ponderous. London is a shapeless city without a center; it sprawls anarchically over 620 square miles and brims over with a variety of neighborhoods and people. One of its sharpest observers, Daniel Defoe, portrayed London in the 18th century much as it could be described today: "It is . . . stretched out in buildings, straggling, confused . . . out of all shape, uncompact and unequal; neither long nor broad, round or square."

London can best be understood not as one city but as a conglomeration of villages that were incorporated whole, one by one, as the monster expanded — Chelsea, Battersea, Paddington, and Hampstead are just a few. Fortunately, all of its important parks and squares have remained inviolate, but not without a struggle, for London's merchant class — its backbone and its pride — often resisted and defeated town planners, ever since Parliament turned down Sir Christopher Wren's splendid plan to rebuild after the Great Fire of 1666. It was royalty and aristocracy who created and preserved the parks — St. James's Park, Hyde Park, Kensington Gardens, Regent's Park, and Kew Gardens were all royal parks — and their enthusiasm became contagious. The passionate regard of Londoners for their green spots has been one of the city's saving graces as it grew so helplessly and recklessly, more in the spirit of commerce than of urban planning.

Today's London — though marred by soulless high-rise intruders of glass and concrete — boasts more greenery than any metropolis could reasonably hope to retain in these philistine times. Aside from its many garden squares and the meticulously tended plots of so many Londoners' homes, the city is punctuated by a series of large parks and commons; besides those already mentioned, there are Wimbledon Common, Richmond Deer Park, Primrose Hill, Hampstead Heath — the list goes on and on. And to make even more certain that citification does not intrude too far into London life, a greenbelt, almost 100 square miles of forest and grassland, virtually encircles the city and, to the chagrin and impatience of developers, is meticulously preserved by law.

London's other natural resource, the river Thames, has not been so fortunate. As any glance at a map will show, London follows the serpentine meanderings of the Thames, England's principal river. Nearly everything of interest in London is on or near the Thames, for London is London because it is a natural port. The river has always been London's mainstay, for centuries its only east–west road, and it has justifiably been said that "every drop of the Thames is liquid history." At the site of the Royal Naval College in Greenwich, for example, there once stood a royal palace where Henry VIII and Elizabeth I were born, and where tournaments, pageants, and banquets were held.

A great river port and a city of gardens, London is also a city of stately squares and monuments, of royalty with its pomp and ceremony, a cosmopolitan city of the first rank. Until World War II, it was the capital of the mammoth and far-flung British Empire upon which, it was said, the sun never set. For many centuries, a powerful Britannia ruled a considerable section of the globe — the largest since Roman times — and the English language spread from the inconsiderable British Isles to become the dominant language all over the world, from North America to India.

If the British Empire has contracted drastically, it has done so gracefully, among memories of its greatest days. And if once-subject peoples hated their oppressor, they still love London, and many have chosen to live there. London is still the center of the Commonwealth of independent nations that were once British colonies, and its cosmopolitan atmosphere owes a great deal to the ubiquity of former colonials. Their presence is felt in the substantial Indian-Pakistani community in the Southall district of West London; in the strong Caribbean flavor in Brixton; in Chinatown in and around Gerrard Street — a hop, skip, and a jump from Piccadilly Circus; in the Cypriot groceries and bakeries of Camden Town; and in the majestic mosque on the fringe of Regent's Park.

A tantalizing diversity of accents flavors the English language here — accents from Australia and Barbados, Bangladesh and Nigeria, Canada and Malaysia, Kenya and South Africa, Sri Lanka and Ireland, Hong Kong and the US. And then the various inflections of Britain itself also are to be heard in the streets of London — the lilt and rasp of cockney, Oxford, Somerset, Yorkshire, the Scottish Highlands, and the Welsh mining towns.

London's somewhat onomatopoeic name derives from the Celtic term *Llyn-din,* meaning "river place," but little is known of London before it was renamed *Londinium* by the Romans in AD 43. The rather fantastical 12th-century historian Geoffrey of Monmouth may have originated the myth — widespread in Shakespeare's day — that London was founded in 1108 BC by Brute, a direct descendant of Aeneas, who named it Troynovant, New Troy, or Trenovant. Even in medieval times, London had grandiose notions of its own importance — a prideful self-image that has been amply justified by history. Nevertheless, yet another chunk of Roman London recently has been uncovered by archaeologists from the *Museum of London.* While excavating the foundation of the 15th-century Guildhall chapel, they found Roman works more than 3 feet wide that have been identified as being from Roman London's missing amphitheater. This, however, is not viewable, though part of the old Roman city wall may be seen near the Tower of London, as can some segments that are in the *Museum of London* (phone: 71-600-3699).

The city was sufficiently prominent for the Norman invader William the Conqueror to make it his capital in 1066. During the Middle Ages, the expansion of trade, population growth, and the energetic activities of its guilds of merchants and craftsmen promoted London's prosperity. Indisputably, London's golden age was the English Renaissance, the 16th century, the time of Queen Elizabeth I, Shakespeare, and Drake's defeat of the Spanish Armada. Most of the Tudor buildings of London were wiped out in the great fire of 1666. Christopher Wren, the architect of genius, undertook to rebuild many buildings and churches, the most outstanding of which is St. Paul's Cathedral. The 18th century, a highly sophisticated age, saw the building of noble homes and stately squares, culminating in the grand expansion program developed between 1811 and 1820 by the prince regent's principal architect, John Nash. One of the best examples of his work is the terrace of largely crown-owned Regency houses surrounding Regent's Park. During the early 19th century, interest continued in homes and squares; only in the Victorian age, the height of the Empire, were public buildings like the Houses of Parliament redesigned, this time in grand and fanciful neo-Gothic style.

London has seen whole catalogues of heroes and villains, crises and conflagrations, come and go, sometimes swallowed whole in the passage of time, sometimes leaving relics. Still on elegant display is stately Hampton Court Palace, the most magnificent of England's palaces, where Henry VIII lived now and again with five of his six wives. There is a spot downtown — in front of the Banqueting House on Whitehall — where another king, Charles I, was beheaded by his subjects, who calmly were committing dreaded regicide 140 years before the presumably more emotional and explosive French across the English Channel even contemplated such a gesture.

London has lived through the unbounded permissiveness of the flamboyantly royal Restoration period (1660–85), when even King Charles II frequented brothels and didn't care who knew it, and it has survived the stern moral puritanism of the Victorian era, when it was downright rude to refer to a *breast* of chicken or a piano *leg*. And more recently, London stood up with exemplary courage under the devastating effects of Nazi bombings, which destroyed a great many buildings and killed thousands of people.

Many of our images of London, taken from old movies, actually mirror its realities: Big Ben rises above the Houses of Parliament, somberly striking the hour; ramrod-straight, scarlet-uniformed soldiers half hide their faces in towering black bearskin hats; clerks (pronounced *clarks*) at the Bank of England still sport the kinds of top hats and tailcoats their predecessors wore for centuries; barristers (lawyers) in court still don wigs and black robes. A few images, however, are outdated: The bowler hat has been slipping steadily out of fashion for years, and rigidly enforced environmental regulations have made London's once-famous pea soup fog a thing of the past.

London's nearly infinite variety of urban moods includes the sturdy edifices lining Whitehall, center of the British government, with Trafalgar Square at its head and Parliament at its foot; the elegant shopping areas of Knightsbridge, Bond Street, Kensington, and the Burlington Arcade; suburban chic in Barnes and Blackheath; handsome squares in Bloomsbury; melancholy mystery in Victoria and Waterloo train stations with their spy-movie atmosphere; the vitality of East End street markets; and the riparian tranquillity of Thameside towpaths in Putney and along Hammersmith Mall.

The British have a talent that amounts to a genius for government — for democracy and political tolerance — a talent that has been demonstrated ever since the Magna Carta was signed in 1215, and one that makes London's ambience easy and relaxed for individualists of all sorts. It is no wonder that the eccentric and inveterate Londoner of the city's 18th-century heyday, Dr. Samuel Johnson, once declared, "When a man is tired of London, he is tired of life, for there is in London all that life can afford."

Johnson's opinion, though somewhat overblown (and open to challenge today), essentially was shared by one of several modern American writers who chose to live in London. Disillusioned with New York, Boston, and Paris, Henry James decided in favor of London in 1881. Somehow he concluded that London was a place eminently suited to human life: "It is not a pleasant place; it is not agreeable, or cheerful, or easy, or exempt from reproach. It is only magnificent. You can draw up a tremendous list of reasons why it should be unsupportable. The fogs, the smoke, the dirt, the darkness, the wet, the distances, the ugliness, the brutal size of the place, the horrible numerosity of society . . . but . . . London is on the whole the most possible form of life."

# LONDON AT-A-GLANCE

**SEEING THE CITY:** London has, for the most part, resisted the temptation to build high. Aside from a handful of modest gestures toward skyscraping, there aren't many towering structures to obscure panoramic overviews of the city from its higher vantage points, which include the following:

**London Hilton International** – There were discreet noises of disapproval from Buckingham Palace when it was realized that the view from the roof bar of the *Hilton* included not only the palace grounds but, with high-powered binoculars, the inside of some of the royal chambers as well. In fact, the view over Mayfair, Hyde Park, and Westminster is breathtaking. 22 Park La., W1A 2HH (phone: 71-493-8000).

**Westminster Cathedral** – Not to be confused with Westminster Abbey. The top of the bell tower of London's Roman Catholic cathedral looks down on a broad expanse of the inner city. An elevator takes visitors up for a token charge (from April to September only). Off Victoria St. near the station, at Ashley Pl., SW1 (phone: 71-834-7452).

**Hampstead Heath** – Climb to the top of Parliament Hill, on the southern rim of this "wilderness" in north London. On a clear day, the view south from the Heath makes the city look like a vast village (for more information, see *Walk 6* in DIRECTIONS).

**South Bank Arts Centre** – On the south bank of Waterloo Bridge is the bunker-like complex of cultural buildings, including the *Royal Festival Hall,* the *Royal National Theatre,* the *National Film Theatre,* the *Hayward Gallery,* and other cultural attractions. For a view of London, look across the Thames — upriver to the Houses of Parliament, downriver to St. Paul's Cathedral.

**Tower Bridge Walkway** – The upper part of one of London's famous landmarks is open to visitors. In addition to the viewing gallery, there is an exhibition on the history of London's bridges and a museum that includes the bridge's Victorian steam pumping engines. Open daily, November through March, 10 AM to 4:45 PM; April through October, 10 AM to 6:30 PM. Admission charge. Tower Hill Underground Station (phone: 71-403-3761 or 71-407-0922).

**St. Paul's Cathedral** – The reward for climbing the 538 steps up to the cathedral's dome — the largest in the world after St. Peter's in Rome — is a panoramic view of London. Galleries are open 10 AM to 4:15 PM weekdays; 11 AM to 4:15 PM Saturdays;

closed Sundays and for special services. Admission charge to cathedral, except on Sundays; admission charge to galleries. St. Paul's, Mansion House Underground Stations (phone: 71-248-2705).

**Docklands –** The development of this area is so extensive that it even includes its own railroad; new apartment, commercial, and office buildings stretch seemingly without end. The *Docklands Light Railway,* a high-tech, overhead train, runs from Tower Hill to Greenwich, speeding over the fast-developing and fascinating terrain. If food shopping is on your agenda, visiting the Docklands will put to rest forever the image of British homemakers buying the family's food in tiny neighborhood greengrocers and small butcher shops. There's a market here called the *Super Store,* a British interpretation of a California supermarket, and the *Billingsgate Market,* originally on Lower Thames Street, has moved here. It's the place where some of London's premier chefs pick out their produce and fresh fish early in the morning, and it's the best place to pick up a side of smoked Scottish salmon to cart home. The Docklands also is home to the *Design Museum* (admission charge; Butler's Wharf, 28 Shads Thames, SE1; phone: 71-403-6933). Walking tours of the Rotherhithe district, where the *Mayflower* returned from its journey in 1621, are offered by local historian Jim Nash; for details, contact *Karisma Travel* (21 Hayes Wood Ave., Hayes, Bromley, Kent BR2 7BG; phone: 81-462-4953; call a week in advance). Further development plans for the Docklands extend to 1998, which will mark the completion of Canary Wharf — including the tallest building in Europe — so there is always something new popping up in this burgeoning community.

 **SPECIAL PLACES/ATTRACTIONS:** Surveying London from the steps of St. Paul's Cathedral at the turn of the 19th century, a visiting Prussian general commented to his English host: "What a place to plunder!" Even those who are less rapacious will appreciate the extraordinary wealth of sights London displays for visitors to inspect. Though some are dispersed in various corners of this vast city, most are clustered reasonably close together in or near the inner districts of Westminster, the City, and Kensington. Twenty Photospot locations — places to stand to get the best photographs of famous sights — have been indicated throughout Westminster with blue-and-white signs fixed to lampposts.

## WESTMINSTER

**Changing of the Guard –** An American who lived in London once said, "There's just no better way to convince yourself that you're in London!" This famous ceremony takes place daily from April to mid-August (alternate days in winter) promptly at 11:30 AM in the Buckingham Palace forecourt, at 11:15 AM at St. James's Palace, and at 11:30 AM at the Tower of London. (In very wet weather, it may be canceled.) Arrive early for a good view, as it can get very crowded.

**Horse Guards –** If you haven't had enough, you can see a new guard of 12 members of the Household Cavalry troop in with trumpet and standard, daily at 11 AM, 10 on Sundays, on the west side of Whitehall. Incidentally, they come from stables not far from Hyde Park and make a daily parade along the south roadway of Hyde Park, past Buckingham Palace, and then on to Trafalgar Square to turn into Whitehall. Their progress is as much fun to watch as the actual ceremony (for more information, see *Walk 1* in DIRECTIONS).

**Buckingham Palace –** The royal standard flies from the roof when the monarch is in residence at her London home. Although George III bought the palace in 1762, sovereigns officially still lived in St. James's Palace around the corner in Pall Mall, and Buckingham Palace did not become the actual principal regal dwelling until 1837, when Queen Victoria moved in. The palace, unfortunately, is open only to invited guests (the *Queen's Gallery* and Royal Mews are open to the public; see below). The queen's summer garden parties are held on the palace lawns. The interior contains magnificently decorated apartments, a superb picture gallery, and a throne room (66 feet long), where foreign ambassadors are received and knights are knighted. The palace grounds contain the largest private garden in London (40 acres). And the gate that originally was built for the entrance, too narrow for the coaches of George IV, now marks the Hyde Park end of Oxford Street and is known as Marble Arch.

**State Visits –** If you aren't going to be in London for the queen's official birthday in June, you might want to see her greet a foreign dignitary in full regalia. This happens quite frequently and is announced in the royal calendar in the *Times*. The queen meets her guest at Victoria Station, and they ride to Buckingham Palace in a procession of horse-drawn coaches, followed by the colorful Horse Guards. Meanwhile, at Hyde Park Corner, the cannoneers on horseback perform elaborate maneuvers before their salute thunders through the whole city.

**Queen's Gallery –** Treasures from the royal art collection are on public display only in this room of the palace. Open Tuesdays through Saturdays from 10:30 AM to 5 PM; Sundays from 2 to 5 PM; closed when exhibitions are being changed, about once a year. Admission charge. Buckingham Palace Rd., SW1 (phone: 71-799-2331).

**Royal Academy –** Housed in a building that resembles a combined mausoleum, railroad station, and funeral parlor are the works of the established, leading fashionable painters of the past. It's also the place where some of the major exhibitions to visit London are mounted. Open daily from 10 AM to 6 PM. Admission charge. Burlington House, Piccadilly, W1 (phone: 71-439-7438).

**Royal Mews –** The mews is a palace alley where the magnificent bridal coach, other state coaches, and the horses that draw them are stabled. The public is admitted on Wednesdays and Thursdays from 2 to 4 PM. Admission charge. Buckingham Palace Rd., SW1 (phone: 71-799-2331).

**St. James's Park –** Parks are everywhere in London, and Londoners love them. This is one of the nicest, where at lunch hour on a sunny day you can see the impeccably dressed London businessmen lounging on the grass, their shoes off and their sleeves rolled up. With its sizable lake (designed by John Nash) inhabited by pelicans and other wild fowl, St. James's was originally a royal deer park, drained under Henry VIII in 1532 and laid out as a pleasure ground for Charles II.

**The Mall –** The wide avenue (pronounced *Mal*), parallel to Pall Mall, is lined with lime trees and Regency buildings and leads from Trafalgar Square to Buckingham Palace. This is the principal ceremonial route used by Queen Elizabeth and her escort of Household Cavalry for the State Opening of Parliament (October/November) and the *Trooping the Colour* (see *Special Events*). It is closed to traffic on Sunday afternoons.

**Trafalgar Square –** One of London's most heavily trafficked squares is built around the towering Nelson's Column — a 145-foot-high monument bearing a 17-foot statue that honors Lord Nelson, victor at the naval Battle of Trafalgar in 1805. At the base of the monument are four huge bronze lions and two fountains. Flanked by handsome buildings, including the *National Gallery* and the 18th-century Church of St. Martin-in-the-Fields (have lunch or tea in the café in the crypt), the square is a favorite gathering place for political demonstrations, tourists, and pigeons.

**Piccadilly Circus –** Downtown London finds its center here in the heart of the theater district and on the edge of Soho. This is the London equivalent of Times Square — lots of it is just as tacky — and at the center of the busy "circus," or traffic circle, is the restored statue of Eros (moved about 40 feet from its original perch), which actually was designed in 1893 as *The Angel of Christian Charity,* a memorial to the charitable Earl of Shaftesbury — the archer and his bow were meant as a pun on his name. The *Trocadero,* a converted 3-story shopping and entertainment complex, has lent Piccadilly a new level of bustle. A recent addition is *Rock Circus* (phone: 71-734-0943), housed on the top 4 floors of the London Pavilion. Rock music's immortals —

from the *Beatles* to the *Who* — are brought to life with surprisingly impressive lighting, narration, and music; it also includes Europe's largest revolving auditorium, where "performances" are offered by rather remarkable robotic figures. It's not quite real life, but a pretty fair approximation. Open Mondays, Wednesdays, and Thursdays from 11 AM to 9 PM; Tuesdays from noon to 9 PM; Fridays and Saturdays from 11 AM to 10 PM. Another popular exhibition is the *Guinness World of Records* display. Open daily from 10 AM to 10 PM (phone: 71-439-7331). Separate admission charges.

**National Gallery** – One of the world's great art museums, this is an inexhaustible feast for art lovers. In the vast collection on display are works by such masters as Uccello, da Vinci, Titian, Rembrandt, Rubens, Cranach, Gainsborough, El Greco, Renoir, Cézanne, and Van Gogh. The just opened Sainsbury Wing highlights Giotto, van Eyck, and Botticelli, among others. The museum has undertaken the rehanging of its entire collection in chronological order. Open Mondays through Saturdays, 10 AM to 6 PM; Sundays, 2 to 6 PM. No admission charge. Trafalgar Sq., WC2 (phone: 71-839-3321).

**National Portrait Gallery** – Right behind the *National Gallery* sits this delightful museum. Nearly every English celebrity from the last 500 years is pictured here, with the earliest personalities at the top and the 20th-century notables at the bottom. Open Mondays through Fridays, 10 AM to 5 PM; Saturdays, 10 AM to 6 PM; Sundays, 2 to 6 PM. Admission charge to special exhibitions only. 2 St. Martin's Pl., WC2 (phone: 71-306-0055).

**Whitehall** – A broad boulevard stretching from Trafalgar Square to Parliament Square, lined most of the way by government ministries and such historic buildings as the Banqueting House (completed in 1622, with a ceiling painted by Rubens) and the Horse Guards (whose central archway is ceremonially guarded by mounted troopers).

Detective novel fans may be interested to know that from 1890 to 1967, Scotland Yard occupied the Norman Shaw Building at the Trafalgar end of Whitehall; it now houses offices for members of Parliament. The Yard has moved to Victoria Street near St. James's Park.

**Downing Street** – Off Whitehall, a street of small, unpretentious Georgian houses includes the official residences of the most important figures in the British government, the prime minister at No. 10 and the chancellor of the exchequer (Britain's secretary of the treasury) at No. 11 (for more information, see *Walk 1* in DIRECTIONS).

**Cabinet War Rooms** – Constructed to resemble its wartime appearance (and filled with its original furnishings), this underground complex of 20 rooms was Winston Churchill's auxiliary command post during World War II, which he used most often during the German Luftwaffe's blitz on London. Of special note are the Map Room, with maps pinpointing the positions of Allied and German troops in the final stages of the war, the Cabinet Room where the prime minister met with his staff, and the cramped Transatlantic Telephone Room (No. 63) used only by Churchill himself. The Cabinet War Rooms are an auxiliary site of London's *Imperial War Museum* (see below). Open daily from 10 AM to 6 PM. Admission charge. Clive Steps, King Charles St., SW1 (phone: 71-930-6961). For more information, see *Quintessential London* in DIVERSIONS.

**Westminster Abbey** – It's easy to get lost among the endlessly fascinating tombs and plaques and not even notice the abbey's splendid architecture, so do look at the structure itself and don't miss the cloisters, which display its Gothic design to advantage. Note also the fine Tudor chapel of Henry VII, with its tall windows and lovely fan-tracery vaulting, and the 13th-century chapel of St. Edward the Confessor, containing England's Coronation Chair and Scotland's ancient coronation Stone of Scone.

Ever since William the Conqueror was crowned here in 1066, the abbey has been the traditional place where English monarchs are crowned, married, and buried. You don't have to be an Anglophile to be moved by the numerous tombs and memorials with their fascinating inscriptions — here are honored (not necessarily buried) kings and queens, soldiers, statesmen, and many other prominent English men and women. Poets' Corner, in the south transept, contains the tombs of Chaucer, Ben Jonson, Tennyson, Browning, and many others — plus memorials to nearly every English poet of note and to some Americans, such as Longfellow and T. S. Eliot.

The abbey is itself a lesson in English history. A church has stood on this site since at least AD 170; in the 8th century, it was a Benedictine monastery. The current early–English Gothic edifice, begun in the 13th century, took almost 300 years to build.

Guided tours are offered six times every weekday and three times on Saturdays. Admission charge to the royal chapels, to Poets' Corner, and to some other sections as well. The nave and cloisters are open daily from 8 AM to 6 PM; Wednesdays from 8 AM to 7:45 PM; the Royal Chapel is open weekdays from 9 AM to 4:45 PM; Saturdays from 9:20 AM to 2:45 PM and from 3:45 to 5:45 PM. Closed Sundays. Broad Sanctuary, off Parliament Sq., SW1 (phone: 71-222-5152).

**Houses of Parliament** – The imposing neo-Gothic, mid-19th-century buildings of the Palace of Westminster, as it is sometimes called, look especially splendid from the opposite side of the river. There are separate chambers for the House of Commons and the House of Lords, and visitors are admitted to the Strangers' Galleries of both houses by lining up at St. Stephen's Entrance, opposite Westminster Abbey. Big Ben, the world-famous 13½-ton bell in the clock tower of the palace, which is illuminated when Parliament is in session, still strikes the hours. Although the buildings are otherwise closed to the public, there are limited tours outside session hours (weekday mornings and Friday evenings). To make tour arrangements, write in advance to *The Public Information Office* (1 Derby Gate, London SW1A 1DG). Particularly impressive are Westminster Hall, with its magnificent hammer-beam roof, and the gold-and-scarlet House of Lords. No admission charge. St. Margaret St., SW1 (phone: 71-219-3000).

**Tate Gallery** – London's fine art museum includes an impressive collection of British paintings from the 16th century to the dawn of the 20th century, as well as modern British and international art. Best of all are masterpieces by Turner, Constable, Hogarth, and Blake. Nicholas Serota, the museum's director, has continued the reorganization of the gallery, arranging the works in chronological order rather than by skill or style. The Turner collection is housed exclusively in the ultramodern Clore Gallery extension. Open Mondays through Saturdays from 10 AM to 6 PM and on Sundays from 2 to 6 PM. Admission charge to special exhibitions only. Millbank, SW1 (phone: 71-821-1313).

**Soho** – This area of London is full of character: lively, bustling, and noisy by day; indiscreetly enticing by night. Its name comes from the ancient hunting cry used centuries ago when the area was parkland. The hunting, in a way, still goes on, particularly by undercover detectives. Soho lacks the sophistication and glamour of its counterparts in Europe, but it's not all sleazy either. The striptease clubs vie for customers with the numerous restaurants, most serving moderately priced food (mostly Italian and Chinese). Soho offers a diversity of entertainments: Shaftesbury Avenue is lined with theaters and movie houses. Gerrard Street abounds with Chinese restaurants, and it is the place to go for *Chinese New Year* celebrations. London's liveliest fruit and vegetable market is on Berwick Street (if you shop here, never touch the produce, as the vendors will get furious). Frith Street is a favorite Italian haunt, the best place for a foaming cappuccino and a view of Italian TV at the *Bar Italia*. Old Compton Street has several good delicatessens, perfect places to buy a picnic lunch to take to Soho Square.

**Covent Garden** – Tucked away behind the Strand, *Covent Garden* was the site of London's main fruit, vegetable, and flower market for over 300 years. The area was immortalized in Shaw's *Pygmalion* and the musical *My Fair Lady* by the scene in which young Eliza Doolittle sells flowers to the ladies and gents emerging from the *Royal*

*Opera House.* The *Opera House* is still here, but the market moved south of the river in 1974 and the *Garden* has since undergone extensive redevelopment. The central market building has been converted into London's first permanent late-night shopping center, with an emphasis on all-British goods. In the former flower market is the *London Transport Museum,* whose exhibits include a replica of the first horse-drawn bus and a steam locomotive built in 1866 (open daily from 10 AM to 6 PM; phone: 71-379-6344). Boutiques selling quality clothes for men and women are springing up all over, along with discos, wine bars, and brasserie-style restaurants. On weekends the whole area is packed with young people. One nice touch: Just to remind everyone of the *Old Covent Garden,* there are about 40 of the original wrought-iron trading stands, from which the home-produced wares of English craftspeople are sold (for more information, see *Walk 4* in DIRECTIONS).

**Bloomsbury** – Well-designed squares — Bloomsbury Square, Bedford Square, Russell Square, and others — surrounded by pretty, terraced houses form this aristocratic district. Within its confines are the *British Museum* and the Centre of the University of London. The Bloomsbury group of writers and artists included Virginia Woolf and her husband, Leonard Woolf; her sister Vanessa Bell and her husband, Clive Bell; Lytton Strachey; E. M. Forster; Roger Fry; and John Maynard Keynes. Living nearby and peripheral to this central group were D. H. Lawrence, Bertrand Russell, and others. Unfortunately, none of the original buildings in Bloomsbury Square have survived, but the garden is still here, and nearby Bedford Square remains complete. Virginia Woolf lived at 46 Gordon Square before her marriage.

**British Museum** – One of the world's largest museums offers a dazzling array of permanent exhibitions — including the legendary Elgin Marbles (from the Parthenon) and the Rosetta Stone. Seven sculpture galleries exhibit some 1,500 Greek and Roman treasures. This magnificent collection includes two of the seven wonders of the ancient world: the Mausoleum of Halicarnassus and the Temple of Artemis at Ephesus. There is an equally impressive parade of temporary displays. The Egyptian and Mesopotamian galleries are especially stunning. The manuscript room of the British Library, within the museum, displays an original copy of the Magna Carta, together with the signatures of a great many famous authors — Shakespeare, Dickens, Austen, and Joyce among them — and numerous original manuscripts, including *Alice's Adventures in Wonderland.* The British Library has an enormous collection, since every book published in Britain must be sent here. If you wish to use the library, consult a copy of the library's catalogue, stocked by major world libraries. Send in your requests with call numbers; many books often take 2 days to arrive from storage or other branches. The library also has a remarkable, gigantic Victorian Reading Room with a huge dome made of cast iron, measuring 140 feet across and 106 feet high. Many of the world's great thinkers and writers worked here, including Marx, Lenin, Gandhi, Yeats, and Dickens. Access to the Reading Room is limited; you must call or write to the museum's British Library Readers' Admissions Office for permission. Open Mondays through Saturdays, 10 AM to 5 PM; Sundays, 2:30 to 6 PM. Admission charge to special exhibitions only. Great Russell St., WC1 (phone: museum, 71-636-1555; library, 71-636-1544).

**Oxford, Regent, Bond, and Kensington High Streets** – London's main shopping streets include large department and specialty stores (*Selfridges, Debenhams, John Lewis, Liberty, D. H. Evans*), chain stores offering good value in clothes (*Marks & Spencer, C & A, British Home Stores, Littlewoods*), and scores of popular clothing chains (*The Gap, Laura Ashley, Benetton, Principles*).

**Burlington Arcade** – A charming covered shopping promenade dating from the Regency period (early 19th century), the arcade contains elegant, expensive shops selling cashmere sweaters (we've seen some here that were 10-ply!), antique jewelry, and other expensive items. One entrance is on Piccadilly (the street, not the circus), the other near Old Bond St., W1.

**Hyde Park –** London's most famous patch of greenery (361 acres) is particularly well known for its Speakers' Corner at Marble Arch, where crowds gather each Sunday afternoon to hear impromptu diatribes and debates. Among the park's other attractions are sculptures by Henry Moore; an extensive bridle path; a cycle path; the Serpentine lake, where boats for rowing and sailing can be rented and where there's swimming in the summer; a bird sanctuary; vast expanses of lawn; and the recently opened *Serpentine* restaurant (phone: 71-402-1142).

**Madame Tussaud's –** The popularity of this wax museum is undiminished by the persistent criticism that its effigies are a little bland, and visitors are quite likely to find themselves innocently addressing a waxwork attendant — or murderer. Madame moved to London from Paris in 1802, when she was 42, crossing the Channel with her waxwork effigies of heads that had rolled during the French Revolution. The current museum includes many modern and historical personalities and the gory Chamber of Horrors, with its murderers and hangmen. Open daily from 10 AM (9:30 AM on Saturdays) to 5:30 PM. Admission charge. Marylebone Rd., NW1 (phone: 71-935-6861).

**London Planetarium –** During their 30-minute shows, visitors travel through space and time under a huge starlit dome. Interesting commentary accompanies the display. The first show begins at 12:20 PM, and they continue every 40 minutes thereafter, with the last one at 4:20 PM (on Saturdays and Sundays, the first is at 10:20 AM and the last at 5 PM). There is also a Laserium concert/light show at varying times in the evening. Guests can save money by purchasing a combination ticket to the planetarium and *Madame Tussaud's* — both at the same address. Open daily. Marylebone Rd., NW1 (phone: 71-486-1121).

## THE CITY

The difference between London and the City of London can be confusing to a visitor. They are, in fact, two distinctly different entities, one within the other. The City of London, usually called only the City, covers the original Roman London. It is now the "square mile" financial and commercial center of the great metropolis. With a Lord Mayor (who serves only in a ceremonial capacity), a police force, and rapidly growing new developments, it is the core of Greater London. The governing council, the London Residuary Body, administers 32 boroughs including the City.

**St. Paul's Cathedral –** The cathedral church of the London Anglican diocese stands atop Ludgate Hill and is the largest church in London. This Renaissance masterpiece by Sir Christopher Wren took 35 years to build (1675–1710). Its domed exterior is majestic, and its sparse decorations are in gold and mosaic. The interior contains particularly splendid choir stalls, screens, and inside the spectacular dome, the "Whispering Gallery," with its strange acoustics. Nelson and Wellington are buried beneath the main floor, and there is a fine statue of John Donne, metaphysical poet and dean of St. Paul's from 1621 to 1631 — he stands looking quite alive on an urn in an up-ended coffin which, typically, he bought during his lifetime and kept in his house. Wren himself was buried here in 1723, with his epitaph inscribed beneath the dome in Latin: "If you seek his monument, look around you."

A gorgeous monument it remains; though damaged by bombs during World War II, it became a rallying point for the flagging spirits of wartime Londoners. More recently, St. Paul's raised British spirits as the site for the wedding of Prince Charles and Lady Diana Spencer in July 1981. The Golden Gallery at the top of the dome, 627 steps from the ground, offers an excellent view of the city. The cathedral is open to tourists on weekdays from 10 AM to 4:15 PM and on Saturdays from 11 AM to 4:15 PM. Admission charge to galleries. St. Paul's Churchyard, EC4 (phone: 71-248-2705).

**Old Bailey –** This is the colloquial name for London's Central Criminal Court, on the site of the notorious Newgate prison. Visitors are admitted to the court, on a space-available basis, to audit the proceedings and to see lawyers (called barristers, in court) and judges clad in wigs and robes. No children under 14 years of age admitted. Open weekdays, 10:30 AM to 1 PM and 2 to 4 PM. No admission charge. Old Bailey, EC4 (phone: 71-248-3277).

**Museum of London** – Exhibits and displays depict London history from the Roman occupation to modern times. The museum is in the Barbican area and was opened in 1976. It includes Roman remains, Anglo-Saxon artifacts, Renaissance musical instruments, a cell from old Newgate prison, Victorian shops and offices, audiovisual re-creation of the 1666 Great Fire, and the Lord Mayor's Golden Coach. Open Tuesdays through Saturdays, 10 AM to 6 PM; Sundays, 2 to 6 PM. No admission charge. 150 London Wall, EC2 (phone: 71-600-3699).

**Barbican Centre for Arts and Conferences** – Served by underground stations Barbican, St. Paul's, and Moorgate, the *Barbican,* which opened in 1982, includes 6,000 apartments, the Guildhall School of Music and Drama, and the restored St. Giles' Church (built in 1390). The *Barbican* also features the 2,026-seat *Barbican Hall,* doubling as conference venue (with simultaneous translation system) and concert hall (*London Symphony Orchestra*); the 1,166-seat *Barbican Theatre* (the *Royal Shakespeare Company*'s London performance venue); a 200-seat studio theatre; sculpture courtyard; art exhibition galleries; seminar rooms; three cinemas; two exhibition halls; a municipal lending library; restaurants and bars. Faced with rising costs, there has been a question as to whether the *RSC* can maintain its London home. At press time, however, there were no plans for the company to leave the *Barbican.* Silk St., EC2 (phone: for guided tours and general information, 71-638-4141, ext. 218; recorded information, 71-628-2295 or 71-628-9760; box office, 71-638-8891).

**Bank of England** – Banker to the British government, holder of the country's gold reserves in its vaults, controller of Britain's banking and monetary affairs, the "Old Lady of Threadneedle Street" is the most famous bank in the world. Bathed in tradition as well as the mechanics of modern high finance, its porters and messengers wear traditional livery. Visits by appointment only. The *Bank of England Museum* here is open daily from 10 AM to 5 PM (from 11 AM on Saturdays and Sundays). No admission charge. Threadneedle St., EC2 (phone: 71-601-4444 for the bank; 71-601-5792 for the museum).

**Mansion House** – The official residence of the Lord Mayor of London, containing his private apartments, built in the 18th century in Renaissance style. It is difficult to gain admission to the house, but you may request permission by writing, well in advance of your visit, to the Principal Assistant Office (Mansion House, London EC4N 8EH). Mansion House St., EC4 (phone: 71-626-2500).

**Lloyd's** – A strikingly dramatic, futuristic building now houses the world's most important seller of international maritime and high-risk insurance. The exhibition gallery overlooking the trading floor is open only to groups who have booked a tour in advance. Corner of Lime and Leadenhall Sts., EC3 N7 DQ (phone: 71-327-5786).

**Stock Exchange** – The second-largest exchange in the world is no longer open to the public. Old Broad St., EC2 (phone: 71-588-2355).

**The Monument** – This fluted Doric column, topped by a flaming urn, was designed by Sir Christopher Wren to commemorate the Great Fire of London (1666) and stands 202 feet tall. (Its height was determined because it was allegedly 202 feet from the bakery on Pudding Lane where the fire began.) The view from the top is partially obstructed by new buildings. Open April through September, weekdays from 9 AM to 6 PM, Saturdays and Sundays from 2 to 6 PM; October through March, open Mondays through Saturdays from 9 AM to 4 PM, closed Sundays. Admission charge. Monument St., EC3 (phone: 71-626-2717). (For more information, see *Walk 3* in DIRECTIONS.)

**Tower of London** – Originally conceived as a fortress to keep "fierce" Londoners at bay and to guard the river approaches, it has served as a palace, a prison, a mint, and an observatory as well. Today, the main points of interest are the Crown Jewels; the White Tower (the oldest building), with its exhibition of ancient arms, armor, and torture implements; St. John's Chapel, the oldest church in London; the Bloody Tower, where the two little princes disappeared in 1483 and Sir Walter Raleigh languished from 1603 to 1616; an exhibit of old military weapons; Tower Green, where two of Henry VIII's queens — and many others — were beheaded; and Traitors' Gate, through which boats bearing prisoners entered the castle. The yeoman warders ("Beef-eaters") still wear historic uniforms. They also give excellent recitals of that segment of English history that was played out within the tower walls. You can see the wonderful Ceremony of the Keys here every night at 9:30 PM; reserve tickets several months ahead. (Send a stamped, self-addressed envelope to Resident Governor Constable's Office, HM Tower of London, EC3N 4AB.) Open March through October, Mondays through Saturdays from 9:30 AM to 6:30 PM, Sundays from 2 to 6 PM; November through February, open Mondays through Saturdays from 9:30 AM to 5 PM; closed Sundays. Admission charge (phone: 71-709-0765, general inquiries; 71-488-5718, for recorded information).

**Fleet Street** – Most native and foreign newspapers and press associations once had offices here — in the center of London's active newspaper world — but none remain because of the exodus to more technologically advanced plants elsewhere. The street also boasts two 17th-century pubs, the *Cock Tavern* (No. 22) and *Ye Olde Cheshire Cheese* (just off Fleet St. at 5 Little Essex St.), where Dr. Samuel Johnson held court for the literary giants of his day (for more information, see *Walk 8* in DIRECTIONS).

**Johnson's House** – In nearby Gough Square is the house where Johnson wrote his famous *Dictionary;* the house is now a museum of Johnsoniana. Open May through September, daily from 11 AM to 5:30 AM; October through April, Mondays through Saturdays from 11 AM to 5 PM; closed Sundays. Admission charge. 17 Gough Sq., EC4 (phone: 71-353-3745).

**Inns of Court** – Quaint and quiet precincts house the ancient buildings, grounds, and gardens that mark the traditional center of Britain's legal profession. Only the four Inns of Court — Gray's, Lincoln's, and the Inner and Middle Temples — have the right to call would-be barristers to the bar to practice law. Especially charming is the still-Dickensian Lincoln's Inn, where young Dickens worked as an office boy. It was in its great hall that the writer later set parts of his fictional law case of Jarndyce vs. Jarndyce in *Bleak House.* John Donne once preached in the Lincoln's Inn chapel, designed by Inigo Jones. The chapel can be seen on weekdays between 12:30 and 2:30 PM; ask at the Gatehouse (Chancery La., WC2; phone: 71-405-1393). Also lovely are the gardens of Lincoln's Inn Fields, laid out by Inigo Jones in 1618. The neo-Gothic Royal Courts of Justice in the Strand, better known as the Law Courts, are home to the High Court and the Court of Appeal of England and Wales, which pass judgment on Britain's most important civil cases. These courts, unlike the Old Bailey, are closed to the public (for more information, see *Walk 5* in DIRECTIONS).

## OTHER LONDON ATTRACTIONS

**Regent's Park** – The sprawling 472 acres just north of the city center include beautiful gardens, vast lawns, a pond with paddleboats, and one of the finest zoos in the world. (Unfortunately, at press time threats were voiced about the zoo's possible closure due to financial problems.) Crescents of elegant terraced homes border the park. No admission charge to the park. London Zoo open November through February, daily from 10 AM to 4 PM; March through October, from 9 AM to 6 PM; open until 7 PM on Sundays and bank holidays. Admission charge (phone: 71-722-3333).

**Camden Passage** – This quaint pedestrian alleyway, lined with antiques and specialty shops, has an open-air market — pushcarts selling curios and antiques — on

Wednesdays, Thursdays (books), and Saturdays. Just off Upper St. in Islington, north of the city, N1.

**Hampstead Heath** – The north London bucolic paradise of wild heathland, meadows, and wooded dells is the highest point in London. Kenwood House, a 17th-century estate on the heath, is the home of the Iveagh Bequest, a collection of art (Gainsborough, Rembrandt, Turner, and others; see *Marvelous Museums* in DIVERSIONS) assembled by the first Earl of Iveagh. Lakeside concerts, both classical and jazz, are held on the grounds in summer (for details, call 71-734-1877).

**Kew Gardens** – Here are the Royal Botanic Gardens, with tens of thousands of trees and other plants. The gardens' primary purpose is to serve the science of botany by researching, cultivating, experimenting with, and identifying plants. There are shaded walks, floral displays, and magnificent Victorian glass greenhouses — especially the Temperate House, with some 3,000 different plants, including a 60-foot Chilean wine palm. Open daily, March through September, from 9:30 AM to 6:30 PM; October through February, from 9:30 AM to 4 PM.. Admission charge (phone: 81-940-1171)

**Portobello Road** – This area is famous for its antiques shops, junk shops, and outdoor pushcarts; it is one of the largest street markets in the world. The pushcarts are out only on Fridays and Saturdays, which are the best and most crowded days for the market. Less well known is *Bermondsey–New Caledonian Market* (Long La. at Tower Bridge Rd., SE1), on Fridays from before dawn; this is where many of the antiques found on Portobello Road or Camden Passage were probably purchased.

**Victoria and Albert Museum** – Born of the *Great Exhibition* of 1851, the museum contains a vast collection of fine and applied arts (probably the largest collection of the latter in the world) — an amalgam of the great, the odd, and the ugly. Especially delightful are the English period rooms. There are superb collections of paintings, prints, ceramics, metalwork, costumes, and armor in the museum, which also contains English miniatures and famous Raphael cartoons. The museum's Henry Cole Wing (named after its founder) houses a broad selection of changing exhibitions, as well as an interesting permanent display of printmaking techniques. The Nehru Gallery, opened in 1990, has the finest collection of Indian art outside of India. Jazz concerts and fashion shows are held in the Italianate Pirelli Garden at the heart of the museum. Open Mondays through Saturdays, 10 AM to 5:50 PM; Sundays, 2:30 to 5:50 PM. Entry donation suggested. Cromwell Rd., SW7 (phone: 71-938-8500; exhibitions information, 71-938-8349).

**Imperial War Museum** – A collection of tanks, planes, cannon, submarines, rockets, artifacts, and war paintings bridging the history of war from Flanders to the Falklands is housed in this 4-floor museum (originally Bethlehem Royal Hospital, hence the word "bedlam"). There are telephones that visitors can pick up to hear people describing their firsthand wartime experiences; and historical films and videos further help to bring wartime events alive. The 20-minute-long "Blitz Experience" confines groups of 20 people to a damp, cramped re-creation of a bomb shelter during a World War II air raid; and "Operation Jericho" is a bumpy simulation of a WWII bombing raid (additional charge for each). Also see the WWI "Trench Experience" (no charge). There is a souvenir shop and a café for light meals and snacks. Open daily from 10 AM to 6 PM; closed *Christmas Eve, Christmas, Boxing Day,* and *New Year's Day.* Admission charge, except on Fridays. Lambeth Rd., SE1 (phone: 71-416-5000).

**Greenwich** – This Thameside borough is traditionally associated with British seapower, especially when Britain "ruled the waves." Here, along Romney Road, is the Royal Naval College, whose beautiful painted hall and chapel are open daily except Thursdays, from 2:30 to 5 PM, when the college is in session. No admission charge (phone: 81-858-2154). Also here is the *National Maritime Museum,* celebrating Britain's illustrious nautical past (see *Marvelous Museums* in DIVERSIONS) and the *Queen's*

*House,* designed by Inigo Jones for Queen Henrietta Maria, wife of Charles I, and reopened in 1990 after extensive restoration. Up the hill is the *Old Royal Observatory,* with astronomical instruments. These three are all open April through September, Mondays through Saturdays from 10 AM to 6 PM, Sundays from 2 to 6 PM; October through March, Mondays through Saturdays from 10 AM to 5 PM, Sundays from 2 to 6 PM (phone: 81-858-4422). Admission charge to each, but a money-saving "Passport" includes entry to these plus the *Cutty Sark,* a superbly preserved 19th-century clipper ship. Open April through September, Mondays through Saturdays from 10 AM to 6 PM, Sundays from noon to 6 PM; October through March, Mondays through Saturdays from 10 AM to 5 PM, Sundays from noon to 5 PM. Cutty Sark Gardens, SE10 (phone: 81-858-3445). Greenwich Park is 200 acres of greenery with splendid views from the hill across to the Docklands and the rest of London. Greenwich Station, *British Rail.*

**Richmond Park** – The largest urban park in Britain is one of the few with herds of deer roaming free. (Hunting them is illegal, though this was once a royal hunting preserve established by Charles I.) It also has large oaks and rhododendron gardens. From nearby Richmond Hill there is a magnificent view of the Thames Valley. Richmond tube stop or *British Rail.*

**Manor Houses** – Six beautifully maintained historic homes are in Greater London. Notable for their architecture, antiques, grounds, and in the case of Kenwood, an 18th-century art collection, these homes are all accessible by bus and underground: Kenwood House (Hampstead tube stop or *British Rail,* Hampstead Heath; open daily; no admission charge; phone: 81-348-1236), Ham House (Richmond tube stop or *British Rail;* closed Mondays; admission charge; phone: 81-940-1950), Chiswick (Turnham Green or Chiswick Park tube stop; open daily; admission charge; phone: 81-995-0508), Syon House (Gunnersbury tube stop, then a No. 237 or No. 267 bus, or *British Rail,* Brentford Central; open daily, except Fridays and Saturdays from *Easter* through September; admission charge; phone: 81-560-0881), and Osterley Park House (Osterley tube stop; closed Mondays; admission charge; phone: 81-560-3918). Apsley House, home of the Duke of Wellington, houses the *Wellington Museum.* It contains many fine paintings, including portraits of the Iron Duke's fellow commanders from the victorious campaign against the French, and a nude(!) statue of Napoleon Bonaparte (open Tuesdays through Sundays from 10 AM to 5 PM; admission charge; 149 Piccadilly, W1).

**Spencer House** – This 1756 mansion owned by the Spencer family — the Princess of Wales is the former Lady Diana Spencer — has recently been restored and opened to the public. There are nine state rooms filled with artwork and furniture from the family's wide collection. The neo-classical state rooms were among the first to be so designed in Europe. Open Sundays for pre-arranged tours only, from 11:30 AM to 5:30 PM; closed during January and August. Admission charge. St. James's Pl., W1 (phone: 71-499-8620).

**Hampton Court Palace** – Along the Thames, this sumptuous palace and gardens are in Greater London's southwest corner. Begun by Cardinal Wolsey in 1514, the palace was appropriated by Henry VIII and was a royal residence for 2 centuries. Its attractions include a picture gallery, tapestries, state apartments, Tudor kitchens — newly restored to the grandeur of Henry VIII's day, re-creating the *Feast of St. John the Baptist* on a midsummer day in 1542 — the original tennis court, a moat, a great vine (2 centuries old), gardens, and a maze. The quickest way to get here is by *British Rail* (32 minutes from Waterloo Station), but you can take a bus or even a boat from Westminster Pier or Richmond during the summer. Open daily, March through October, from 9:30 AM to 6 PM; November through February, from 9:30 AM to 4:30 PM. Admission charge. East Molesey, Surrey (phone: 81-977-8441).

**Freud Museum** – This house was the north London home of the seminal psychiatrist after he left Vienna in 1938. His antiquities collection, library, desk, and famous couch are all on display. Open Wednesdays through Sundays, noon to 5 PM. Admission charge. 20 Maresfield Gardens, NW3 (phone: 71-435-2002).

**Highgate Cemetery** – The awe-inspiring grave of Karl Marx in the eastern cemetery (open daily from 10 AM to 4:45 PM during the summer, 10 AM to 3:45 PM during the winter) attracts countless visitors. Entrance to the western cemetery, with its overgrown gravestones and catacombs of the not-so-famous, is by guided tour only. Admission charge. Highgate Hill, NW3 (phone: 81-340-1834 for times).

**Thames Flood Barrier** – A massive and intriguing defense structure across the river at Woolwich Reach near Greenwich. Boats regularly leave Barrier Gardens Pier (or the riverside promenade nearby) for visits up close. Visitors are not allowed on the barrier itself, but audiovisual displays at the visitors' center, on the river's south bank just downstream, explain its background and illustrate the risk to London of exceptionally high tides. Open weekdays from 10:30 AM to 5 PM, weekends to 5:30 PM. Admission charge. Accessible from London by road, by river (from Westminster Pier to Barrier Gardens Pier), and by rail (to Charlton Station). 1 Unity Way, Woolwich (phone: 81-854-1373).

■**EXTRA SPECIAL:** Windsor Castle is the largest inhabited castle in the world. It is the queen's official residence, and was first built by William the Conqueror in 1066 after his victory at the Battle of Hastings. Among the royal sovereigns buried here are Queen Victoria and Albert, her beloved consort. Windsor looks like a fairy-tale castle in a child's picture book: The huge Norman edifice looms majestically above the town; visitors feel awed and enchanted as they climb up the curving cobblestone street from the train station, past pubs and shops, toward Henry VIII's Gateway. The castle precincts are open daily, and there's a regular changing of the guard. The State Apartments, which can be toured when they're not in use, are splendidly decorated with paintings, tapestries, furniture, and rugs. There is also an exhibition of drawings by Leonardo da Vinci, Michelangelo, and Raphael, and a room displaying Queen Mary's dollhouse. Separate admission charges. For information, call 753-831118.

The castle is bordered by 4,800 acres of parkland on one side and the town on the other. The Savill Gardens — 35 acres of flowering shrubs, rare flowers, and woodland — make for a lovely summer walk. Open daily. Admission charge (phone: 784-435544). While the town still has a certain charm, heavy tourism is beginning to have a deleterious effect. Across the river is Eton — considered by some to be the more attractive town — which is the famous home of the exclusive boys' school founded by Henry VI in 1440.

The train from Paddington stops right in the center of Windsor (travel time is 39 minutes), or there's a *Green Line* coach from Victoria (1½ hours).

Don't miss taking one of the many boat trips along the Thames to places like Marlow, Cookham, or Henley (where the first rowing regatta in the world was held in 1839). The Royal Windsor Safari Park is also located southwest of London. It's an easy 45-minute car ride (exit 3 off the M3; exit 6 off the M6). Once a royal hunting ground, it's now a drive-through zoo, whose residents include baboons, camels, rhinos, cheetahs, and Bengal tigers. Be forewarned: In summer the park is very popular and traffic is bumper-to-bumper. An alternative would be to take the safari bus. Open daily. Admission charge (phone: 753-869841).

For a spectacular side trip out of London, there is nothing quite like Oxford and Stratford-upon-Avon, Shakespeare's birthplace — both of which can be seen in a 1-day organized bus tour. Otherwise you can choose one; the regular bus from Victoria Coach Station to Stratford (90 miles) travels via Oxford (65 miles), so you can catch a glimpse of the ancient colleges if you try hard (for information, call *National Express Coach;* phone: 71-730-0202).

Shakespeare's birthplace is still an Elizabethan town, and even if there's no time to see a play at the *Shakespeare Memorial Theatre,* the Tudor houses, with their overhung gables and traditional straw roofs, are a very pleasant sight. The poet's birthplace is a must, as is his grave at charming Holy Trinity Church. The Great Garden of New Place, said to contain every flower that Shakespeare mentioned in his plays, and Anne Hathaway's Cottage (his wife's previous home) are both enjoyable (for tourist information, call 789-293127).

Oxford is England's oldest university town; its fine Gothic buildings have cloistered many famous Englishmen. Most of the great colleges are on High Street (the High) or Broad Street (the Broad). See Magdalen (pronounced *Mawd*-lin) College, Christ Church, the Bodleian Library, St. Edmund Hall, and the marvelous *Ashmolean Museum of Art;* be sure to look in a bookstore, too — *Blackwells* on Broad Street is one of the finest in the world. Students usually guide the university tours (for tourist information, call 865-726871).

Another highly recommended day trip, less ambitious than Stratford and Oxford, is Cambridge, only 1 hour from London by train. Cambridge is even more delightful than Oxford because the town takes full advantage of the river Cam. So don't fail to walk along "the Backs" — the back lawns of several colleges, leading down to the river; or better yet, rent a canoe or a punt, a flat-bottomed boat that is propelled by a long pole. (It's easier than it sounds.) The town has two parallel main streets that change their names every 2 blocks; one is a shopping street and the other is lined with colleges. Don't miss *Heffers* on Trinity Street; it's the biggest branch of the best bookstore in Cambridge. Stroll through the famous colleges — King's, Trinity, Queens, Jesus, Magdalene, and Clare. King's College Chapel is a 15th-century Gothic structure that is a real beauty. The *Fitzwilliam Museum* is noted for its art and antiquities. Also see at least one garden and one dining hall (for tourist information, call 223-322640).

# LOCAL SOURCES AND RESOURCES

**TOURIST INFORMATION:** In the US, contact the British Tourist Authority (40 W. 57th St., New York, NY 10019; phone: 212-581-4700). The London Visitor and Convention Bureau is the best source of information for attractions and events once you get to London. Its information center, in the forecourt of Victoria British Rail Station, is open Mondays through Saturdays, 8 AM to 7 PM; Sundays, 8 AM to 5 PM, later in peak summer months. Many leaflets and brochures about the city's landmarks and events are available; staff are also on hand to answer questions on what to do, how, and when. Other branches are at the tube station at Heathrow Airport Terminals 1, 2, and 3 (8 AM to 6:30 PM), *Harrods* and *Selfridges* stores (during store hours), and the Tower of London (*Easter* to November only). A telephone information service is offered weekdays, 9 AM to 6 PM (phone: 71-730-3488), but it is very busy. Accommodations and tours can be reserved by telephone using credit cards, Mondays through Fridays 9 AM to 6 PM (phone: 71-824-8844).

The British Travel Centre books travel tickets, reserves accommodations and theater tickets, and sells guidebooks. They have numerous free leaflets that include fascinating information (for movie trivia buffs, pick up the "Movie Map," which guides you to famous film locations). It offers a free information service, including an information hotline covering the whole of Britain. There also is an All-Ireland Information Desk, a Welsh Tourist Office, and a National Trust Shop. Open weekdays, 9 AM to 6:30 PM; Saturdays, 9 AM to 5 PM; Sundays, 10 AM to 4 PM. 4 Lower Regent St., W1 (phone: 71-730-3400).

Among the most comprehensive and useful guidebooks to London are the *Blue Guide to London* (Benn); *London Round the Clock* (CPC Guidebooks); *Londonwalks* (Holt, Rinehart & Winston); and a series of guides available from *Time Out* (Time Out Ltd.). *Naked London* (Queen Anne Press) lists the city's more unusual, less visited sights for dedicated sleuths. The annual *Good Food Guide* and *Egon Ronay's Guide to Hotel and Restaurants* are available in most bookstores. For detailed information on 200 London museums, including maps, consult the *London Museums and Collections Guide* (CPC Guidebooks). The *Shell Guide to the History of London* (Michael Joseph) bristles with exciting, accurate details on the city. *London: Louise Nicholson's Definitive Guide* (Bodley Head) comes surprisingly close to the claims of the title. Susie Elms's *The London Theatre Scene* (Frank Cook) gives fair coverage of an essential aspect of the city. For incurable Anglophiles, *The London Encyclopedia* (by Benjamin Weinreb) is a must. A new guide called *Permanent Londoners: An Illustrated Guide to the Cemeteries of London* lists the locations of the graves, along with biographical notes, of some of the more famous Londoners buried in the city. The book is available from Chelsea Publishing Co. (PO Box 130, Post Mills, VT 05058-0130; phone: 802-333-9073). Another new book called *Amazing London,* published by the British Tourist Authority, lists numerous bargains to help a tourist's dollars go farther. It also provides discounts of up to 50% in certain shops, restaurants, and tourist attractions. For a free copy, contact the British Tourist Authority (40 W. 57th St., New York, NY 10019; phone: 212-581-4700). The *Travel Bookshop* (25 Cecil Court, WC2N 4EZ; phone: 71-836-9132) has a wide selection of guidebooks and travel information. It's possible to get secondhand books here and to trade your own books as well.

*London A-Z* and *Nicholson's Street Finder,* inexpensive pocket-size books of street maps (available in bookstores and from most "newsagents"), are very useful for finding London addresses. Also helpful are maps of the subway system and bus routes and the *London Regional Transport Visitors Guide* — all available free from the London Transport information centers at several stations, including Victoria, Piccadilly, Charing Cross, Oxford Circus, and Heathrow Central, and at the ticket booths of many other stations (phone: 71-222-1234 for information).

The US Embassy is at 24-31 Grosvenor Sq., W1 (phone: 71-499-9000).

**Local Coverage** – Of London's several newspapers, the *Times,* the *Sunday Times,* the *Observer* (Sundays only), the *Guardian,* the *Independent,* and the *Daily Telegraph* are the most useful for visitors. Also helpful are the weekly magazines *City Limits, Time Out,* and *New Statesman.* The *Evening Standard* is the paper most read by Londoners. For business news, read the *Financial Times* (daily) and the *Economist* magazine (weekly).

 **TELEPHONE:** London has two area codes. The area code for inner London is 71; for outer London, 81. All telephone numbers listed in this chapter, therefore, include the correct city code. When calling from one area code to another within London or from elsewhere within Great Britain, dial either 071 or 081 before the local number.

The procedure for calling London from the US is as follows: dial 011 (the international access code) + 44 (the country code) + the city code + the local number.

The procedure for calling the US from London is as follows: dial 010 (the international access code) + 1 (the US country code) + the area code + the local number. For instance, to call New York from London, dial 010 + 1 + 212 + the local number. For calling from one British city to another, simply dial 0 + the city code + the local number; and for calls within the same city code coverage area, simply dial the local number.

For emergency service dial 999 (much as you would dial 911 in the US). An alternative may be to dial 100 for an operator who can connect you to emergency services. For further information on what to do in the event of an emergency, see *Medical and Legal Aid and Consular Services,* in GETTING READY TO GO.

As in the US, to call from most British pay phones you will need either a pocketful of change or a telephone credit card. The Phonecard service offered by *British Telecom* gives travelers a convenient alternative at over 20,000 special phones nationwide. Note that calls made from these phones can be made *only* with Phonecards. When scanning a line of pay phones or phone booths, it helps to know that cash phones generally are marked in yellow and Phonecard phones are labeled and marked in green.

Phonecards, which function much as telephone credit cards, are available in 20, 40, 100, and 200 units; these cards cost £2, £4, £10, and £20, respectively, and are good for the equivalent amount in calls. (The value of each card is holographically encoded on the card.) Cards are inserted into the phone at the beginning of a call, and the appropriate charge is subtracted — the number of units remaining on the card appears on the phone's digital display throughout the call. If the units are about to be used up, the display will flash and a tone will sound — at which point you can insert a new card and continue your call uninterrupted. Phonecards are sold at major transportation centers (airports, train stations, and so on), post offices, and *BritRail* and some tourist information offices, as well as at gas stations, newsstands, major shopping centers, and numerous stores. Look for the green "Phonecard, Buy Yours Here" signs. For further information, contact *British Telecom,* 81 New Gate St., London EE1 AJA, England (phone: 71-356-5000).

Phones marked with a large "M" are part of the *Mercury* system, another, less common telephone card service (*British Telecom*'s cards won't work in these). Cards for use in *Mercury* phones are available at airports, hotels, stores, and shopping centers. They are available in £1, £2, £4, £5, and £10 denominations. One of the advantages of the *Mercury* phones is that they also accept *American Express, MasterCard (or Access),* and *Visa* cards. For further information, contact *Mercury,* Gretton House, 3rd Floor, 28-30 Kirby St., London EC1, England (phone: 71-528-2000).

Although you can use a telephone company credit card number on any phone, pay phones that take major credit cards — such as *Mercury* phones (mentioned above) — are increasingly common worldwide, particularly in transportation and tourism centers. Also now available is the "affinity card," a combined telephone calling card/bank credit card that can be used for domestic and international calls. Cards of this type include the following:

> *AT&T/Universal* (phone: 800-662-7759). Cardholders can charge calls to the US from overseas.
>
> *Executive Telecard International* (phone: 800-950-3800). Cardholders can charge calls to the US from overseas, as well as between most European countries.
>
> *Sprint Visa* (phone: 800-446-7625). Cardholders can charge calls to the US from overseas.

Similarly, *MCI VisaPhone* (phone: 800-866-0099) can add phone card privileges to the services available through your existing *Visa* card. This service allows you to use your *Visa* account number, plus an additional code, to charge calls on any touch-tone phone in the US and Europe.

**GETTING AROUND: Boat** – The *RiverBus Partnership,* a high-speed riverboat service, links east London to west, between London City Port and Chelsea Harbour (including the London "City" Airport). It runs at approximately 20-minute intervals, weekdays from 7 AM to 10 PM, calling at eight piers. Exchange Tower, 1 Harbour Exchange Sq., E14 (phone: 71-512-0555).

For a leisurely view of London from the Thames, tour boats leave roughly every half hour from Westminster Pier (at the foot of Westminster Bridge) and from Charing Cross Pier (on Victoria Embankment); they sail (*Easter* through September) upriver to Kew or downriver to the Tower of London, Greenwich, and the massive Thames flood barrier. An inclusive ticket covering a round-trip boat ride from central London to Greenwich and entry to the *National Maritime Museum,* the *Old Royal Observatory,* and the *Cutty Sark* clipper is available for about $10 from the British Travel Centre, the Victoria Tourist Information Centre, and at Charing Cross, Westminster, and Tower piers. A journey along Regent's Canal through north London is offered (summers only) by *Jason's Trip* (opposite 60 Blomfield Rd., Little Venice, W9; phone: 71-286-3428). For further information about these and other boat trips, contact the London Tourist Board or the Convention Bureau's River Boat Information Service (phone: 71-730-4812).

**Bus and Underground** – The London public transport system seems to be getting more and more sluggish these days, and you'll hear many Londoners complaining about it, but it is still reasonably efficient and will get you where you're going. The subway, called the underground or tube, and bus lines cover the city pretty well — though buses suffer from traffic congestion, and the underground is notoriously thin south of the Thames. (Avoid rush-hour traffic, which is hideous, from 8:30 to 9:30 AM and from 5 to 6 PM.) The tops of London's famous red double-decker buses do, however, offer some delightful views of the city and its people. The underground is easy to understand and to use, with clear directions and poster maps in all stations. Pick up free bus and underground maps from tourist offices or underground ticket booths. The fares on both trains and buses are set according to length of the journey. On most buses, conductors take payment after you tell them where you're going; some require that you pay as you enter. Underground tickets are bought on entering a station. Retain your ticket; you'll have to surrender it when you get off (or have to pay again), and bus inspectors make spot checks to see that no one's stealing a free ride. There are also *Red Arrow* express buses, which link all the main-line *British Rail* stations, but you'll have to check stops before you get on. With just a few exceptions, public transport comes to a halt around midnight; it varies according to underground line and bus route. If you're going to be traveling late, check available facilities. For 24-hour travel information, call 71-222-1234.

A London Transport Visitor Travelcard can be purchased in the US from travel agents and *BritRail Travel International* offices in New York, Dallas, and Los Angeles, or in London from *London Regional Transport* travel information centers. The card provides unlimited travel on virtually all of London's bus and underground networks and costs about $4 for 1 day (available only in London), $15 for 3 days, $21 for 4 days, and $35 for 7 days. If purchased in the US, a book of discount vouchers for many of the city's sights is included; for purchase in London, a passport-size photo must be provided.

One of the least expensive and most comprehensive ways to tour the city is to take the *Original London Transport Sightseeing Tour,* a 2-hour unconducted bus tour, which leaves every hour from four sites: Marble Arch, Piccadilly Circus, Baker Street tube station, and Victoria Station (phone: 71-227-3456). Other guided bus tours are offered by *American Express* (phone: 71-930-4411), *Frames* (phone: 71-837-6311), *Harrods* (phone: 71-581-3603), and *Thomas Cook* (phone: 71-499-4000).

**Car Rental** – Most rental agencies have desks at the airports. For more information on renting a car in London, see "Car Rental" in *Traveling by Plane,* GETTING READY TO GO.

**Helicopter Flights** – See London from the air. Sightseeing tours are available (prices vary and start at around $250). The standard flight includes an aerial tour of the major

London sites; special views available on request. Make a reservation with *C.B. Helicopters,* Battersea (phone: 71-228-3232).

**Taxi** – Those fine old London cabs are gradually being supplemented with more "practical" models. It is one of life's great tragedies. Although dashboard computers in cabs are becoming increasingly more common, too, London cabbies seem generally pleased with the new system; the computers allow communication between driver and dispatcher so that the cab's home office knows who's empty and who's closest to a prospective fare. Riders will be happy to know that the computer also allows drivers to check on possible traffic problems and to obtain basic route instructions. Whether you end up in a computerized or "regular" cab, taxi fares in London are increasingly expensive (though you don't mind the price so much if you're riding in the big, old comfortable vehicles), and a 15% tip is customary.

Tell a London cabbie where you're going *before* entering the cab. When it rains or late at night, an empty cab (identifiable by the glow of the roof light) is often very difficult to find, so it is wise to carry the telephone number of one or more of the cab companies that respond to calls by phone. There are also many "minicab" companies that do not respond when hailed on the street, nor do they use meters. They operate on a fixed fare basis between their home base and your destination, and you have to call their central office to book one. Hotel porters or reception desks usually can make arrangements to have such a car pick you up at a specified time and place. Be aware that taxi rates are higher after 8 PM (and sometimes even higher after midnight) and on weekends and holidays.

Several firms and taxi drivers offer guided tours of London; details are available at information centers. You can arrange for the personal services of a member of London's Guild of Guides by phoning the London Visitor and Convention Bureau's Guide Dept. (phone: 71-730-3450).

*London Taxi Video Tours* provides a unique service in which a knowledgeable and obliging driver/guide will escort from 1 to 5 people on a 3-hour tour of London, driving them from place to place in one of the city's wonderful, old, big, black cabs. The guide videotapes his group, capturing them strolling London's streets, visiting historic sites, talking to a London policeman, watching the Changing of the Guard. The videotape, which includes perky background music, is later presented to travelers in a system compatible with American VCRs. The tour, including the video, costs about $205 (extra copies are about $33). An all-day tour also is available for about $330. Special theme tours (Victorian and macabre London, the haunts of the "Elephant Man," and "Sweeney Todd" territory) and custom-designed tours also are available. Reservations advised. 25 Stanway Rd., Benfleet, Essex SS7 5UX (phone: 268-566330).

**Train** – London has 11 principal train stations, each the starting point for trains to a particular region, with occasional overlapping of routes. The ones you are most likely to encounter include King's Cross (phone: 71-278-2477), the departure point for northeast England and eastern Scotland, including Edinburgh; Euston (phone: 71-387-7070), serving the Midlands and north Wales, with connections to Northern Ireland and the Republic, northwest England, and western Scotland, including Glasgow; Paddington (phone: 71-262-6767), for the West Country and south Wales, including Fishguard and ferries to Rosslare, Ireland; Victoria (phone: 71-928-5100), for Gatwick Airport and, along with Charing Cross Station (phone: 71-928-5100), for departures to southeast England; and Liverpool St. Station (phone: 71-928-5100), for departures to East Anglia and to Harwich for ferries to the Continent, including Scandinavia. All of these stations are connected via London's underground.

*BritRail's* Travelpak transportation program is intended for travelers who wish to venture out of London. It includes round-trip journeys from Gatwick or Heathrow airports to central London; the London Explorer; and a 4-day *BritRail* pass for unlimited train travel within Britain (15-day and 1-month passes also are available). Maps and timetables are also included. *BritRail* Travelpaks must be obtained before leaving the US, from any North American *BritRail* office. Write *BritRail,* 630 Third Ave., New York, NY 10017 (phone: 212-599-5400).

For a special treat, take a day trip on the luxurious British *Pullman* cars of the *Venice Simplon–Orient Express.* You can see the spas, castles, and more in southwest England on trips to Bath, Bristol, and Salisbury. Or take the trip through beautiful Kent, enjoying a sumptuous, 4-course luncheon as you wind through the countryside. For additional information: 1155 Avenue of the Americas, New York, NY 10036 (phone: 800-524-2420; 212-302-5006 in New York City; 71-834-8122 in London).

**Walking Tours** – A trained guide can show you Shakespeare's London or that of Dickens or Jack the Ripper — many different themes are offered. These reasonably priced tours last up to 2 hours, generally in the afternoon or evening. *City Walks* offers several tours, including a Sherlock Holmes Trail of Mystery and Whodunit Tour departing from the Baker Street underground station, Baker Street exit, on Tuesdays at 10:30 AM (phone: 71-937-4281). *Citisights* (phone: 81-806-4325) start from many places, including the *Museum of London* (London Wall). *Streets of London* (phone: 81-882-3414) tours start from various underground stations. *Londoner Pub Walks* (phone: 81-883-2656) start from Temple underground station (*District* and *Circle* lines) on Fridays at 7:30 PM. *London Walks* (phone: 71-435-6413) provides tours leaving from a variety of points. A tour of the Docklands' Rotherhithe district is offered by local historian Jim Nash (see the "Docklands" in *Seeing the City,* above). Informative books on London walking tours include *Londonwalks* (Holt, Rinehart & Winston), *Guide to Literary London* (Batford) by George Williams, and *Birnbaum's Great Britain 1992* (HarperCollins). *Time Out* also has day-by-day listings of walks in each issue.

**Especially for Kids** – If you're traveling *en famille* and have the urge to be alone but don't want to deprive your offspring (all ages) of what London and its immediate countryside have to offer, *Take-a-Guide* may be the answer. They will provide a car with a driver-guide especially knowledgeable in the ways and wiles of young folk for half- or full-day tours. It's costly: in London, $212 for a half day; $350 for a full day; or in the countryside, $250 for a half day; $500 for a full day. Contact them in the US at 800-223-6450; 212-628-4823 in New York City; 71-221-5475 in London.

 **LOCAL SERVICES: Baby-sitting Services** – Nannies are quite easily available in London. Two of the baby-sitting agencies are *Childminders* (phone: 71-935-9763 or 71-935-2049) and *Universal Aunts Ltd.* (phone: 71-371-9766). Whether the sitter is hired directly or through an agency, ask for and check references.

**Dentist** – *Eastman Dental Hospital,* 256 Gray's Inn Rd., WC1 (phone: 71-837-3646).

**Dry Cleaner/Tailor** – *Jeeves* (8-10 Pont St., SW1; phone: 71-235-1101); *Anderson Sheppard* (30 Savile Row, W1; phone: 71-734-1420).

**Limousine Service** – *Guy Salmon,* 23 Bryanston St., W1 (phone: 71-408-1255).

**Medical Emergency** – *Middlesex Hospital* is among the most central of London's hospitals and provides 24-hour emergency service (Mortimer St., W1; phone: 71-636-8333). In cases of extreme emergency, dial 999.

**Messenger Service** – *Quicksilver,* 227 Liverpool Rd., N1 (phone: 71-734-6126).

**National/International Courier** – *DHL International* (181 The Strand, WC2, and Orbital Park, Great Southwest Rd., Hounslow, Middlesex; phone: 81-890-9000); *Federal Express* (9 Elms La., Unit 4, SW8; phone: 71-622-3933 or toll-free in England, 800-123800). *British Airways* operates *Speedbird Express* (World Cargo Centre, Hounslow, Middlesex; phone: 81-562-6279 or 81-562-6229).

**Office Equipment Rental** – *Office Installations,* 11A The Mall, W5 (phone: 81-579-6771).

**Pharmacy** – *Boots* (Piccadilly Circus; phone: 71-734-6126). The local police stations have lists of 24-hour pharmacies in their neighborhoods.

**Photocopies** – *Kall Kwik*, at several locations, including 21 Kingly St., W1 (phone: 71-434-2471).

**Post Office** – The main post office (London Chief Office, King Edward Building, King Edward St., EC1; phone: 71-239-2000) is open Mondays through Fridays from 8:30 AM to 6:30 PM. A centrally located branch, off Trafalgar Square (24 William IV St., WC2; phone: 71-930-9580), is open Mondays through Saturdays from 8 AM to 8 PM.

**Secretary/Stenographer** – *Drake Business Centre*, 136 Regent St., W1 (phone: 71-437-6900).

**Teleconference Facilities** – The *Inter-Continental* hotel (1 Hamilton Pl., W1; phone: 71-409-3131) has a worldwide teleconference link in its Mercury video conferencing studio (phone: 71-491-7824, direct line).

**Telex** – *Kensington Business Centre* is open from 8:30 AM to 8 PM. 9-11 Kensington High St., W8 (phone: 71-938-1721 or 71-938-2151).

**Other** – Business services: *Business Centre* (next to Terminal 2, Heathrow Airport; phone: 81-759-2434); *Channel 5*, which also provides direct mail services (331 Goswell Rd., EC1; phone: 71-833-2732). Camera rental and repair: *Keith, Johnson, and Pelling* (Great Marlborough St., W1; phone: 71-439-8811). Jewelry rental: *Robert White* (22 Tavistock St., WC2; phone: 71-240-3111). Unisex hair salon: *Vidal Sassoon* (60 S. Molton St., W1; phone: 71-491-8848). Tuxedo rental: *Moss Bros.* (Bedford St., WC2; phone: 71-240-4567). Fur rental: *Herman* (30 Maddox St., W1; phone: 71-734-3804).

 **SPECIAL EVENTS:** Dates vary marginally from year to year and should be checked — together with details — with the London Visitor and Convention Bureau. In late March/early April, the Oxford and Cambridge rowing "eights" race through the waters from Putney to Mortlake, an important competition for the two universities, whose respective teams practice for months beforehand. The world-famous *Chelsea Flower Show* takes place in late May. In early June, enjoy the annual *Trooping the Colour*, England's most elaborate display of pageantry — a Horse Guards' parade, with military music and much pomp and circumstance — all in celebration of the queen's official birthday. You can see some of the parade without a ticket, but for the ceremony you must book before March 1 by writing to the Brigade Major (Headquarters, Household Division, Horse Guards, Whitehall, SW1) — do not send money. The 2-week-long *Greenwich Festival*, also held in June, includes mime and dance performances, poetry readings, a wide variety of music, and children's events. (For more details, see *The Best Festivals* in DIVERSIONS.) The *Grosvenor House Antiques Fair* is held for 10 days every June at the hotel on Park Lane. Late June heralds the *Wimbledon Lawn Tennis Championship* — the world's most prestigious — complete with a member of the royal family presenting the prizes. The *City of London Festival* is held for 2½ weeks in July within the Old City's square mile. It features choirs, orchestras, chamber groups, and leading soloists of international repute, along with a popular jazz program, dance, street theater, and a wide range of exhibitions. The *Henley Royal Regatta*, in early July (at Henley-on-Thames, a 1-hour train ride from London), is an international rowing competition and one of the big social events of the year. Watch from the towpath (free) or from within the *Regatta* enclosure (fee). The *Royal Tournament*, a military pageant, takes place at Earl's Court for 3 weeks in July. The *Early Music Centre Festival* — featuring orchestral, chamber, and choral music — is usually held sometime between the end of September and early November. October or November is the time for the *State Opening of Parliament*; *Guy Fawkes Day* is on November 5, when fireworks and bonfires mark the anniversary of the plot to blow up both Houses of Parliament and King James I in 1605; and on the second Saturday in November, the *Lord Mayor's Procession* is held, in which the new lord mayor, who rides in a golden carriage, is followed by bands and wacky, colorful floats. On the first Sunday in November, the *London-to-Brighton Veteran Car Run* features shiny antique autos undertaking the 50-mile drive. On *Remembrance Sunday,* the Sunday nearest to November 11 (*Armistice Day*), a moving and solemn parade of veterans passes before the queen and lays red poppy wreaths at the base of the Cenotaph, on Whitehall.

 **MUSEUMS:** Many of London's museums and galleries have no admission charge; others charge about $1.50 to $3. A number of the museums are described in *Special Places.* Others of note include the following:

**Bethnal Green Museum of Childhood** – Impressive collection of more than 4,000 toys, including dolls and dollhouses, games, and puppets. Open Mondays through Thursdays and Saturdays from 10 AM to 5:50 PM; Sundays from 2:30 to 5:50 PM. No admission charge. Cambridge Heath Rd., E2 (phone: 81-980-3204).

**Courtauld Institute Galleries** – A remarkable collection of French Impressionist and post-Impressionist paintings is now in a new home. Open Mondays through Saturdays, 10 AM to 6 PM; Sundays, 2 to 6 PM. Admission charge. Somerset House, the Strand, WC2 (phone: 71-873-2526).

**Design Museum** – Examples of everyday items from today's consumer society are on display at this museum in the Docklands. Teakettles, tables and chairs, cars and bikes are all part of the permanent exhibit explaining the development of such items' design. There is also a library, lecture theater, and riverside café. Open daily, except Mondays, from 11:30 AM to 6:30 PM. Admission charge. Butler's Wharf, SE1 (phone: 71-403-6933).

**Dickens's House** – Manuscripts of early works, first editions, and personal memorabilia. Open Mondays through Saturdays, 10 AM to 5 PM. Admission charge. 48 Doughty St., WC1 (phone: 71-405-2127).

**Dulwich College Picture Gallery** – Works by European masters in one of England's most beautiful art galleries. The college itself boasts such famous alumni as P. G. Wodehouse and Raymond Chandler. Open Tuesdays through Fridays, 10 AM to 1 PM and 2 to 5 PM; Saturdays, 11 AM to 5 PM; Sundays, 2 to 5 PM. Admission charge. College Rd., SE21 (phone: 81-693-5254).

**Ecological Museum** – The history of the earth is represented in tremendous collections of rocks, fossils, and exhibits on the latest theories. Open Mondays through Saturdays, 10 AM to 6 PM; Sundays, 11 AM to 6 PM. Admission charge. Exhibition Rd., SW7 (phone: 71-938-8765).

**Florence Nightingale Museum** – Opened in 1989, this museum is not for nurses only. It offers a fascinating look at the life of the "Lady with the Lamp." Open Tuesdays through Sundays, including bank holidays, from 10 AM to 4 PM (last admission). Admission charge. 2 Lambeth Palace Rd., SE1 (phone: 71-620-0374).

**Hayward Gallery** – Temporary exhibitions of British and international art. Open Tuesdays and Wednesdays from 10 AM to 8 PM; Thursdays through Mondays from 10 AM to 6 PM. Admission charge. At the *South Bank Arts Centre* on Belvedere Rd., SE1 (phone: 71-928-3144).

**Institute of Contemporary Arts** – Exhibitions of up-to-date British art, film, theater, manifesto. Open daily, noon to 10 PM. Admission charge. Nash House, Duke of York Steps, The Mall, SW1 (phone: 71-930-3647).

**Jewish Museum** – Art and antiques illustrating Jewish history. Closed Mondays, Saturdays, and Jewish and bank holidays. No admission charge. Woburn House, Upper Woburn Pl., WC1 (phone: 71-388-4525).

**London Toy and Model Museum** – This charming Victorian building houses a fine collection of model trains and mechanical toys. Open Tuesdays through Saturdays from 10 AM to 5:30 PM; Sundays from 11 AM to 5:30 PM. Admission charge. October House, 23 Craven Hill, W2 (phone: 71-262-7905).

**Museum of Garden History** – Set in tiny St. Mary-at-Lambeth Church, the museum houses a collection of antique gardening tools and horticultural exhibits. A 17th-century–style garden (out back) contains a tulip tree and trumpet honeysuckle. Captain Bligh — who lived down the road — is buried right in the garden's center! Open the first Sunday in March to the second Sunday in December, Mondays through Fridays from 11 AM to 3 PM and Sundays from 10:30 AM to 5 PM. No admission charge. Lambeth Palace Rd., SE1, across the Thames from Parliament (phone: 71-373-4030).

**Museum of Mankind** – Ethnographic exhibitions. Open Mondays through Saturdays from 10 AM to 5 PM; Sundays from 2:30 to 6 PM. No admission charge. 6 Burlington Gardens, W1 (phone: 71-323-8043).

**Museum of the Moving Image** – The museum has over 50 exhibits and over 1,000 clips from various old and recent films and TV shows. There's also a good bit of movie memorabilia, including Charlie Chaplin's hat and cane and fine movies ignored by big distributors. Open Tuesdays through Saturdays, 10 AM to 8 PM; Sundays, 10 AM to 6 PM; closed Mondays. Admission charge. *South Bank Arts Centre,* SE1, underneath the Waterloo Bridge, next to the *Royal Festival Hall* (phone: 71-928-3535).

**Musical Museum** – One of Europe's most comprehensive collections of pianos and mechanical musical instruments, all in good working condition. Open April through October, Saturdays and Sundays from 2 to 5 PM. Admission charge. 368 High St., Brentford, Middlesex (phone: 81-560-8108).

**Natural History Museum** – Exhibits of native wildlife, plants, fossils, and minerals. Open Mondays to Saturdays from 10 AM to 6 PM; Sundays from 11 AM to 6 PM. Admission charge. Cromwell Rd., SW7 (phone: 71-589-6323).

**Royal Air Force Museum** – A full exhibition of planes from the time of the Wright Brothers to the present. Open daily from 10 AM to 6 PM. Admission charge. Grahame Park Way, NW9 (phone: 81-205-2266).

**Science Museum** – The development of science and industry, including an "Exploration of Space" exhibit. Open Mondays through Saturdays, 10 AM to 6 PM; Sundays, 11 AM to 6 PM. Admission charge. Exhibition Rd., SW7 (phone: 71-589-3456).

**Sir John Soane's Museum** – Its eclectic collection of arts and antiques, stuffed into the architect's unusually designed home, includes Hogarth's series *The Rake's Progress.* Open Tuesdays through Saturdays from 10 AM to 5 PM. No admission charge. 13 Lincoln's Inn Fields, WC2 (phone: 71-405-2107).

**Theatre Museum** – Britain's newest collection of theatrical material has been given its own home. Everything from circus to pop, grand opera to mime, straight theater to Punch and Judy and pantomime is here, as well as an excellent informal café-restaurant on the main floor. Open Tuesdays through Sundays, 11 AM to 7 PM. Admission charge. 1E Tavistock St., WC2 (phone: 71-836-7891).

**Wallace Collection** – Sir Richard Wallace's fine collection of European paintings, sculpture, porcelain, and armor. Open Mondays through Saturdays from 10 AM to 5 PM; Sundays from 2 to 5 PM. No admission charge. Hertford House, Manchester Sq., W1 (phone: 71-935-0687).

**Whitechapel Art Gallery** – An East End haven for modern art, including works by Moore, Hepworth, and Hockney. Temporary exhibitions range from contemporary British artists to Third World and ethnic minority artists. Open 11 AM to 5 PM, Wednesdays to 8 PM; closed Mondays and bank holidays. No admission charge. 80 Whitechapel High St., E7 (phone: 71-377-0107).

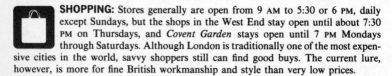 **SHOPPING:** Stores generally are open from 9 AM to 5:30 or 6 PM, daily except Sundays, but the shops in the West End stay open until about 7:30 PM on Thursdays, and *Covent Garden* stays open until 7 PM Mondays through Saturdays. Although London is traditionally one of the most expensive cities in the world, savvy shoppers still can find good buys. The current lure, however, is more for fine British workmanship and style than very low prices.

The favorite items on any shopping list in London are cashmere and Shetland knitwear; fabric (tweeds, blends, men's suitings); riding gear; custom-made men's suits, shirts, shoes, and hats; shotguns; china and crystal; umbrellas; antiques; sporting goods; English food specialties (jams and marmalade, various blended teas, Stilton cheese, shortbread, and others). Books published by British houses, once a fine buy, are now far higher in price, and you probably will do better to buy the US editions. For secondhand books, though, London still hides treasures. Charing Cross Road is a good place to start, and even pricey establishments may have basements with long out of print paperbacks in good condition, along with unfashionable Victoriana at very inexpensive prices. See Sheppard's *Directory of Second-Hand and Antiquarian Bookshops of the British Isles* for tips. But as all bargain hunters know, there is no substitute for your own voyages of discovery.

Devoted bargain hunters recognize that the best time to buy British is during the semi-annual sales that usually occur from *Boxing Day* (December 26) through the early part of the new year and again in early July. The *Christmas/New Year* sales offer by far the best bargains in the city, and the crowds can be the equal of the low prices. Many stores remain open on *New Year's Day* to accommodate the bargain hunters, and the best-publicized single sale is that held by *Harrods* for 3 weeks beginning the first Wednesday in January. That opening day is an event in itself.

Be sure to take your passport when you shop, and always inquire about the VAT refund application forms when your total purchases in a shop are over £50, about $83. The VAT (value added tax) is a 17.5% surcharge payable at the sales counter, but foreign customers usually will be reimbursed for it at home. *Chequepoint* money exchange in London will cash VAT refund checks 24 hours a day, but you'll have to pay for the privilege; there are three branches: 548 Oxford St., 222 Earl's Court Rd., and 71 Gloucester Rd. For purchases at any of the 10,000 shops displaying the London Tax Free Shopping logo, retailers issue vouchers that will be stamped by Customs when you leave the country and then posted to LTFS (21-24 Cockspur St., SW1); a refund is issued in local currency in as few as 4 days.

Though scattered about the city, the most appealing shops tend to center in the West End area, particularly along Old and New Bond Streets, Oxford, South Molton, Regent, and Jermyn Streets, and Piccadilly. Other good shopping areas are the King's Road, Kensington High Street, and Kensington Church Street, along with Knightsbridge and Covent Garden.

This is a city of markets; we have already described Portobello Road and Camden Passage in *Special Places.* Also worthy of note is *Camden Lock Market* (Camden High St., NW1) on Saturdays and Sundays for far-out clothes, leather items, antiques, and trinkets. The restored *Jubilee Market,* on the south side of *Covent Garden* piazza, is one of the largest indoor markets in the country. It features antiques and a flea market on Mondays; housewares, clothing, and jewelry Tuesdays through Fridays; and crafts on weekends. Another good choice for the real antiques connoisseur is the *Bermondsey–New Caledonian Market,* open on Fridays before dawn — bring a flashlight (at Bermondsey St. and Long La., off Tower Bridge Rd., SE1). Or get up early on a Sunday morning and head for the East End to sample a typically English transport café ("caff") breakfast at *Fred's* (40 Aberfeldy St., E14; phone: 71-987-6084) before tackling the very famous *Petticoat Lane* (Middlesex St., E1) for food, inexpensive clothes, crockery, and even the proverbial kitchen sink.

The following stores are only a sampling of London's treasure houses:

**Alexander Juran –** This business, started in Prague during the reign of Emperor Franz Josef II, has unattractive showrooms but wonderful merchandise, including textiles, rugs, and carpets. 74 New Bond St., W1 (phone: 71-493-4484 or 71-629-2550).

**Anderson and Sheppard –** Reputable "made-to-measure" tailor for men's clothes. 30 Savile Row, W1 (phone: 71-734-1420).

*Antiquarius Antique Market* – Wide variety of antique items from over 170 vendors. 135-141 King's Rd., SW3 (phone: 71-351-5353).

*Antique Porcelain Company Ltd.* – For 18th-century English porcelain and other varieties. 149 New Bond St., W1 (phone: 71-629-1254).

*Aquascutum* – Famous for raincoats and jackets for men and women. 100 Regent St., W1 (phone: 71-734-6090).

*Asprey & Company* – Fine jewelry, silver, and luggage. 165-169 New Bond St., W1 (phone: 71-493-6767).

*Austin Reed* – Classic English menswear, plus an old-fashioned barber shop in the basement. Some women's wear, too. 103 Regent St., W1 (phone: 71-734-6789).

*Bates* – A gentlemen's hatter, and our favorite. Check out the eight-part caps. 21A Jermyn St., SW1 (phone: 71-734-2722).

*Body Shop* – More than 150 different beauty products (perfume, soap, hair and skin care products — famous for not having been tested on animals), from the worldwide chain that started in Brighton. There are several locations throughout the city. One of the main stores is at 32 Great Marlborough St., W1 (phone: 71-437-5137).

*Bond Street Antique Centre* – Everything from antique jewelry and watches to silver and porcelain. 124 New Bond St., W1 (phone: 71-351-5353).

*Browns* – Designer clothes for men and women in seven shops along the tiny, pedestrians-only South Molton St., W1 (phone: 71-491-7833).

*Burberrys* – Superb, expensive, men's and women's raincoats and traditional clothes, and home of the now nearly ubiquitous plaid that began life as a raincoat lining. 18 Haymarket, SW1 (phone: 71-930-3343).

*Caroline Charles* – Perfect women's styles for *Ascot* and other very social events. 56-57 Beauchamp Pl., SW3 (phone: 71-589-5850).

*Chelsea Antique Market* – London's first antiques market still has a fine selection and reputation. 253 King's Rd., SW3 (phone: 71-352-1424).

*Church's Shoes* – Superior men's shoes in various locations, including 58-59 Burlington Arcade, W1 (phone: 71-493-8307).

*Collets* – One of the best places to find musical recordings from eastern Europe, particularly folk tunes. 129-131 Charing Cross Rd., WC2 (phone: 71-734-0782).

*Conran's* – Terence Conran has transformed the beautiful Michelin Building into a larger, more exclusive and expensive version of his well-known *Habitat* stores. However, the export of larger furniture and furnishings is probably better arranged through a US branch. 81 Fulham Rd., SW3 (phone: 71-589-7401).

*Cordings* – Sportswear for the quintessential country squire. They've also recently added a fine line of women's wear, from linen suits to riding gear. 19-20 Piccadilly, W1 (phone: 71-734-0830).

*Courtenay House* – Pricey but elegantly designed women's wear; particularly beautiful ladies' sweaters and silky lingerie. 22 Brook St., W1 (phone: 71-629-0542).

*David Shilling* – His one-off (a tad eccentric) hat creations always create a stir at *Ascot*. 44 Chiltern St., W1 (phone: 71-935-8473).

*Dillon's* – London's most scholastic bookstore, partly owned by London University. 1 Malet St., WC1 (phone: 71-636-1577).

*Disney Store* – Selling Disney-related characters, including videos, stationery, clothes, jewelry, watches, and cuddly things. 140-144 Regent St., W1 (phone: 71-287-6558).

*Douglas Hayward* – A reputable made-to-order tailor. 95 Mount St., W1 (phone: 71-499-5574).

*Dress Circle* – If the music of show biz is what you're after, here are original recordings from big and small hits (and total flops), plus pressings of Judy Garland, Bing Crosby, Peggy Lee. 57-59 Monmouth St., WC2 (phone: 71-240-2227).

*Farlows* – Perhaps the best spot in London to buy the completely waterproof and windproof Barbour jackets and hats. 5 Pall Mall, SW1 (phone: 71-839-2423).

*Feathers* – French and Italian designer clothing for women. 40 Hans Crescent, SW1 (phone: 71-589-0356).

*58 Dean Street Records* – Offers a wide selection of show tunes and movie soundtracks, and the staff is very helpful. 58 Dean St., W1 (phone: 71-734-8777).

*Filofax Shop* – The famous brand-name personal organizers. 21 Conduit St., W1 (phone: 71-499-0457).

*Floris* – Old-fashioned English scents, soaps, potpourri, and more in a charming Victorian shop. 89 Jermyn St., SW1 (phone: 71-930-2885).

*Fortnum & Mason* – Boasts designer originals (of the rather dowdy variety), an appealing soda fountain–cum–restaurant, and one of the most elegant grocery departments in the world (where the staff wears striped morning trousers and swallowtail coats). 181 Piccadilly, W1 (phone: 71-734-8040).

*Foyle's* – London's largest bookstore. 119 Charing Cross Rd., WC2 (phone: 71-437-5660).

*Grays Antique Market* – The hundreds of stalls here and at the annex down the street sell everything from antique playing cards to 16th-century furniture. 1-7 Davies Mews, W1, and 58 Davies St., W1 (phone: 71-629-7034).

*Grosvenor Prints* – Over 100,000 prints on many subjects. 28-32 Shelton St., *Covent Garden*, WC2 (phone: 71-836-1979).

*Gucci* – Outposts of the famous Italian fashion, leather goods, and shoe manufacturer are found at 27 Old Bond St., W1 (phone: 71-629-2716), and at 17-18 Sloane St., SW1 (phone: 71-235-6707).

*Habitat* – Up-to-the-minute designs with realistic prices for furniture and household goods. 196 Tottenham Court Rd., W1 (phone: 71-631-3880), and 206 King's Rd., SW3 (phone: 71-351-1211).

*Hackett* – These elegant, but warmly welcoming, shops cater to men's sartorial and tonsorial needs. From togs for the most formal occasion, to a first class shave. There are several branches: 65b New King's Rd., SW6 (phone: 71-731-2790); 26 Eastcheap, EC3 (phone: 71-626-0707); and 1-2 Holborn Bars, EC1 (phone: 71-405-1767).

*Halcyon Days* – The best place to find authentic enameled Battersea boxes — both antique and brand-new. 14 Brook St., W1 (phone: 71-629-8811).

*Hamleys* – The largest toy store in the world. 188 Regent St., W1 (phone: 71-734-3161).

*Harrods* – The ultimate department store, although it does tend to be quite expensive. It has everything, even a mortuary and a bank, and what it doesn't stock it will get for you. The "Food Halls" particularly fascinate visitors, and traditional British merchandise is available in abundance. For those interested in trendy styles, it has the *Way In* boutique. Its annual January sale is legendary. 87-135 Brompton Rd., Knightsbridge, SW1 (phone: 71-730-1234).

*Harvey Nichols* – Princess Di's favorite luxury department store, specializing in women's haute couture. Knightsbridge, SW1 (phone: 71-235-5000).

*Heal's* – Furniture and fabrics in the best modern designs. (It also has a popular lunch-meeting restaurant.) 196 Tottenham Court Rd., W1 (phone: 71-636-1666).

*Henry Sotheran Ltd.* – Now incorporates *Cavendish Rare Books.* The large stock includes books on voyages and travel, Weinrab architectural books, finely bound literature, early English and continental titles. 2 Sackville St., W1 (phone: 71-439-6151).

*Herbert Johnson* – Men's and women's hats. 30 New Bond St., W1 (phone: 71-408-1174).

*Irish Linen Co.* – Plain and fancy bed and table linen and handkerchiefs. 35 Burlington Arcade, W1 (phone: 71-493-8949).

*Jaeger* – Tailored (and expensive) men's and women's clothes. 204 Regent St., W1 (phone: 71-494-3101), and 163 Sloane St., SW1 (phone: 71-235-2505).

*James Lock and Company, Ltd.* – The royal hatters. They fitted a crown for the queen's coronation, and they'll happily fit you for your first bowler. Plus hats for fishermen, hunters, groundskeepers. 6 St. James's St., SW1 (phone: 71-930-8874).

*James Purdey and Sons* – The place to go for custom-made shotguns and other shooting gear. 57 S. Audley St., W1 (phone: 71-499-1801).

*James Smith and Sons* – Believed to be the oldest umbrella shop in Europe, it was opened in 1830 by James Smith, and in 1857 it moved to its current address. Besides umbrellas, it also carries walking sticks and whips. A couple of blocks from the *British Museum.* 53 New Oxford St., WC1 (phone: 71-836-4731).

*Jasper Conran* – Top British designer clothes from Sir Terence Conran's son. 303 Brompton Rd., SW3 (phone: 71-823-9134).

*John Keil* – Lovely, expensive antiques. 154 Brompton Rd., SW3 (phone: 71-589-6454).

*John Lewis* – Good, basic department store, "never knowingly undersold" and particularly noted for its fabrics and household goods. 278 Oxford St., W1 (phone: 71-629-7711).

*John Lobb* – World-famous for men's made-to-order shoes — at stratospheric prices — that will last 10 years or more, with proper care. 9 St. James's St., SW1 (phone: 71-930-3664).

*Joseph* – One of the trend-setting shopping spots selling everything from luggage and housewares to men's and women's clothing, now with several branches around London. Try the largest, 77 Fulham Rd., SW3 (phone: 71-823-9500), or the one at 26 Sloane St., SW1 (phone: 71-235-5470).

*Justin De Blank* – Excellent specialty foods, especially cheese and take-out dishes. 42 Elizabeth St., SW1 (phone: 71-730-0605).

*Kent & Curwen* – The place to buy authentic cricket caps, Henley club ties, and all sorts of similarly preppy raiment. 39 St. James's St., SW1 (phone: 71-409-1955), and 6 Royal Arcade (for *Wimbledon* wear), W1 (phone: 71-493-6882).

*Laura Ashley* – A relatively inexpensive women's boutique specializing in romantically styled skirts, dresses, and blouses. 256 Regent St., W1 (phone: 71-437-9760), plus other branches including 47-49 Brompton Rd., SW1 (phone: 71-823-9700).

*Liberty* – Famous for print fabrics. Scarves and ties a specialty. 210 Regent St., W1 (phone: 71-734-1234).

*Lillywhites* – The whole gamut of sporting goods. Piccadilly Circus, SW1 (phone: 71-930-3181).

*London Silver Vaults* – An extraordinary maze of antique silver and jewelry shops belowground, housed in what once were real vaults. (A few shops sell new silver or silver plate, too.) Browse around first; prices range from astronomical to affordable, and some shops offer items at considerably lower prices than similar pieces fetch on New Bond and Conduit Streets. 53-54 Chancery La., WC2 (phone: 71-242-3844).

*Lucy B. Campbell* – Decorative prints from the 17th to the 19th centuries. 80 Holland Park Ave., W11 (phone: 71-229-4252).

*Mallett and Son* – Specializes in fine English antique furniture, but carries a wide variety of other items, too. 40 New Bond St., W1 (phone: 71-499-7411).

*Mandy's* – For all kinds of Irish music — *Clancy Brothers, ceilidh,* country, and *Chieftains*-style. 161 High Rd., NW10 (phone: 81-459-2842).

*Marks & Spencer* – Locally nicknamed "Marks & Sparks," this chain specializes in clothes for the whole family, made to high standards and sold at very reasonable prices. Its sweaters (especially cashmere and Shetland) are among the best buys in Britain; plus linens and their own cosmetics line. 458 Oxford St., W1, and many other branches (phone: 71-935-7954).

**McAfee** – Good selection of fine men's shoes. 17-18 Old Bond St., W1 (phone: 71-499-7343).

**Moss Bros.** – Men's formal attire (including dress tartans) and high-quality riding clothes for sale and hire. 88 Regent St., W1 (phone: 71-494-0666), and 27 King St., WC2 (phone: 71-497-9354).

**Partridge Ltd.** – Fine (but expensive) antiques. 144 New Bond St., W1 (phone: 71-629-0834).

**Paul Smith** – Britain's number one men's designer has two adjacent shops in *Covent Garden.* 43-44 Floral St., WC2 (phone: 71-379-7133).

**Peter Jones** – Another good, well-stocked department store, offering moderately priced, tasteful goods. Sloane Sq., SW1 (phone: 71-730-3434).

**Pickering and Chatto** – For antiquarian books on many topics. 17 Pall Mall, SW1 (phone: 71-930-2515).

**Prestat** – The best chocolates in all of London. Try the truffles. 14 Princes Arcade, SW1 (phone: 71-629-4838).

**Reject China Shop** – Good buys in slightly (invisibly) irregular, name-brand china. Glassware, crystal, and flatware, too. For a fee, the shop will ship your purchases back home. 34 Beauchamp Pl., SW3 (phone: 71-581-0737), or 134 Regent St., W1 (phone: 71-434-2502).

**Scotch House** – Famous for Scottish cashmeres, sweaters, tartans — a wide selection of well-known labels. 2 Brompton Rd., SW1 (phone: 71-581-2151), and many branches.

**Selfridges** – This famous department store offers somewhat less variety than *Harrods,* but it has just about everything, too — only a little less expensive. The extensive china and crystal department carries most patterns available. 400 Oxford St., W1 (phone: 71-629-1234).

**Shellys Shoes** – Wide selection of trendy street footwear from thigh-high suede boots to platform shoes. 159 Oxford St., W1 (phone: 71-439-8717).

**Shirin** – The best designer cashmeres in town. 51 Beauchamp Pl., SW3 (phone: 71-581-1936).

**Simpson (Piccadilly)** – Classic and safe English looks for men and women, including their own famous "Daks" label. 203 Piccadilly, W1 (phone: 71-734-2002, or toll-free in the UK, 800-282-188).

**S. J. Phillips** – Silver, jewelry, and more from the 16th to the early 19th centuries. 139 New Bond St., W1 (phone: 71-629-6261).

**Smythson of Bond Street** – The world's best place to buy diaries, notepads, and calendars, many in Florentine marbled paper; also exotic ledgers in which to record odd data. 54 New Bond St., W1 (phone: 71-629-8558).

**Sotheby's** – The world's oldest art auctioneer, interesting to look at even if you don't plan to buy. They auction books, porcelain, furniture, jewelry, and works of art — at times, even such odd items as vintage cars and wines. Viewing hours are between 9:30 AM and 4:30 PM on weekdays. 34 New Bond St., W1 (phone: 71-493-8080).

**Swaine, Adeney, Brigg, and Sons** – Riding gear and their famous pure silk umbrellas. 185 Piccadilly, W1 (phone: 71-734-4277).

**Temple Gallery** – Specializes in Byzantine, Greek, and early Russian icons. 6 Clarendon Cross, W11 (phone: 71-727-3809).

**Thomas Goode and Company** – London's best china and glass shop first opened in 1827. Even if you don't plan to buy anything, you may want to look at their beautiful 1876 showroom. 19 S. Audley St., W1 (phone: 71-499-2823).

**Turnbull and Asser** – Famous for their made-to-order shirts, but they also sell ready-made luxury menswear, as well as women's wear next door. 71-72 Jermyn St., SW1 (phone: 71-930-0502).

*Twinings* – Tea — and (almost) nothing but — in bags, balls, and bulk. 216 Strand, WC2 (phone: 71-353-3511).

*Vigo-Sternberg Galleries* – For tapestries from the 16th to the 19th centuries. 37 S. Audley St., W1 (phone: 71-629-8307).

*Waterstone's* – Look for the maroon canopy of this huge chain of bookstores, whose instant success is due mainly to enterprising, well-informed staff and late, late hours (it's open till midnight in Edinburgh, for example). There are many branches, including ones on 68-69 Hampstead High St., NW3 (phone: 71-794-1098), 99-101 Old Brompton Rd., SW7 (phone: 71-581-8522), 121-125 Charing Cross Rd., WC2 (phone: 71-434-4291), and 193 Kensington High St., W8 (phone: 71-937-8432).

*W. Bill Ltd.* – Shetland sweaters, knit ties, argyle socks, club mufflers, gloves. Two locations: 28 Old Bond St., W1 (phone: 71-629-2554) and 93 Old Bond St., W1 (phone: 71-629-2837).

*Wedgwood* – Porcelain. 158 Regent St., W1 (phone: 71-734-7262).

*Westaway and Westaway* – Cashmere and Shetland wool kilts, sweaters, scarves, and blankets. 65 Great Russell St., WC1, and around the corner at 29 Bloomsbury, WC1 (phone: 71-405-4479).

*Whiteleys of Bayswater* – Once a department store rivaling *Harrods,* the original building has undergone a total renovation and is now a beautiful, enclosed Edwardian mall housing a branch of just about every shop found on Bond Street or Piccadilly. The top tier holds a "Food Court," offering cafés, bars, and restaurants. Both stores and restaurants are open daily (from 10 AM to 10 PM and 10 AM to midnight, respectively). Queensway, W2 (phone: 71-229-8844).

**SPORTS AND FITNESS:** Soccer (called football hereabouts) and cricket are the most popular spectator pastimes, but London offers a wide variety of other sports.

**Cricket** – The season runs from mid-April to early September. The best places to watch it are at *Lord's Cricket Ground* (St. John's Wood Rd., NW8; phone: 71-289-1615), and *The Oval* (Kennington, SE11 5SS; phone: 71-582-6660).

**Fishing** – Several public ponds right in London are accessible to the angler. A permit is required from the Royal Parks Department (The Storeyard, Hyde Park, W2; phone: 71-262-5484). The department also can provide information on where to fish.

**Fitness Centers** – *Barbican Health & Fitness Centre* (97 Aldersgate St., EC2; phone: 71-374-0091); *Pineapple Dance Studios* (7 Langley St., WC2; phone: 71-836-4004); *Holmes Place Health Club* (188a Fulham Rd., SW10; phone: 71-352-9452); the *Albany* (Little Albany St., NW1; phone: 71-383-7131); *Earls Court Gym* (254 Earls Court Rd., SW5; phone: 71-370-1402); and several other locations around town, as well as in several hotels.

**Golf** – Aside from private clubs, for which membership is required, there are several municipal courses, some of which rent clubs. Try *Pickett's Lock Center* (Pickett's Lock La., N9; phone: 81-803-3611), *Addington Court* (Featherbed La., Addington, Croydon; phone: 81-657-0281), and *Beckenham Place Park* (Beckenham, Kent; phone: 81-650-2292). *Wentworth* (Virginia Water, Surrey; phone: 344-2201) and *Sunningdale* (Ridgemount Rd., Sunningdale, Berkshire; phone: 990-21681) are two of the best courses in England, and are within driving distance of London. A letter from your home club pro or president (plus a polite phone call) may gain access to their courses during the week.

**Greyhound Racing** – *Wembley Stadium* (Stadium Way, Wembley; phone: 81-902-8833, ext. 3346), and others. There are evening races, so check the afternoon newspapers for details.

**Horseback Riding** – Try *Bathurst Riding Stables* (63 Bathurst Mews, W2; phone: 71-723-2813) and *Ross Nye's Riding Establishment* (8 Bathurst Mews, W2; phone: 71-262-3791).

**Horse Racing** – Nine major racecourses are within easy reach of London, including *Epsom,* where the *Derby* (pronounced *Dar-*by) is run, and *Ascot,* where the *Royal Ascot* races take place — both in June. The flat racing season is from March to November; steeplechasing, August to June. Call the *Jockey Club* (42 Portman Sq., W1; phone: 71-486-4921) for information.

**Ice Skating** – There is the *Queen's Ice Skating Club* (17 Queensway, W2; phone: 71-229-0172) and *Silver Blades Ice Rink* (386 Streatham High Rd., SW16; phone: 81-769-7861). Skates are for rent at both rinks.

**Jogging** – Most pleasant for running are Hyde Park, bordered by Kensington Road, Park Lane, and Bayswater Road; Hampstead Heath, North London; and Regent's Park, bordered by Prince Albert Road, Albany Street, Marylebone Road, and Park Road. Do not jog after dark.

**Rugby** – An autumn-through-spring spectacle at *Rugby Football Ground,* Whitton Rd., Twickenham (phone: 81-892-8161).

**Soccer** – *The* big sport in Britain. The local football season is autumn to spring and the most popular local clubs are *Arsenal* (*Highbury Stadium,* Avenell Rd., N5; phone: 71-226-0304); *Chelsea* (Stamford Bridge, Fulham Rd., SW6; phone: 71-381-6221); and *Tottenham Hotspur* (White Hart La., N17; phone: 81-808-8080). As a spectator, be careful at games. Buy a seat rather than standing space. Violence and overcrowding have been major problems in recent years.

**Swimming** – Several excellent indoor public pools include *Swiss Cottage Center* (Adelaide Rd., NW3; phone: 71-586-5989); *Putney Swimming Baths* (376 Upper Richmond Rd., SW15; phone: 81-789-1124); and *The Oasis* (167 High Holborn,, WC1; phone: 71-836-9555). There is outdoor swimming in the Hyde Park Serpentine, and Hampstead Heath, in the summer.

**Tennis** – Aside from private clubs, more than 50 London public parks have tennis courts available to all. Get information from the London Visitor and Convention Bureau (phone: 71-730-3488).

 **THEATER:** London remains the theater capital of the world, with about 50 theaters regularly putting on plays in and around its West End theater district and a vigorous collection of "fringe" theaters in various parts of town. Best known, and most accomplished, are the two main repertory theater companies — the *Royal National Theatre Company* at the *Royal National Theatre* (South Bank, SE1; phone: 71-928-2252) and the *Royal Shakespeare Company (RSC)* at the *Barbican Centre* (The Barbican, EC2; phone: 71-638-8891); from time to time, both present dazzling versions of classics and new plays, although they sometimes trade on their reputations — the *National* mistaking dreariness for realism, and the *RSC,* stuffiness for stability. (For reliable critical reviews, consult *Time Out* magazine and the *Guardian's* Michael Billington.) Shakespearean plays also are performed in summer at the open-air theater in Regent's Park, NW1 (phone: 71-935-5756).

In the West End, presentations include both first class and second-rate drama and comedy, a fair sprinkling of farce (for which the British have a particular fondness), and the best imports from the American stage. Visitors from the US often find attending theater in London easier — and a little less expensive — than it is at home. Except for the small handful of runaway box-office successes, tickets usually are available for all performances. In most cases, you can reserve by telephone, but tickets must be picked up well before curtain time. The *West End Theatre Society* operates a half-price ticket kiosk in Leicester Square. It posts a list of shows for which remaining seats may be purchased at half price on the day of the performance. Ticket agencies that offer tickets to all shows, charging a small commission, include *Keith Prowse & Co.* (phone: 81-741-9999; in the US, 800-669-7469; in New York City, 212-398-1430), *Ticketmaster* (phone: 71-379-4444), *London Theatre Bookings* (96 Shaftesbury Ave.; phone: 71-439-3371/

4061), and *First Call* (phone: 71-240-7200). A phone service, *Theatreline,* offers information on a wide variety of West End performances (phone: 836-430959 for plays; 836-430960 for musicals; 836-430961 for comedies; 836-430962 for thrillers; 836-430963 for children's shows; 836-430964 for opera, ballet, and dance); calls can be placed from anywhere in Great Britain, and there is a service charge per call — about 60¢ to 80¢ in Great Britain, depending on the time of day. Another service, *Theatre Tonight,* offers tickets for sold-out performances. Available from noon to 6 PM, tickets can be bought by phone with a Visa card for same-night performances; no booking fee or ticket surcharge (phone: 71-753-0333).

The quality of London's fringe theater varies from accomplished and imaginative to amateurish. Theaters in pubs are at the *King's Head* (115 Upper St., Islington, N1; phone: 71-226-1916), and at the *Bush* (in the *Bush Hotel,* Shepherd's Bush Green, W6; phone: 81-743-3388). The *Riverside Studios* (Crisp Rd., Hammersmith, W6; phone: 81-748-3354), the *Tricycle Theatre* (269 Kilburn High Rd., NW6; phone: 71-328-1000), and the *New End Theatre* (27 New End, Hampstead, NW3; phone: 71-794-0022) have established reputations for the excellence of their productions, which often move on to the West End and sometimes even directly to Broadway. Also keep an eye on the *Donmar Warehouse* for major transfers from the *Edinburgh Festival Fringe* or for exciting avant-garde companies such as *Cheek by Jowl* (41 Earlham St., *Covent Garden,* WC2; phone: 71-240-8230). Lunchtime fringe theater presentations offer an alternative to sightseeing on rainy days.

A visit to *St. Martin's* is now tantamount to seeing a major London landmark, as it houses the late Agatha Christie's *The Mousetrap;* transferred from the *Ambassadors* next door, there's a fresh cast each year, and it's been running since 1952 — the longest run ever in nightly theater. The play is an exciting, tantalizing, and mildly frightening mystery-thriller. If you tell whodunit, you are ruined socially. West St., Cambridge Circus, WC2 (phone: 71-836-1443).

For those interested in musical nostalgia, the recently refurbished *Players Theatre* (in Villiers St., WC2, just off the Strand at Charing Cross station; phone: 71-839-1134) offers old-fashioned Victorian music hall entertainment.

Check *Time Out* or *City Limits* for comprehensive lists, plot summaries, and theater phone numbers. Daily papers list West End performances.

Show tours to London are very popular in season; see your travel agent for package deals. If you want to reserve specific tickets before you arrive in London, there are agencies in the US that keep a listing of what's on in London. For a service charge of about $5 per ticket, they will sell you the best seats only. Contact *Edwards & Edwards* (One Times Square Plaza, New York, NY 10036; phone: 212-944-0290 or 800-223-6108) or *Keith Prowse & Co.* (234 W. 44th St., New York, NY 10036; phone: 212-398-1430 or 800-669-7469). (For more London theater listings, see *The Performing Arts* in DIVERSIONS.)

The best of London's ballet performances are presented at *Covent Garden,* the *Coliseum,* and at *Sadler's Wells* (Roseberry Ave., EC1; phone: 71-278-8916), though the original company has moved to Birmingham, as well as at *The Place* (17 Duke's Rd., WC1; phone: 71-387-0031), home of the *London Contemporary Dance Theatre* and the *London School of Contemporary Dance.* Details about concert, recital, opera, and ballet performances are listed in the arts sections of the Sunday newspapers. Tickets to London ballet performances can be obtained in the US by contacting *Edwards & Edwards* (One Times Square Plaza, New York, NY 10036; phone: 212-944-0290 or 800-223-6108).

 **CINEMA:** London may not be the equal of Paris as a movie metropolis, but many say it's stronger when it comes to very good, little-known films, often from the US or Commonwealth countries. British film is startling in both similarities and contrasts to that of the US. In Great Britain, Chaplin, Hitchcock, and Laughton are regarded as English. The *British Film Institute* (21 Stephen St., W1; phone: 71-255-1444) has an incomparable British and international film library, administers the National Film Archive, contains first class documentation and filmographic material, and publishes the monthly *Film Bulletin* and the quarterly *Sight and Sound,* as well as running the *London Film Festival* (November), which takes place in the *National Film Theatre* (*NFT*) on the South Bank near Waterloo Station and Bridge (phone: 71-928-3232). Membership is required at the *NFT* (about 80¢ a day or $15.70 for a year), but it's well worth it for its two cinemas; wide variety of old and new British, US, and international movies; good film bookshop; and eating facilities. The success of the *NFT*'s *London Film Festival* in past years testifies to the high caliber of London's critics, who include the *Evening Standard*'s Alexander Walker, the *Guardian*'s Derek Malcolm, the *Financial Times*'s Nigel Andrews, and above all, the *Observer*'s Philip French; the *Film Festival* appoints one of them as its *supremo* of the year.

As with the theater, there are big divisions between West End and fringe (or independent) cinema. The West End strives for probable box-office smash hits, so look for long lines at Friday openings, and head for early showings, some of which begin not long after noon. Monday admission prices are less expensive. One word of warning: West End movie house prices are not inexpensive: Admission to a long-running film (at a theater on the Haymarket) cost us £6.50 (about $10.75) last winter. The widest selection of films under one roof can be found at *Whiteleys,* an enclosed mall with eight cinemas (Queensway, W2; phone: 71-792-3303). For sheer comfort, the *Curzon Mayfair* in the West End (on Mayfair's Curzon St., W1; phone: 71-465-8865) is unbeatable for both low-budget and commercial films. The most exciting film fare usually is found in independents, and sometimes you must travel to remote parts of London to see outstanding work in an almost empty cinema. If independent films interest you, check what's showing in places like *Everyman* (at Hampstead; phone: 71-435-1525); the luxurious, comfortable *Barbican Centre Cinemas* (phone: 71-638-8891); *Screen* (Baker St., W1; phone: 71-935-2772); *Screen on the Green* (at Islington; phone: 71-226-3520); and *Screen on the Hill* (in Hampstead; phone: 71-435-3366). All feature late-night showings and children's screenings on Saturdays (as do the *Barbican* and *NFT*). In some cases you may have to pay moderate club fees. Most British cinemas now ban smoking. Telephone the theaters for show times.

The *Museum of London,* near the *Barbican* (phone: 71-600-3699), and the *Museum of the Moving Image* (phone: 71-928-3535), alongside the *National Film Theatre,* also show films. Since showings are not regular, it is best to call ahead or to check in *Time Out.*

**MUSIC:** Few cities offer a greater variety of musical performances — both classical music and the many varieties of popular music. For classical fare, the focus of attention is the *South Bank Arts Centre* with its three concert halls, *Royal Festival Hall, Queen Elizabeth Hall,* and the *Purcell Room* (phone: 71-928-3191 for all three); the *Barbican Hall,* home of the *London Symphony Orchestra* (phone: 71-638-4141); and the *Royal Albert Hall* (Kensington Gore, SW7; phone: 71-589-8212). The latter is the home of the *Henry Wood Promenade Concerts,* or more simply, "the *Proms,*" an 8-week series of orchestral concerts that has been a popular feature of the London summer scene (July to September) for decades. Tickets are inexpensive because the *Proms* came into being to give students and other people who are not affluent an opportunity to dress up and be part of a grand musical event. The performances are tops (some broadcast live by the BBC), and the SRO audience is large and enthusiastic. *Wigmore Hall* (Wigmore St., W1; phone: 71-935-2141) is best known for recitals of chamber music and performances by some of the world's most accomplished instrumental and vocal soloists. Concerts also are often held in the dignified, splendid setting of St. John's Church (Smith Sq., SW1; phone: 71-222-1061).

During the summer, outdoor concerts are given at Kenwood, Crystal Palace, and Holland Park, and bands play in many of London's parks.

Operas at the *Royal Opera House, Covent Garden* (Floral St., WC2; phone: 71-240-1066), are internationally famous. The *English National Opera Company,* whose performances are always in English, is at the *London Coliseum* (St. Martin's La., WC2; phone: 71-836-3161). If you wish to obtain opera tickets before departing from the US, contact the agency *Edwards & Edwards* (One Times Square Plaza, New York, NY 10036; phone: 212-944-0290 or 800-223-6108).

Although superstar musicians and vocalists usually appear in the city's larger halls, good live popular music can be heard in London's music pubs. Among the best of them are the *Dublin Castle* (94 Parkway, NW1; phone: 71-485-1773); *King's Head* (4 Fulham High St., SW6; phone: 71-736-1413); *Hare and Hounds* (181 Upper St., N1; phone: 71-226-2992); and *Half Moon* (93 Lower Richmond Rd, SW15; phone: 81-788-2387).

If you are interested in purchasing tickets in the US to see pop and rock musicians who will be appearing in London, contact *Keith Prowse & Co.,* 234 W. 44th St., New York, NY 10036 (phone: 800-669-7469 or 212-398-1430 in New York City).

**NIGHTCLUBS AND NIGHTLIFE:** There was a time when they virtually rolled up the sidewalks in London at 11 PM. Now there's a very lively and often wild nightlife, including nightclubs, jazz clubs, historical feast entertainments, and gambling casinos. Some wind up around midnight; most go on until well into the early morning hours. In Covent Garden and still-trendy-after-all-these-years Chelsea, particularly along King's and Fulham roads, are fashionable pubs, wine bars, and restaurants. Two nightclubs with cabarets are *The Talk of the Town* (Drury La., WC2; phone: 71-408-1001) and *L'Hirondelle* (199 Swallow St., W1; phone: 71-734-1511). The best jazz clubs are *Ronnie Scott's* (47 Frith St., W1; phone: 71-439-0747) and *The 100 Club* (100 Oxford St., W1; phone: 71-636-0933). For jazz and a slice, try *Pizza Express* (10 Dean St., W1; phone: 71-437-9595), or *Pizza on the Park* (11 Knightsbridge, SW1; phone: 71-235-5550). *Dingwalls* (Camden Lock, Chalk Farm Rd., NW1; phone: 71-267-4967) and the *Town and Country Club* (9 Highgate Rd., NW5; phone: 71-284-0303) have a continually changing program of much-acclaimed performers of rock music.

For a special (if touristy) treat, London offers the *medieval banquet,* complete with traditional meals served by costumed waiters and waitresses. Menus resemble those of traditional Elizabethan feasts, and there is period music, horseplay, occasional mock sword fights, Shakespearean playlets, and other light entertainment. Try *Tudor Rooms* (17 Swallow St., W1; phone: 71-240-3978); *Beefeater* (St. Katherine Dock, E1; phone: 71-408-1001); and *Cockney Cabaret* (6 Hanover St., W1; phone: 71-408-1001).

The disco scene is an ever-changing one, and many places — such as expensive and exclusive *Annabel's* (44 Berkeley Sq., W1; phone: 71-629-3558) — are open only to members. Clubs of the moment include the *Hippodrome* (Charing Cross Rd., WC2; phone: 71-437-4311); *Stringfellows* (16-19 Upper St. Martin's La., WC2; phone: 71-240-5534); *Legend's* (29 Old Burlington St., W1; phone: 71-437-9933); *Crazy Larry's* (Lots Rd., SW10; phone: 71-376-5555); *Tramp* (40 Jermyn St., SW1; phone: 71-734-0565), where the chic social set meets to disco (members only); and *Limelight* (136 Shaftesbury Ave., W1; phone: 71-434-0572). A smart addition to the West London night scene is the *Broadway Boulevard* club in Ealing, particularly convenient for guests at the nearby Heathrow hotels (phone: 81-840-0616).

Female impersonators regularly perform at the *Jongleurs Cabaret Club* (at the *Coronet,* Lavender Gardens, SW11; phone: 71-585-0955), and the *Black Cap* (171 Camden High St., NW1; phone: 71-485-1742). Phone for details.

# BEST IN TOWN

 **CHECKING IN:** One way to help you select the type of hotel that fits your personal needs is to become familiar with Britain's official hotel classification system, which enables prospective guests to determine the minimum facilities provided by a given hostelry. The system consists of six classifications, from five crowns (the highest rating) through one crown, to simply, "listed" (the lowest rating). The crown system indicates the *range and types* of facilities and services offered by an establishment.

This classification scheme (maintained collectively by the tourist boards of England, Scotland, and Wales) applies to all types of accommodations, from luxury hotels to humble bed and breakfast establishments. The crown rating is posted outside the premises, but before relying on it entirely in choosing a bed for the night, it is important to note two characteristics of the scheme. For one thing, it is voluntary: An establishment requests (and pays for) inspection and rating by the pertinent tourist board, and not all hotels in Britain have yet done so or even intend to do so. For another, the crowns merely guarantee the existence of the facilities and services rated; they do not assess the quality. Thus, a five-crown hotel could be a clean, comfortable, but characterless place to sleep, while a listed accommodation might be simple yet above average in charm, run with attention to detail and a high degree of hospitality.

No matter what their crown rating, all participating establishments are required to supply adequate heating according to the season and to serve breakfast. In any London hotel, whether participating or not, breakfast is apt to be included in the quoted price of the room, and it usually is a full one of juice, coffee or tea, rolls, cereal, eggs, and bacon or sausage, although there is a growing tendency to substitute a continental breakfast (coffee and rolls) or to charge separately for the full one.

Hotels with four rooms or more are required to display minimum and maximum room prices in a manner that clearly shows what is included. If it is not clear, be sure to ask in advance what the final tab will be, since the extras can add considerably to the bill. A service charge of 10% to 15% may be added to bills at some properties in addition to the compulsory 17.5% value added tax (VAT).

**Bed and Breakfast** – More and more small hotels have opened up in converted townhouses. Some offer bed and breakfast only, while others have restaurants. The *Aster House* and *Pembridge Court* are hostelries that have received top ratings from the British Tourist Authority (see below for additional information on both). The BTA (phone: 212-581-4700, for information in the US) has a useful list of bed and breakfast hotels.

Reservations for bed and breakfast accommodations in London also can be made through the London Tourist Board. Travelers can make reservations by phone or mail using an *American Express, MasterCard,* or *Visa* credit card. If you do write, be sure to specify how many individuals will be staying, what part of London you prefer, and the price range you have in mind; leave ample time for a response. All reservations must be made at least 6 weeks in advance. Contact the London Tourist Board (26 Grosvenor Gardens, Victoria, London SW1, England; phone: 71-824-8844). In addition, once in Britain, travelers also can make reservations by credit card by calling the 24-hour *Bed and Breakfast Great Britain Hotline* at 491-578803.

The *Worldwide Bed and Breakfast Association* publishes *The Best Bed & Breakfast in the World 1992–93,* a guide to over 800 member establishments throughout England, Scotland, and Wales. The book costs $15.95, and purchase includes an $18 discount that may be applied toward the cost of a stay in London. Found in bookstores, it also can be ordered from the distributor, Globe Pequot Press (138 W. Main St., Box Q, Chester, CT 06412; phone: 800-243-0495). The *Worldwide Bed & Breakfast Association* also acts as a booking service for the properties listed; contact the association at PO Box 134, London SW10 9EH, England (phone: 81-742-9123 for information and reservations, 24 hours).

Another useful source of information on bed and breakfast establishments overseas is the *Bed & Breakfast Reservations Services Worldwide,* a trade association of B&B reservations services, which provides a list of its members for $3. To order the most recent edition, contact them at PO Box 39000, Washington, DC 20016 (phone: 800-842-1486).

Still another alternative to conventional hotel accommodations is to stay in one of 500 private homes and apartments through a program called "Your Home in London." These vary from a single in a bed and breakfast establishment for $30 a night to a 2-bedroom apartment in central London for $140 a night. For information in the US, call 301-269-6232. The *Bulldog Club* is a good resource for very upscale bed and breakfast accommodations, and functions exclusively for its members (annual membership costs about $50 per person). It has contacts with a variety of period homes in London's busy city center or calmer, surrounding neighborhoods. For additional information: 35 The Chase, London SW4 0NP (phone: 71-622-6935; fax: 71-720-2748). Or contact their North American office: 6 Kittredge Ct., Richmond Hill, Ontario, Canada L4C 7X3 (phone: 416-737-2798; fax: 416-737-3179).

**Apartments and Homes –** An attractive alternative for the visitor content to stay in one spot for a week or more is to rent one of the numerous properties available in London. These offer a wide range of luxury and convenience, depending on the price you want to pay. One of the advantages to staying in a house, apartment (usually called a "flat" overseas), or other rented vacation home is that you will feel much more like a visitor than a tourist.

Known to Europeans as a "holiday let" or a "self-catering holiday," a vacation in a furnished rental has both the advantages and disadvantages of living "at home" abroad. It can be less expensive than staying in a first class hotel, although very luxurious and expensive rentals are available, too. It has the comforts of home, including a kitchen, which can mean potential savings on food. Furthermore, it gives a sense of the country that a large hotel often cannot. On the other hand, a certain amount of housework is involved because if you don't eat out, you have to cook, and though some rentals (especially the luxury ones) include a cleaning person, most don't. (If the rental doesn't include daily cleaning, arrangements often can be made with a maid service.)

For a family, two or more couples, or a group of friends, the per-person cost — even for a luxurious rental — can be quite reasonable. Weekly and monthly rates are available to reduce costs still more. But best of all is the amount of space that no conventional hotel room can equal. As with hotels, the rates for properties in some areas are seasonal, rising during the peak travel season, while for others they remain the same year-round. To have your pick of the properties available, you should begin to make arrangements for a rental at least 6 months in advance.

There are several ways of finding a suitable rental property. For those who want to make their own arrangements, the British Tourist Authority and the English tourist board provide information on self-catering holidays.

Many tour operators regularly include a few rental packages among their offerings; these generally are available through a travel agent. In addition, a number of companies specialize in rental vacations. Their plans typically include rental of the property (or several properties, but usually for a minimum stay per location), a rental car, and airfare.

The companies listed below rent properties in London. They handle the booking and confirmation paperwork and can be expected to provide more information about the properties than that which might ordinarily be gleaned from a short listing in an accommodations guide.

*At Home Abroad* (405 E. 56th St., Apt. 6H, New York, NY 10022; phone: 212-421-9165). Handles apartments. Photographs of properties can be requested by mail for a $50 registration fee.

*British Travel Associates* (PO Box 299, Elkton, VA 22927; phone: 800-327-6097 or 703-298-2232). Arranges apartment rentals, as well as stays in bed and breakfast establishments.

*Castles, Cottages and Flats* (7 *Faneuil Hall Marketplace,* Boston, MA 02109; phone: 617-742-6030). Handles apartment rentals. Small charge ($5) for receipt of main catalogue, refundable upon booking.

*Country Homes and Castles* (4092 N. Ivy Rd., Atlanta, GA 30342; phone: 404-231-5837; or 900 Wilshire Blvd., Suite 830, Los Angeles, CA 90017; phone: 213-629-4861). This company specializes in large, elegant properties — apartments and private homes.

*Eastone Overseas Accommodations* (198 Southampton Dr., Jupiter, FL 33458; phone: 407-575-6991). Handles flats.

*Europa-Let* (PO Box 3537, Ashland, OR 97520; phone: 800-462-4486 or 503-482-5806). Offers apartments.

*Heart of England Cottages* (PO Box 878, Eufala, AL 36072-0878; phone: 205-687-9800). Offers apartments and private home rentals.

*Hideaways International* (15 Goldsmith St., PO Box 1270, Littleton, MA 01460; phone: 800-843-4433 or 508-486-8955). Rents apartments in London, and cottages in the surrounding countryside.

*Hometours International* (1170 Broadway, New York, 10001; phone: 800-367-4668 or 212-689-0851). Handles apartments.

*The Independent Traveller Thorverton* (Exeter EX5 5NU, England; phone: 392-860807). Handles apartments.

*International Lodging Corp.* (300 1st Ave., Suite 7C, New York, NY 10009; phone: 212-228-5900). Rents flats.

*Livingstone Holidays* (1720 E. Garry Ave., Suite 236, Santa Ana, CA 92705; phone: 714-476-2823). Handles flats.

*London Apartments, Ltd.* (5 Hidden Valley Rd., Lafayette, CA 94549; phone: 800-366-8748 or 510-283-4280). Rents flats.

*Rent a Vacation Everywhere* (*RAVE;* 328 Main St. E., Suite 526, Rochester, NY 14604; phone: 716-454-6440). Rents flats.

*Vacances en Campagne* (PO Box 297, Falls Village, CT 06031; phone: 800-533-5405). Rents apartments. A catalogue is available for $5.

*VHR Worldwide* (235 Kensington Ave., Norwood, NJ 07648; phone: 201-767-9393, locally; 800-NEED-A-VILLA). Rents flats.

*Villas International Ltd.* (605 Market St., Suite 510, San Francisco, CA 94105; phone: 800-221-2260 or 415-281-0910). Handles flats.

When considering a particular vacation rental property, look for answers to the following questions:
- How do you get from the airport to the property?
- What size and number of beds are provided?
- How far is the property from whatever else is important to you, such as museums or nightlife?
- How far is the nearest market?

- Are baby-sitters, cribs, bicycles, or anything else you may need for your children available?
- Is maid service provided daily?
- Is air conditioning and/or a phone provided?
- Is a car rental part of the package? Is a car necessary?

Before deciding which rental is for you, make sure you have satisfactory answers to all your questions. Ask your travel agent to find out or call the company involved directly.

If you are particularly interested in service flats (furnished apartments with close-to-traditional hotel services — mostly daily maid service), contact *Eastone Overseas Accommodations* (198 Southampton Dr., Jupiter, FL 33458; phone: 407-575-6991) or *Home Tours International* (1170 Broadway, Suite 614, New York, NY 10001; phone: 212-689-0851 or 800-367-4668). Service flats range from the very elegant to the very modest at a bed and breakfast establishment.

**Home Exchanges** – Still another alternative for travelers who are content to stay in one place during their vacation is a home exchange: The Smith family from Chicago moves into the home of the Hansen family in London, while the Hansens enjoy a stay in the Smiths' home. The home exchange is an exceptionally inexpensive way to ensure comfortable, reasonable living quarters with amenities that no hotel could possibly offer; often the trade includes a car. Moreover, it allows you to live in a new community in a way that few tourists ever do: For a little while, at least, you will become something of a resident.

Several companies publish directories of individuals and families willing to trade homes with others for a specific period of time. In some cases, you must be willing to list your own home in the directory; in others, you can subscribe without appearing in it. Most listings are for straight exchanges only, but each directory also has a number of listings placed by people interested in either exchanging or renting (for instance, if they own a second home). Other arrangements include exchanges of hospitality while owners are in residence or youth exchanges, where your teenager is put up as a guest in return for your putting up their teenager at a later date. A few house-sitting opportunities also are available. In most cases, arrangements for the actual exchange take place directly between you and the foreign host. There is no guarantee that you will find a listing in the area in which you are interested, but each of the organizations given below includes British homes among its hundreds or even thousands of foreign listings.

*Home Base Holidays* (7 Park Ave., London N13 5PG, England; phone: 81-886-8752). For $42 a year, subscribers receive four listings, with an option to list in all four.

*Intervac US/International Home Exchange Service* (Box 190070, San Francisco, CA 94119; phone: 415-435-3497). For $45 (plus postage), subscribers receive copies of the three directories published yearly, and are entitled to list their home in one of them; a black-and-white photo may be included with the listing for an additional $10. A $5 discount is given to travelers over age 62.

*Loan-A-Home* (2 Park La., Apt. 6E, Mt. Vernon, NY 10552; phone: 914-664-7640). Specializes in long-term (4 months or more — excluding July and August) housing arrangements worldwide for students, professors, businesspeople, and retirees, although its two annual directories (with supplements) carry a small list of short-term rentals and/or exchanges. $35 for a copy of one directory and one supplement; $45 for two directories and two supplements.

*Vacation Exchange Club* (PO Box 820, Haleiwa, HI 96712; phone: 800-638-3841). Some 10,000 listings. For $50, the subscriber receives two directories — one in late winter, one in the spring — and is listed in one.

*World Wide Exchange* (1344 Pacific Ave., Suite 103, Santa Cruz, CA 95060; phone: 408-476-4206). The $45 annual membership fee includes one listing (for house, yacht, or motorhome) and three guides.

*Worldwide Home Exchange Club* (13 Knightsbridge Green, London SW1X OJZ, England; phone: 71-589-6055; or 806 Brantford Ave., Silver Spring, MD 20904; no phone). Handles over 1,500 listings a year worldwide. For $25 a year, you will receive two listings, as well as supplements.

*Better Homes and Travel* (formerly *Home Exchange International*), with offices in New York, Los Angeles, London, Paris, and Milan, functions differently in that it publishes no directory and shepherds the exchange process most of the way. Interested parties supply the firm with photographs of themselves and their homes, information on the type of home they want and where, and a registration fee of $50. The company then works with its other offices to propose a few possibilities, and only when a match is made do the parties exchange names, addresses, and phone numbers. For this service, *Better Homes and Travel* charges a closing fee, which ranges from $150 to $500 for switches from 2 weeks to 3 months and from $300 to $600 for longer switches. Contact *Better Homes and Travel* at 30 E. 33rd St., New York, NY 10016 (phone: 212-689-6608).

**Home Stays** – If the idea of actually staying in a private home as the guest of a British family appeals to you, an organization arranging home stays is *In the English Manner,* which specializes in home stays with British families, who open their homes to guests. Prospective hosts have been visited by the company to assure that only those genuinely interested in meeting foreigners and making their stay a memorable experience participate. Hosts, in fact, are probably better screened than guests, who need merely supply the company with family members' names and ages, occupations, special interests, and other pertinent data, such as allergies. The company then selects a few possible hosts and lets the client make the final decision. There is a minimum stay of 3 nights, which can be divided among three different families if desired, but no maximum stay, except what is mutually agreeable to both hosts and guests. The entire cost of the stay is paid in advance. Meals that guests decide upon in advance also are prepaid; meals and other extras decided upon during the stay are paid in cash on departure (to avoid embarrassment, the company advises clients beforehand what the hosts charge). The program is not for budget travelers (the double occupancy rate ranges from expensive to very expensive) but the homes — about 80 of them — are not ordinary; they include several country houses, some larger stately homes, and a castle. Single rates are available, and there are reductions for children. Contact *In the English Manner* at PO Box 936, Alamo, CA 94507 (phone: 415-935-7065 in California; 800-422-0799 elsewhere in the US).

For more information on home stays, see the British Tourist Authority's informative, free booklet, *Stay with a British Family,* which lists agencies that arrange for foreigners to stay in a British home, as well as a listing of many specific homes with brief descriptions and pertinent information. Another publication that lists home stay opportunities is *Wolsey Lodges: Welcome to an Englishman's Home.* This brochure lists private homes, mostly in village and country locations, linked by the "Wolsey Lodges" banner. For a copy of this publication, write to *Wolsey Lodges,* 17 Chapel St., Bildeston, Suffolk 1P7 7EP, England.

You also might be interested in a publication called *International Meet-the-People Directory,* published by the *International Visitor Information Service.* It lists several agencies in a number of foreign countries (37 worldwide, 18 in Europe, including Great Britain) that arrange home visits for Americans, either for dinner or overnight stays. To order a copy, send $5.95 to the *International Visitor Information Service* (733 15th St. NW, Suite 300, Washington, DC 20005; phone: 202-783-6540). For other local organizations and services offering home exchanges, contact the local tourist authority.

Note that members of the *English-Speaking Union* are eligible for a 30% discount at the *Chesterfield* hotel, as well as for discounts on numerous functions at the *Union's* headquarters in London and other *E-SU* offices around the world. For more information regarding membership and activities, contact the *English-Speaking Union* in the US (16 E. 69th St., New York, NY 10021; phone: 212-879-6800) or in London (Dartmouth House, 37 Charles St., W1; London WIX 8LX; phone: 71-491-2622).

■**A warning about telephone surcharges in hotels:** A lot of digits may be involved once a caller starts dialing beyond national borders, but avoiding operator-assisted calls can cut costs considerably and bring rates into a somewhat more reasonable range — except for calls made through hotel switchboards. One of the most unpleasant surprises travelers encounter in many foreign countries is the amount they find tacked on to their hotel bill for telephone calls, because foreign hotels routinely add on astronomical surcharges. (It's not at all uncommon to find 300% or 400% added to the actual telephone charges.)

Until recently, the only recourse against this unconscionable overcharging was to call collect when phoning from abroad or to use a telephone credit card — available through a simple procedure from any local US phone company. (Note, however, that even if you use a telephone credit card, some hotels still may charge a fee for line usage.) Now, *American Telephone and Telegraph (AT&T)* offers *USA Direct,* a service that connects users, via a toll-free number, with an *AT&T* operator in the US, who will then put the call through at the standard international rate. Another feature of this service is that travelers abroad can reach US toll-free (800) numbers by calling a *USA Direct* operator, who will connect them. Charges for all calls made through *USA Direct* appear on the caller's regular US phone bill. To reach *USA Direct* in Great Britain, dial 0-800-890011, and wait for the *AT&T* operator to come on the line. For a brochure and wallet card listing the toll-free number for other countries, contact International Information Service, *AT&T Communications,* 635 Grant St., Pittsburgh, PA 15219 (phone: 800-874-4000).

*AT&T* also has put together *Teleplan,* an agreement among certain hoteliers that sets a limit on surcharges for calls made by guests from their rooms. *Teleplan* currently is in effect in selected hotels in London. *Teleplan* agreements stipulate a flat amount for credit card or collect calls (currently between $1 and $10), and a flat percentage (between 20% and 100%) on calls paid for at the hotel. For further information, contact *AT&T*'s International Information Service (address above).

It's wise to ask about surcharges *before* calling from a hotel. If the rate is high, it's best to use a telephone credit card, or the direct-dial service discussed above; make a collect call; or place the call and ask the party to call right back. If none of these choices is possible, make international calls from the local post office or special telephone center to avoid surcharges. Another way to keep down the cost of telephoning from London is to leave a copy of your itinerary and telephone numbers with people in the US so that they can call you instead.

Visitors arriving in London between early spring and mid-autumn without hotel reservations are in for an unpleasant experience. For many years now, there has been a glaring shortage of hotel rooms in the British capital during the prime tourist season, which each year seems to begin earlier and end later. (For a small fee, the Tourist Information Centre at Victoria Station Forecourt, or at the underground station in Heathrow, will try to help you locate a room. For credit card reservations, call 71-824-8844 Mondays through Fridays, 9 AM to 6 PM.) This fact, plus years of general inflation and the difficulty of finding suitable hotel staff, are largely responsible for often excessive hotel charges, generally out of keeping with other costs in Britain. As a rule, very expensive and expensive hotels do not include any meals in their prices; moderate and inexpensive hotels generally include continental breakfasts. In our selections below, prices — with bath, English breakfast, VAT, and a 10% service charge sometimes included — are $350 and up (sometimes way up) for a double room in a very expensive hotel; $200 to $325 for a double room in an expensive hotel; $135 to $190, moderate; and $85 to $130, inexpensive.

*Berkeley* – Remarkably understated, this 160-room hotel in Knightsbridge manages to preserve its impeccably high standards while keeping a low profile. Soft-spoken service complements the tastefully lavish, traditional English decor. There also is a health club and a new gymnasium. Business facilities include 24-hour room service, meeting rooms for up to 220, concierge, foreign currency exchange, secretarial services, translation services, photocopiers, cable television news, and express checkout. Wilton Pl., SW1 (phone: 71-235-6000; fax: 71-235-4330; telex: 919252). Very expensive.

*Claridge's* – This plush 190-room outpost for visiting royalty, heads of state, and other distinguished and/or affluent foreigners is an Art Deco treasure. The line of chauffered limousines outside the main entrance sometimes makes traffic seem impenetrable. Wrought-iron balconies and a sweeping foyer staircase help provide a stately setting for one of London's most elegant hostelries. Liveried footmen serve afternoon tea. Business facilities include 24-hour room service, meeting rooms for up to 250, concierge, foreign currency exchange, secretarial services, audiovisual equipment, photocopiers, computers, cable television news, translation services, and express checkout. Brook St., W1 (phone: 71-629-8860; fax: 71-499-2210; telex: 21872). Very expensive.

*Connaught* – A touch too sober for high livers; a trifle too formal for the rough-and-ready crowd. But there aren't many hotels left in the world that can rival it for welcome, elegance, and comfort — particularly in its luxurious suites. The food served in the restaurant and the *Grill,* rated one Michelin star, is an experience all its own (see *Eating Out*). Business facilities include 24-hour room service, 2 private dining rooms, concierge, and foreign currency exchange. Carlos Pl., W1 (phone: 71-499-7070; fax: 71-495-3262). Very expensive.

*Dorchester* – The grande dame is back after a 2-year closure for a total face-lift, and she looks better than ever. All 252 rooms and 55 suites were refurbished and redecorated (the bed linen is extra special; the bathrooms, superbly designed). Behind the scenes, renovation involved hidden necessities like wiring, plumbing, triple glazing on the Park Lane side, and air conditioning. Best of all, the service is topnotch. Once again you can take tea in the pink marble *Promenade* and eat in the *Grill* and *Terrace* restaurants. Additions include the *Oriental* restaurant, which specializes in authentic Cantonese food, and the exclusive basement nightspot — the *Dorchester Club,* which requires membership 48 hours in advance. Business facilities include 24-hour room service, meeting rooms for up to 1,000, concierge, foreign currency exchange, secretarial services, audiovisual equipment, photocopiers, computers, cable television news, translation services, a health club, and express checkout. Park La., W1 (phone: 71-629-8888; fax: 71-409-0114; telex: 887704). Very expensive.

*Forty-Seven Park Street* – One of our most cherished secrets, these 54 suites, or "service flats," are a favorite of folks who are staying for more than a few days; the accommodations are not-so-small apartments perfect for extended visits. Breakfast alone is worth crossing the Atlantic, since "room service" here is provided by the elegant *Le Gavroche* restaurant, which flourishes downstairs (see *Eating Out*). Owned by the Roux Brothers, who also own the restaurant (and the

*Wayside Inn* out in Bray), the furnishings are luxurious in the best English taste. The location, roughly between Hyde Park and Grosvenor Square, also is ideal. Business facilities include 24-hour room service, meeting rooms for up to 24, concierge, foreign currency exchange, secretarial services, photocopiers, computers, and translation services. 47 Park St., W1 (phone: 71-491-7282; fax: 71-491-7281; telex: 22116). Very expensive.

**Grosvenor House** – This 454-room grande dame facing Hyde Park has a health club, a swimming pool, some interesting shops, the much-lauded *Pavilion* restaurant (see *Eating Out*), the *Park Lounge,* which serves traditional afternoon teas, and the exclusive *Crown Club* on the top floor for members only — usually businesspeople who require special services — with rooms, suites, a lounge, and complimentary extras. Business facilities include 24-hour room service, meeting rooms for up to 1,500, concierge, foreign currency exchange, secretarial services, audiovisual equipment, photocopiers, translation services, and express checkout. Park La., W1 (phone: 71-499-6363; fax: 71-629-9337; telex: 24871). Very expensive.

**Inn on the Park** – Don't be deceived by the modern exterior; everything is traditional (and wonderful) within. A fine example of the superb service routinely offered by members of the Four Seasons chain, the 228 rooms are comfortable, tastefully furnished, and spacious. The breakfast buffet is delightful; the restaurant is first-rate. Business facilities include 24-hour room service, meeting rooms for up to 450, concierge, foreign currency exchange, secretarial services, audiovisual equipment, photocopiers, computers, translation services, and express checkout. Hamilton Pl., off Piccadilly, W1 (phone: 71-499-0888; fax: 71-499-5572; telex: 22771). Very expensive.

**Inter-Continental** – Smack-dab in the middle of the West End, right on Hyde Park Corner, with windows overlooking the route of the Royal Horse Guards as they go cantering off for the Changing of the Guard each morning. Its 490 well-proportioned rooms are equipped with refrigerated bars. Modern and comfortable, particularly the Art Deco *Le Soufflé* restaurant, but the location is the chief lure. Business facilities include 24-hour room service, meeting rooms for up to 1,000, concierge, foreign currency exchange, secretarial services, audiovisual equipment, photocopiers, computers, translation services, and express checkout. 1 Hamilton Pl., Hyde Park Corner, W1 (phone: 71-409-3131; fax: 71-493-3476; telex: 25853). Very expensive.

**Lanesborough** – This brand-new luxury hotel at Hyde Park Corner, just steps from the Wellington Gate in the tony Belgravia area, is built within the landmark structure that was St. George's Hospital from 1734 to 1980. The interior design re-creates the feeling of an elegant 19th-century residence. There are 95 superbly appointed guestrooms which include 46 suites, some with steam showers and Jacuzzis. The more formal *Dining Room* offers traditional English food, while the *Conservatory* serves light meals for breakfast and lunch, and traditional afternoon tea. The Library and the Withdrawing Room both have bars. The location is one of the best in the city. Business facilities include 24-hour room and butler service, concierge, secretarial services, in-room fax machines, 2-line telephones, and cable television news. Knightsbridge and Grosvenor Crescent (phone: 71-259-5599, or 214-871-5400 in the US; fax: 71-259-5606). Very expensive.

**Langham Hilton** – Originally opened in 1865 as "the first grand hotel of London," it was known for its "rising rooms" (elevators) and famous guests, including Mark Twain, Toscanini, and Oscar Wilde. Following World War II, it was converted to BBC offices and studios, but after a multi-million-dollar renovation, restoring many original Victorian features, it reopened last year as a 385-room hotel. Several restaurants include the *Palm Court,* serving light meals and snacks around-the-clock, and *Tsar's,* specializing in vodka and caviar. Business facilities include

24-hour room service, meeting rooms for up to 500, concierge, foreign currency exchange, secretarial services, audiovisual equipment, photocopiers, computers, cable television news, translation services, and express checkout. Portland Pl., W1 (phone: 71-636-1000; in the US, 800-223-1146; fax: 71-323-2340; telex: 21113). Very expensive.

**London Hilton International** – Well situated off Hyde Park Corner, near shopping and theater, this contemporary high-rise offers comfortable accommodations (450 rooms) and spectacular views of the park and the city. Special attention to executives includes a multilingual switchboard, secretarial staff, office equipment, and private dining rooms. There's every conceivable service, plus 3 restaurants — *Windows on the World*, with a view; *Trader Vics* (Polynesian); and the *Brasserie*. Business facilities include 24-hour room service, meeting rooms for up to 1,000, concierge, foreign currency exchange, secretarial services, audiovisual equipment, photocopiers, computers, translation services, and express checkout. 22 Park La., W1 (phone: 71-493-8000; 71-493-4957; telex: 24873). Very expensive.

**Park Lane** – If you don't mind the noise of the city streets, the site of this hotel, in the heart of the West End, is appealing. Some of the 320 rooms have views of Green Park across the street. *Bracewell's* restaurant is an elegant dining spot. Business facilities include 24-hour room service, meeting rooms for up to 500, concierge, foreign currency exchange, secretarial services, audiovisual equipment, photocopiers, computers, translation services, and express checkout. Piccadilly, W1 (phone: 71-499-6321; fax: 71-499-1965; telex: 21533). Very expensive.

**Ritz** – The fellow who was heard to mutter snootily, "Nobody stays at the *Ritz* anymore," was off base, especially since renovations have restored much of the old luster and certainly got the "bugs" out. With 130 rooms, it now ranks among London's finest stopping places, and it's hard to find another hotel in London with more elegant surroundings. Tea here is a very pleasant experience; in probably the most formal and elegant tearoom in the city, gracious white-tied waiters carry silver trays to serve guests in the lovely Louis XIV–style *Palm Court* (reservations necessary at least 2 weeks in advance for weekends and 1 week in advance for weekdays). The dining room is equally splendid, with its elegant interior columns, opulent ceiling frescoes, and the view of Green Park. Once again, after a bit of a slump, the fare almost matches the elegant surroundings. Business facilities include 24-hour room service, meeting rooms for up to 50, concierge, foreign currency exchange, secretarial services, audiovisual equipment, photocopiers, computers, cable television news, and translation services. Piccadilly, W1 (phone: 71-493-8181; fax: 71-493-2687; telex: 257200). Very expensive.

**St. James's Club** – For about $400 for the first year ($250 thereafter) and an introduction by a member, you can join this exclusive residential club in the heart of London (though you don't need to bother for your first stay). Guests have full use of club suites. Some very good food is served in the downstairs dining room. Business facilities include 24-hour room service, meeting rooms for up to 30, concierge, foreign currency exchange, secretarial services, audiovisual equipment, photocopiers, computers, and translation services. 7 Park Pl., SW1 (phone: 71-629-7688; fax: 71-491-0987; telex: 298519). Very expensive.

**Savoy** – A favorite of film and theater performers, some of whom check in for months, the hotel celebrated its 100-year anniversary in 1989. Still one of London's top addresses, its 200 rooms are overseen by armies of chambermaids and porters, and the reputation of its famous *Savoy Grill* (see *Eating Out*) has been restored through a beautiful resuscitation of the decor and a revitalization of the kitchen. More casual than the *Savoy Grill*, the *Upstairs Bar* serves primarily seafood and offers 44 different vintages of wine. The *River* restaurant has a wonderful view of the gardens and the Thames. Tea is served in the spacious Thames Foyer, where guests relax in posh, comfortable sofas and chairs in a garden-theme setting with a pianist playing background music; hotel guests are served in an exclusive tea-room. The Thames Suites are the most beautiful accommodations in the city. Business facilities include 24-hour room service, meeting rooms for up to 500, concierge, foreign currency exchange, secretarial services, computers, cable television news, translation services, and express checkout. The Strand, WC2 (phone: 71-836-4343 or 71-836-3719; fax: 71-872-8894; telex: 24234). Very expensive.

**22 Jermyn Street** – London's fashionable menswear street has also had a fashionable hotel since 1990. Wedged up a long passageway between a hatmaker and a shirtmaker, there are 18 rooms which are really suites, furnished with antiques, elegant curtains, and marble bathrooms. It's so English that guests expect valets at the guestroom doors — and get them! There's no restaurant, but many of London's best eateries are moments away. Business facilities include 24-hour room service, concierge, secretarial services, fax machines in the rooms, and photocopiers. 22 Jermyn St., SW1 (phone: 71-734-2353; fax: 71-734-0750; telex: 261085). Very expensive.

**Windsor** – This brand-new Ritz-Carlton property is opening this May in what was the *Great Central* hotel, built in 1899. It has 308 guestrooms, which include 58 suites. The rooms all have marble baths, safe deposit boxes, thick bathrobes, and color television sets, and many have working fireplaces. There is a restaurant, café, and lobby lounge serving tea and drinks, as well as a swimming pool and health and fitness center. The Club level offers a private lounge and concierge staff, complimentary continental breakfast, light lunch, afternoon tea, cocktails with hors d'oeuvres, and late evening sweets and cordials. Business facilities include 24-hour room service, meeting rooms for up to 200, concierge, secretarial services, audiovisual equipment, photocopiers, and translation services. 222 Marylebone Rd., NW1 (phone: 71-499-4050; fax: 71-409-0880). Very expensive.

**Abbey Court** – In the Notting Hill Gate area near Portobello Market, this elegant hotel has 22 bedrooms of various sizes, all with private bath, TV sets, hair dryers, and trouser presses. The flowers on display in the common areas are especially lovely. Breakfast is served in the room, and 24-hour room service also is available. No restaurant. Business facilities include concierge, secretarial services, and photocopiers. 20 Pembridge Gardens, W2 (phone: 71-221-7518; fax: 71-792-0858; telex: 262172). Expensive.

**Basil Street** – A relic with a reputation for graceful, old-fashioned service and beautiful antique furnishings to match. It draws a faithful international clientele who, if they can reserve one of its 94 smallish rooms, prefer staying here to patronizing any of the modern, impersonal, newer hotels. It has a women's health club and sits just down the street from *Harrods*. Business facilities include 24-hour room service, meeting rooms for up to 300, concierge, foreign currency exchange, audiovisual equipment, and photocopiers. 8 Basil St., SW3 (phone: 71-581-3311; fax: 71-581-3693; telex: 28379). Expensive.

**Beaufort** – Tranquil and very elegant, it is composed of two Victorian houses in Beaufort Gardens, the heart of fashionable Knightsbridge. It offers 28 comfortable and attractively decorated rooms, each with a plenitude of facilities: stereo/cassette player; TV set; direct-dial phone; hair dryer; magazines and books; a decanter of brandy; and even a teddy bear for the youngsters. Breakfast is brought on a tray each morning. Convenient to restaurants and shops (*Harrods* is just around the corner). Business facilities include concierge and photocopiers. 33 Beaufort Gardens, SW3 (phone: 71-584-5252; fax: 71-589-2834; telex: 929200). Expensive.

**Blake's** – A row of Victorian townhouses has been transformed into this charming 52-room hotel, where many employees wear stylish uniforms. There's black antique furniture on the lower level, while the upper floors are decorated in pale gray and pastels. The bathrooms are made of marble, and business facilities include a topnotch restaurant, laundry service, 24-hour room service, concierge, foreign currency exchange, secretarial services, and photocopiers. Popular with show-biz folk. 33 Roland Gardens, SW7 (phone: 71-370-6701; fax: 71-373-0442; telex: 813500). Expensive.

*Britannia* – Mahogany furniture, velvet armchairs, rooms painted in colors you might choose at home — all very tasteful and solid, despite the anonymity of the spacious foyer with the pretentious chandeliers. This is where the American Embassy — also on the square — often puts up visiting middle-ranking State Department officials. The 354 rooms all have private bath. A link in the Inter-Continental chain. Business facilities include 24-hour room service, meeting rooms for up to 120, concierge, foreign currency exchange, secretarial services, audiovisual equipment, photocopiers, computers, cable television news, translation services, and express checkout. Grosvenor Sq., W1 (phone: 71-629-9400; fax: 71-629-7736; telex: 23941). Expensive.

*Brown's* – As English as you can get, retaining pleasing, quaint, Victorian charm, and not at all marred by heavy, sturdy furniture or the somewhat hushed atmosphere. Strong on service. If it's an English tea you're after, this is the place (tie and jacket required). Business facilities include 24-hour room service, meeting rooms for up to 80, concierge, foreign currency exchange, and photocopiers. Dover St., W1 (phone: 71-493-6020; fax: 71-493-9381; telex: 28686). Expensive.

*Cadogan Thistle* – Very comfortable, older, 69-room place, redolent of Edwardian England. Oscar Wilde was arrested here, and Lillie Langtry, who was having an affair with the Prince of Wales (later Edward VII), lived next door. The furniture and decor are original, but modern conveniences are offered as well. Business facilities include 24-hour room service, meeting rooms for up to 40, concierge, foreign currency exchange, secretarial services, photocopiers and express checkout. 75 Sloane St., SW1 (phone: 71-235-7141; fax: 71-245-0994; telex: 267893). Expensive.

*Capital* – Only a stone's throw from *Harrods,* this 45-room hotel has been beautifully refurbished and is a member of the prestigious Relais & Châteaux group. All rooms have air conditioning, color TV sets, radios, and elegantly appointed bathrooms — and the beds have the best pillows in England! There is an intimate lounge, a lively bar, and an excellent French restaurant (see *Eating Out*). Business facilities include 24-hour room service, meeting rooms for up to 24, concierge, foreign currency exchange, secretarial services, photocopiers, and cable television news. 22 Basil St., SW3 (phone: 71-589-5171; in the US, 800-926-3199; fax: 71-225-0011; telex: 919042). Expensive.

*Cavendish* – Famous as the *Bentinck,* the hotel run by Louisa Trotter (in real life, Rosa Lewis) in the TV series "The Duchess of Duke Street," this very modern replacement offers one of the most attractive locations in central London, near Piccadilly. Its 254 rooms are comfortable, though hardly elegant. Business facilities include 24-hour room service, meeting rooms for up to 200, concierge, foreign currency exchange, secretarial services, audiovisual equipment, photocopiers, computers, cable television news, translation services, and express checkout. Jermyn St., SW1 (phone: 71-930-2111; fax: 71-839-2125; telex: 263187). Expensive.

*Chesterfield* – In the heart of Mayfair and near Hyde Park, this small, rebuilt Georgian mansion has a certain exclusive elegance. Its 110 bedrooms are thoroughly modernized and well equipped. Amenities include a restaurant, a wood-paneled library, and a small bar that opens onto a flower-filled patio. Business facilities include 24-hour room service, meeting rooms for up to 150, concierge, foreign currency exchange, photocopiers, and express checkout. 35 Charles St., W1 (phone: 71-491-2622; fax: 71-491-4793; telex: 269394). Expensive.

**Churchill** – Always thought of as an "American"-style hotel, it remains a favorite among travelers headed to London from the US. Inside, a turn-of-the-century mood is reflected in the discreet decor, which is undergoing a $50-million roof-to-roadway renovation. This is a well-run, efficient 430-room place, with a pleasant restaurant and a snack room that serves the best bacon and eggs in London. Business facilities include 24-hour room service, meeting rooms for up to 200, concierge, foreign currency exchange, secretarial services, photocopiers, computers, cable television news, translation services, and express checkout. Portman Sq., W1 (phone: 71-486-5800; fax: 71-486-1255; telex: 264831). Expensive.

**Conrad Chelsea Harbour** – Hilton hotels (the US branch, not the international chain) has opened in Chelsea Harbour, overlooking the Thames. Each of the 160 suites has a living room, 3 telephones, and a mini-bar. Guests can take advantage of the hotel's health club, complete with a heated indoor swimming pool, saunas, and steamrooms. There are 18 shops and restaurants, including the *Compass Rose,* which serves international and continental fare, and the less formal *Broadwood Lounge,* for breakfast and light meals. *Drakes* bar is open nightly. Business facilities include 24-hour room service, meeting rooms for up to 200, concierge, foreign currency exchange, secretarial services, photocopiers, computers, cable television news, and express checkout. Chelsea Harbour, SW10 (phone: 71-823-3000; 800-HILTONS in the US or 800-268-9275 in Canada; fax: 71-351-6525; telex: 919222). Expensive.

**Draycott** – The 26 rooms here are each distinctively decorated. While there's no restaurant, there is 24-hour room service, as well as a drawing room. Staying here is like living in a fashionable London townhouse, and guests must register as members upon their first visit. Business facilities include meeting rooms for up to 15, concierge, foreign currency exchange, secretarial services, photocopiers, and computers. 24-26 Cadogan Gardens, SW3 (phone: 71-730-6466; fax: 71-730-0236). Expensive.

**Drury Lane Moat House** – Near the theater district and fashionable *Covent Garden,* this 153-room hotel is ultramodern with a cool, sophisticated decor and an elegant bar. Business facilities include 24-hour room service, meeting rooms for up to 100, concierge, foreign currency exchange, secretarial services in English, audiovisual equipment, photocopiers, computers, translation services, and express checkout. 10 Drury La., High Holborn, WC2 (phone: 71-836-6666; 71-831-1548; telex: 881395). Expensive.

**Dukes** – Despite its modest size (only 38 rooms and 26 suites), this is an establishment where nobility and prestige shine through. The exterior has an exquisite Edwardian façade, there's a peaceful flower-filled courtyard, and some suites are named for former dukes. A virtual total reconstruction has produced accommodations of great taste and warmth, and the snug location, down a quiet cul-de-sac, does its best to make guests feel protected and private. Afternoon tea is a formal affair served in the lounge or the elegant dining room. Piccadilly, Buckingham Palace, Trafalgar Square, Hyde Park Corner, and the shops of Bond Street and the Burlington Arcade are all within walking distance. Now owned by Cunard, which also operates the nearby *Ritz* and *Stafford.* Business facilities include 24-hour room service, meeting rooms for up to 150, concierge, foreign currency exchange, secretarial services, audiovisual equipment, photocopiers, translation services, and express checkout. 35 St. James's Pl., SW1 (phone: 71-491-4840; fax: 71-493-1264; telex: 28283). Expensive.

**Edwardian International** – The first 5-star hotel at Heathrow Airport manages to deliver an English country-house feel despite its location and size (460 rooms, 17 suites). *Henley's* restaurant serves British favorites (steak and kidney pie), as well as Italian and French dishes. The *Brasserie* is open from 6:30 AM to 11 PM for light, quick meals, while the Leisure Centre has a full gym, a swimming pool, a sauna, and hairdressing facilities. Business facilities include 24-hour room service, concierge, foreign currency exchange, secretarial services, audiovisual equipment, photocopiers, computers, cable television news, and translation services. Bath Rd., Hayes, Middlesex (phone: 81-759-6311; fax: 81-759-4559; telex: 23925; in the US, 800-447-7011). Expensive.

**Forte Crest St. James'** – Formerly the *Cavendish* and now a member of the Forte group, this very modern property offers one of the most attractive locations in central London, near Piccadilly. Its 254 rooms are comfortable, though hardly elegant. There are 2 restaurants and a pleasant bar. Business facilities include 24-hour room service, meeting rooms for up to 200, concierge, foreign currency exchange, secretarial services, audiovisual equipment, photocopiers, computers, cable television news, translation services, and express checkout. Jermyn St., SW1 (phone: 71-930-2111; fax: 71-839-2125; telex: 263187 CAVHTL G). Expensive.

**Halcyon** – A $15-million restoration brought the two Belle Epoque mansions that are the foundations of this property back to their original glamour. Some of the 44 guestrooms feature four-poster beds and Jacuzzis, plus all modern conveniences. Its *Kingfisher* restaurant is among London's best hotel dining spots. Business facilities include 24-hour room service, meeting rooms for up to 120, concierge, foreign currency exchange, secretarial services, audiovisual equipment, photocopiers, translation services, and express checkout. 81 Holland Park, W11 (phone: 71-727-7288; fax: 71-229-8516; telex: 266721). Expensive.

**Halkin** – This intimate, newly constructed property in the Belgravia area, right near Buckingham Palace and Hyde Park, boasts 41 individually designed rooms and suites, furnished with a mixture of contemporary and antique pieces. The hotel's restaurant looks out over a pretty garden, and serves fine French food. Business facilities include 24-hour room service, meeting rooms for up to 50, concierge, secretarial services, photocopiers, cable television news, fax machines in each room, and translation services. 5-6 Halkin St., SW1 (phone: 71-333-1000; in the US, 800-345-3457; fax: 71-333-1100). Expensive.

**Hyde Park** – The only hotel set in Hyde Park, this establishment — formerly apartments during Victorian times — played host to Rudolph Valentino in the 1920s and George VI and Queen Elizabeth in 1948. The recently redecorated 186 spacious bedrooms and suites are furnished with antique furniture and modern bathrooms. Some rooms also have spectacular views of the park (and some have air conditioning). Marble stairs, chandeliers, and plants are all part of the hotel's elegant decor. Visit the *Park Room,* with huge windows providing panoramic views of Hyde Park, for delicious meals, including breakfast and afternoon tea. There is also a grillroom, and a drawing room. Business facilities include 24-hour room service, meeting rooms for up to 250, concierge, foreign currency exchange, secretarial services, audiovisual equipment, photocopiers, and translation services. 66 Knightsbridge, SW1 (phone: 71-235-2000; fax: 71-235-4552; telex: 262057). Expensive.

**Londonderry** – Overlooking Hyde Park, its 3 penthouse suites and 150 rooms have just undergone a renovation, and there is a new health club. Business facilities include 24-hour room service, meeting rooms for up to 130, concierge, foreign currency exchange, secretarial services, photocopiers, and express checkout. Park La., W1 (phone: 71-493-7292; fax: 71-495-1395; telex: 263292). Expensive.

**London Marriott** – Close to the American Embassy and West End shopping, it's bright and busy, and it has a full range of facilities — lounge, bar, 2 restaurants, shops, 223 very comfortable rooms, and good service. Business facilities include 24-hour room service, meeting rooms for up to 1,000, concierge, foreign currency exchange, secretarial services, audiovisual equipment, photocopiers, computers, cable television news, and translation services. Grosvenor Sq., W1 (phone: 71-493-1232; fax: 71-491-3201; telex: 268101). Expensive.

**Mayfair Holiday Inn** – Renovation hasn't damaged the hotel's Regency style, unusual for this chain. Sitting in London's most prestigious neighborhood, it has 192 rooms, the à la carte *Berkeley* restaurant, and an evening pianist in the *Dauphin* cocktail bar. Business facilities include 24-hour room service, meeting rooms for up to 70, concierge, foreign currency exchange, secretarial services, photocopiers, and computers. 3 Berkeley St., W1 (phone: 71-493-8282; fax: 71-629-2827; telex: 24561). Expensive.

**Le Meridien** – Located between the Royal Academy and Piccadilly Circus, the lofty, Edwardian marble entrance hall leads to the 284 rooms and 24 suites. Many of the accommodations here are on the smallish, dark side. The *Terrace* restaurant, on the second floor, has a glass roof, and the space beneath the hotel has been transformed into a very good health club. There is also a less formal restaurant, a bar, and a cocktail lounge. Afternoon tea in the lounge is accompanied by a harpist. Business facilities include 24-hour room service, meeting rooms for up to 100, concierge, foreign currency exchange, secretarial services, audiovisual equipment, photocopiers, computers, cable television news, translation services, and express checkout. Piccadilly, W1 (phone: 71-734-8000; fax: 71-437-3574; telex: 25795). Expensive.

**Montcalm** – A smaller, elegant hostelry that has a lovely façade, a warm-toned and understated interior, and topnotch service. Its 114 rooms have all the usual comforts, and its 6 suites are especially luxurious. There's a bar, and in *Les Célébrités* restaurant, chef Gary Houiellbecq brings to bear all the skills that he employed at the acclaimed *Compleat Angler* in Marlow. Business facilities include 24-hour room service, meeting rooms for up to 70, concierge, foreign currency exchange, secretarial services, audiovisual equipment, photocopiers, computers, and express checkout. Great Cumberland Pl., W1 (phone: 71-402-4288; fax: 71-724-9180; telex: 28710). Expensive.

**Mountbatten** – The life and times of Earl Mountbatten of Burma is the theme throughout this refurbished, wonderfully eccentric hotel's public rooms, all with exhibitions of various mementos from India. All 127 rooms feature Italian marble bathrooms, satellite color TV, and in-house movies, while 7 suites have whirlpool baths. A purely vegetarian tea (scones without animal fat) is served in the country-house–style drawing room decorated with oak paneling and a fireplace. Business facilities include 24-hour room service, meeting rooms for up to 75, concierge, foreign currency exchange, secretarial services, audiovisual equipment, photocopiers, computers, and translation services. Monmouth St., *Covent Garden,* WC2 (phone: 71-836-4300; fax: 71-240-3547; telex: 298087). Expensive.

**Pelham** – These two mid-Victorian townhouses in South Kensington offer 35 stylish (though smallish) rooms and 2 suites — all individually decorated and all with private bath, a TV set, and telephone. There is also a restaurant and 2 lounges. Business facilities include 24-hour room service, a small meeting room, concierge, foreign currency exchange, and secretarial services. Cromwell Pl., SW7 (phone: 71-589-8288; fax: 71-584-8444; telex: 881-4714). Expensive.

**Royal Court** – Clean and comfortable, the 102-room establishment has a courteous, helpful staff, at the head of London's fashionable Chelsea shopping and residential district and within quick, easy reach of the rest of the action in town. Business facilities include 24-hour room service, meeting rooms for up to 40, concierge, foreign currency exchange, secretarial services, audiovisual equipment, photocopiers, computers, and express checkout. Sloane Sq., SW1 (phone: 71-730-9191; fax: 71-824-8381; telex: 296818). Expensive.

**Selfridges** – Just behind the department store of the same name, it's modern in both furnishings and tone, but its housekeeping needs upgrading. 298 rooms. Convenient for shopping. Business facilities include 24-hour room service, meeting rooms for up to 200, concierge, foreign currency exchange, secretarial services, audiovisual equipment, photocopiers, translation services, and express checkout. Orchard St., W1 (phone: 71-408-2080; fax: 71-409-2295; telex: 22361). Expensive.

**Stafford** – In a surprisingly quiet side street close to the city center, this is where many American television and newspaper organizations often lodge visiting correspondents to give them efficient, friendly, British small-hotel management at its best. Owned by Cunard, the hostelry's 62 rooms have been refurbished in smashing style. Enjoy tea in the cozy drawing room, complete with fireplaces and comfortable furniture. Business facilities include 24-hour room service, meeting rooms for up to 30, concierge, foreign currency exchange, secretarial services, photocopiers, computers, and cable television news. 16 St. James's Pl., SW1 (phone: 71-493-0111; fax: 71-493-7121; telex: 28602). Expensive.

**Sterling Heathrow** – A first-rate addition to Heathrow Airport, with its own covered walkway to Terminal 4. Designed by Michael Manser, it is shaped like a steel parallelogram, with a 5-story glass atrium enclosing a waterfall, as well as 3 restaurants. The 400 rooms have everything from trouser presses to an in-room review of accounts and express checkout — on your TV screen. The health club has a pool, gym, steamroom, and a sauna. Business facilities include 24-hour room service, meeting rooms for up to 200, concierge, foreign currency exchange, secretarial services, audiovisual equipment, photocopiers, cable television news, and express checkout. Terminal 4, Heathrow Airport, Hounslow, Middlesex (phone: 81-759-7755; fax: 81-759-7579). Expensive.

**Whites** – What used to be three 19th-century merchant bankers' private homes have been transformed into one of London's most charming small hostelries, with 54 rooms. It has personality that the larger ones lack — a cobbled forecourt, a glass-and-iron-covered entryway, even a wood-paneled writing room where tea is served in the afternoon. Choose a room at the front, overlooking Hyde Park, and take breakfast on the balcony. Business facilities include 24-hour room service, meeting rooms for up to 30, concierge, foreign currency exchange, secretarial services, audiovisual equipment, photocopiers, and computers. Lancaster Gate, W2 (phone: 71-262-2711; fax: 71-262-2147; telex: 24771). Expensive.

**Dorset Square** – Set on a lovely garden square (formerly Thomas Lord's own private cricket grounds) in the heart of London, this Georgian house is one of the city's more charming hotels. Guests can choose from 37 rooms. There is 24-hour room service and photocopiers. 39-40 Dorset Sq., NW1 (phone: 71-723-7874; fax: 71-724-3328; telex: 263964). Expensive to moderate.

**Fenja** – In this classic Victorian townhouse, each of the 14 bedrooms is named for a writer or artist with associations in the vicinity (Jane Austen, Hilaire Belloc, Henry James, John Singer Sargent). There are private baths/showers with luxury fittings, and crystal decanters filled with liquor. Business facilities include meeting rooms for up to 14, foreign currency exchange, secretarial services, and photocopiers. 69 Cadogan Gardens, SW3 (phone: 71-589-7333; fax: 71-581-4958; telex: 934272). Expensive to moderate.

**Hilton International Kensington** – A bit out of the way, this modern 605-room hotel offers a great deal of comfort at prices below those of most international Hiltons. An executive floor was added in 1990, which offers separate check-in and checkout and complimentary breakfast in a private lounge. Facilities include a traditional restaurant (with a lavish Sunday brunch), a Japanese restaurant, and a piano lounge. Rooms are well designed and well maintained. Business facilities include 24-hour room service, meeting rooms for up to 250, concierge, foreign currency exchange, secretarial services, audiovisual equipment, photocopiers, computers, and express checkout. 179-199 Holland Park Ave., W11 (phone: 71-603-3355; fax: 71-602-9397; telex: 919763). Expensive to moderate.

**Number Sixteen** – Housed in four adjoining townhouses, this is a delightfully comfortable spot with an accent on personal service. The 36 rooms feature fresh flowers and full baths/showers. Continental breakfast is served in all rooms, some of which have terraces leading to the conservatory and garden. There is a small bar. Because of its quiet atmosphere, it is not suitable for small children. Photocopiers available. 16 Sumner Pl., SW7 (phone: 71-589-5232; fax: 71-584-8615; telex: 266638). Expensive to moderate.

**Academy** – Not far from the University of London and the *British Museum,* this 32-room property scores for its handy location. Colorful modern art and pretty floral curtains and bedspreads make rooms cheery whether they are on the ground floor or upstairs (in what was once the attic). Paperbacks can be borrowed from the library, which overlooks a small patio garden at the back. The stylish restaurant and bar are in the basement. 17-21 Gower St., WC1 (phone: 71-631-4115; 800-678-3096, in the US; fax: 71-636-3442; telex: 24364). Moderate.

**Copthorne Tara** – Situated on a quiet corner of Kensington, this 831-room giant is just minutes from the bustling High Street and within walking distance of the *Albert Hall,* the *Victoria & Albert Museum,* and the *Natural History Museum,* and just a short jog from Kensington Gardens. The rooms are on the small side, but all have color TV sets and many have hair dryers. There are 4 restaurants, a nightclub, a baby-sitting service, and a garage. Business facilities include 24-hour room service, meeting rooms for up to 500, concierge, foreign currency exchange, secretarial services, audiovisual equipment, photocopiers, computers, and express checkout. Wright's La., W8 (phone: 71-937-7211; fax: 71-937-7100; telex: 918834). Moderate.

**Cranley** – Sister hotel of *One Cranley Place* (see below), this is larger, with 41 rooms and plusher furnishings. The unusual decor is bolder than most townhouse hotels, described by the American owner as "gutsy." With CNN, microwaves in the kitchenettes, plus showers and firm mattresses straight from the US, the aim is to make you feel at home. Secretarial services and photocopiers are available. 10-12 Bina Gardens, SW5 (phone: 71-373-0123; fax: 71-373-9497; in the US, phone: 800-553-2582 or 313-995-4400; fax: 313-995-1050). Moderate.

**Diplomat** – Small and charming, with an 1882 white façade, it has 27 rooms — all with private baths. It is comfortable, friendly, and affordable. There is a breakfast room, but no restaurant. In Belgravia at 2 Chesham St., SW1 (phone: 71-235-1544; fax: 71-259-6153; telex: 926679). Moderate.

**Durrants** – This elegant Regency-style hotel has a splendid location behind the *Wallace Collection,* and is only a few minutes' walk from the Oxford Street shopping district. It has been family-run for over 70 years, and all 95 rooms have retained their character while being kept comfortably up to date. Business facilities include 24-hour room service, meeting rooms for up to 45, concierge, foreign currency exchange, audiovisual equipment, and photocopiers. George St., W1 (phone: 71-935-8131; fax: 71-487-3510; telex: 894919). Moderate.

**Embassy House** – This Edwardian building, on a wide tree-lined street in Kensington, is very near the *Albert Hall,* the *Victoria & Albert Museum,* and the *Natural History Museum,* and an easy walk from *Harrods* and Hyde Park. There are 69 rooms, and although the decor is modern, there are elaborate high ceilings and elegant staircases. There's also a restaurant and bar. Business facilities include 24-hour room service, concierge, foreign currency exchange, secretarial services, and photocopiers. 31 Queen's Gate, SW7 (phone: 71-584-7222; fax: 71-589-8193; telex: 914893). Moderate.

**Gatwick Hilton International** – Part of the airport's expansion program, this 552-

room hotel provides much-needed accommodations for the ever-increasing number of visitors using the Gatwick gateway. Connected to the terminal by an enclosed walkway. Business facilities include 24-hour room service, meeting rooms for up to 400, concierge, foreign currency exchange, secretarial services, audiovisual equipment, photocopiers, computers, and express checkout. There also are 2 restaurants, bars, a health club, and lounge service. Gatwick Airport (phone: 293-518080; fax: 293-28980; telex: 877021). Moderate.

*Gore* – Ten-foot-tall potted palms and a collection of 5,000 prints on the walls set the tone in this 54-room hostelry, just 5 minutes from *Albert Hall* and the shopping on Kensington High Street. Wall safes are an unusual addition to conveniences such as hair dryers and mini-bars in the rooms. Ask to see, if not stay in, the Judy Garland room, with its carved medieval-style bed. The *Bistro 190* on the ground floor is a popular dining spot. Business facilities include 24-hour room service, meeting rooms for up to 20, concierge, foreign currency exchange, secretarial services, audiovisual equipment, photocopiers, and express checkout. 189 Queen's Gate, SW7 (phone: 71-584-6601; fax: 71-589-8127; telex: 296244). Moderate.

*Harewood* – Small and modern, this property is well maintained by a pleasant and efficient staff. Some of its 93 rooms have private terraces. Restaurant and wine bar. Business facilities include 24-hour room service, meeting rooms for up to 100, concierge, foreign currency exchange, secretarial services, audiovisual equipment, and photocopiers. Harewood Row, NW1 (phone: 71-262-2707; fax: 71-262-2975; telex: 297225). Moderate.

*Hazlitt's* – Formerly the nurses' quarters for the Royal Women's Hospital during Victorian times, this row of three adjacent terrace houses now serves as a cozy bed and breakfast establishment. The National Trust building has 23 rooms, each individually decorated in Victorian flavor and each with private bath. Hung on the walls are 2,000 prints depicting Victorian London. Photocopiers are available. 6 Frith St., W1 (phone: 71-434-1771; fax: 71-439-1524). Moderate.

*L'Hotel* – Owned by the same folks who own the wonderful *Capital* just a few steps away, this comfortable 12-room bed and breakfast hotel has a New England colonial–style decor, with pine furniture and a huge patchwork quilt hung over the stairs. All rooms have mini-bars and kettles for making tea or coffee; 4 rooms have fireplaces. Breakfast is served in *Le Metro* bistro next door, and laundry and dry-cleaning services are available. Business facilities include meeting rooms for up to 24, foreign currency exchange, secretarial services, audiovisual equipment, photocopiers, translation services, and express checkout. 28 Basil St., SW3 (phone: 71-589-6286; fax: 71-225-0011). Moderate.

*One Cranley Place* – Set among a row of Regency houses in South Kensington, this charming and personal establishment is like a private home. Unique antique pieces furnish the individually decorated rooms (from double rooms to luxury double suites), and fireplaces in rooms and common areas make for an exceptionally cozy atmosphere. Some rooms overlook the quiet mews at the back, and there is a small garden. Breakfast is served in the dining room or guests' rooms; tea and light snacks also are available. Business facilities include 24-hour room service, concierge, secretarial services, and photocopiers. 1 Cranley Pl., SW7 (phone: 71-589-7944; fax: 71-225-3931; in US, 800-553-2582 or 313-995-4400; fax: 313-995-1050). Moderate.

*Pastoria* – In the very center of the West End, near all theaters, this pleasant, comfortable little hotel has 58 rooms, all with baths and TV sets; it also has a bar and a restaurant. Business facilities include 24-hour room service, meeting rooms for up to 60, concierge, foreign currency exchange, secretarial services, photocopiers, and translation services. St. Martin's St., WC2 (phone: 71-930-8641; fax: 71-925-0551; telex: 25538). Moderate.

**Pembridge Court** – Recommended by bed and breakfast aficionados, this cozy Victorian townhouse has a variety of room sizes, from large doubles to tiny singles. Each room has a private bath and phone. The hotel is particularly pleasant for cat lovers, since two resident ginger cats normally greet new arrivals. The bistro serves English breakfasts and French fare for dinner. Business facilities include meeting rooms for up to 20, concierge, foreign currency exchange, secretarial services, and photocopiers. 34 Pembridge Gardens, W2 (phone: 71-229-9977; fax: 71-727-4982; telex: 298363). Moderate.

**Portland Bloomsbury** – Around the corner from the entrance to the *British Museum,* this little gem opened in 1990. All 26 bedrooms and the 1 suite have plush furnishings and white tiled bathrooms with hair dryers. The elegant basement restaurant serves Italian food and looks out onto a small garden. Business facilities include 24-hour room service, meeting rooms for up to 20, concierge, foreign currency exchange, secretarial services, photocopiers, translation services, and express checkout. 7 Montague St., WC1 (phone: 71-323-1717; fax: 71-636-6498). Moderate.

**Portobello** – Antiques are a main feature in this hostelry, converted from two Victorian row houses, located near the Portobello antiques market. The 25 rooms come in all shapes and sizes, and most have simple but attractive military-style mahogany furniture; the "Special Rooms" have four-poster beds. Bathrooms tend to be quite small. There is an informal restaurant and bar in the basement. The atmosphere is friendly and relaxing throughout. Business facilities include 24-hour room service, secretarial services, photocopiers, and express checkout. 22 Stanley Gardens, W11 (phone: 71-727-2777; fax: 71-792-9641; telex: 268349 Port G). Moderate.

**Ramada Inn** – All 501 rooms have private baths and in-house movies. There's also a comfortable Victorian pub. Business facilities include meeting rooms for up to 1,750, concierge, foreign currency exchange, secretarial services, audiovisual equipment, photocopiers, computers, translation services, and express checkout. Lillie Rd., SW6 (phone: 71-385-1255; fax: 71-381-4450; telex: 917728). Moderate.

**Royal Horseguards Thistle** – Overlooking the Thames and offering good views of the South Bank, its 376 rooms provide a good base for those interested in the changing of the Buckingham Palace guard, Westminster Abbey, and the Houses of Parliament. Riverside rooms have balconies, and there's a pleasant terrace. Business facilities include 24-hour room service, meeting rooms for up to 100, concierge, foreign currency exchange, secretarial services, audiovisual equipment, photocopiers, computers, translation services, and express checkout. 2 Whitehall Ct., SW1 (phone: 71-839-3400; fax: 71-925-2263; telex: 917096). Moderate.

**White House** – A very big place with 577 rooms, converted from apartments, it's in a quiet spot near Regent's Park. Modernized and efficiently run, it has a coffee shop and wine bar. Business facilities include 24-hour room service, meeting rooms for up to 100, concierge, foreign currency exchange, secretarial services, audiovisual equipment, photocopiers, computers, translation services, and express checkout. Albany St., NW1 (phone: 71-387-1200; fax: 71-388-0091; telex: 24111). Moderate.

**Wilbraham** – A charming, 52-room bed and breakfast establishment, just around the corner from Sloane Square. Business facilities include foreign currency exchange, secretarial services, and photocopiers. 1 Wilbraham Pl., SW1 (phone: 71-730-8296). Moderate.

**Claverley** – Named the "Best Bed and Breakfast Hotel" in 1987 by the British Tourist Authority, this establishment, in the middle of London, has 36 rooms, 30 of which have private baths; some rooms have four-poster beds. All bedrooms have floral decor, and each has a heated towel rack in the bathroom. Guests are invited to help themselves to newspapers, coffee, tea, and cookies in the reading room. A fine British breakfast is served in the morning. Just a block from *Harrods*. Photocopiers are available. 13 Beaufort Gardens, SW3 (phone: 71-589-8541; fax: 71-730-6815). Moderate to inexpensive.

**Aster House** – One of the top bed and breakfast properties (according to the BTA) in London, this unpretentious, family-run establishment has 14 rooms with private shower; 1 has a four-poster bed and fireplace. Enjoy breakfast in the conservatory under blooming bougainvillea. In South Kensington. 3 Sumner Pl., SW7 (phone: 71-581-5888; fax: 71-584-4925). Inexpensive.

**Blandford** – Another pleasant bed and breakfast establishment, this one has 33 rooms, decorated in pastel greens and pinks, each with a color TV set and direct-dial telephone. An English breakfast is served in the morning, and complimentary newspapers are offered. There is 24-hour room service available. 80 Chiltern St, W1 (phone: 71-486-3103; fax: 71-487-2786; telex: 262594). Inexpensive.

**Delmere** – Nearly 200 years old, this lovely hostelry was designed by architect Samuel Pepys Cockerell, a student of Benjamin H. Latrobe, who designed the south wing of the Capitol building in Washington, DC. Its 40 rooms are equipped with private showers or baths, hair dryers, and the makings for tea and coffee. There is also a bar and a restaurant, *La Perla,* serving Italian food. The staff, mostly from Holland, is very friendly. Paddington Station, where trains depart to Bath and south Wales, is a mere 5-minute walk away. So is Hyde Park. Business facilities include 24-hour room service, small meeting rooms, concierge, foreign currency exchange, secretarial services, photocopiers, and computers. 130 Sussex Gardens, W2 (phone: 71-706-3344; fax: 71-262-1863; telex: 8953857). Inexpensive.

**Ebury Court** – A small hotel with smallish but cozy rooms and an intimate atmosphere (the owners dine with guests in the restaurant). Its faithful clientele testifies to its comfort, suitability, and "country house in London" touches. Hard to beat — all things considered — in a town where hotel prices tend to be unreasonable. Fewer than half of the 39 rooms have a private bath or shower. There are meeting facilities for up to 40, a concierge, and photocopiers. 26 Ebury St., SW1 (phone: 71-730-8147; fax: 71-823-5966). Inexpensive.

**Hotel 167** – Another bed and breakfast place, it is housed in a brick Victorian building and has been lovingly and uniquely furnished with both modern and antique pieces, along with a color scheme of soft grays and creams. Double rooms include private bath, and singles have baths opposite the rooms. Conveniently located near good shopping on Fulham Road, the *Victoria & Albert Museum,* and the Gloucester Road underground station. 167 Old Brompton Rd., SW5 (phone: 71-373-0672; fax: 71-373-3360). Inexpensive.

**Hotel la Place** – Fine bed and breakfast establishment with 24 rooms, including private baths, TV sets, and king-size or two double beds; some rooms also have mini-bars. British breakfast is served in the morning. Business facilities include 24-hour room service, meeting rooms for up to 20, concierge, secretarial services, and photocopiers. 17 Nottingham Pl., W1 (phone: 71-486-2323). Inexpensive.

**Observatory House** – Once owned by Count Dangerville of France (and many members of royalty have slept here since), this bed and breakfast establishment in Kensington has been renovated in Victorian decor. All 26 rooms have private showers, color TV sets, telephones, trouser presses, and tea and coffee supplies. Some rooms are for nonsmokers only. Business facilities include foreign currency exchange, secretarial services, photocopiers, and computers. 37 Hornton St., W8 (phone: 71-937-1577; fax: 71-938-3585; telex: 914-9172). Inexpensive.

**St. Giles** – Formerly a *YMCA* hostel, the lodging facilities have been transformed, renovated, and expanded into a hotel of over 600 rooms. Guests have free use of the pool at the *Y,* and access to the sauna and other facilities, all located in the lower section of the building containing the hotel. Close to the *British Museum* and Oxford Street shopping district. There are photocopiers and a concierge. Bedford Ave., WC1 (phone: 71-636-8616; fax: 71-631-1031; telex: 22683). Inexpensive.

**Winchester** – Near Victoria Station, this bed and breakfast place is in an old townhouse with a Victorian-style façade. The 18 bedrooms include modern bathrooms with showers, color TV sets, and radios. Guests are treated to an English breakfast in the morning. 17 Belgrave Rd., SW1 (phone: 71-828-2972; fax: 71-828-5191; telex: 26974). Inexpensive.

 **EATING OUT:** Once upon a time, few London restaurants were ever known for the excellence of their cooking — and some visitors of times past might call that a charitable understatement. But there's been a notable transformation in recent years. While restaurants offering really good English cooking — and not simply "chips with everything" — are still not easy to find (some are listed below), there has been a veritable explosion of good foreign restaurants in town (many of which are also noted below). A new telephone service, *Dining By Numbers*, offers 24-hour information on hundreds of London restaurants, grouped by region. A map is available from *Direct Dialing* (29 Dean St., W1V 6LL; phone: 71-287-3287). For restaurants in central London, call 71-839-12345-1; inner London, call 71-839-12345-2, and outer London, call 71-839-12345-3.

A meal for two will cost $150 and up at a restaurant listed as very expensive; $100, expensive; $50 to $75, moderate; and $40 and under, inexpensive. Prices do not include drinks, wine, or tips. Most London restaurants have developed the continental habit of automatically adding a service charge to the bill, so make certain you're not tipping twice.

**Bibendum** – Located on the second floor of the former Michelin Building, it was stylishly renovated by Sir Terence Conran of the *Habitat* chain of stores. Chef Simon Hopkinson's good taste evokes English dreams of France, and he serves the best roast beef in town. Open daily for lunch and dinner. Reservations necessary. Major credit cards accepted. Michelin House, 81 Fulham Rd., SW3 (phone: 71-581-5817). Very expensive.

**Connaught Grill** – Although there are two dining rooms at the *Connaught* hotel that share the same kitchen, it is the *Grill* that has one Michelin star. Very dignified and very proper, it has a fine reputation for both its fine food and elegant service. Frankly, these guys carry stuffy to sometimes excessive lengths, but it's hard not to appreciate the masterful culinary performance; and though the wine list is conservative, you won't find more expertly prepared liver and bacon in the city. The setting — lots of rich paneling and crystal chandeliers — matches the distinction of the menu. Closed weekends and holidays. Reservations essential. Major credit cards accepted. At the *Connaught Hotel*, Carlos Pl., W1 (phone: 71-499-7070). Very expensive.

**Le Gavroche** – Probably the best French restaurant in London and, according to *Guide Michelin*, one of the best in the entire country, with three stars to its credit (only one other establishment in Britain has received such a high rating). The food is classic French; many of the dishes by those chefs extraordinaires, the Roux brothers, qualify as genuine masterpieces. Try the *pot au feu Albert*, a fine, rich casserole. Closed weekends and from late December to late January. Reservations essential (well in advance). Major credit cards accepted. 43 Upper Brook St., W1 (phone: 71-408-0881). Very expensive.

**L'Arlequin** – A tiny establishment that offers unusual and innovative Gallic cooking by proprietor Christian Delteil, who reputedly makes the best sorbets in London. Also try either the ravioli of lobster or the divine stuffed cabbage. Closed weekends, 3 weeks in August, and 1 week in winter. Reservations essential. Major credit cards accepted. 123 Queenstown Rd., SW8 (phone: 71-622-0555). Expensive.

*Le Bistroquet* – A chic, French-ish brasserie. Ceiling fans rotate and spiky-haired waiters and waitresses whiz between tables as fish dishes cooked in parchment are cut open, filling the air with the scent of capers and fresh fennel. Open daily. Reservations necessary. Major credit cards accepted. 273-275 Camden High St., NW1 (phone: 71-485-9607). Expensive.

*Capital* – The elegant, comfortable, small dining room in this hotel near *Harrods* offers well-chosen, admirably prepared French dishes. Some discriminating Londoners consider it the best place to dine in town. Shuns the aren't-you-lucky-to-get-a-table attitude flaunted by some of the other better London restaurants. Open daily for lunch and dinner. Reservations necessary. Major credit cards accepted. 22-24 Basil St., SW3 (phone: 71-589-5171). Expensive.

*Cavaliers'* – Sue and David Cavaliers' restaurant, south of the river in upwardly mobile Battersea, serves French fare prepared by an accomplished British chef. Closed Sundays and Mondays. Reservations essential. Major credit cards accepted. 129 Queenstown Rd., SW8 (phone: 71-720-6960). Expensive.

*Chez Nico* – London's rage for the new has a leader in Nico Ladenis, England's first love-to-be-hated culinary star. This temperamental talent specializes in gutsy flavors and ample portions that have earned this eatery two Michelin stars. (For a less formal atmosphere, try *Very Simply Nico;* see below.) Closed Saturdays and Sundays. Reservations essential. Major credit cards accepted. 35 Great Portland St., W1 (phone: 71-436-8846). Expensive.

*Gay Hussar* – Among the best Hungarian restaurants this side of Budapest, its substantial menu offers a varied selection: chicken ragout soup, goulash, roast pork, and lots more. The food here is extremely filling as well as delicious. Informal atmosphere, with a regular clientele drawn from London's newspaper and publishing world. Closed Sundays. Reservations essential. Major credit cards accepted. 2 Greek St., W1 (phone: 71-437-0973). Expensive.

*Green's* – Pinstripes and bowlers rule at this establishment, which serves the best oysters in London, and some would say the best English food. Open daily. Reservations necessary, at least 4 days in advance during the week. Major credit cards accepted. 36 Duke St., SW1 (phone: 71-930-4566). Expensive.

*Greig's Grill* – Formerly the *Guinea Grill,* this small, unimposing restaurant substitutes displays of its fresh food — steaks, chops, fresh vegetables — for a menu. The food, cooked with care, is as good as ever — the Scottish beef is the best in London — but the service is right out of "Fawlty Towers." Closed Sundays. Reservations necessary. Major credit cards accepted. 26 Bruton Pl., W1 (phone: 71-629-5613). Expensive.

*Harvey's* – The current wild boy — long hair, bad language, and all — is the chef, Marco Pierre White, at this eatery. If he's in the right mood, he'll cook up a dream: oysters with *tagliatelle* and pigeon from Bresse. Open Tuesdays through Saturdays for lunch and dinner. Reservations essential. Major credit cards accepted. 2 Bellevue Rd., Wendsworth Common, SW1 (phone: 81-672-0114). Expensive.

*Hilaire* – Once serving only superb French food, this spot now also offers impressive English dishes, imaginatively prepared and charmingly served. Closed Saturdays for lunch and Sundays. Reservations essential. Major credit cards accepted. 68 Old Brompton Rd., SW7 (phone: 71-584-8993). Expensive.

*Ivy* – Since 1911, this has been one of *the* restaurants of London's theater elite. A change of ownership has brought it a new lease on life, plus specially commissioned works of contemporary art that contrast with the stained glass and oak paneling. International specialties are served along with British classics like grilled Dover sole, Cumberland sausages, and smoked salmon with scrambled eggs. Open daily from noon to 3 PM and from 5:30 PM to midnight. Reservations essential. Major credit cards accepted. 1 West St., London WC2H 9NE (phone: 71-836-4751). Expensive.

**Ken Lo's Memories of China** – The premier Chinese eatery in London, where Ken Lo, well-known Chinese author and tennis player, and his chefs prepare a wide range of fine dishes from all regions of China, from dim sum to Szechaun-style food. Closed Sundays and bank holidays. Reservations advised. Major credit cards accepted. 67 Ebury St., SW7 (phone: 71-730-7734); and a new location at Harbour Yard, Chelsea Harbour, SW 10 (phone: 71-352-4953). Expensive.

**Leith's** – A fine continental restaurant in an out-of-the-way Victorian building northwest of Kensington Gardens, this spot serves very good entrées, hors d'oeuvres, and desserts as part of a fine prix fixe dinner. An excellent vegetarian menu is also available, and its wine selection is very good. Open daily for dinner. Reservations essential. Major credit cards accepted. 92 Kensington Park Rd., W11 (phone: 71-229-4481). Expensive.

**Pavilion** – In the *Grosvenor House* hotel, it serves English fare, including Dover sole, salmon, and lamb; the starter buffet features such treats as king-size prawns, cold salmon, and salads. Situated at the front of the hotel, the spacious, bright, and airy dining room offers a fine view of Hyde Park. Open daily for breakfast, lunch, and dinner. Reservations advised for lunch and dinner on Sundays. Major credit cards accepted. *Grosvenor House,* Park La., W1 (phone: 71-499-6363). Expensive.

**Rue St. Jacques** – Lavishly decorated with huge gold-framed mirrors. The food is marked by rich cream sauces. A delicous vegetarian main course also is available. Pricey, but well worth it. The formality stretches to a jacket-and-tie requirement and a doorman who provides parking service. Closed Saturdays for lunch and Sundays. Reservations necessary. Major credit cards accepted. 5 Charlotte St., W1 (phone: 71-637-0222). Expensive.

**Savoy Grill** – Renowned as a celebrity watching ground, but actually inhabited mostly by a male, business clientele. Although the menu features some classic French dishes, the English grills and roasts are its specialty. The lovely, restored decor resembles a luxurious ship's dining room (first class, natch) of 50 years ago. Perfect for after theater. Closed Saturday lunch and Sundays. Reservations essential. Major credit cards accepted. At the *Savoy Hotel,* The Strand, WC2 (phone: 71-836-4343). Expensive.

**Sutherlands** – Don't be put off by the plain exterior. This place is for serious food lovers, and has been awarded a Michelin star for innovative dishes that range from *courgette* (zucchini) flowers stuffed with chicken mousse and ringed with wild mushroom sauce to a chocolate truffle torte with marmalade mousse. Fine wine list. Closed Saturday lunch and Sundays. Reservations essential. Major credit cards accepted. 45 Lexington St., W1 (phone: 71-434-3401). Expensive.

**Tante Claire** – Run by chef Pierre Koffman and his wife, Annie, this establishment has been awarded two Michelin stars, as well as many other honors. While fish dishes are the chef's specialty, everything — especially the duck, calf's liver, and *pied de cochon farci aux morilles* (pig's foot stuffed with foie gras and mushrooms) — is excellent. The prix fixe lunch is a remarkably good value at around $45. Closed weekends. Reservations essential. Major credit cards accepted. 68 Royal Hospital Rd., SW3 (phone: 71-352-6045). Expensive.

**Wilton's** – Good food, skillfully prepared, elegantly served in a plush, rather formal Victorian setting. Game, fish, oxtail, steak and kidney pie — what the best of English cooking can be all about. Closed Saturday lunch, Sundays, and 3 weeks in August. Reservations necessary. Major credit cards accepted. 55 Jermyn St., SW1 (phone: 71-629-9955). Expensive.

**Langan's Brasserie** – Still trendy after all these years, and still a haunt for celebrities. Ask for a downstairs table and take your time studying the lengthy menu. (For a lighter menu, try *Langan's Bistro;* see below.) Closed Saturdays and Sundays for lunch. Reservations necessary. Major credit cards accepted. 1 Stratton St., W1 (phone: 71-493-6437). Expensive to moderate.

*Alastair Little* – This spot is not so new but still chic, and many find the chef here to be the most natural cook in the city, offering an eclectic menu featuring French, Japanese, and Italian dishes. Open for lunch and dinner Mondays through Fridays; Saturdays for dinner only; closed Sundays. Reservations advised. No credit cards accepted. 49 Frith St., W1 (phone: 71-734-5183). Moderate.

*Bloom's* – Specializing in Jewish food, it has a bright and bustling atmosphere, a bit like the dining room of a large hotel, with waiters who almost — but not quite — throw the food at you. The popular take-out counter serves the best hot salt beef (like corned beef) sandwiches in town. House wine is Israeli. Closed Friday evenings and Saturdays. Reservations advised. Major credit cards accepted. 130 Golders Green Rd., NW11 (phone: 81-455-1338), and 90 Whitechapel High St., E1 (phone: 71-247-6001). Moderate.

*Bombay Brasserie* – At lunchtime there is an Indian buffet; at dinner, classic cooking from the Bombay region. Parsi dishes, rarely found outside of India itself, are also included. And the setting is lovely, with lots of banana plants, wicker chairs, and ceiling fans. Popular with both the American and British show-biz colonies. Open daily. Reservations essential. Major credit cards accepted. Courtfield Close, Courtfield Rd., SW7 (phone: 71-370-4040). Moderate.

*Camden Brasserie* – The daily specials are posted on a board outside this restaurant, located in an increasingly fashionable part of town. Among the selections are meats and fish grilled over an open fire. Open daily for lunch and dinner. Reservations necessary. Major credit cards accepted. 216 Camden High St., NW1 (phone: 71-482-2114). Moderate.

*Chuen Cheng Ku* – At this huge restaurant in the heart of Chinatown, the overwhelming majority of the clientele is Chinese. The specialty here is dim sum, served every day until 6 PM. Also try the pork with chili and salt, duck webs, steamed lobster with ginger, and shark fin soup. Open daily. Reservations necessary. Major credit cards accepted. 17 Wardour St., W1 (phone: 71-437-1398). Moderate.

*Clarke's* – It's London's answer to the Bay Area's *Chez Panisse,* set dinner menus of California-style cooking in a lovely, light, basement eatery. Open Mondays through Fridays for lunch and dinner; closed weekends. Reservations necessary. Major credit cards accepted. 124 Kensington Church St., W8 (phone: 71-221-9225). Moderate.

*Kensington Place* – One of the hot tickets in town, set behind a huge glass front, so you can see and be seen. A mix of "Californian new English" cookery from partridge and cabbage to foie gras, oysters, and delicious desserts. Frenzied atmosphere, sensible wine list. Open daily. Reservations necessary. Major credit cards accepted. 201 Kensington Church St., W8 (phone: 71-727-3184). Moderate.

*Langan's Bistro* – Serves slightly simpler and less expensive dishes prepared in the same style as *Langan's Brasserie.* Closed Sundays and Saturdays for lunch. Reservations advised. Major credit cards accepted. 26 Devonshire St., W1 (phone: 71-935-4531). Moderate.

*Porters* – A very English eatery in *Covent Garden,* it's famous for home-cooked pies — steak, mushroom, and vegetable are the specialties (and an acquired taste). The kitchen, bar, and basement are more spacious since the restaurant's total redecoration. Open daily. Reservations advised, especially for lunch. Major credit cards accepted. 17 Henrietta St., WC2 (phone: 71-836-6466). Moderate.

*River Café* – The eloquent Northern Italian dishes and the Thameside location here are best appreciated at lunch. Open daily except Mondays for lunch, and Saturdays and Sundays for dinner. Reservations essential. Major credit cards accepted. Thames Wharf, Rainville Rd., W6 (phone: 71-381-8824) Moderate.

**Rules** – Approaching its bicentennial, this eatery has been at the same site since 1798. The Lillie Langtry Room, upstairs where the actress dined with the Prince of Wales (later King Edward VII), is reserved for private parties. The downstairs retains its Victorian atmosphere and decor. Walls are covered with signed photographs and cartoons of actors and authors. Once a *must* for visitors to London, the quality of its food has seesawed over recent years. The menu remains decidedly British, from feathered game amd game fish in season to treacle sponge pudding. Open daily from noon to midnight. Reservations essential. American Express, MasterCard, and Visa accepted. 35 Maiden La., WC2 (phone: 71-836-5314). Moderate.

**Shezan** – Just below street level, this quiet brick and tile spot prepares some very fine Pakistani food. Specialties include marinated-in-yogurt *murg tikka Lahori* (chicken cooked in a tandoor, or clay oven) and *kabab kabli* (minced spiced beef). An enthusiastic staff will explain the intricacies of tandoori cooking, help with your order, and lavish excellent service upon you. Closed Sundays. Reservations necessary. Major credit cards accepted. 16 Cheval Pl., SW7 (phone: 71-589-7918). Moderate.

**Stephen Bull** – For value, it was the most successful opening back in 1989. This clean-cut, modern eatery offers creatively prepared food, as well as service pared to essentials for true enjoyment and sensible tabs. Open for lunch and dinner Mondays through Fridays; for dinner only, on Saturdays; closed Sundays. Reservations necessary. Major credit cards accepted. 5-7 Blandford St., W1 (phone: 71-486-9696). Moderate.

**Sweetings** – A special London experience, this traditional fish restaurant is one of the great lunchtime attractions in London's financial district. You may have to sit at a counter with your lobster, brill, or haddock, but it will be fresh and perfectly prepared. Open weekday lunchtime only; no reservations, so expect a wait. Major credit cards accepted. 39 Queen Victoria St., EC4 (phone: 71-248-3062). Moderate.

**Tate Gallery Restaurant** – Who would expect one of London's better dining establishments to be in a fine art museum? But here it is — a genuine culinary outpost (leaning toward French cuisine), with a very good wine list. Enjoy the famous Rex Whistler murals as you sip. Lunch only. Closed Sundays. Reservations essential. No credit cards accepted. *Tate Gallery,* Millbank, SW1 (phone: 71-834-6754). Moderate.

**Thai Pavilion** – The staff may have limited familiarity with English at this place in Soho, but the decor is pretty, and the beef with sesame, fish cakes in chili sauce, and chicken with peanut sauce are worth the effort to be understood. Try one of the Thai beers to cool off the roof of your mouth. Open daily. Reservations advised. Major credit cards accepted. 42 Rupert St., W1 (phone: 71-287-6333). Moderate.

**Trattoo** – An airy, attractive eatery, just off Kensington High Street, it serves very good Northern Italian food — from a variety of pasta to *saltimbocca* or *fegato all veneziana.* Closed Sundays for lunch. Reservations advised. Major credit cards accepted. 2 Abingdon Rd., W8 (phone: 71-937-4448). Moderate.

**La Trattoria dei Pescatori** – A busy atmosphere pervades this place, whose decor includes a boat, terra cotta tiles, copper pans, and chunky ceiling beams. The menu is enormous, with trout, halibut, salmon, shrimp, turbot, and lobster appearing in several guises. A typical specialty is *misto dei crostacei alla crema* — Mediterranean prawns, scallops, shrimp, and mussels sautéed with onions and herbs, simmered in fish stock and asti, with a touch of cream. Closed Sundays. Reservations necessary. Major credit cards accepted. 57 Charlotte St., W1 (phone: 71-580-3289). Moderate.

**Treasure of China** – In a landmark Georgian building in historic Greenwich, it's a leader in original Peking and Szechuan cooking. Owners Tony Low and Roger Norman offer a selective daily menu, as well as superb banquets celebrating Chinese festivals. Open daily. Reservations essential. Major credit cards accepted. 10 Nelson Rd., SE10 (phone: 81-858-9884). Moderate.

**Very Simply Nico** – It's Nico Ladenis's not-so-snooty steak-and-chips joint. Open for lunch and dinner; closed Sundays. Reservations necessary. Major credit cards accepted. 48A Rochester Row, SW1 (phone: 71-630-8061). Moderate.

**Wheeler's** – One of the chain of London seafood restaurants with the same name, this is the original and the best of the lot. It's an old-fashioned, narrow establishment, on 3 floors, which specializes in a variety of ways of preparing real Dover sole. The oyster bar on the ground floor is our favorite perch for savoring bivalves and smoked salmon. Closed Sundays. Reservations advised. Major credit cards accepted. Duke of York St. at Apple Tree Yard, SW1 (phone: 71-930-2460). Moderate.

**Chiang Mai** – Thai restaurants used to be a rarity in London. This one has always been easy to spot since it's the only eatery in Soho (and probably the whole of Britain) with a carved wooden elephant poised on the sidewalk. The menu offers such dishes as coconut chicken and galanga soup. Those unfamiliar with northern Thai cooking should inquire about the spiciness of individual dishes before ordering. Open daily. Reservations advised. Major credit cards accepted. 48 Frith St., W1 (phone: 71-437-7444). Moderate to inexpensive.

**HQ** – Live jazz is the main attraction at this restaurant/wine bar in trendy Camden Lock. Its location above the arts and crafts shops affords guests good views of the canal and weekend street performers. Open daily for dinner. Reservations necessary. Major credit cards accepted. Commercial Pl., SW1 (phone: 71-485-6044). Moderate to inexpensive.

**Kalamaras Taverna** – A small friendly eatery with authentic Greek food, prepared under the watchful eye of the Greek owner. The menu here is more varied than in most of the other Greek/Cypriot restaurants in London. Open Mondays through Saturdays for dinner. Reservations advised. Major credit cards accepted. 76 and 66 Inverness Mews, W2, off Queensway. No. 66 has no liquor license (phone: 71-727-5082 or 71-727-9122). Moderate and inexpensive, respectively.

**Kettner's** – As you check your coat, you have to make your choice — a bottle of champagne at the bar (25 labels in stock), a humble but tasty salad in the brasserie-style café, or a pizza in the beautifully furnished dining room reminiscent of an Edwardian hotel. In Soho. Open daily, noon to midnight. Reservations unnecessary. Major credit cards accepted. 29 Romilly St., W1 (phone: 71-437-6437). Moderate to inexpensive.

**Khyber** – A wide selection of Indian Punjabi specialties, as well as tasty vegetarian dishes, are served here. Try the *pannir,* mild cheese cooked with peas, meat, and spices, and the *aloo gobi,* a cauliflower dish. Open daily. Reservations advised. Major credit cards accepted. 56 Westbourne Grove, W2 (phone: 71-727-4385). Moderate to inexpensive.

**Last Days of the Raj** – This popular eatery on the eastern fringe of *Covent Garden* serves dishes from India's Punjabi region. Punjabi cuisine is rather mild, and one of its specialties is meat prepared tandoori style — marinated in yogurt and spices, then baked in a special clay oven. Some kind of tandoori cooking is usually on the menu in addition to other specials, which change every few months. The exotic mango-based cocktails are powerful, and the service is extremely friendly. Be sure to dine at the Drury Lane *Raj,* as other restaurants are now trading on the original restaurant's good name. Open daily. Reservations essential. Major credit cards accepted. 22 Drury La., WC2 (phone: 71-836-1628). Moderate to inexpensive.

*Smollensky's Balloon* – This American-owned cocktail bar/restaurant with a 1930s piano-bar atmosphere is guaranteed to make you feel homesick. Steaks and fries figure importantly on the menu, offset by some interesting vegetarian dishes. Real family fun. Open daily, noon to 11:45 PM; Sundays noon to 10:30 PM. Reservations unnecessary. Major credit cards accepted. 1 Dover St., W1 (phone: 71-491-1199). There is a second branch at 105 Strand, WC2 (phone: 71-497-2101). Both moderate to inexpensive.

*Street Fish Shop* – For decent salmon, as well as traditional fish and chips. Open for lunch and dinner; closed Monday evenings and Sundays. Reservations unnecessary. Major credit cards accepted. 324 Upper St. (phone: 71-359-1401). Moderate to inexpensive.

*Bangkok* – Known for its *saté* — small tender slices of beef marinated in a curry and soy sauce and served with a palate-destroying hot peanut sauce. From your butcher block table you can watch your meal being prepared in the windowed kitchen. Closed Sundays. Reservations unnecessary. Major credit cards accepted. 9 Bute St., SW7 (phone: 71-584-8529). Inexpensive.

*Calabash* – West African fare gives this place a unique position on London's restaurant map, especially since it's in the bubbling *Covent Garden* district. The service is accommodating and helpful, and the food is both good and different. Closed Sundays. Reservations advised. Major credit cards accepted. Downstairs at London's *Africa Centre,* 38 King St., WC2 (phone: 71-836-1976). Inexpensive.

*Chicago Pizza Pie Factory* – A decade ago, an American advertising executive turned his back on the US ad world to bring London deep-dish pizza Windy City–style, along with Budweiser beer and chocolate cheesecake. Londoners beat a path to his door and haven't yet stopped clamoring to get in. Open daily. Reservations unnecessary. Major credit cards accepted. 17 Hanover Sq., W1 (phone: 71-629-2669). Inexpensive.

*Cosmoba* – A small and friendly family-run Italian restaurant that is basic in every respect — except for its food. Tucked down a tiny alleyway and always packed with regulars. Closed Sundays. Reservations advised. Major credit cards accepted. 9 Cosmo Pl., WC1 (phone: 71-837-0904). Inexpensive.

*Cranks* – There are several branches of this self-service vegetarian restaurant. All are popular and serve good homemade desserts, as well as salads, quiches, and other hot food. Drop in for coffee or afternoon tea. Some of the more central branches include 8 Marshall St., W1 (phone: 71-437-9431), open for dinner Mondays through Saturdays; 11 The Market, *Covent Garden,* WC2 (phone: 71-379-6508), open daily; Tottenham St., W1 (phone: 71-631-3912), closed Sundays; Unit 11, Adelaide St., WC2 (phone: 71-836-0660), closed Sundays; 23 Bartlett St., W1 (phone: 71-495-1340), closed Sundays; and Great Newport St., Leicester Sq. (phone: 71-83605226), open daily. Reservations advised. Major credit cards accepted. Inexpensive.

*Dove* – Boasting a nice riverside spot, it serves good as well as filling pub grub and good Fullers beer. Open daily. Reservations unnecessary. Major credit cards accepted. 19 Upper Mall, Hammersmith, W6 (phone: 81-748-5405). Inexpensive.

*Dumpling Inn* – This Peking-style restaurant serves excellent Oriental dumplings, and most of the other dishes are equally good. Try the fried seaweed; it's got lots of vitamins and tastes terrific. The service, though efficient, is a bit brisk. Open daily. Reservations unnecessary. Major credit cards accepted. 15A Gerrard St., W1 (phone: 71-437-2567). Inexpensive.

*Geales'* – Truly fresh English fare, including fish and chips, is served in a setting that looks like a 1930s tearoom. Go early, because this spot is no secret. Closed

Sundays and Mondays and the last 3 weeks in August. Reservations unnecessary. Major credit cards accepted. 2 Farmer St., W8 (phone: 71-727-7969). Inexpensive.

**Hard Rock Café** – The original. An American-style eating emporium with a loud jukebox and good burgers. It's always crowded, and the lines stretch well out into the street. As much a T-shirt vendor (at the shop around the corner) these days as a restaurant. Open daily. No reservations. Major credit cards accepted. 150 Old Park La., W1 (phone: 71-629-0382). Inexpensive.

**My Old Dutch** – This authentic Dutch pancake house serves endless varieties of sweet and savory pancakes on genuine blue Delft plates. Loud music. Open daily. Reservations necessary only for parties of eight or more. Major credit cards accepted. 132 High Holborn, WC1 (phone: 71-242-5200). Inexpensive.

**Standard** – Possibly the best Indian restaurant value in London, so it tends to get crowded quickly. Open daily. Reservations advised. Major credit cards accepted. 23 Westbourne Grove, W2 (phone: 71-727-4818). Inexpensive.

**Tuttons** – Serving food all day, it's a very popular and lively brasserie in a former *Covent Garden* warehouse, and a handy snack spot for theatergoers. Open from 10 AM to 11:30 PM, Sundays through Thursdays; 10 AM to midnight, Fridays and Saturdays. Reservations advised. Major credit cards accepted. 11 Russell St., WC2 (phone: 71-836-4141). Inexpensive.

**Widow Applebaum** – Not an authentic New York delicatessen, but this place serves pretty good herring, cold cuts, chopped liver, potato salad, dill pickles, and apple pie. Closed Sundays. Reservations unnecessary. Major credit cards accepted. 46 S. Molton St., W1 (phone: 71-629-4649). Inexpensive.

 **SHARING A PINT:** There are several thousand pubs in London, the vast majority of which are owned by the six biggest brewers. Most of these pubs have two bars: the "public," which is for the working man who wants to get on with the business of drinking, and the "saloon" or "lounge," which makes an attempt at providing comfort and may serve food and wine as well as beer. Liquor at the latter may cost more. Among the means by which pubs are appraised is the brand and variety of draft brews that spew forth from its taps. The extraordinary variety can easily perplex the uninitiated. There's ale: bitter, mild, stout; and lager, whose varying tastes provide a perfect excuse to linger longer in pubs you find particularly convivial. Eating in a crowded pub is not always easy because the limited number of tables are barely large enough to hold all the empty beer glasses, let alone food. Pub food is hearty but not especially imaginative: a ploughman's lunch, which is a hunk of bread and cheese plus a pickle; cottage pie, which is ground meat with mashed potatoes on top, baked in the oven; sausages; and sandwiches. The number (and quality) of pubs serving more upscale food is increasing, since British law has recently expanded opening hours for pubs offering food; the law used to require pubs to close for several hours during late afternoon to early evening, whereas now most open at 10:30 or 11 AM and remain open until 11 PM.

Here are the names of pubs where we like to raise a pint or two: *Dirty Dick's* (202 Bishopsgate, EC2) is offbeat but popular, with fake bats and spiders hanging from the ceilings, sawdust on the floor, and good bar snacks; and *Sherlock Holmes* (10 Northumberland St., WC2) is the pub that Holmes's creator, Arthur Conan Doyle, used to frequent when it was still the *Northumberland Arms,* and which he mentioned in *Hound of the Baskervilles.* A glass-enclosed replica of Holmes's Baker Street study is there, along with Holmes memorabilia. The *Audley* (41 Mount St., W1) is our favorite luncheon stop in the high-rent district, with fine sandwiches and salad plates in an atypically hygienic environment. Other fine spots include the *Antelope* (22 Eaton Terrace, SW1), where the Bellamys (or even Hudson, their butler) might have sipped a lager on the way home to nearby 165 Eaton Place; the *Grenadier* (18 Wilton Row,

SW1), perhaps the poshest pub site in town, just off Belgravia Square; *Admiral Codring-
ton* (17 Mossop St., SW3) is large and Victorian, with brass beer pumps, engraved
mirrors, and good food; *Dickens Inn* by the Tower (St. Katherine's Way, E1) is a
converted warehouse overlooking a colorful yacht marina and serving shellfish snacks;
*George Inn* (77 Borough High St., SE1) dates from 1676 and retains the original gallery
for viewing Shakespearean plays in the summer; *The Flask* (77 Highgate West Hill, N6)
serves drinks at three paneled bars and on its outside patio; *The Lamb* (94 Lambs
Conduit St., WC1) is also paneled and hung with photos of past music hall performers;
*Museum Tavern* (49 Great Russell St., WC1) is across the road from the *British
Museum* and decorated with hanging flower baskets; *Princess Louise* (208 High Hol-
born, WC1) has live music, cabaret, and a wine bar upstairs with good food; *Bull and
Bush* (North End Way, NW3) owes its fame to the Edwardian music hall song "Down
at the Old Bull and Bush." Former customers include Thomas Gainsborough and
Charles Dickens. It has an outdoor bar and barbecue for balmy summer evenings.
*Prospect of Whitby* (57 Wapping Wall, E1), the oldest riverside pub in London, was
once the haunt of thieves and smugglers (now it draws jazz lovers); *Ye Olde Cheshire
Cheese* (5 Little Essex St., EC4, just off Fleet St.) is a 17th-century pub, with paneled
walls and sawdust floors, that's popular with the Fleet Street set. On the south bank
of the Thames, in the district of the Docklands called Rotherhithe, are two special pubs,
the *Mayflower* and the *Angel;* the former has been around since the days in the 17th
century when the *Mayflower* left for the New World and returned to Rotherhithe;
today, the partially rebuilt Tudor inn is still a good spot to enjoy beer and ale. The
*Angel* is set on stone pillars overlooking the Thames, and the cozy, dark interior hasn't
changed much since the days when it was patronized by Samuel Pepys and Captain
Cook.

 **WINE BARS:** Growing in popularity on the London scene, they serve wine
by the glass or bottle, accompanied by such light fare as quiche and salad,
and occasionally full meals. Prices tend to be lower in wine bars than in
restaurants, and tables can often be reserved in advance. Here's a selection
of the finest: *Café Suze* (1 Glentworth St., NW1) combines rustic decor with good
homemade food; *Cork and Bottle* (44-46 Cranbourn St., WC2) is patronized by the
London wine trade and has a classical guitarist providing background music; *Draycott's*
(114 Draycott Ave., SW3) has tables grouped outside on the pavement and is frequented by the smart London set; *Ebury Wine Bar* (139 Ebury St., SW1), in the heart
of Belgravia, serves good food (try the English pudding) and offers live music nightly;
*Le Bistroquet* (273-275 Camden High St., NW1) is one of London's trendiest spots,
popular with the city's yuppies; *Shampers* (4 Kingly St., W1) is near the famous *Liberty*
department store, and sometimes has a classical guitarist in the evenings; *Skinkers* (42
Tooley St.) is an atmospheric spot with sawdust on the floor, serving hearty food; *Crown
Passage Vaults* (20 King St.) is renowned for its potted shrimp — to be eaten with a
glass of montagny or pouilly vinzelles; *Bar des Amis* (11-14 Hanover Pl., WC2) is a
crowded watering hole in fashionable *Covent Garden; Crawford's* (10-11 Crawford St.,
W1) is a lively basement bar serving full cold buffet lunches and suppers; *Brahms and
Liszt* (19 Russell St., WC2) always has good wines, food, and music; *Julie's* (137
Portland Rd., W11) has become a landmark for aging flower children of the 1960s;
*El Vino* (47 Fleet St., EC4), once a journalists' haunt famous for refusing to serve
women at the bar, is now full of legal eagles and PR folk in a nice Old World
atmosphere.

# DIVERSIONS

# For the Experience

## Quintessential London

London is a city of contrast and paradox. The cockney trader setting up his "fruit and veg" stall as dawn breaks over St. Martin's and Bow is every bit as much a Londoner as the aristocratic gentleman reading the *Times* in the lofty peace of his Mayfair club — as is the teenager scavenging the bustling secondhand markets of Camden and Portobello.

For the city's charm is not locked in any specific tourist areas, museums, or expensive excursions. It creeps up and surrounds you before you've even attempted to officially "do" London. A stop for a drink at a riverside pub, enjoying the view along with a few locals on lunch break; a shortcut down a cobbled back street between hectic junctions; or mingling with a throng of theatergoers in neon-lit Piccadilly — each and all reveal a part of the real London, one best absorbed at your own pace.

The essence of London is in the air and in the people who breathe it, making it as exciting to visit for the 50th time as it is for the first. As Dr. Johnson said over 200 years ago, "When a man is tired of London, he is tired of life."

**A DAY AT LORD'S:** Though the rules of cricket are totally incomprehensible to most people who are not British born and bred, anyone can enjoy the unique atmosphere of a day at Lord's — cricket headquarters near Regent's Park — especially if the weather is warm. (Some Americans say it's a lot like baseball — without the hot dogs.) In the center of its large expanse of immaculately mown grass, 15 men dressed in white — called "flanneled fools" by Kipling — perform the game's complicated rituals. The two men in coats are the umpires; the two with bats are part of the team that is "in" (up) trying to score "runs" (the other nine members of the team are in the pavilion, or dugout, awaiting their turn at bat). The bowler (pitcher) tries to get the batsmen "out" by hitting the wickets (2 wooden posts behind the batsman) with the bowled ball. The rest of the men on the field try to catch a hit before it bounces. For his part, the batsman is trying to hit the ball and prevent it from hitting the wicket. Everyone cheers when a batsman hits a ball to the boundary (the equivalent of the outfield wall) for 4 runs, or better still if the ball gets there without bouncing (6 runs). After the bowler throws the balls 6 times from one end (this is called an "over"), the bowling changes ends and all the fielders move around. During this British version of a seventh-inning stretch, spectators can also move around; during play, however, they are expected to remain seated.

For the uninitiated, 1-day matches are the most exciting, because the batsmen have to score quickly and the prize money is high. The 5-day international test matches or 3- and 4-day county ones are definitely for the connoisseur. (Many spectators listen to the radio commentary on earphones as they watch the game.)

The day-long matches begin at 10 AM; everything stops at lunchtime, when spectators and players alike fill the neighboring pubs and coffee shops. Many people bring picnic lunches, eating on blankets laid out on the adjoining "nursery" practice area. There is also a tea break around 4 PM. Another diversion is to stroll to the practice nets to watch batsmen warming up, or behind the pavilion where autograph hunters stand waiting for their favorite players to emerge. Play usually ends around 6:30 or 7 PM, and everyone heads home to rest up for the next day's match.

**BESPOKE TAILORING:** Savile Row, a narrow street near Piccadilly Circus, is lined with gentlemen's tailors, but if you're in search of the perfect "bespoke" suit, nowhere equals *Gieves and Hawkes* (at No. 1). Alongside the Union Jack above its entrance, three royal coats of arms mark the fact that it is "by appointment," indicating that the queen, the Duke of Edinburgh, and the Prince of Wales are all regular customers. Inside, the rooms are of dark wood with imposing, large mirrors, resembling a gentlemen's club. Some of the street's other tailors will do rush jobs for customers in only a few days' time, but garments at *Gieves* take between 6 and 8 weeks to complete. The only concession they are prepared to make — *if* a customer is only in London for a few days and *if* the tailors can manage to fit it into their schedule — is to offer a first fitting within a few days of the order being placed. Called "bespoke" because the suit is "spoken for" — planned — on a one-to-one client-to-tailor basis, these custom-made clothes carry a hefty price tag — anywhere from $1,500 to as much as £1,500.

First a formally dressed consultant helps the customer decide exactly what he wants, taking into account such things as his general shape, stature, lifestyle, and personality. A cutter then takes the measurements he needs to produce the paper pattern from which the tailor will work. Deciding on the fabric is usually the most difficult step, as there is a vast selection of cloths in all sorts of weights, colors, shades, and patterns from which to choose.

Incidentally, *Gieves* is pronounced with a hard "G" and rhymes with "leaves." But Robert Gieves, the fifth generation of his family to work here, says they do not mind if someone says "Jeeves," as — like P. G. Wodehouse's famous butler — they *are,* after all, there to help a gentleman be seen at his very best.

**BOATING UP THE THAMES:** Threading like a ribbon through the heart of London, the Thames — from its narrowest point to its widest, at bucolic Richmond — offers some of the best views of the city. Upstream, where the river is narrower, the banks are lined with lovely private homes; the towering cityscape can be seen in the distance. In the evening, the lights twinkle from the Palace of Westminster as members of Parliament diligently work through the night. In the more rural areas, joggers and equestrians can be seen along the tree-lined towpath. A boat trip provides one of the best ways to appreciate many of London's famous sights — an unobstructed view of Big Ben, the majesty of the Houses of Parliament — and provides a much less cluttered perspective than walking or riding a bus. It is also by far the most relaxing way of traveling through the busy capital.

Boat trips go either downstream past the Tower of London and Docklands toward Greenwich, or upstream toward Kew and Hampton Court, where the landscape is more rustic. The most central place to board is Westminster Pier, where boats depart every 30 minutes in season to Greenwich and Kew; there are four each morning to Hampton Court. As each boat carries about 100 passengers, there's rarely a wait to board — except in summer. Depending on the tide, trips take about 45 minutes to Greenwich (the new Riverbus for commuters takes less time, but costs more) or 90 minutes to Kew, plus another 2 hours on to Hampton Court.

A commentator describes the sites along the way. Upstream past the House of Parliament, the first landmarks are Lambeth Palace, home of the Archbishop of Canterbury, and in complete contrast, the now empty Battersea Power Station. This huge brick building, with its four tall chimneys, is now an empty shell after an ambitious plan to transform it into a theme park was abandoned due to a shortage of funds. London bridges are notable throughout, many old and ornate, with interesting histories of their own. The shore is lined with churches, their lofty spires reflected in the water, as well as stately mansions and schools. The stretch between Putney and Mortlake is where the famous Oxford-Cambridge boat race takes place every spring. Kew, where the river skirts the famous botanical gardens, is a good place to disembark — especially for those who fancy a walk along the towpath.

The first of the Thames's locks is at Richmond, a particularly English-looking spot. As you wait for the lockkeeper to open the electrically powered gates, there is an opportunity to pass the time of day with many onlookers and members of other boat crews. The next lock, Teddington, built in 1811, marks the dividing line between the tidal and non-tidal stretches of the Thames. From here, the river winds around Thames Ditton Island and on to Hampton Court; its landing stage was specially designed by the architect Lutyens in 1933 to harmonize with the palace, which dates to 1514. A stroll through the building and its extensive gardens, which include the famous maze, is the perfect complement to a river trip.

**BRITISH LIBRARY:** Unless you are at least 21 years old and an academic scholar doing research, you are not allowed more than a quick glimpse into the British Library's huge Reading Room in the *British Museum*. Visitors can walk through briefly, accompanied by a guard, on the hour between 11 AM and 4 PM. The first sight of the room's spectacular 106-foot-high, pale blue, domed ceiling, and the rows upon rows of leather-bound books — whose combined colors resemble an autumn hillside — that fill every inch of the circular walls is truly mesmerizing. The dome, 140 feet across, is only 2 feet smaller than the world's largest — the Pantheon in Rome; its bottom rim has the room's opening date, 1857, inscribed around it in large gold Roman numerals. Dickens researched the background for his novels here, and this is where Karl Marx worked on *Das Kapital.*

The atmosphere is hushed as researchers pore over their volumes at leather-topped tables, with dimly lit desk lamps. In all, the library holds 18 million volumes for reference, including a copy of everything published in Britain since 1757, from great literature to computer catalogues and sheet music. There is space for only a fraction of the books to be displayed on its three floors; the rest are stored in other areas, some in other buildings, so researchers may have to wait anywhere from 2 hours to 2 days to have their book request filled. Within the next 5 years, however, the library is scheduled to move to new premises at St. Pancras, and the room will revert to being part of the *British Museum.*

Some of the library's most treasured possessions are on display in the nearby Granville and King's Libraries and Manuscript Saloon. Among them is a copy of the Magna Carta (sealed in 1215), the beautifully calligraphed and illustrated Lindisfarne Gospels (made ca. 698), and Shakespeare's First Folio. The impressive collection of autographs includes those of Milton, Wordsworth, the Brontës, Michelangelo, Galileo, and Leonardo da Vinci. Musical scores and stamp collections can be found here as well.

**CABINET WAR ROOMS:** Two floors below street level, protected by 10 feet of solid concrete, lie the Cabinet War Rooms, Winston Churchill's top-secret — and bombproof — headquarters during the Second World War. Built in a warren of basement corridors under government offices in Great George Street near the Houses of Parliament, they have been preserved almost as they were when the war ended.

Nineteen of the rooms — seen through glass panels — are open to the public. Their dingy, peeling beige paint, faded maps, and piles of papers and files heaped on simple tables and desks all give a sense of the gloomy wartime atmosphere — and of the history that was made here. Each room is dominated by massive red girders installed to support the heavy bombproof ceilings.

In the Cabinet Room — where Churchill presided over 100 meetings of the War Cabinet — 24 chairs are squeezed in around a row of tables covered in heavy, dark blue police-uniform cloth (the only material available during the war). Churchill himself sat on a wooden chair in front of a large map of the British Empire. Above the doorway, two small electric bulbs, red and green, indicated whether an air raid was in progress.

Along the corridor is the tiny Transatlantic Telephone Room, where the prime minister could telephone President Roosevelt at the White House on a "hotline," fitted with one of the earliest scrambler devices (not visible). An emergency candle stands on the table beside the tin Churchill used for his cigar butts. On the wall, a large clock has an extra hour hand indicating Washington, DC, time.

Also on view are a series of makeshift bedrooms and offices outfitted with old-fashioned typewriters and duplicating machines. Around the walls of the Map Room hang the maps used during the final stages of the war, including one on which the movement of warships and convoys was plotted.

Churchill's own small bedroom is particularly interesting to see, though against all advice, he rarely stayed here; he hated to be confined underground, even at the height of the bombing. Its narrow bed is covered with a faded blue quilt. A map on the wall shows the location of Britain's airports, vulnerable beaches, barrage-balloon sites, and torpedo defenses. Also in the room is the large brown desk from which he made many of his famous radio broadcasts. Looking at it, one can almost hear his famous voice defiantly declaring, "We shall not flag or fail whatever the cost may be."

**INNS OF COURT:** Today, Charles Dickens would find little changed at Gray's Inn or at Lincoln's Inn, where he worked as an office boy. Not inns in the usual sense, they are places where barristers are trained and have their offices. Though close to the busy thoroughfare of High Holborn and the Royal Courts of Justice in the Strand, the inns are quiet, peaceful places. Their courtyards and gardens are lined with elegant town-houses, a dining hall, a library, and a chapel. Dark-suited lawyers — men and women, young and old — stride purposefully to and from their offices clutching files of documents. Look through the windows: Every desk seems to be covered with piles of papers and books, and occasionally — a sign of the times — a word processor.

Strolling around, you notice ornate old lampposts, rows of tall chimneys, and perhaps a faded notice stating, "The servants of the Inn have orders to remove all hawkers, disorderly people and those causing a nuisance." Quaintest of all are the carefully hand-painted lists of names beside each doorway. Everyone's title is included, usually a simple Mr. or Miss, but sometimes you can spot a Professor, Judge, or Honorable.

Except for the chapels, with their old wooden pews and colorful stained glass windows, the Inns are working places, and the buildings are not open to the public. Be sure to visit *Windy & Son,* the tiny legal bookshop at the Carey Street entrance to Lincoln's Inn. Almost the only change since it first opened in 1830 seems to be that "oil" has been added to the traditional subjects such as "matrimonial," "contract," and "libel" marked on its densely packed shelves.

**POETS' CORNER:** Shakespeare stands with his arm resting on a stack of books on one side of Poets' Corner in Westminster Abbey. Around him are the graves and memorials of most of Britain's great poets, as well as some writers and musicians. Though the Bard is buried at Stratford-upon-Avon, Chaucer, Dickens, and Handel are among those whose actual graves are here. Despite its name, the area is not a "corner" at all. Instead, it fills the lofty transept on the south side of the nave, alongside the spot where Britain's kings and queens are crowned. Also gracing the area are two beautiful 13th-century wall paintings, which were uncovered in 1936.

High overhead loom the ornate stone arches of the abbey's walls and ceiling, with their magnificent stained glass windows. But upon further inspection, it is the famous names on the inscriptions that catch the eye. Dr. Johnson, Wordsworth, the Brontë sisters, D. H. Lawrence, Lewis Carroll, Edward Lear, John Masefield, and Dylan Thomas — to name a few. Some are commemorated by statues, but most by memorial tablets on the walls or massive inscribed flagstones set in the floor.

It is a particularly special place to be — surrounded by the great names and the memory of all the famous writings born from them — when one of the abbey staff hourly calls for silence throughout the great church and requests that everyone stand still for a moment of private prayer. "Let the peace of Westminster Abbey speak to you," he says.

**REMEMBRANCE SUNDAY:** No city in the world can equal London in its penchant for pomp and circumstance, its great national ceremonies with centuries-old tradition of pageantry and soul-stirring music. Each year in November, the queen leads Britain in paying homage to its war dead in a solemn ceremony (comparable to *Memorial Day* in the US) that takes place at the Cenotaph on Whitehall at 11 AM on the nearest Sunday to the 11th, the anniversary of the end of World War I. Dressed in black, and surrounded by her family and the nation's top political and military leaders, the queen lays a wreath of red Flanders poppies on the Cenotaph, the tall white column that is Britain's national war memorial. Beforehand, military bands play traditional songs, and then, as Big Ben chimes 11 o'clock in nearby Parliament Square, 2 minutes of silence are observed, followed by a short religious service. Though the area immediately around the Cenotaph is filled with officials and service detachments, everyone can get a good view of the long march that follows.

The parade begins with groups of current military personnel, followed by representatives of uniformed organizations — such as the police force and London's busmen — commemorating the fact that they kept their services running even at the height of the blitz. Last comes a seemingly endless column of civilian men and women — often with medals on their chests — "old comrades" marching proudly by to pay tribute to their fallen friends. Most poignant of all are the blind and the handicapped in wheelchairs, each turning his or her head upon passing the Cenotaph, many laying wreaths, covering the steps in a sea of red — "every leaf a life."

Around the same time each year, London also celebrates the *State Opening of Parliament,* when the queen rides in state in a procession of ancient gilded coaches from Buckingham Palace to the Palace of Westminster. There the House of Lords and the Members of Parliament assemble to hear her read a speech written by the government outlining its plans for the forthcoming session. Her route takes her down the Mall, across Horse Guards Parade, and into Whitehall, providing plenty of photo ops.

**THE PROMS:** During the annual *Henry Wood Promenade Concerts* at the *Royal Albert Hall,* a night at "the *Proms"* is a must for any music lover. The concerts take place daily (except some Sundays) from mid-July to mid-September. Most of the seats for popular programs are sold out well in advance, but inexpensive standing-room tickets — a *Proms* specialty — are always available on the day of performance. These enable the "promenaders" to wander freely through the hall's circular ground floor — just in front of the orchestra platform — from which all the seats are removed, just to accommodate them. It is a festive event, where many young college and music students can be found enjoying the inexpensive standing-room tickets ($2 to $3), while the older, more sedate crowd enjoys the music from the plush red chairs in the surrounding two tiers of ornate curtained boxes and the balcony. (The *Royal Albert* accommodates about 8,000 people.)

Promenaders manage to stand remarkably still, as if spellbound, while each piece is played. A traditional part of the final "Last Night" (for which tickets are in such demand that there has to be a lottery), however, is to link arms and sway to such well-known, quintessentially British tunes as "Land of Hope and Glory" and "Jerusalem." Participants dress up in fancy hats and flowers, while Union Jacks, banners, and balloons wave amidst the crowd and everyone joins in the singing. Much cheering, clapping, and loud calls for encores accompany the festivities. The huge organ at the end of the rotunda seems to preside over all the activities.

The famous conductor Henry Wood started the *Proms* in 1912, in hopes of bringing classical music to a broader audience. Now they are run by the BBC, whose *Symphony Orchestra* performs at many of the concerts, joined by an impressive roster of internationally known orchestras and soloists. Most evenings, expect to hear a mixture of musical styles, from baroque to contemporary — sometimes including a premier performance.

**CHRISTMAS SHOPPING AND JANUARY SALES:** Like the Grand Bazaar of Istanbul, the souks of Marrakesh, and the Agora of ancient Athens, the crowded sidewalks of Oxford, Regent, and Bond Streets—and the Brompton Road—provide one of the world's great shopping experiences. They fuse into a shopping mall of fame and frenzy, offering the finest names in everything and an unsurpassed array of specialized retailers of tobaccos and tweeds, silver and salmon, Scottish wool and Irish linen. Try *Liberty* for the perfect paisley to cover your bed, *Hamleys* for a battery-operated model of a 1940s Rolls-Royce, *Fortnum & Mason* for truffled liver pâté, and *Selfridges* for just about anything else. If you can't live without something nobody else could have, tour the galleries and gilded boutiques of Bond Street, and stop in at that ultimate purveyor of the unique—*Sotheby's* auction house. To make the best of *Harrods'* month-long January sale, you'll have to bundle up, join the queue of local housewives and visiting sheiks, and wait for hours for the doors to open on the sale's first day, the first Wednesday in January. But if you sleep through dawn or foolishly stop for breakfast, you'll still find plenty of bargains on everything from china to Chippendale.

**LAWN TENNIS CHAMPIONSHIP, Wimbledon:** *Wimbledon* is to sports what *Claridges* hotel is to shelter, the most elegant possible fulfillment of a basic human need. The Duke of Kent presides, and total silence reigns as rows of eyes follow the to-and-fro of the little yellow ball. Connoisseurs savor strawberries between serves, and appraise each measured swing. The ballboys and girls move in a fluid dash, scoop, toss, and kneel, and the players, all still dressed in crisp white, scuff, scurry, charge, and leap across the green velvet of lovingly rolled, mowed, and watered grass. To win this tournament, players must be at home with the slick turf and the quick bounce of the ball that can surprise even a master accustomed to gritty clay. Each year's final handshake across the net evokes ghosts of *Wimbledon's* past—Pat Cash vaulting into the grandstand to kiss his family before accepting the cup, a teenage Bjorn Borg surrendering himself to joy after an icy victory, Martina Navratilova raising her record ninth *Wimbledon* trophy above her head, the flawless and freckled Rod Laver, Big Bill Tilden, Helen Wills Moody. . . .

**AFTERNOON TEA AND AN EVENING AT THE THEATER:** One cannot live by bread alone, so at a full-scale cream tea at the *Savoy* hotel, you may have to eat cake—as well as buttered scones and crumpets, finger sandwiches with watercress, cucumber, and egg salad, clotted cream, strawberry jam, and the ubiquitous English "cuppa." It is symptomatic of the effort to Anglicize the exotic that, just as the British brought sheep to Australia and cricket to India, so, too, did an infusion made from the dried leaves of an East Asian shrub become England's national beverage. Five o'clock tea is England at its Englishest, with courteous gossip, starched white aprons, and polite but firm exclusion of the rain and mist outside. From the trellised summer Art Deco decor and domed gazebo of the *Savoy's* Thames Foyer, step quickly through the dark London winter to the warm plushness of a West End theater—the glow of chandeliers, and the dazzle of the hottest ticket in town. Here, in the *Theatre Royal* in the Haymarket, or the *Drury Lane,* or the farther-flung *Royal National Theatre,* is kept the flame of the English-speaking stage, a light passed down from Shakespeare to the *Royal Shakespeare Company,* connecting the reign of Elizabeth I with that of Elizabeth II.

# London's Grand Hotels

Like the great transatlantic liners that were once the centerpiece of European travel, the great hotels of London seem destined to disappear, to be gradually replaced by more practical concrete palaces. And when the world has finally been transformed into one gigantic *Holiday Inn,* we will look back longingly on the grand hotels' shimmering chandeliers, their lordly tail-coated concierges, the neat rows of shoes in their corridors awaiting morning massages. Already, these hotels belong more to the past than the present — still extant only by some strange quirk of fate. So enjoy them while you can, these gracious temples of excess, and damn the expense — which is usually monstrous. But don't think of it as just the cost of a hot bath, a night's sleep, and a morning's coffee. When you start your day with a turn through those historic revolving doors, you somehow see the whole of the surrounding city from a different, far more glittering perspective.

Some notes on getting the most from your stay: Remember that, as a rule, the more princely a hotel, the more regal the surcharges applied to telephone calls (300% is not unheard of) — so call collect when you can, use a phone credit card, or telephone from the nearest post office. You can dine out on the difference. Consider, moreover, the story of the irascible New Yorker, a guest at one of London's most fabulous hostelries, who refused to pay the automatic 18% service charge because he said he hadn't had any service. And he won.

Here are some of the London's finest dormitories, on whose crested stationery there will be a good deal to write home about.

**BLAKE'S:** Popular with visiting Hollywood royalty, this 52-room complex of Victorian townhouses offers charming accommodations in an Old World setting: Many of the rooms are decorated in shades of gray, with antique furniture, rich wood floors, four-poster beds, and marble baths. Also offered here is some of the most attentive service in town — as befits modern moguls. It also boasts one of the city's first-rate restaurants. Information: *Blakes,* 33 Roland Gardens, London SW7 3PF, England (phone: 71-370-6701; fax: 71-373-0442; telex: 813500).

**CAPITAL:** In addition to having the very best pillows in Elizabeth's England, this intimate hostelry, just steps from *Harrods* in bustling Knightsbridge, has cozy rooms with Ralph Laurenish decor, a wonderful wood-paneled bar, and is the site of one of the finest dining places in London (see *London's Best Restaurants*). Don't be put off by its ultramodern exterior, a design-in-haste from the 1970s; once inside, you'll find everything according to British tradition, taste, and tact. And for travelers who keep score on such matters, it's one of only two hostelries in London that is a member of the prestigious Relais & Châteaux group. Information: *Capital,* 22 Basil St., London SW3 1AT, England (phone: 71-589-5171, 800-926-3199 in the US; fax: 71-225-0011; telex: 91904).

**CLARIDGE'S:** With India and Australia gone, here is the final bastion of the British Empire. Despite its sober red brick façade, its supreme, traditional elegance is as much a part of the London experience as the Horse Guards and the Crown Jewels. When visiting royalty is in residence here — which is often — the flags of their countries are flown outside, beside the Union Jack. The concierge, however, accords the same personalized attention to kings and commoners alike: Regulars will find their favorite soap and shampoo — even their pillow preference — waiting in their rooms. If it's winter, try for one of the suites with a working fireplace. Information: *Claridge's,* Brook St., London W1A 2JQ, England (phone: 71-629-8860; fax: 71-499-2210; telex: 21872).

**CONNAUGHT:** Another stronghold of 19th-century Britain, luxurious and intimate, that soon will have you feeling like a distinguished guest at Lord Hyphen's townhouse. Most impressive are those small details that set this place apart from the ordinary — like tea served in a private lounge reserved only for guests, and the white linen mats laid out every night at your bedside (heaven forbid that you should have to step down onto a carpet, or worse yet, a wood floor!). Small — with a tenaciously faithful clientele — it sometimes seems to be booked several generations in advance. Don't be put off by the hauteur; they've earned it. There's a restaurant on the premises, but it's the *Connaught's* excellent *Grill* that has earned a Michelin star (see *London's Best Restau-*

*rants*). Information: *The Connaught,* Carlos Pl., Mayfair, London W1Y 6AL, England (phone: 71-499-7070; fax: 71-495-3262).

**DORCHESTER:** The grande dame of London hostelries is better and more elegant than ever following a 2-year-long refurbishment. All 252 rooms and 55 suites have beautiful bed linen and superbly designed bathrooms with Italian marble. Best of all, the service is fit for a king. Treat yourself to tea in the pink marble *Promenade* and dinner in the *Grill* and *Terrace* restaurants. The brand-new *Oriental* restaurant specializes in authentic Cantonese food, and there is an exclusive basement nightspot — the *Dorchester Club,* which requires membership 48 hours in advance. The *Dorchester Spa,* managed by Elizabeth Arden, is a luxurious health club where guests can unwind; also offered here are several beneficial treatments such as Sea Therapy, Seaweed Body Wrap, aromatherapy, reflexology, facials, and body massages — ah, the indulgence of it all. Information: *Dorchester,* Park La., London W1Y 3DH, England (phone: 71-629-8888; fax: 71-409-0114; telex: 887704).

**DUKES:** Set in a cul-de-sac in the heart of St. James's, this small (38-room and 26-suite) Victorian enclave (it's two buildings joined together), with its geranium-filled window boxes, offers all the comforts of home, but with all the attentive service one leaves home for. More like flats than hotel suites, accommodations have separate dining areas (room service here is an elegant affair, with the ghost of "Upstairs Downstairs" hovering nearby); some also have kitchenettes. There's a charming lounge for tea time, and a restaurant. Home was never like this. Information: *Dukes,* 35 St. James's Pl., London SW1A 1NY, England (phone: 71-491-4840; fax: 71-493-1264; telex: 28283).

**FORTY-SEVEN PARK STREET:** This suites-only establishment just off Grosvener Square is more like a private apartment dwelling than a hotel; even the lobby is more like one you'd expect to find in an elegant home. Popular among diplomats and well-heeled travelers planning on a longish stay, each "flat" is individually — and beautifully — decorated. And the best part of this homey-elegant ambience is the staff: Aside from handling everything from procuring tickets to sold-out shows or seats at "booked" restaurants, they'll stock your kitchen for you. If you don't feel like cooking, room service is available from none other than three-Michelin-star *Le Gavroche* (see *London's Best Restaurants*) in the adjoining building! Information: *Forty-Seven Park Street,* London W1Y 4EB, England (phone: 71-491-7282; fax: 71-491-7281; telex: 22116).

**RITZ:** The fellow who was heard to mutter snootily, "Nobody stays at the *Ritz* anymore," was off-base. Recent renovations have restored it to much of its former glory; Monsieur Ritz himself would be proud to know that this remains one of London's most elegant hostelries. The guestrooms and the decor are splendid and the service impeccable. Tea here is as vital a British ritual as the coronation. Try to have cocktails on the terrace — if the sun comes out. Information: *The Ritz,* Piccadilly, London W1V 9DG, England (phone: 71-493-8181; fax: 71-493-2687; telex: 257200).

**SAVOY:** This hostelry is to theater what the *Sacher* in Vienna is to music. On The Strand, and very near *Covent Garden* and Waterloo Bridge, this grande dame (she turned 100 in 1989) remains one of *the* places to stay in London; its lobby is often a *Who's Who* of the international entertainment world. The atmosphere is gently Edwardian, but the management is contemporary — and adept at catering to the demands of plutocrats from every part of the planet. The refurbished Thames Suites are London's most beautiful digs. The showerheads alone are worth the price of admission. In addition, there's a private salon where guests can have tea; the *River* restaurant, which offers a splendid view of the Thames and the Houses of Parliament; and the legendary *Savoy Grill,* an ideal spot to rub elbows with theater and movie stars at after-theater dinner. Information: *Savoy,* The Strand, London WC2R 0EU, England (phone: 71-836-4343 or 71-836-3719; fax: 71-872-8894; telex: 24234).

# London's Best Restaurants

 The image most Americans have of British food is that of a massive roasted haunch of beef, surrounded by plainly prepared (and often overcooked) vegetables, mashed potatoes, and a little gravy. No elaborate sauces or sharp flavors. Unfortunately, cost has driven the roast beef of old England into decline, but you still can sample its splendor in "carvery" rooms in major London hotels, where huge joints of beef, pork, and lamb are featured. Many "medieval banquet" restaurants also serve meals styled to resemble feasts of the past — from the 16th century to Victorian times. These, however, aim more for drama than for authenticity, and the visitor must go elsewhere for genuine "Olde English" dishes. In an effort to promote traditional foods and recipes, the British Tourist Authority created the "Taste of England, Scotland, and Wales" distinction. You'll see this noted on many menus, and tourist board booklets list the establishments that serve traditional fare.

It also should be noted that it is very possible to enjoy what can be fairly termed nouvelle English cooking: more imaginative and certainly lighter fare. A sprinkling of Michelin stars even can be found in London, and the variety of ethnic choices ranges from first-rate continental cooking to the more exotic flavors of fine Indian and Thai dishes.

Regardless of your craving — be it a banquet fit for a king (or queen) served by white-gloved waiters, fish and chips wrapped in newspaper, or even a pizza — there's no reason to go hungry here. Below, a few of our favorite places; we feel they represent the true spirit of the city — and serve up some pretty fine fare as well.

**CAPITAL:** Serving the best pâté this side of the English Channel, this hotel dining room specializes in gracious service and fine French fare. For an appetizer, try the scallop and lobster emince with ginger and tarragon sauce. Entrées include filet of brill in watercress sauce, duck with foie gras, and roast lamb with herb and tarragon sauce. Even if you aren't staying at the hotel, try to make this one of your London dinner stops. We guarantee you won't regret it. Information: *Capital Hotel Restaurant,* 22-24 Basil St., London SW3 1AT, England (phone: 71-589-5171).

**CONNAUGHT GRILL:** With one Michelin star, the *Grill* is every bit as well mannered as you'd expect of a place so thoroughly steeped in British tradition. The best dishes on the menu are those on which the empire was founded: roast beef and Yorkshire pudding, Lancashire hot pot, gooseberry pie. After dinner, you will feel as if the gentlemen should retire to the library with a glass of port and a cigar; many still do. Closed weekends and holidays. Information: *Connaught Hotel,* Carlos Pl., London W1Y 6AL, England (phone: 71-499-7070).

**DUMPLING INN:** Located in the heart of Soho's Chinatown, this not-so-grand eatery lacks both gracious service and elegant atmosphere. What it does have — and what makes it worth your while — are dumplings. Terrific little triangles stuffed with almost anything you can imagine are steaming hot — and irresistible. A dozen or so of these tasty tidbits — steamed or fried — will keep body and soul content through any rainy (or sun-filled) London day. And if you're warding off a slight chill, try the hot and sour soup. Information: *Dumpling Inn,* 15A Gerrard St., London W1V 7LA, England (phone: 71-437-2567).

**LE GAVROCHE:** After over 70 years of rating restaurants, the *Guide Michelin* gave its first three-star rating in Britain to this most French of restaurants. It is owned and run by Albert Roux, a former chef for the Rothschild family and once the chef in the royal household. The wine card is exceptionally long and inviting (listing over 400 items, including a 1945 Château Lafite-Rothschild for about $1,000, though many modest vintages are available for less than $25). Closed weekends, and late December to early January. Information: *Le Gavroche,* 43 Upper Brook St., London W1Y 1PF, England (phone: 71-408-0881).

**GREIG'S GRILL:** Superlative steak — and plenty of it — is the order of the day at this rather plain place, formerly the *Guinea Grill* (the owner of the original *Guinea Grill* — which still exists several doors away — is its headwaiter, and most of the staff left and moved down the street and assumed its present identity). The menu is "in the raw." Diners get to choose their meal from a display of raw Scottish beef (you've never tasted anything this good) or lamb chops, or smoked salmon, plus an array of artichokes (always) and asparagus (in season), and you can order what just may be the world's biggest and best baked potato. Open late, this is a good place for an after-theater feast. Save room for the Turkish Delight, brought to the table after dinner. Closed Sundays. Information: *Greig's Grill,* 26 Bruton Pl., London W1X 7AA, England (phone: 71-629-5613).

**WATERSIDE INN, Bray-on-Thames, Berkshire:** Three Michelin stars are still rare in England. Yet this establishment's claim to being one of the only two honorees is just part of the reason to make a detour to the village of Bray, not far from Windsor Castle and 27 miles west of London. Michel Roux (a French chef with embassy experience and service for the best private families before he opened London's renowned *Le Gavroche* with his brother Albert) chose to open his Thameside country restaurant in a setting that provides a feast for the eyes before the feast for the palate begins. In spring, enormous red tulips are in bloom all around, flowering cherry trees line the river, and swans circle past as though summoned by a magic wand. In summer, aperitifs are served on the terrace and in two delightful summer houses, and the sight of weeping willows and boats on the water may distract a diner — momentarily — from the extraordinary menu. Monsieur Roux is ceaselessly inventive. Among his enduring specialties are *tronçonnettes de homard* (chunks of lobster in a white port wine sauce); warm oysters served in a puff pastry case, garnished with bean sprouts, raspberry vinegar butter sauce, and fresh raspberries; a medium-rare roast duckling pierced with cloves and served with a honey-flavored sauce; and a Grand Marnier–infused soufflé laid atop orange sauce and garnished with orange segments. The wine list, which counts no fewer than 400 bin numbers, is first-rate, and some of the restaurant's personal touches are charming — for example, *foie gras tartelettes, gravlax* salmon, and haddock quiche served with cocktails. The cost of all this is "rather dear," as the British would say, but less than its equivalent in Paris and well worth it for a memorable occasion. Closed Mondays, Tuesday lunch, Sunday dinner from October through *Easter,* and for 7 weeks starting December 26. A private dining room, serving eight people, can be hired. No guestrooms. Details: *Waterside Inn,* Ferry Rd., Bray-on-Thames, Berkshire SL6 2AT, England (phone: 628-20691).

**WHEELER'S:** Whether you climb the narrow stairs to any one if its 3 floors of dining rooms for some of the most inventively prepared Dover sole or Scotch salmon served anywhere in the British isles, or opt to perch at the bar on the ground floor where they shuck oysters to order, this is one of the best places for seafood in all of London. Unpretentious — it's located in a narrow, old-fashioned building in an alley off Duke Street — it has a comfortable, easygoing atmosphere not found in those oh-so-elegant white-glove establishments. Manager John Nalty just *loves* Americans. Closed Sundays. Information: *Wheeler's,* Duke of York St., London SW1, England (phone: 71-930-2460).

# Afternoon Tea

 That great British institution, afternoon tea, had been given up for lost a few years ago. The cost of the ingredients and the extensive labor required had soared just as weight watchers began to question the healthfulness of the scones and pastries habit that their parents and grandparents had always taken for granted. But like another great British favorite, fish and chips, which for a brief moment was also put down as a thing of the past, afternoon tea has survived and has actually enjoyed a resurgence in popularity. Lots of harried Londoners have given up the rat race, moved to the country, and converted barns and old cottages into quainter-than-quaint tea shops where you can get the kinds of set afternoon teas of which dreams are made — those wonderful teas whose passing was so vigorously lamented until just recently.

The reasons for this revival are hard to gauge, but simple economy may be among them. As the prices of full meals climb, tea becomes increasingly attractive to most vacationers, who know that they can get by on nothing more than a full breakfast in their hotel and a relatively inexpensive tea in some country café. Nostalgia, in the form of a stubborn refusal to abandon tradition even in the face of stern realities, may also figure. As an afternoon meal, tea was first served in the late 18th century by the Duchess of Bedford to entertain her guests between the early lunches and late dinners at her house parties. It soon became an integral part of everyday life. A whole industry grew up around the manufacture of teacups and saucers, cake stands, tea forks for the cakes, silver teapots, sugar bowls and tiny silver tongs, linens, and the like. In Victorian days, less aristocratic families developed elaborate teatime rituals around the new meal; at a time when Britons seemingly lived to eat rather than the other way around, it was quite natural to nosh away the otherwise gustatorily empty late-afternoon hours. "Everything stops for tea" became a popular English saying, and the World War I poet Rupert Brooke wrote about it, referring to a tea garden at Grantchester, near Cambridge. (That tea garden still exists, after all these years, in a sun-dappled meadow close to where the undergraduates leave their punts.)

Beginning around the turn of the century, when Miss Cranston established the nation's first tearoom in Sauchiehall Street, Glasgow, running tea gardens and tea shops was considered a respectable occupation for spinsters, and the foods served at tea today still reflect their genteel touch. Honey and country preserves, particularly strawberry jam, show up on the tea tables, along with biscuit-like scones. In Devon and Cornwall, thick clotted cream — too stiff for pouring — invariably accompanies the cakes; strawberry teas, a summertime specialty, include a bowl of the luscious red fruit. Visitors to country districts, especially in the midlands and the north of England, will often encounter "farm teas," repasts that include enough salad, ham, fish, and other fairly substantial edibles to allow them to skip the evening meal and still not go to bed with a rumbling stomach.

As served in its most elaborate form at some London hotels, afternoon tea may take a couple of hours to come to the end of the procession of comestibles — thin sandwiches filled with cucumbers, watercress, or smoked salmon; warm scones with cream and preserves; and delicate pastries, not to mention the good selections of fine China and India brews. A round of the best London teas would take in the following:

*Brown's,* 19-24 Dover St., W1 (phone: 71-493-6020).
*Daquise,* 20 Thurloe St., SW7 (phone: 71-589-6117).
*Dorchester,* Park La., W1 (phone: 71-629-8888).
*Dukes,* 35 St. James's Pl., SW1 (phone: 71-491-4840).
*Grosvenor House,* 86-90 Park La., W1 (phone: 71-499-6363).

*Hyde Park,* 66 Knightsbridge, SW1 (phone: 71-235-2000).
*Joe's Café,* 126 Draycott Ave., SW3 (phone: 71-225-2217).
*Maison Bertaux,* 28 Greek St., W1 (phone: 71-437-6007).
*Meridien,* Piccadilly, W1 (phone: 71-734-8000).
*Mountbatten,* Monmouth St., WC2 (phone: 71-836-4300).
*Pâtisserie Valerie,* 44 Old Compton St., W1 (phone: 71-437-3466).
*Ritz,* Piccadilly, W1 (phone: 71-493-8181).
*Savoy,* The Strand, WC2 (phone: 71-836-4343).
*Stafford,* 16 St. James's Pl., SW1 (phone: 71-493-0111).
*Waldorf,* Aldwych, WC2 (phone: 71-836-2400).

For those who prefer taking tea at home, *Home Hosting (GB)* offers travelers the opportunity to enjoy the experience of an English cream tea with a London family at their home. For more information, contact *Home Hosting (GB),* 754 The Square, Cattistock, Dorchester, Dorset DT2 OJD, England (phone: 300-20671; fax: 300-21042).

# Pub Crawling

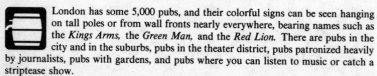

London has some 5,000 pubs, and their colorful signs can be seen hanging on tall poles or from wall fronts nearly everywhere, bearing names such as the *Kings Arms,* the *Green Man,* and the *Red Lion.* There are pubs in the city and in the suburbs, pubs in the theater district, pubs patronized heavily by journalists, pubs with gardens, and pubs where you can listen to music or catch a striptease show.

Yet only a fraction of them have the kind of decor and atmosphere that measure up to most Americans' idea of what British pubs are like. Some do have dark paneling, a long mahogany bar, and an abundance of engraved glass mirrors and gleaming brass fittings, but they're the exception rather than the rule.

Though some of the worst abuses of the recent past — the superabundance of Formica and other plastics, loud jukeboxes, and the battery of electronic games that bleep and squeal above the noises of good cheer encouraged by a draft from the pressurized aluminum keg — have begun to disappear in pubs in London, the garden-variety British pub generally reflects many of the more obnoxious intrusions of 20th-century civilization.

Paradoxically, it doesn't seem to matter. Just as an American neighborhood tavern can be entertaining even when the floor is ugly green tile, the bar stools covered with plastic, and the lighting murky, the pub is a center of social life here. It also is becoming a focus of culinary activity — a decided change over earlier years, when "pub grub" meant a sandwich, a mashed potato–topped ground meat concoction known as cottage pie, or a ploughman's lunch consisting of a hunk of bread and cheese, plus a pickle. Nowadays, with the burgeoning interest in good food and the proliferation of wine bars, many pubs are setting aside rooms especially for more ambitious sit-down meals, including meats, unusual salads, and homemade desserts.

Before setting off on that most convivial of pleasures, the pub crawl, there are a number of facts a visitor should keep in mind:

*Pub crowds vary.* London pubs usually attract a mixed crowd. At lunchtime, pubs are invariably filled with people from nearby offices and workplaces. In the evenings they're usually emptier and, apart from those in the West End theater district, mostly filled with locals.

*Pub hours have changed.* Following a relaxation in licensing a year or two back, most pubs are now open from 11 AM to 11 PM Mondays through Saturdays, noon to 3 PM and 7 to 10 PM on Sundays.

*Beer is not the name of the brew.* The sheer variety of drafts can perplex newcomers. Londoners talk of lagers and of ales and of their subtypes, rather than "beer." Lager is made from a yeast that sinks to the bottom of the brewing tank during fermentation (rather than rising to the top like the yeast used in traditional ales). It also is activated at a lower temperature, so the product stays clear instead of turning cloudy when cooled. Typically, lagers are also lighter in color and body, fizzier, drier, and taste more of malt than of hops. But there are exceptions, because many lagers are made to taste like ales and vice versa.

*Ales fall into several distinct categories.* Bitter, usually served on draft, has a good, strong, brown color, a frothy head, and a taste that tends to be sharp or earthy (owing to a large proportion of hops in the brew). The terms "special" and "best," applied to bitters, refer not to quality but to strength. So-called pale and light ales are the bottled versions of bitter; pale is likely to be the stronger. Mild ale, yet a different brew, is made from a recipe that calls for more sugar and less hops. Served on draft, it is usually sweeter and dark brown to black. Brown ale is like a bottled version of mild. Stouts — brews made from well-roasted, unmalted barley — are all very dark and sometimes sweet; Guinness, Ireland's most famous drink, is thick and rich like all stout, but not at all sweet.

At one time, pubs in London served only keg beers, which have been filtered and pasteurized at the brewery and packed under pressure. But because of the "real ale" movement of the past few years, most pubs now also serve brews that are still fermenting when they are delivered. Unlike keg beers, real ales require careful handling, but the taste warrants the effort.

The best guide to pubs is the *Good Beer Guide,* published under the aegis of the active Campaign for Real Ale (CAMRA) and available for £5.95 (about $9.80) from its offices at 34 Alma Rd., St. Albans, Hertfordshire AL1 3BW, England (published in the US under the title *The Best Pubs of Great Britain,* by Globe Pequot Press, Old Chester Rd., Chester, CT 06412; $12.95). This guide lists over 5,000 pubs that serve the better brews. The annually revised *Good Pub Guide,* published by Consumers' Association and Hodder & Stoughton (£9.95/about $16.40), also is recommended.

The following selection, which includes some of the very best, most unusual, and most atmospheric pubs, describes the variety of places travelers to London will turn up when they prowl into its various neighborhoods.

**ALBERT:** Prince Albert stands holding a flower on the sign outside this smart but genuine Victorian pub, which has gaslamps and wrought-iron balconies on its mellow brick façade. Originally one of the street's most distinguished buildings, it now looks rather small and fragile compared with the towering modern office blocks that have replaced the rows of small shops once surrounding it. Inside, the walls are decorated with Victorian prints. Office workers crowd in on weekdays at lunchtime, particularly for the interesting range of bar snacks. There is a small, excellent-value carvery upstairs that's popular with politicians, who are only minutes away from the Houses of Parliament. The stairs leading to the carvery are lined with photographs of Britain's prime ministers dating back to the last century, along with a large portrait of Queen Victoria. The restaurant also offers superb breakfasts, notably a feast called Full English, of which porridge, kippers, and kidneys are only a part. Victoria Street, SW1 (phone: 71-222-5577).

**AUDLEY:** In London's higher-rent Mayfair district, this large establishment sits on the corner of South Audley and Mount Streets, only a block from the American Embassy at Grosvenor Square. Its cleanliness makes it a major luncheon favorite, and sitting on one of the stools at the counter is a special treat. The 40-seat restaurant on the first floor serves traditional English fare. The large bar and cold carvery offer first class sandwiches and, for dessert, a fresh and feisty nugget of Stilton. The conversation varies substantially from room to room, and it's fun to move between the two very different groups of customers. The Victorian decor, with its garish ornamentation, provides a very pleasant environment. This is one of the places where you're most likely to run into a friendly accent from home. 41 Mount St., W1 (phone: 71-499-1843).

**DIRTY DICK'S:** When his fiancée was killed on the eve of their wedding day, the Dirty Dick in question, one Nathaniel Bentley, went into seclusion and lived out his life in isolation and ever-increasing squalor in the apartments that now make up the downstairs section of this pub at 202 Bishopsgate. The spiders and bats that used to swing from the walls and ceiling in the downstairs bar as reminders of the weird, Dickensian story have been relegated to a small museum area, and the place is a pleasant enough spot to begin an evening. The area above, rebuilt in 1745 and now more of a wine bar, lends itself to other functions. Galleried and spacious, with wood everywhere and sawdust on the floors, it's plain rather than plush (much like the East End surrounding it), and in its dark and clubby way, it is a supremely restful place to quench a thirst after a hectic Sunday morning's bargaining along nearby Petticoat Lane. 202 Bishopsgate, EC2 (phone: 71-283-5888).

**GRENADIER:** This is a very special stopping place in a most unlikely location. To get there, it's necessary to ignore a barrier and coachman, forbidding obstacles whose purpose actually is to keep cars, not pedestrians, out of this narrow, mews-style residential street just off Wilton Crescent, only a block from Belgrave Square. The military moniker derives from the time when this was the Officers' Mess for the Duke of Wellington's soldiers. The exterior is chauvinistically red, white, and blue, featuring a bright sentry box, and access from the north is via narrow Old Barracks Yard. Since it's an ideal place to stop for lunch after a trip to *Harrods* or a boutique browse up Brompton Road, the clientele is unceasingly posh. A tiny bar is at the front, with a rare pewter-topped counter. The two back rooms serve as an intimate candlelit restaurant. The place is reportedly haunted by a ghost who seems to make his presence known especially during September. The resident specter is purported to be a young officer who was caught cheating at cards and was ruthlessly beaten by his fellow officers. But he's apparently a relatively stable spirit and seldom disturbs drinkers or diners. 18 Wilton Row, SW1 (phone: 71-235-3074).

**YE OLDE CHESHIRE CHEESE:** The perfect place to stop and rest during a tour of the nearby Inns of Court, made familiar in those murky scenes on PBS's presentation of Dickens's *Bleak House*. This makes the nip down the narrow alley (beside 145 Fleet Street) to the pub door all the more evocative; it's easy to imagine the London of a century or so ago. Samuel Johnson lived around the corner, and his intimate circle — notably Boswell, Reynolds, and Gibbon — frequented "The Cheese." The character of the pub has remained remarkably intact despite its place on many tourist itineraries. The wooden stairs are narrow and the downstairs bar always several drinkers deep, but somehow the bumping and squeezing past are part of the fun. On a very cold winter's afternoon, a bowl of beef barley soup can be a special savior and the warmth of the roaring fire upstairs a consummate joy. Those interested in unusual beer brands should try a pint of Marston's Pedigree or a mug of Merrie Monk. 5 Little Essex St., EC4 (phone: 71-353-6170).

**SHERLOCK HOLMES:** Forget about Baker Street; this Northumberland Street pub, which Arthur Conan Doyle knew when it was called the *Northumberland Arms* hotel (and in which he set an early scene in his *Hound of the Baskervilles*), is the nearest most people will ever come to the great man. Drawings and photographs of actors playing Holmes and of scenes from Holmes works, and all manner of other Holmesiana, adorn the downstairs bar; upstairs, on the way to a first-floor restaurant, there's a replica of his Baker Street study, cleverly walled off by glass. The collection of memorabilia was assembled in 1951 by the Sherlock Holmes Society of London for the *Festival of Britain,* and this smart and congenial pub provides it with an excellent home. 10 Northumberland St., WC2 (phone: 71-930-2644).

**EL VINO:** A wine bar rather than a pub, this Fleet Street establishment deserves special mention as a bastion of City tradition. From its earliest years, for allegedly chivalrous reasons, women were not allowed to stand at the bar (a High Court action financed by the Equal Opportunities Commission has changed all that). Men must wear jacket and tie, and women must wear skirts or dresses (never trousers). The magnificently polished Victorian setting makes it almost impossible to imagine a more Dickensian scene. Fleet Street may no longer be the center of Britain's newspaper industry (since the various proprietors decided they could no longer afford its outdated practices and technology), but it is still a tony crowd of writers and barristers that savors the varied offerings of wine, both plain and fortified. 47 Fleet St., EC4 (phone: 71-353-6786).

**SPANIARDS INN, Hampstead:** Perfectly positioned on Spaniards Road between the east and west sides of Hampstead Heath, this establishment attracts Sunday walkers, visitors to nearby Kenwood House, wealthy local residents, and casual passersby. The building, with its large outdoor garden dotted with wooden tables and chairs, is quite pretty. The labyrinthine interior has low-ceilinged rooms paneled in oak and warmed by open fires. Bar food consists of unexceptional rolls, meat pies, and hot daily specials. Spaniards Rd., NW3 (phone: 81-455-3276).

# Shopping Spree

No matter where the dollar stands relative to the pound, the lure of shopping in Britain is irresistible, and the choice of where to go and what to buy is greatest in London. The range invariably wakens the dormant consumer in even the most monastic visitor. Sooner or later he finds himself walking around with a bulging carrier bag, rummaging feverishly through the sale scarves at *Liberty* on Regent Street, or shuffling past the bric-a-brac stalls on Portobello Road. Shopping has become such an institution among travelers here that the English word for it has found its way into the other European languages. Oxford Street on a Saturday is the West's most teeming bazaar.

Quality, durability, and what the natives are fond of calling "value for money" are the norm. And the best buys are still those articles in which craftsmanship counts: riding equipment, humidors, umbrellas, china, crystal, fireplace tongs, and other items essential to every well-equipped Victorian household. When it comes to clothing, there are many trendy designers in London today.

## WHERE TO SHOP

You can find good buys all over London, provided you know where to look.

**CHAIN STORES:** Some of the great British chain stores are as dedicated to quality as their Bond Street betters. For clothing, *Marks & Spencer* is a prime example of attractive prices and vast selection. The linen and sweaters, especially those in cashmere, lamb's wool, and Shetland wool, are among Britain's best buys. (But get there early before the aisles become impassable with the day's blizzard of buyers.) Also stop at *Boots* for cosmetics, pharmaceuticals, and sundries; *Sainsbury's* for food products; *Habitat* for designer items for the home; *W. H. Smith's* for newspapers, magazines, and stationery supplies; and *Mothercare* for children's clothes.

**POST-CHRISTMAS AND JULY SALES:** These British events have the stature of *Wimbledon* or a royal family christening. Travel agents are now packaging tours to the sales with the promise that participants' savings in discounts will cover the cost of the trip. The winter sale at *Harrods* that begins the first Wednesday in January is a ritual no devout shopper can afford to miss, and values can be breathtaking. Some stores stay open on *New Year's Day* to accommodate the throngs. But beware of smaller stores that stock their racks with cut-rate merchandise specially acquired for a sale event.

**DEPARTMENT STORES:** For department store shopping, there's no place like London. First, it's the home of *Harrods,* whose motto is *Omnia, Omnibus, Ubique* (Everyone, Everything, Everywhere). This giant among emporiums offers everything from pianos to straight pins. It has a butcher, a bank, a library, a kennel — and whatever it doesn't have, it will order. (There is a joke about a man who requested an elephant, only to be asked whether he preferred African or Indian.) The January and July sales are world-famous. Brompton Rd., Knightsbridge, SW1 (phone: 71-730-1234).

*Peter Jones,* where the King's Road meets Sloane Square, is a popular emporium that carries just about everything, from washing machines to children's Wellington boots. Sloane Square, SW1 (phone: 71-730-3434).

*Harvey Nichols & Co. Ltd.,* a stone's throw from *Harrods,* is a favorite among London's fashion-conscious women shoppers, but it also carries menswear. The basement has great "young" clothes and super sales, and there's a café on the third and ground floors. Knightsbridge, SW1 (phone: 71-235-5000).

*Selfridges* claims "all the needs of civilized life under one roof." The variety is somewhat smaller than at *Harrods,* but the prices generally are lower. The china and crystal department is extensive and the Miss Selfridge department particularly lively. 400 Oxford St., W1 (phone: 71-629-1234).

*Fortnum & Mason,* which was founded by a footman and a greengrocer from the 18th-century court of Queen Anne, makes high art of selling fashions, fragrances, fine tableware, clothing, and groceries. The royal coats of arms proudly displayed on the front of the building show how extensively the queen and her family shop here. Jams and preserves, tea, crocks of Stilton cheese — all sold on the ground floor by salesmen in swallowtail coats — are specialties. Their *St. James* restaurant is popular for lunch and traditional afternoon tea. 181 Piccadilly, W1 (phone: 71-734-8040).

**SPECIAL SHOPPING STREETS AND DISTRICTS:** Endowed with special character and verve, some streets invite shoppers to linger and browse. These areas may be brassy, quaint, or even supremely grand — whatever, these areas offer strollers a real spectacle made up partly of the stores, partly of fellow shoppers. Whether buying or just looking, everyone will find these streets worth a walk.

Beauchamp Place (pronounced *Beech*-um), a short walk from *Harrods,* off the Brompton Road, is a boutique-filled block known for designer clothes and jewelry, trendy shops and shoppers.

New Bond and Old Bond Streets, laid out by Sir Thomas Bond in 1686, would leave even an oil sheik yearning for more of the kinds of luxury items that are specialties at these places. The area was fashionable as early as the Regency days of Beau Brummel and friends; back then, there was an establishment that offered aspiring dandies lessons in tying cravats.

Regent Street, which runs parallel to Bond Street between Oxford and Piccadilly circuses, is as elegant as its shops' façades. It originally was planned as a grand processional between Regent's Park and the regent's palace, to divide Mayfair from Soho. *Liberty* and *Hamley's* are just two of its retail landmarks.

Crowded Oxford Street has department stores — *Selfridges, John Lewis* ("never knowingly undersold"), *Debenhams, D. H. Evans,* and *Marks & Spencer,* among others.

The pedestrian streets are special fun. Carnaby Street, which made its name in the

1960s, and Rupert Street are lively, though terribly tacky. South Molton Street, off Oxford Street, has become a fashion center. Chairs and umbrellas preside over much of the sidewalk in the summer.

*Covent Garden,* London's longtime vegetable market district, has undergone tremendous redevelopment, and the central market building, which stays open late, concentrates on wares from Britain. The whole area is crammed with trendy boutiques stocked with clothing for men and women, not to mention wine bars, restaurants, discos, and the like.

The *Burlington Arcade,* a charming covered Regency shopping promenade, is another must. It dates from the early 19th century and is crammed with shops piled elegantly with cashmeres, antiques, and other costly wares. Off Piccadilly near Old Bond St., W1. The *Princes* and *Piccadilly Arcades* on the other side of the street are shorter but similar.

## BEST BUYS

Britain may be one of the last holdouts against everything synthetic. Some of the products and shops are of superior quality, which puts them on the road to obsolescence, like the great ocean liners. So shoppers should yield to temptation and shop for the classics — the finest china, the softest cashmere, the sturdiest shoes — while they can still get them. London is a perfect — though sometimes pricey — place for indulgence.

**BOOKS:** Don't leave London without buying at least one book. Rare and secondhand volumes are available and well priced. Addicted browsers will have to be dragged out of the following haunts:

*Foyle's* is the largest general bookstore in London — it's enormous. 119 Charing Cross Rd., WC2 (phone: 71-437-5660).

*Henry Sotheran Ltd.,* which was founded in York in 1761 and moved to London in 1815, now incorporates *Cavendish Rare Books.* The large stock, handsomely shelved in 100-year-old bookcases, includes books on voyages and travel, Weinrab architectural books, finely bound literature, early English and continental titles, and volumes on maritime history, mountaineering, and polar exploration. A knowledgeable staff is on hand to offer guidance. 2 Sackville St., W1 (phone: 71-439-6151).

*Hatchard's,* narrow and utterly classic and founded in 1797, is London's oldest bookseller — and one of the most civilized. It currently stocks more than 150,000 titles on its 4 floors. It has several branches, but the main store is at 187 Piccadilly, W1 (phone: 71-439-9921).

*Robin Greer,* a member of the *Antiquarian Booksellers Association,* specializes in rare books, particularly illustrated children's books, including fairy tales and other tales of wonder. By appointment only. 30 Sloane Court W., SW1 (phone: 71-730-7392).

*Maggs Bros. Ltd.*'s welcoming staff will help you find your way through 5 floors of antiquarian books on travel, military and naval history, and 17th-century English literature. 50 Berkeley Sq., W1 (phone: 71-493-7160).

**CHINA:** The world's best pottery and porcelain has been produced in England since the 18th century, and many of the famous brands can be found in London.

*Thomas Goode and Company* occupies showrooms built in 1844, and the lavishly set tables that fill the 13 rooms evoke visions of pheasant, champagne, and brilliant conversation. All the most famous names in china and crystal can be found here under one imposing roof. It's London's best china and glass shop. 19 S. Audley St., W1 (phone: 71-499-2823).

The *Reject China Shops* offer slightly irregular brand-name china at such reduced prices that they're a bargain even when shipping charges are included. First-quality china, crystal, and gifts from Coalport, Aynsley, and Spode are also available at good prices. 134 Regent St., W1 (phone: 71-434-2502), 34 Beauchamp Pl., SW3 (phone: 71-581-0737), and 183 Brompton Rd., SW3 (phone: 71-581-0739).

**CHOCOLATE:** The English have long been famous for what's known as confectionery — creams, marzipan, truffles, fudge, and other irresistible sweets. A Mocha Baton, said to be Prince Philip's favorite, can be purchased at *Charbonnel et Walker* in London. This establishment, founded in 1875 and a Royal Warrant holder, "enrobes" its creations' interiors with dark chocolate (bittersweet plain) and white chocolate — nothing so humdrum as milk chocolate. The round white *boîtes blanches* (white boxes) traditionally hold gold-foil-covered chocolates emblazoned with letters and numbers; purchasers make a selection to spell out a message in a special circular box. 28 Old Bond St., W1 (phone: 71-491-0939).

*Prestat* is a center for the richest of truffles. Brandied cherries, milk and dark chocolate. 14 Princes Arcade, SW1 (phone: 71-629-4838).

*Rococo Chocolates* is London's most eccentric candy store. Offerings range from the serious (fresh cream truffles, pralines, and Swiss chocolates made in London) to the sublimely imaginative (for example, sugar engagement rings). A sugar chandelier hangs from the ceiling, and every summer a new artist makes candy creations. Tea served in summer by appointment only. 321 King's Rd., SW3 (phone: 71-352-5857).

**CRYSTAL AND GLASS:** The manufacture of crystal in England is centered in the west midlands; in Scotland, it's at Penicuik near Edinburgh. But outstanding items can be purchased in London.

*Thomas Goode and Company,* described above in the section on china, also sells the best crystal. 19 S. Audley St., W1 (phone: 71-499-2823).

*Lawley's* has a wide selection of well-known china and crystal including Wedgwood and Waterford Crystal. 154 Regent St., W1 (phone: 71-734-2621).

**CURIOSITY SHOPS:** London is a wonderful source for eccentric items that elsewhere might never even have been imagined.

*Anything Left-Handed* offers tools designed specifically for the left-handed person — can openers, over 30 types of scissors, potato peelers, special mugs, pens (including italic and calligraphic writing sets), knitting guides, corkscrews, bread knives, and boomerangs, among other items. 65 Beak St., W1 (phone: 71-437-3910).

*Naturally British* will make you feel as if you've traveled all over the country, even if you never leave London. Its stock includes dolls from Dorset, glass from the Lake District, woolen shirts from Wales, hand-knits from Scotland, and many wooden items such as rocking horses and traditional pub games. 13 New Row, *Covent Garden,* WC2 (phone: 71-240-0551).

**DESIGN:** The best of British craft and design is available at the following London shops:

The *Design Centre* offers exhibitions of British design and an extensive bookshop of architecture, graphics, and more. The young designers' center upstairs is particularly interesting. 28 Haymarket, SW1 (phone: 71-839-8000).

*Conran's,* in the magnificently restored Michelin Building on Fulham Road, displays designer furnishings upstairs; downstairs, everything from Oriental treasures to *Valentine's Day* cards are found. Stop in at the *Oyster Bar,* or book reservations at *Bibendum,* the popular restaurant upstairs. Michelin House, 81 Fulham Rd., SW3 (phone: 71-589-7401).

The *General Trading Company* has a profusion of serious items with a streak of colorful fun, including shower curtains, mugs, stationery, cookware — and, of course, the ubiquitous Filofax. 144 Sloane St., SW1 (phone: 71-730-0411).

**DESIGNER CLOTHING:** Britain offers the ultimate in things traditional — and the fantastic. And London is headquarters for all this, never more so than since a young royal named Diana took British fashion under her wing.

The client list at *Bellville Sassoon* reads like a chapter from *Debrett's,* and the Princess of Wales, who chose a saucy sailor dress for her first official picture with the queen, is a loyal customer. The specialty is glamorous evening wear in fabrics and prints specifically designed for the shop. 73 Pavilion Rd., SW1 (phone: 71-235-3087).

*Zandra Rhodes,* a fearlessly original designer, makes elaborate and intricate garments of hand-printed or hand-embroidered silk chiffon or organza with hand-pleating, ruffles, or other unusual details and extravagant shapes. The prices are even more extravagant. Beaded stoles, beaded sweatshirts, and stockings are also available. 14a Grafton St., W1 (phone: 71-499-3596).

Other London designer showrooms worth visiting are *Katharine Hamnett* (20 Sloane St., SW1; phone: 71-823-1002); *Jasper Conran* for women's fashion (303 Brompton Rd., SW3; phone: 71-823-9134) or men's fashions (2 Berners St., W1; phone: 71-637-9891); and *Nicole Fahri* (193 Sloane St., SW1; phone: 71-235-0877).

**FABRICS:** The yard goods available in London will bring out the seamstress in even the least handy traveler — from luscious woolens in the colors of an Irish landscape to fine lawn reminiscent of an English meadow in springtime. *Laura Ashley* (several stores, including 256 Regent St., W1; phone: 71-437-9760) has cloth steeped in the English country look.

In London, the name *Liberty* is synonymous with printed fabrics in cotton, wool, and silk. The scarves and ties are beautiful, and the store's façade — romantic and half-timbered — is equally appealing. 210 Regent St., W1 (also 340A King's Rd., SW3; phone: 71-734-1234).

**FOODSTUFFS AND LIQUOR:** Jams and marmalades, blended teas, Stilton cheese, shortbreads, and other edibles for sale throughout the city make wonderful souvenirs and presents.

At old-fashioned, wood-paneled *Ferns,* the carved mahogany shelves are crammed with teas, tea caddies, and more, and the drawers are packed with beans of all types. Since many of these are roasted on the premises, you can smell the coffee from several doors down. 27 Rathbone Pl., W1 (phone: 71-636-2237).

*Fortnum & Mason* is the British Empire's most elegant grocery store: The staff wear swallowtail morning coats, and the wine department is noteworthy for its breadth and for the rarity of its selections. 181 Piccadilly, W1 (phone: 71-734-8040).

*Harrods* is a must, if only for the experience. The gigantic Food Halls, reminiscent of a late-Victorian cathedral, will leave visitors salivating. From poultry to pâtés, plum pudding to pork (the pigs are raised to the store butchers' own standards), *Harrods* has it all. The wine selection, one of London's largest, ranges from the insignificant and inexpensive to the superb and very costly. There also are dozens of pure, single-malt, Scotch whiskies. Brompton Rd., Knightsbridge, SW1 (phone: 71-730-1234).

*Justin De Blank* sells excellent quality specialty foods, including whole-grain bread baked in century-old ovens on the premises and a wide array of English cheeses, among them Stilton and Shropshire blue. 42 Elizabeth St., SW1 (phone: 71-730-0605).

*Paxton and Whitfield,* a pungent paean to cheese housed in a little black-beamed 17th-century building, shows cheeses the way some shops display jewelry. There are cones and cubes large and small, pepper-covered logs of goat cheese, cakes with rinds of gray and tan, huge wheels of snowy brie, light-gold cheddar, peach-colored cheshires, deep gold derbies, and more — all of it superb. Established in 1797, the firm has held the Royal Warrant since 1973. 93 Jermyn St., SW1 (phone: 71-930-0250).

*Twinings* offers tea (as well as coffee) in bags, balls, and bulk. 216 Strand, WC2 (phone: 71-353-3511).

**GUNS:** London is the source for precision arms. At *Holland and Holland,* gunmaking is high art, and many of the customers choose their weapons with more care than they would choose a home. The curious will want to peek in, if only to inspect the binoculars, the folding earmuffs, and other appurtenances of hunting and shooting, and to see the England that used to be — and obviously still is for some. 33 Bruton St., W1 (phone: 71-499-4411).

*James Purdey and Sons,* Royal Warrant holders and distinguished gunmakers who have been in business for over a century, have served royalty. Prince Philip and Prince Charles are both supplied from these quiet and dignified premises. Many a sportsman dreams of owning one of the house's beautifully worked metal-and-walnut creations. 57 S. Audley St., W1 (phone: 71-499-1801).

*J. C. Field & Stream* features an immaculate and extensive stock of new, rare, and collectible firearms — from antique Purdeys to Holland & Holland and W. W. Greener models. 604 Fulham Rd., SW6 (phone: 71-736-0015).

**HATS:** The traditional cool, damp weather has led to the evolution of a number of distinctive kinds of headgear here. London is home to some of the finest makers.

*James Lock and Company,* an institution since 1686, is the royal purveyor. The company has fitted a crown for the queen's coronation — and they'll fit a visitor for his first bowler. Bankers, tycoons, politicians, actors, horse owners, and trainers have all been hatted here. 6 St. James's St., SW1 (phone: 71-930-5849).

Travelers who fancy a tweed cap or a black topper to protect against the London weather will want to stop at *Edward Bates,* founded by George Bates just after the turn of the century and still in the family. Presiding over the premises — in top hat — is Binks, a huge tabby cat who resided here from 1921 to 1926 and was preserved, after his demise, by a first class taxidermist. 21A Jermyn St., SW1 (phone: 71-734-2722).

The *Hat Shop* sells berets, cloches, deerstalkers, fedoras, flying caps, panamas, pillboxes, tam-o'-shanters, even baseball caps with earflaps, along with hats made by designers. 58 Neal St., *Covent Garden,* WC2 (phone: 71-836-6718).

**JEWELRY:** Beautiful jewelry is available all over London. Nearly every antiques shop, for instance, sells jewelry, and more and more craft workers are using silver and gold.

For fine jewelry, silver, and luggage, visit *Asprey & Company* (165-169 New Bond St., W1; phone: 71-493-6767); *Mappin & Webb* specializes in fine gold and silver jewelry (106 Regent St., W1; phone: 71-734-5842). The *London Silver Vaults* house a fine selection of antique silver and jewelry shops (53-54 Chancery La., WC2; phone: 71-242-3844).

**MAPS AND PRINTS:** A map of an area just visited makes a fine and eminently packable souvenir, and antique maps are a specialty at many stores. A beautiful print can bring many hours of enjoyment at home — all the better if it's an old one. Again, London offers the widest selection and the highest quality.

*Colnaghi* is a respected specialist in fine drawings and paintings, and prices are commensurate with quality. 14 Old Bond St., W1 (phone: 71-491-7408).

*Stanford's* is the principal destination of map seekers, whether they want a topographical map of the mountains they've just walked, a yachting chart for an area they want to cruise, or a road map of the byways just cycled. It may well be, as the proprietors contend, the world's largest map shop. Landsat pictures, world maps, atlases, and globes are all available. 12 Long Acre, WC2 (phone: 71-836-1321).

**MENSWEAR:** When it comes to clothing, what Paris is to women, London is to men — it has the finest of everything. Herewith, a few of our selections:

*Anderson and Sheppard* is just one of the city's celebrated made-to-measure tailors. 30 Savile Row, W1 (phone: 71-734-1420).

*Douglas Hayward,* one of the most distinctive tailors in London, makes bespoke suits for an exclusive clientele. A boutique stocks knitwear, luggage, and accessories. 95 Mount St., W1 (phone: 71-499-5574).

*Gieves and Hawkes,* over 200 years old, provides traditional English tailoring at its best, along with "the complete gentleman's wardrobe," from formal dress to the proper attire for hunting and fishing. The queen, Duke of Edinburgh, and Prince Charles are all regular patrons. 1 Savile Row, W1 (phone: 71-434-2001), and 18 Lime St., EC3 (phone: 71-283-4914).

*Hackett* means elegant shops catering to men's sartorial and tonsorial needs. From togs for the most formal occasion, to a first class shave. There are several branches, including 65b New King's Rd., SW6 (phone: 71-731-2790).

*Harvie and Hudson* offers men's shirts made to order, not to mention a selection of all-silk ties designed and colored to coordinate with the shirts. 77 and 97 Jermyn St., SW1 (phone: 71-930-3949). There is also a branch at 55 Knightsbridge, SW3 (phone: 71-235-2651).

*Turnbull and Asser,* which has catered to the likes of Prince Charles, makes the Rolls-Royce of shirts to order; it provides a shirttail long enough to reach to mid-thigh, so that it stays tucked even after many hours at a desk. 71 Jermyn St., SW1 (phone: 71-930-0502).

**MUSIC:** *Chappell* is London's largest supplier of sheet music, from Bach to rock. It also sells pianos, electronic keyboards, guitars, and metronomes. 50 New Bond St., W1 (phone: 71-491-2777).

**PAPER GOODS:** England is the source of some of the world's most beautiful stationery, and in London, the quality and selection of paper goods are unparalleled.

*Paperchase,* a delightful shop, deals in beautiful wrapping paper, unique greeting cards, posters, prints, kites, toys and games, hand-marbled papers, and more. 213 Tottenham Court Rd., W1 (phone: 71-580-8496), and 167 Fulham Rd., SW3 (phone: 71-589-7839).

*Frank Smythson* has personalized writing paper and visiting cards, sealing waxes, diaries, calendars, and leather-bound pocket notebooks specially designed for wine connoisseurs, golfers, fishermen, gardeners, travelers, and so on. Everything is in exquisite taste. The queen patronizes the firm. 44 New Bond St., W1 (phone: 71-629-8558).

**PERFUME:** France may be more famous for its scents, but the English have a nose for them as well, and the fragrances are equally subtle and appealing. They make light, inexpensive gifts for men and women alike. There are some luscious spots in the capital to stock up on the country's most celebrated perfume.

*Floris,* for instance, has been blending flower-based perfumes since 1730, when Jermyn Street was a cobbled, unlit byway, and the young Spaniard Juan Famenias Floris sailed to England from Minorca. The shop, which holds two Royal Warrants, now sells delicious-smelling powder in boxes and tins, potpourris, toilet water and perfume, bath essences and soaps. 89 Jermyn St., SW1 (phone: 71-930-2885).

*Penhaligon's* Victorian shops offer an extensive range of classical scents, toilet water, soap, and bath oils for ladies and gentlemen — along with antique scent bottles and old English silver for the dressing table. They hold Prince Philip's Royal Warrant. 41 Wellington St., WC2, and three other locations (phone: 71-836-2150).

*Taylor of London,* founded in 1887, offers English floral fragrances, not only as perfume and toilet water, but also as scented sachets, soap, pomanders, and potpourris. Available at finer department stores.

**RAINWEAR:** The best-quality rainwear in the world is available in London. The umbrellas ("bumbershoots"), in particular, are durable and distinguished. Herewith, the shrines of the rainy day:

*Aquascutum,* established in 1851, is famous for its tailored raincoats and classic English clothes. 100 Regent St., W1 (phone: 71-734-6090).

*Burberrys* is home for the superb but expensive men's, women's, and children's raincoats with the omnipresent and often imitated beige-and-red-plaid linings. 18 Haymarket, SW1 (phone: 71-930-3343).

*James Smith and Sons* is Europe's oldest purveyor of umbrellas and one of Great Britain's few specialty shops for umbrellas and walking sticks. Shoppers who don't like anything they see can have the company make something up to their specifications. 53 New Oxford St., WC1 (phone: 71-836-4731).

*Swaine, Adeney, Brigg, and Sons* is one of the last extant firms to make umbrellas in pure silk. Handmade antique and modern walking sticks, along with riding gear and probably London's largest selection of attaché cases. A large selection of handmade luggage is also available. 185 Piccadilly, W1 (phone: 71-734-4277).

**RIDING EQUIPMENT:** Horse-mad country that it is, England offers some of the best riding equipment on earth.

*Gidden's of London,* founded in 1806, sells saddles and other riding equipment to the queen. On 3 floors, near New Bond St. at 15d Clifford St., W1 (phone: 71-734-2788).

**SHOES:** In London there are still places to have a pair of shoes made to order, but patience is required, since the labor can take months. People with time to wait can choose from a seemingly unlimited variety of wonderfully high-quality footgear.

*John Lobb* will custom-make both men's and women's shoes (for an average of $1,700 a pair) that, with proper care, will likely last longer than the wearer. Still in the family that founded it in 1849, the shop's rich scent of leathers, the superb workmanship, and the opportunity to view Queen Victoria's own lasts make a visit well worthwhile, even if you buy nothing more than a tin of the shop's celebrated shoe cream. 9 St. James's St., SW1 (phone: 71-930-3664).

*McAfee* offers a good selection of fine men's shoes. 17-18 Old Bond St., W1 (phone: 71-499-7343).

*Church's,* over a century old, mass manufactures footwear with consummate care — and the results are first class. 58-59 Burlington Arcade, W1 (phone: 71-493-8307), and 163 New Bond St., W1 (phone: 71-493-8307).

**SILVER:** Though bargains and outright steals are few and far between, London still offers a chance to find beautiful bits and pieces of this precious metal.

The *London Silver Vaults* are an extraordinary maze of antique silver and jewelry shops belowground, in what once were real vaults (a few shops do sell silver plate, too). Browse around first; prices range from affordable to astronomical. 53-54 Chancery La., WC2 (phone: 71-242-3844).

**SPORTING GOODS:** The great outdoors figures so strongly in leisure activities here that it's not surprising to find an abundance of excellent equipment for the sportsman's pleasure.

*Lillywhites* has equipment on a half-dozen floors for some 3 dozen sports, from cricket (the avocation of its mid-19th-century founder, James Lillywhite) to Ping-Pong to polo. It's the largest store of its kind in the country and has held a Royal Warrant since 1955. Piccadilly Circus, SW1 (phone: 71-930-3181).

**TOBACCO:** The Englishman's grasp of the world of tobacco is immediately evident at two London shops:

*Alfred Dunhill* offers the best in precision lighters, pipes, tobacco, and cigars. Claiming to provide almost anything that a man can carry or wear, its offerings include luxury leather accessories, watches, writing instruments, and classically styled casual clothes. The Humidor Room features Havana and other cigars for connoiseurs. The store is redolent with the many fragrances of sweetly scented tobacco. 30 Duke St. (near Piccadilly), SW1 (phone: 71-499-9566).

*James Fox* specializes in cigars from around the world, including Havana, and most brands are represented. Another draw for the connoisseur is the use of humidifying rooms, where cigars mature to peak condition. 2 Burlington Gardens, W1 (phone: 71-493-9009).

**TOYS:** The first stop in London for parents and other doters is *Hamleys,* whose 6 floors make it the world's largest toy shop. There are magicians doing tricks, demonstration models whizzing, dolls walking and talking, teddy bears 6 inches to 6 feet begging to be cuddled, electronic games blipping and bleeping, and trains of every gauge whistling along their tracks. (No fewer than six on the ground floor encircle the escalators and stop at famous London landmarks.) Additions to the ground floor include a coffee shop, sweetshop, and a branch of *Lillywhites* for children's sports equipment. *Young Hamleys* specializes in playthings for youngsters under 6. Elsewhere there are board games, computers, and a *Model Centre* that offers scaled-down versions of practically anything. The selection is astonishing, to say the least. 188 Regent St., W1 (phone: 71-734-3161).

The *Disney Store* sells (what else?) Disney — everything from Mickey and Minnie mugs to Pluto pen and pencil sets. This branch of the Disney store chain does the second-largest volume in the world. 140-144 Regent St., W1 (phone: 71-287-6558).

*Pollock's Toy Museum* may have a museum upstairs, but downstairs there are all manner of things to take home, including miniatures, little theaters in the Victorian style to cut out, and teddy bears and reproduction toys from Victorian and Edwardian times. 1 Scala St., W1 (phone: 71-636-3452).

**WOOLENS:** The tweeds, plaids, and knits of Britain are justly famous, and nearly every department store carries them. Wool is a way of life as well as an attraction for tourists.

*Scotch House,* founded in 1834, has not only plaids but also lamb's wool, Shetland pullovers, classic cashmeres, and 57 other styles of cashmere, as well as 350 different tartans in pure wool. This may be London's best single source for woolen items. 2 Brompton Rd., Knightsbridge, SW1, and other locations (phone: 71-581-2151).

*Westaway and Westaway* has traditional pullovers in cashmere and lamb's wool at particularly good prices. Some are hand-knit, and there's not a synthetic thread in the place. A second shop around the corner specializes in hand-knits and designer knits, and adjacent premises are devoted entirely to woolens made in the Shetland Islands. 65 Great Russell St., WC1, and around the corner at 29 Bloomsbury, WC1 (phone: 71-405-4479 or 71-405-2128).

# LONDON'S MARKETS

Never pass up a chance to wander through one of London's bustling markets. The stalls are a painter's palette of colors — scarlets, yellows, and bright greens. Oranges and tomatoes keep company with spinach and celery — and often garish crockery and inexpensive clothes, too. The hoarse shouts and rough accents of the traders, women as well as men, add to the colorful atmosphere as they extoll the wonders of their bargains and the astonishing competitiveness of their prices. Smells of flowers, cheese, and fish, each aroma blending with the next, assail the passerby. Markets, big and small, exist both in the center of London and in many of its suburbs. At *Christmas,* fruit stands are often joined by stands selling holiday decorations and wrapping paper at very low prices. A useful guide is *London Street Markets,* by Debra Shipley and Mary Peplow (Shire Publications, £1.25).

**BERWICK STREET:** Incongruously set amidst the bright lights and striptease shows of Soho, this narrow street's double row of stalls offers probably the best values in fruit and vegetables in all of London. It has had a reputation for selling exotic imported items since the 1880s, when tomatoes and grapefruit first appeared here. Lunchtime is the liveliest time to go, when office workers join the local residents and tourists; but for real bargains go around 5 PM, when the last of the day's perishable goods are sold off inexpensively. Open Mondays through Saturdays. Berwick Street, Soho, W1.

**CAMDEN LOCK:** Clothing, crafts, and items from the 1930s and 1940s are crammed together on this crowded canalside piazza. Trendy young folk arrive by the thousands on Sundays to deck themselves out in the latest regalia — from rhinestone-studded boots to earrings. If being in the forefront of inexpensive contemporary fashion is important to you (or to some teenager near and dear to your heart), this is the place to see and buy. Linger, too, in one of the area's many cafés. Camden Town, NW1.

**COVENT GARDEN AND JUBILEE MARKET:** Although the present market hall, with its decorative cast-iron work and glass roofs, was constructed in 1830, the first market piazza was laid out here in 1631 by Inigo Jones for the fourth Earl of Bedford. The wholesale fruit and vegetable operation moved away in 1974 to Nine Elms, and after years of public outcry, plans to demolish the old buildings and replace them with characterless office blocks were abandoned. Instead, the area was extensively refurbished and quickly became one of London's liveliest spots, both during the day and at night. A plan to close the underground station was also abandoned; instead the station is being enlarged. The stalls, barrows, and small shops sell mainly crafts, clothes, and gifts, while all around the perimeter are cafés, wine bars, and small restaurants. Buskers and street artists perform on the cobbled roadway. Open daily. Covent Garden, WC2.

**EARL'S COURT EXHIBITION CENTRE SUNDAY MARKET:** A favorite haunt for students and young people, this market has a good selection of secondhand clothes and bric-a-brac, as well as electrical goods, fruit, and vegetables. Open Sunday mornings. Lillie Road, SW6.

**KENSINGTON MARKET:** A warren-like indoor emporium of small shops and stalls; the traders here are mostly young, and sell as well as wear an unusual selection of fashionable clothes and accessories, both new and secondhand. Open Mondays through Saturdays. 49-53 Kensington High Street, W8. *Hyper,* across the road, is more expensive, more way out, and a haven for young designers.

**LEADENHALL:** Held in a fine Victorian arcade with splendid cast-iron work, this food market specializes in game, poultry, fish, and cheese. Situated next to the ultra-modern Lloyds Building in the heart of the City; many of its customers are London's yuppies. Open Mondays through Fridays. Gracechurch Street, EC5.

**LEATHER LANE:** Well over 100 stalls sell everything from household wares to clothes and groceries. Surrounded by office blocks, it is particularly busy at lunchtime. Open Mondays through Fridays. Leather Lane, Holborn, EC1.

**PICCADILLY MARKET:** In the forecourt of St. James's Church on the south side of Piccadilly, this small market is a particularly convenient place at which to find interesting bric-a-brac as well as paintings, craft items, and secondhand clothes. Open Fridays and Saturdays. Piccadilly, W1.

# Gambling

 Thanks to the Betting and Gaming Act, gambling has been legal in Britain since 1960, after being strictly outlawed for more than a century. Even so, it is only permitted in "bona fide clubs," of which it's necessary to be a member (for a cost of a modest few pounds). It's possible to go as a member's guest, but guests are allowed only to watch. Once you become a member, there's still a 24-hour period before you can actually gamble. (Be sure to allow about 2 days to go through all the formalities.)

There are at least 25 casinos in London, and the most common games are roulette, blackjack, baccarat, and punto banco. As the laws do not permit casinos to advertise, would-be gamblers have to rely on word of mouth to find out where they are. The Soho, Mayfair, and Knightsbridge areas sport the greatest number of gaming houses. Hotel porters are a great source of information on the subject, and will usually suggest such places as the *Ritz Club* (next to the *Ritz* hotel in Piccadilly; phone: 71-491-4678), the *Palm Beach* (Berkeley Sq.; phone: 71-493-6585), the *Golden Nugget* (Shaftesbury Ave.; phone: 71-439-0099), and the *Cromwell Mint* (Cromwell Rd.; phone: 71-589-4041). Also consult the yellow pages under the heading "Clubs and Associations," as it lists them alongside all sorts of other organizations — from yoga groups to knitting circles. Opening times are noon to 4 AM every day except *Christmas Day* and *Boxing Day.*

# For the Body

## Tennis

Britain practically closes down in late June and early July, the fortnight of the *All England Lawn Tennis Championships* at *Wimbledon*. Ticket scalpers do a brisk trade outside the gate (and even advertise in the personal columns of the newspapers), and those who aren't lucky enough to secure tickets stay home and watch the competition on television. (For travelers, the best source of tickets is one of the package programs offered by British ticket broker/tour operator *Keith Prowse & Co.,* 234 W. 44th St., New York, NY 10036; phone: 800-669-7469; in New York City, 212-398-1430).

This passion has definitely had its effect on the number of participants in the sport, and the population of courts and players has soared in the last few years. Although tennis still has a long way to go before it becomes the national mania in Britain that it is in the US, there are now hundreds of thousands of players, and courts in London's parks — although usually crowded — aren't hard to find.

### WHERE TO PLAY

Municipal courts abound in London parks. In addition, many of the more luxurious hotels have their own courts. The best source of information, including lists of affiliated private tennis clubs where visiting players may be able to get a game, is *Britain's Lawn Tennis Association,* Queens Club, West Kensington, London W14 9EG, England (phone: 1-385-4233).

**INSIDE OUT TENNIS, Hammersmith:** For players at all levels, there are short courses based on the Inner Tennis concept developed in the US, which addresses motivation and outlook as well as physical skills. Course prices, if staying more than 1 day, include accommodations in a highly rated nearby hotel. Details: *Inside Out Tennis,* 6 Adam and Eve Mews, London W6 6UJ, England (phone: 71-938-3365).

### WHERE TO WATCH

The big deal is unquestionably the *All England Lawn Tennis Championships,* which will take place this year from June 22 to July 5 (excluding June 28) at the *All England Lawn Tennis and Croquet Club* in Wimbledon. Still a magnet to players who compete for much bigger cash prizes elsewhere, this tourney is an experience even for those who have never held a racquet. Grass courts, strawberry teas, and the legendary *Centre Court* make for such a spectacle that visitors may find the world class matches that are going on quietly on all the outlying lawns no more than a diversion. Advance seat tickets for *Centre Court* and *Number One Court* are distributed by lottery. Ticket applications, available from the end of September 1991, can be obtained by sending a self-addressed, stamped envelope to the *All England Lawn Tennis and Croquet Club* (PO Box 98, Church Rd., Wimbledon SW19 5AE, England). The club must receive completed forms by midnight, January 31. For the first 9 days of the tournament, some tickets are available on the day of play for *Number One Court;* for *Number Two Court* and the remaining outside courts, tickets are always available on the day of play. For more details, contact the *All England Lawn Tennis and Croquet Club* (phone: 81-946-2244); a self-addressed, stamped envelope or international postage coupons should be included with any correspondence.

By far the most certain and efficient means of seeing the match of your choice is to purchase one of the many packages of Britain's *Keith Prowse & Co.* (234 W. 44th St., New York, NY 10036; phone: 800-669-7469; in New York City, 212-398-1430), which offers a wide range of selections for first-week, second-week, and men's and women's finals play. Similar offerings with close-to-the-court grandstand seats are available for the *Stella Artois* (men's) championships at *Queens Club* in *Wimbledon.*

# Horsing Around

Britain is among the world's most horse-mad nations — and has been practically ever since the Romans, and later the Normans, brought horses to Britain many centuries ago. There were races as early as the 12th century at London's *Smithfield Market.* Period romances speak of races between knights and noblemen. Later, Henry VIII and James I kept stables (the latter's at *Newmarket*), and from James II on down, English monarchs have been horse fanciers. Elizabeth II, who keeps a stable and rides regularly, can be at her most animated when urging on her horse. Princess Anne, who ranks in the international class in the demanding game of 3-day eventing, used to compete in shows all over the country with her now-estranged husband, Captain Mark Phillips, who also conducts equestrian weekends at the *Gleneagles* hotel's equestrian center, which he helped plan.

London still loves its horses. In Hyde Park, riders have their own special soft track alongside part of the roadway. In the early morning, there are almost as many equestrians as there are joggers. For a taste of the country, while staying well within the city limits, there's the huge Richmond Park south of the Thames. There, riders can lose themselves in its expansive rural acres amidst deer and sheep.

*Ross Nye's Riding Establishment* (8 Bathurst Mews, W2; phone: 71-262-3791) takes groups of all levels out in Hyde Park, or gives individual lessons there. *Roehampton Gate Stables* (Priory Lane, SW15; phone: 81-876-7089) offers the same in Richmond Park. Both welcome visitors.

**HORSE OF THE YEAR SHOW, Wembley, near London:** Hunters, hacks, and ponies show up in October for this premier fixture of the British equestrian calendar. The Horse Personalities of the Year awards are always popular, but the whole event presents a wonderful display of horseflesh, an equine extravaganza if ever there was one. Details: *Horse of the Year Show, Wembley Arena,* Wembley HA9 0DW, England (phone: 81-902-8833, or for tickets, 81-902-1234).

**ROYAL ASCOT, Ascot, Berkshire:** The June meeting at this racecourse on the southern edge of Windsor Great Park, 25 miles west of London, has enjoyed royal patronage ever since Queen Anne drove over to watch the first races on the *Ascot Common* in 1711 — and it is still considered a high point of the London social season. Ascot is where Eliza Doolittle (of George Bernard Shaw's *Pygmalion* and Lerner and Loewe's *My Fair Lady*) first encountered high society; things are as oh-so-social even today. In the Royal Enclosure — the pricey part of the seating area — men wear top hats and morning coats, and women, their smartest dresses and hats. Models come here hoping to catch a photographer's eye and launch a career; while other females, including more than one dowager, show up in bonnets that some might call preposterous. The sovereign and members of the royal family drive in state carriages from Windsor Castle on each day of the 4-day meeting. The key race in the meeting is the *Ascot Gold Cup* — a 2½-mile race that ranks as one of the most important of British flat racing's season. The *King George VI and the Queen Elizabeth Stakes,* a 1½-miler first run in 1951, takes place each July. Packages that include admission to the Grandstand Enclosure and the Paddock for the *Ascot Gold Cup* are available from *Keith Prowse & Co.* (234 W. 44th St., New York, NY 10036; phone: 800-669-7469; in New York City, 212-398-1430). Other details: *Ascot Racecourse,* Ascot, Berkshire SL5 7JN, England (phone: 344-22211).

# Cruising London's Waterways

Of all the nation's rivers, the Thames warrants special attention because of its navigability and accessibility. Stretching across the breadth of the southern part of the country and navigable for about 125 miles, the Thames winds its long way through pastoral green landscapes punctuated by villages so quaint you'll think you've stepped into a photograph from *National Geographic;* there are lovely estates, grand old houses, medieval churches, marvelously well-tended gardens — and even a few gray cities where the roar of traffic may blot out the memory of the birdsongs that accompany you the rest of your trip. As John Burns once commented, "Every drop of the Thames is liquid history." Commercial traffic along most of the Thames's navigable length is light, and the current is almost nonexistent in most seasons. A recorded announcement of Thames River cruises can be heard by calling the River Boat Information Service of the London Tourist Board (phone: 71-730-3488).

There are also regular *RiverBus* services (Exchange Tower, 1 Harbour Exchange Sq., E14; phone: 71-512-0555) that link Charing Cross with Greenwich and the City Airport in Docklands; in rush hour they extend to Chelsea Harbour, too. As these trips are mainly for commuters, there's no commentary about the sites along the way.

Another cruisable waterway that is much longer and narrower than the Thames is London's old canal system. It offers quiet towpath walks, leisurely trips in cruisers or "narrowboat" barges, and a chance to see some fascinating industrial archaeology — old bridges, canal buildings, and abandoned wharves. When Britain's canals were first dug around 200 years ago, they provided much-needed arteries for the country's rapidly growing industries. Until then, transport had been limited primarily to horse-drawn wagons.

Initially, canals prospered, but with the dawn of the railroad age the barge became almost obsolete (though a few barge owners struggled on, some even into the 1950s). The canal system was left to rot, forgotten by everyone except a few fishermen, walkers, and people who used them as a place to dump unwanted items like old mattresses and refrigerators.

In recent years, however, the canals have enjoyed a renaissance: Locks have been restored, towpaths cleared, and bridges painted. Now a trip on one of them can be a real pleasure — and very relaxing, too, as the maximum speed is 4 miles per hour. From here one can see London from another vantage point — the backs of houses, ends of gardens, and the remains of the original hand-built wharves and warehouses.

The main canal route through London is a 28-mile, U-shape section near the north bank of the Thames, at Kew to the west and at Limehouse below Tower Bridge. Near the Kew end, it links with the main Grand Union Canal, which slowly winds its way north to Birmingham. Trips ply the stretch between Camden Lock, where the water drops 8 feet, and Little Venice, an affluent area of elegant homes and elaborate houseboats. In between there's plenty to see along the twisting route, sections of which cut through the middle of the London Zoo, a long wooded area in Regents Park, and the Maida Vale tunnel. The main starting points are Little Venice (near Warwick Avenue underground station) or Camden Lock (near Camden Town station).

There are also well-equipped boats that can be hired for week-long trips, during which passengers live on board and operate the boat and locks themselves. For information, call *Blakes Holidays* (phone: 603-782911) or *Hoseasons Holidays* (phone: 502-500505). A convenient starting point from which to savor London's northwestern outskirts is Berkhamsted, where *Bridgewater Boats* (phone: 442-863615) has a selection of luxurious boats named after T. S. Eliot's famous cats.

# Freewheeling by Two-Wheeler

Bicycling may not be everyone's idea of the best transportation around London, and in fact it can prove a nightmare to newcomers not forewarned about patterns of traffic flow and congestion. But it's also true that there's no better way of seeing the real London — away from the main thoroughfares used by most buses and taxicabs. Traveling by bike, more than any other mode of transport, will provide a good feel for the way London's "villages" all fit together.

The London Cycling Campaign's excellent booklet *On Your Bike* (£5/about $9, including postage) is full of maps of central London on which are designated streets good for bicycling, as well as the official cycle routes through the city. Though aimed at Londoners who use their bikes as transportation, it can be useful to sightseers as well — and serves as an excellent primer on English laws pertaining to cyclists and on cycling safety, maintenance, and repairs. Cycling shops are also listed. In addition, the Campaign publishes a bimonthly newsletter providing up-to-date information on cycling in London, as well as a listing of shops where L.C.C. members can get a 10% discount. Fold-out cycling route maps of south, east, and northwest London (£1/about $1.80 each) are also available. Details: *London Cycling Campaign*, 3 Stamford St., London SE1 9NT, England (phone: 71-928-7220).

# For the Mind

## Marvelous Museums

 It has often been said that when King Charles I was executed in 1649, and Parliament auctioned off his collection of paintings and other treasures, Britain lost its heritage. But the growth of the great national collections, beginning as early as the 17th century with the founding of Oxford's *Ashmolean Museum,* more than made amends. This included the collecting mania of the 18th and 19th centuries — when the rich were really rich and gentlemen made careers of their hobbies, accumulating not only the fine art of Western Europe, but also trifles and prizes from the farthest corners of the empire. Today, Britain — and especially London — is home to a staggering agglomeration of artwork from all over the world. And although some of these treasures are privately owned, the majority are on display in the nation's great museums.

Britain's museums usually are well conceived and designed to provide ideal space and lighting for the works on display. And despite recent cutbacks in government support of the arts, many museums have no admission charge (donations are suggested) and are open to the public every day except principal holidays. There usually also are special lecture programs designed as much for experts in the fields as for beginners seeking a greater appreciation of what they've seen and admired. Local newspapers and museum calendars are good sources for details.

A museum can be a great deal more pleasurable if a few simple guidelines are kept in mind. Visitors should plan several short visits to a large museum rather than one long one, stay for about an hour, and take in no more than a dozen fine works. There's no fatigue quite like aching, yawny museum fatigue — once described as the dread "museum foot" — and when it has set in, merely sitting for 3 minutes in front of a Rubens won't cure it. Travelers should be well rested when they visit important collections — preferably as soon as the museum opens, before the crowds have arrived. If possible, they should know what they want to see before beginning their rounds, so as not to clutter the experience with too many bleeding saints and blustery seascapes. Most museums publish excellent pamphlets and booklets to steer visitors to the more worthwhile works in their collections.

And everyone should visit an art gallery or an auction house occasionally — just as a reminder that once it was all for sale.

**BRITISH MUSEUM:** Founded in 1753 around the lifetime accumulations of Sir Hans Sloane, a British physician and naturalist, this vast institution is Britain's largest and most celebrated, consecrated to the whole of human history. Trying to cover it all in a single visit is like trying to master nuclear physics while in a barber's chair. The crown jewels of the collection are the renowned *Elgin Marbles,* massive sculpture and reliefs from the Parthenon that Lord Elgin brought, in the early 19th century, from the Turkish sultan and carted off to safe, civilized England, where they were purchased by the government for £35,000 and presented to the museum. Other treasures on display include the *Rosetta Stone,* the black basalt tablet that provided the key to Egyptian hieroglyphs; the *Royal Gold Cup;* the deep blue and white cameo-cut *Portland Vase,* a great marvel of the glassmaker's art dating from Roman times; gold and silver objects from the Sutton Hoo Burial Ship, found at an East Suffolk archaeological excavation; the *Tomb of Mausolus* from Halicarnassus, which brought the word "mausoleum" into the English language; the *Temple of Diana* from Ephesus; and many mummies, among them the one that is widely (and erroneously) believed to have occasioned the legends of the curse of the mummy's tomb.

Seven sculpture galleries exhibit some 1,500 Greek and Roman treasures, including two of the seven wonders of the ancient world and representing the bulk of the museum's Greek and Roman collection. Man Before Metals provides an enthralling look at the art and technology of the Stone Age. The departments of Western Asiatic Antiquities and Oriental Antiquities are magnificent. The *Magna Carta* is on view in the Manuscript Saloon of the British Library (a separate institution since 1973, though still housed in the *British Museum*), and the King's Library houses a Gutenberg Bible. Depending on what is on display at the time, visitors may see such wonders as the sketchbooks of Dürer or da Vinci, manuscripts of famous composers' most famous works and of *Alice's Adventures in Wonderland,* plus the signatures of Shakespeare, Dickens, and Joyce.

The British Library Reading Room, where Karl Marx did research for *Das Kapital,* is accessible only to those who come well recommended (preferably by a scholar of some note) and who apply in advance for a ticket, or to those who pay about $25 to join the National Art Collections Fund. But visitors may view the Reading Room for a few minutes, on the hour (11 AM to 4 PM) with a warder. The rest of the museum also is overwhelming; guidebooks to various parts of the collections, for sale in the main lobby, are good investments, as are detailed guides to single aspects of the offerings. Open Mondays through Saturdays from 10 AM to 5 PM and on Sundays from 2:30 to 6 PM. No admission charge (except for special exhibits). Details: *British Museum,* Great Russell St., London WC18 3DG, England (phone: 71-636-1555; for the library, 71-636-1544).

   **COURTAULD INSTITUTE GALLERIES:** At first, this institution, established in 1932 to teach art history to University of London students, might not appear to be very special. Yet like a good many museums of its type, this one is approachable and enjoyable in ways that its far larger and more widely known counterparts can never be. The setting, in Somerset House, replete with Oriental rugs and handsome furnishings, is lovely. The works in the collections are the bequests of industrialist Samuel Courtauld (whose generosity also benefited the *Tate Gallery*), as well as Lord Lee of Fareham and art critic Roger Fry (who organized London's first post-Impressionist exhibition in 1910). The excellent assemblage of Impressionist and post-Impressionist works includes Manet's *Bar at the Folies-Bergère* and *Le Déjeuner sur l'Herbe;* van Gogh's *Artist with His Ear Cut Off* and *Peach Trees in Blossom;* Cézanne's *Lake of Annecy* and one rendering of the easily recognizable *Card Players;* Tahitian scenes by Gauguin; and wonderful works by Bonnard, Renoir, and Seurat. There are early Italian paintings from the Gambier-Parry Bequest and the superb Princes Gate Collection of Flemish and Italian Old Masters. Open Mondays through Saturdays from 10 AM to 6 PM and Sundays from 2 to 6 PM. Admission charge. Details: *Courtauld Institute Galleries,* Somerset House, The Strand, London WC2 5DN, England (phone: 71-873-2526).

   **DULWICH PICTURE GALLERY:** Tucked away in Dulwich, a quiet, leafy, almost rural (but easily accessible — 11 minutes by train) suburb of southeast London, this gallery — decorated and hung in the best Regency manner — boasts a collection of Old Masters worthy of a capital city anywhere. The nation's oldest public picture gallery, it contains works bequeathed by the great Shakespearean actor-manager Edward Alleyn, the founder of Dulwich College, plus nearly 400 others from the collection of the French-born art dealer Noël Joseph Desenfans. Many of these had been collected at the behest of Poland's King Stanislas, who abdicated before they could be delivered (or paid for). Among others, there are works by such Dutch painters as Rembrandt, Cuyp, and Hobbema; by 17th- and 18th-century British portraitists such as Gainsborough and Reynolds; by the Flemish painters Rubens and Van Dyck; by the Frenchmen Claude, Poussin, Watteau, and Charles LeBrun; and by Italians such as Raphael, Veronese, Tiepolo, and Canaletto. The austerely neo-classical building that houses the collection was built in 1811 and often is considered to be the masterpiece of its architect, Sir John Soane. Open Tuesdays through Fridays from 10 AM to 1 PM and from 2 to 5 PM, on Saturdays from 11 AM to 5 PM, and on Sundays from 2 to 5 PM; guided tours are offered on Saturdays and Sundays at 3 PM. Admission charge. Details: *Dulwich Picture Gallery,* College Rd., London SE21 7AD, England (phone: 81-693-5254).

**GUARDS MUSEUM:** This small museum at Wellington Barracks, close to Buckingham Palace, houses exhibits of memorabilia relating to the Brigade of Guards, beginning with those of the oldest of the five regiments, the Grenadiers, formed in the 1660s. Exhibits include uniforms and weapons, but there are unexpected items, too. A cat-o-nine tails and a spring-loaded set of dye needles that was used to tattoo a large "D" under the arm of deserters give some idea of what corporal punishment ca. 1660 was all about. Among the uniforms on display is a black tunic that King George VI had made for the queen in 1942 when (as a 16-year-old) Princess Elizabeth was made Colonel of the Grenadier Guards. Beside it is one of her scarlet tunics from the annual Trooping the Colour ceremony on Horse Guards Parade. Open daily except Fridays from 10 AM to 4 PM. Admission charge. Details: *Guards Museum,* Birdcage Walk, London SW1E 6HQ, England (phone: 71-930-4466).

**HORNIMAN MUSEUM:** Though founded over 100 years ago by Frederick Horniman, the famous tea merchant, this international heritage museum all about conservation is up-to-the-minute on current environmental issues. In a striking Art Nouveau building whose clock tower is a South London landmark, the exhibits illustrate the cultures, traditions, and changing living conditions of the peoples of the world. Several religions are covered as well, and there's an excellent natural history collection including an aquarium where endangered species of fish are bred. There are also displays of masks, puppets, and musical instruments. Outside is a 16-acre park with exotic gardens and nature trails. Open daily from 10:30 AM to 5:50 PM, Sundays from 2 to 5:50 PM. Parking daily from 8 AM to dusk. No admission charge. Details: *Horniman Museum,* London Rd., Forest Hill, London SE23 3PQ, England (phone: 81-699-2339).

**IMPERIAL WAR MUSEUM:** Tanks, planes, cannon, submarines, rockets, artifacts, and war paintings are housed in this 4-floor museum, which covers the history of war from Flanders to the Falklands. Wartime events are brought to life on films, videos, and telephones that visitors can pick up to hear people describing their firsthand wartime experiences. The 20-minute-long "Blitz Experience" confines groups of 20 people in a damp, cramped re-creation of a bomb shelter during a World War II air raid, while "Operation Jericho" is a bumpy simulation of a World War II bombing raid; also see the WWI "Trench Experience" (no additional admission charge for the Trench Experience). A souvenir shop and a café are also on the premises. Open daily from 10 AM to 6 PM; closed *Christmas Eve, Christmas, Boxing Day,* and *New Year's Day.* Admission charge, except on Fridays. Details: *Imperial War Museum,* Lambeth Rd., London SE1 6HZ (phone: 71-416-5000).

**IVEAGH BEQUEST:** The collection, assembled by the first Earl of Iveagh, includes works by Cuyp, Gainsborough, Hals, Rembrandt, Reynolds, Romney, Turner, Vermeer, and others. What makes this institution particularly interesting is its setting, a late-17th-century house remodeled beginning in 1764 by the Scottish architect Robert Adam. It's a marvelously stately neo-classical villa that was scheduled for demolition until it was rescued in 1925 by the first Earl of Iveagh, who then presented the house and the better part of his own collection to the nation. It has the atmosphere of an 18th-century English country house, and in summer frequently offers chamber recitals, poetry readings, and open-air concerts. Open daily from 10 AM to 4 PM in winter and until 6 PM from *Easter* to September. No admission charge. Details: *Iveagh Bequest,* Kenwood, Hampstead La., London NW3 7JR, England (phone: 81-348-1286).

**MUSEUM OF MANKIND:** Only the collections of Berlin's *Ethnographic Museum* can rival those of the *British Museum,* which are housed in this structure next to the Burlington Arcade in Piccadilly. By far the largest part of its holdings of items relating to African, American, Asian, and Pacific cultures is brought out of the relative limbo of the reserve areas only for special theme exhibitions. However, a selection of the greatest treasures is normally on display, including items such as bronzes from Nigeria, Maori jade ornaments, and a crystal skull probably made by the Aztec. There's also a café. Open Mondays through Saturdays from 10 AM to 5 PM and on Sundays from 2:30 to 6 PM. No admission charge. Details: *Museum of Mankind,* 6 Burlington Gardens, London W1X 2EX, England (phone: 71-323-8043).

**MUSEUM OF THE MOVING IMAGE:** What goes on behind the camera is the theme of this lively museum about the history of film and television. Opened in 1988, it's an exciting glass and steel structure sandwiched under the arches of Waterloo Bridge beside the *National Film Theatre* in the *South Bank Arts Centre* complex. The 50 exhibition areas mix state-of-the-art technology with old-fashioned showmanship. It's all here, from Charlie Chaplin clips to esoteric foreign-language films, from Dr. Who's daleks to newsreels. And it's possible to take part in the exhibits in addition to simply looking at them, as there's an abundance of hands-on opportunities. To make the most of these, however, it's necessary to arrive early, before it gets too crowded. Open Tuesdays through Saturdays from 10 AM to 8 PM, Sundays from 10 AM to 6 PM. Admission charge. Details: *Museum of the Moving Image,* Waterloo, London SE1 8XT, England (phone: 71-928-3535).

**NATIONAL GALLERY:** Among the greatest art museums in the world, the *National Gallery* was instituted in 1824, when the connoisseur Sir George Beaumont convinced the government to buy the 3 dozen–plus paintings put up for sale after the death of the wealthy Russian-born merchant-collector John Julius Angerstein — among them Rembrandt's *The Woman Taken in Adultery* and *The Adoration of the Shepherds,* Rubens's *The Rape of the Sabine Women,* and Titian's *Venus and Adonis.* Subsequent gifts and acquisitions have endowed it with a collection that is remarkably balanced and which represents a cross section of the chief schools of Western European art from Giotto to Picasso. The recent addition of the Sainsbury Wing, an austere $60-million annex serenely ensconced in Trafalgar Square's northwest corner, provides ample space to properly display 250 paintings — including works by Dürer, van Eyck, and Raphael — of this extraordinary collection. Artistic jewels such as Leonardo da Vinci's great cartoon *The Virgin and Child with St. Anne and St. John the Baptist,* Botticelli's *Venus and Mars,* Raphael's *Crucifixion,* and van Eyck's *Arnolfini Marriage* glow on the walls. The balance of the museum's collections — over 2,000 treasures in all — have been reorganized and regrouped according to nationality and now hang in chronological order in the museum's main building. Nearly every item the museum owns is on view at all times. An elaborate computer system enables visitors to locate any painting housed here. Homan Potterton's *A Guide to the National Gallery* (available at the gallery shop) makes an erudite — and delightful — companion to a visit. Open Mondays through Saturdays from 10 AM to 6 PM, Sundays from 2 to 6 PM. No admission charge. Details: *National Gallery,* Trafalgar Sq., London WC2 5DN, England (phone: 71-839-3321).

**NATIONAL MARITIME MUSEUM:** In a royal park by the Thames in Greenwich, this was England's first Palladian building. A beautifully proportioned white structure designed in 1616 by Inigo Jones for James I's consort, Anne of Denmark, this institution tells the story of Britain's long involvement with the sea. There are scores of pictures and silver, porcelain and uniforms, swords and medals, ship models and dioramas. Galleries in the West Wing explore "Discovery and Seapower" and the "Development of the Warship," and the world's largest ship in a bottle is on display in Neptune Hall. There, too, are the steam paddle tug *Reliant,* which rests after a career on the Manchester Ship Canal; the *Donola,* a 60-foot steam launch; and the smaller *Waterlily.* Next door in the Barge House, Prince Frederick's barge glitters in golden livery. Another must: the uniform that Lord Nelson wore when he was shot at the Battle of Trafalgar in 1805, complete with bullet hole and bloodstains. Finally, the *Old Royal Observatory* — the home of the Greenwich Meridian, which divides the western hemisphere from the eastern — is centered around Sir Christopher Wren's 1675 Flamsteed House and has exhibits that illustrate the history of nautical astronomy, timekeeping, and Greenwich mean time. The refracting telescope here is the largest in the United Kingdom and is available to visitors. Also in Greenwich, don't miss the *Cutty Sark,* once the fastest clipper in existence; and the *Gipsy Moth IV,* the 53-foot ketch that, in 1966–67, bore Sir Francis Chichester — solo — around the world. Open April through September, Mondays through Saturdays from 10 AM to 6 PM, Sundays from 2 to 6 PM; October through March, Mondays through Saturdays from 10 AM to 5 PM, Sundays from 2 to 6 PM. Admission charge. Details: *National Maritime Museum,* Romney Rd., Greenwich, London SE10 9NF, England (phone: 81-858-4422).

**NATIONAL PORTRAIT GALLERY:** Established in 1856, this museum is devoted to the portraits of the most important figures in British arts, letters, history and politics, military life, science, and various other fields. In all, over 9,000 likenesses, arranged chronologically, stare down at visitors from the walls. Elizabeth I is there as a young woman and a dowager, not far from Shakespeare, Mary Queen of Scots, Thomas More, Cardinal Wolsey, Essex, Leicester, and Raleigh. The list of authors portrayed reads like the table of contents of a literature text — Pepys, Milton, Dryden, Pope, Swift, Boswell, Johnson, Tennyson, Dickens, the Brontë sisters, Wilde, Auden, Shaw, and more. Especially since the 1984 opening of a series of galleries devoted to post–World War I portraiture, there's far too much to see in one visit — but it's difficult not to want to give it a try. Special exhibits on historical themes or individual artists are frequently mounted as well. Open Mondays through Fridays from 10 AM to 5 PM, Saturdays from 10 AM to 6 PM, and Sundays from 2 to 6 PM. Admission charge to special exhibitions only. Details: *National Portrait Gallery,* St. Martin's Pl., London WC2H 0HE, England (phone: 71-306-0055).

**QUEEN'S GALLERY:** The British Royal Collection — one of the world's greatest — remained outside the experience of the common man until 1962, when this gallery was created at Buckingham Palace, and even now only a fraction is on view. But the exhibitions that are mounted here never fail to impress, whether they are devoted to a subject such as royal children, animal paintings, or British soldiers; to single artists — da Vinci or Gainsborough or Canaletto or Holbein, to name a quartet of past shows; or to groups of painters — the Italians or the Dutch, for instance. Exhibitions change about once a year. Open Tuesdays through Saturdays from 10:30 AM to 5 PM and Sundays from 2 to 5 PM (last ticket sold at 4:30 PM all days). Admission charge. Details: *Queen's Gallery,* c/o the Lord Chamberlain's Office, St. James's Palace, London SW1A 1AA, England (phone: 71-930-4832).

**SIR JOHN SOANE'S MUSEUM:** On the north side of central London's largest square (a haunt of lawyers since the 16th century), it occupies two houses designed by the great architect Sir John Soane (1753–1837) and is a remarkable survival of an early museum. The rooms, ingeniously designed, have curious lighting effects and are packed with objects that were arranged in a very personal manner by Soane himself. The place is full of surprises that the plain and fairly straightforward exterior does not foretell.

In the Library, for instance, the spaces behind the flying arches are mirrored, so that a visitor is left with the impression of more space than actually exists. The Monk's Yard, a "Gothick fantasy," is concocted of bits of masonry from the old Palace of Westminster; the Monk's Parlour houses Flemish woodcarvings, casts from medieval sculptures and buildings, and architectural models of some of Soane's own designs; the Sepulchral Chamber contains the alabaster sarcophagus discovered in the tomb of Seti I (d. 1290 BC) by G. B. Belzoni in 1817, and purchased by Soane in 1824 for £2,000 after *British Museum* authorities decided they could not afford it, having just bought the *Elgin Marbles;* and the shallow-domed Breakfast Room displays ingenious use of mirrors and indirect lighting.

All in all, the place is a hodgepodge — but who ever said a house had to be otherwise? Visitors should not miss Hogarth's famous series *The Rake's Progress,* which recounts the life and hard times of one Tom Rakewell, and his four-part political satire *The Election,* both installed in a small gallery with hinged walls. The Library contains the world's greatest collection of 17th- and 18th-century architectural drawings — works by Sir Christopher Wren, Robert Adam, George Dance, Soane, and many others. There is also a Model Room, open by request, that houses Soane's collection of cork, plaster, and wooden architectural models. (Visits to the Library, Drawings Collection, and Model Room are by appointment.) Open Tuesdays through Saturdays from 10 AM to 5 PM. No admission charge. Details: *Sir John Soane's Museum,* 13 Lincoln's Inn Fields, London WC2A 3BP, England (phone: 71-405-2107).

**TATE GALLERY:** Built in 1897 on the site of Millbank Prison, the gift of the sugar broker and art collector Sir Henry Tate, this national collection of British painting and 20th-century painting and sculpture was established less than half a century after the *National Gallery,* when bequests had swelled the size of the latter's collection to an extent that there was no longer room to house all the paintings — 282 oils and 19,000 watercolors by Turner, among them. Tate bequeathed his own collection plus £80,000 to house it, art dealer Sir Joseph Duveen gave additional funds, and the museum was on its way. A major extension was opened in 1979 that increased exhibition space by half, and in 1990, the museum's director, Nicholas Serota, continued the reorganization of the gallery, arranging the works in chronological order. The magnificent Clore Gallery — designed by James Stirling and set in a newer wing — houses the Turner Collection. Often overlooked is the fact that the *Tate* also houses one of the world's best collections of French post-Impressionist works; and the sculpture collection offers excellent examples of the artistry of Rodin, Maillol, Mestrovic, Moore, and Epstein. The British Collection contains the world's most representative collection of works by Blake, as well as works by Hogarth, George Stubbs, John Constable, and the Pre-Raphaelites. The Modern Collection includes works of conceptual, minimal, optical, kinetic, British figurative, pop, and abstract art; it incorporates the most extensive survey of British art of its period in any public collection, including selected examples of very recent art. Rothko, Nevelson, Bacon, Ernst, and Picasso are all represented. Rex Whistler, the noted trompe l'oeil painter, is responsible for the decor of the gallery's excellent restaurant. A northern branch of the *Tate Gallery* is at Liverpool's Albert Dock. Open Mondays through Saturdays from 10 AM to 6 PM and on Sundays from 2 to 6 PM. No admission charge, except for special exhibitions. Details: *Tate Gallery,* Millbank, London SW1P 4RG, England (phone: 71-821-1313; 71-821-7128 for recorded information).

**VICTORIA AND ALBERT MUSEUM:** An offspring of the *Great Exhibition* of 1851, this museum was originally a repository of the world's finest craftsmanship. Many of the galleries have undergone recent renovations. The collection, dating from ancient times, was intended to lend inspiration to leatherworkers and ceramists, furniture makers and woodcarvers, architects and dressmakers, silversmiths and goldsmiths, and other artisans working in the applied arts in the 19th century. Though the original function has not been abandoned even today, the collections are a bit more wide-ranging (and recently were the subject of furious in-house debate that resulted in the resignations — some of them not altogether voluntary — of several of the museum's curators); they encompass not only textiles and furniture but also watercolors and paintings — among them John Constable's *Salisbury Cathedral from the Bishop's Grounds;* the collections of British art (which include the Constable Collection, presented to the museum by the artist's daughter) stand out for their scope and comprehensiveness. Of particular interest are the Raphael cartoons (designs for tapestries for the Sistine Chapel), the period rooms, Queen Elizabeth I's virginals, the world's oldest known teapot, and the intricately carved, abundantly graffiti-covered *Great Bed of Ware*, which Shakespeare's Sir Toby Belch mentioned in *Twelfth Night* and (measuring about 11 feet square) was purportedly big enough to sleep a dozen couples, half of them at the head, the other half at the foot. Also on exhibit is the Chippendale furniture once owned by David Garrick, pieces by designer William Morris and his followers, Marie-Antoinette's music stand, Russian imperial jewels, patchwork quilts, medieval hangings, and tiles and stained glass. The museum's Henry Cole Wing (named after its founder) houses a broad selection of changing exhibitions, as well as an interesting permanent display of printmaking techniques. The Nehru Gallery, opened in 1990, has the finest collection of Indian art outside of India. There's also a restaurant and super museum shop. Open Mondays through Saturdays from 10 AM to 5:50 PM and Sundays from 2:30 to 5:50 PM. Donations suggested. Details: *Victoria and Albert Museum*, Cromwell Rd., London SW7 2RL, England (phone: 71-938-8500, 71-938-8441 for recorded information).

**WALLACE COLLECTION:** The fourth Marquess of Hertford, who died in 1870 after living most of his life in Paris, had one major criterion in collecting: "I only like pleasing paintings," he claimed. But what he called "pleasing" included works of many types — Italian, Dutch, French, Flemish, and Spanish, as well as British — that are now displayed at Hertford House, his former townhouse off Oxford Street, which contains not only the works he amassed, but also the ones he inherited, since the collection was first put together by his great-grandfather in the 18th century and enlarged in the two succeeding generations. The museum's French furniture from the 17th and 18th centuries is very fine, as are the considerable numbers of 18th-century French clocks and the collections of miniatures, gold boxes, and Sèvres porcelain. Painters whose works are represented include Boucher, Canaletto, Fragonard, Gainsborough, Guardi, Hals, Rembrandt, Reynolds, Rubens, Titian, Van Dyck, Velázquez, and Watteau. The famous collection of Oriental and European armor was formed principally by Sir Richard Wallace, the illegitimate son of the fourth Marquess of Hertford. His widow, Lady Wallace, bequeathed the vast collection to the nation in 1897. Open Mondays through Saturdays from 10 AM to 5 PM and Sundays from 2 to 5 PM. No admission charge. Details: *Wallace Collection*, Hertford House, Manchester Sq., London W1M 6BN, England (phone: 71-935-0687).

# The Performing Arts

 When the summer festival season ends, winter's cultural whirlwind begins. London has lately become something of a dance capital, hosting not just its own progeny — among them the *Royal Ballet* and the *London Festival Ballet* — but also visiting companies from home and abroad. *The Royal Opera House, Covent Garden*, ranks among the world's greats. And there's always music in the air, whether it's classical — and played by a symphony orchestra, a chamber group, or a soloist — jazz, or the most traditional folk works. Above all, the city is a hotbed of dramatic affairs, with literally hundreds of offerings in hundreds of playhouses. The dozens of theaters in the West End (London's Broadway) regularly mount ostensibly commercial productions (although many, as a result of British theater's fondness for the experimental, have a long way to go before they make money). The tradition of eclecticism and experimentation has put the English theater at the forefront of world drama.

With all this going on, deciding on an evening's entertainment (or an afternoon's — or even a morning's, for that matter) can pose some problems. When it comes to theater, one man's meat is another's moan, so before settling on a play, visitors should ask a friend or check newspapers such as the *Guardian* or the *Observer* or well-regarded tourist magazines such as *What's On* or the BTA's monthly theater guide, the *London Planner*.

We've given a sampling of halls that culture buffs will find worth going out of their way to visit, but there are many others. It's possible to order tickets in advance of arrival in London directly through the individual box offices and through *Keith Prowse & Co.* (234 W. 44th St., New York, NY 10036; phone: 212-398-1430 or 800-669-7469, except in New York City). This organization, which has been in business for over 200 years, is the world's largest entertainment ticket agency and sells some 53,000 tickets a week; its allocations range from a fifth to nearly half of all the seats at London theaters. Tickets to theater and major festival events also can be booked in advance through *Edwards & Edwards* (One Times Square Plaza, New York, NY 10036; phone: 212-944-0290 or 800-223-6108, except in New York City).

**BARBICAN CENTRE:** An apparent tribute to modern architecture, this 1982 structure looks like a maze of concrete towers and corridors from the outside. Inside, the lavish decor, the complex design, the exciting potential of the building, and the breadth of artistic activity generated are overwhelming. The *Royal Shakespeare Company* performs here on occasion, as does the *London Symphony Orchestra*. There are two theaters, cinemas, an art gallery, two shops, a magnificent conservatory of plants, and a concert hall that hosts regular performances of classical music, opera, and more. The *Waterside Café,* which offers snacks by the fountains in summer, *Café on Six* (the *Barbican*'s wine bar), and the more formal *Searcey's* all make for a delightful interlude. Details: *Barbican Centre,* Silk St., London EC2Y 8DS, England (phone: 71-638-4141 for general information; 71-638-8891 for the box office).

**LONDON COLISEUM:** There's a sense of occasion surrounding any visit to this floridly Edwardian, 2,358-seat theater, London's largest, at the foot of St. Martin's Lane near St. Martin-in-the-Fields Church and the *National Gallery.* The interiors are all alabaster and marble, bronze and splendid gleaming mahogany, as posh as those of the ships that once crisscrossed the Atlantic when the theater was first opened. Diaghilev's *Ballet Russe* performed here, as did Sarah Bernhardt, Mrs. Patrick Campbell, Ellen Terry, and a child star named Noël Coward. The impresario who conceived the place even staged tennis matches and rodeos to keep it filled. Since 1968, the *English National Opera Company,* which stages classic and contemporary operas in English, has called it home, and is in residence from August to June. Details: *English National Opera,* London Coliseum, St. Martin's La., London WC2N 4ES, England (phone: 71-836-3161).

**LYRIC THEATRE HAMMERSMITH:** Though Victorian in style, this theater blends gracefully into its modern shopping center surroundings in Hammersmith's King Street. Classical productions and new plays are presented in the main theater, and the smaller adjacent Studio presents an adventurous program of modern and foreign works. Details: *Lyric Theatre Hammersmith,* King St., London W6 0QL, England (phone: 71-741-2311).

**MERMAID THEATRE:** Founded by actor Bernard Miles in 1951, this theater acquired its present permanent home on the site of an old warehouse on the banks of the Thames 8 years later. It soon gained a reputation for presenting adventurous works, and now is completely self-supporting. Details: *Mermaid Theatre,* Puddle Dock, Blackfriars, London EC4 V3DB, England (phone: 71-410-0102).

**OLD VIC:** Architects, bombs, and ill-advised alterations had left the *Old Vic* nothing short of a mishmash when a Canadian named "Honest" Ed Mirvish bought it sight unseen a few years ago and commenced transforming it into one of the most elegant, attractive, and comfortable theaters in central London. The façade was returned to its 1818 incarnation, complete with brick arches, and the interior was restored to a semblance of its 1880s self. Boxes, ceiling, proscenium arch, and tier fronts were elaborately painted in shades of ivory, apricot, coral, pewter, and gold and silver. Velvet house curtains were installed, and the entire auditorium was decked out in wallpaper and carpeting with a period flavor. The house now produces its own subscription season, and beginning in 1988, Jonathan Miller took over as artistic director, which ensured interesting — if controversial — theater. Miller resigned in 1991, and the theater was searching for his replacement at press time. The remarkable restoration alone makes a visit worthwhile. Details: *Old Vic,* Waterloo Rd., London SE1 8NB, England (phone: 71-928-7616).

**OPEN AIR THEATRE (REGENT'S PARK):** It's hard to find a more pleasant way to spend a summer evening in London than to take in a performance of Shakespeare (or a musical) in this lovely amphitheater in the woods near Queen Mary's Rose Garden. Established in 1932, it quickly became an institution among London theatergoers, and actors from Vivien Leigh to Jeremy Irons have played here. Since 1962, the *New Shakespeare Company* has made its home here and offers three plays, two by Shakespeare, every summer. The newer auditorium, which opened in 1975, provides plenty of space for a bar, which serves such fare as Puck's Fizz and mulled wine, barbecue, and a cold buffet. Details: *Open Air Theatre,* Regent's Park, London NW1 4NP, England (phone: 71-486-2431).

**RIVERSIDE STUDIOS:** This modern arts center alongside the Thames in Hammersmith offers a lively program of drama, music, dance, film, exhibitions, and children's programs in attractive surroundings, which make the *Riverside* well worth a visit. Details: *Riverside Studios,* Crisp Rd., London W6 9RL, England (phone: 81-748-3354).

**ROYAL ALBERT HALL:** Designed in the classical amphitheater style, and opened by Queen Victoria in 1871 as a memorial to her late consort, Prince Albert of Saxe-Coburg, this almost round house is truly splendid and imposing, with a seating capacity of 5,500. The domed building, a quarter of a mile in circumference, has terra cotta moldings imposed on a red brick exterior, an immense Grand Organ, and three tiers of boxes. All kinds of concerts, from a Bach "B Minor Mass" to a spine-tingling, cannon-throttled "1812 Overture," will fill it up. The *Henry Wood Promenade Concerts* ("the *Proms*" in local parlance) are particularly special and attract crowds every night from July to September. The *Proms* programs feature music from all eras. Traditionally, the last night concludes with familiar British music, including Elgar's "Pomp and Circumstance March No. 1." The *BBC Symphony Orchestra* performs here during most of the season, but every year appearances are made by most of the other major British orchestras, as well as visits by some of the world's most prestigious ensembles, such as the *Vienna Philharmonic,* the *Amsterdam Concertgebouw,* the *Leipzig Gewandhaus,* and the *New York Philharmonic.* Most concerts at the *Hall* have remarkably low ticket prices. The *Hall* also has hosted such popular artists as Frank Sinatra, John Denver, Paul Simon, and Eric Clapton. And it's also a venue for championship boxing, tennis tournaments, and grand balls. Details: *Royal Albert Hall,* Kensington Gore, London SW7 2AP, England (phone: box office, 71-589-8212; administration/tours, 71-589-3203).

**ROYAL COURT THEATRE:** One of the most famous of London's small stages, this one has made theatrical history more than once — first around 1904, with Harley Granville Barker's stagings of Arthur Pinero farces and George Bernard Shaw plays, and again in the late 1950s, when George Devine's *English Stage Company* presented John Osborne's *Look Back in Anger.* Even today, the theater is associated with very modern works, and produces the plays of such contemporary writers as Caryl Church-ill, Edward Bond, and Snoo Wilson. And despite the chronic shortage of money, standards are always high. The *Royal Court* is a great place for spotting talent, and the audience is lively. Ron Hutchinson's *Rat in the Skull,* Michael Hastings's *Tom and Viv,* and Wallace Shawn's *Aunt Dan and Lemon* started here before heading for the West End and New York, and its latest *Hamlet* was pronounced revolutionary. Details: *Royal Court,* Sloane Sq., London SW1W 8AS, England (phone: 71-730-1745).

**ROYAL FESTIVAL HALL:** Opened in 1951, London's premiere concert hall seats an audience of 3,000. It is part of the *South Bank Arts Centre,* which also includes the nearby *Royal National Theatre,* the *National Film Theatre,* the *Museum of the Moving Image* (*MOMI*), Jubilee Gardens, riverside walkways, the *Hayward Gallery,* and two smaller halls, the 1,065-seat *Queen Elizabeth Hall* and the 370-seat *Purcell Room.* In addition to an annual program of 1,200 events that feature most major performers on the international music and lyric arts scenes, there are free foyer exhibitions and lunchtime concerts. Shops and dining facilities are open all day. Details: *Royal Festival Hall,* South Bank, London SE1 8XX, England (phone: 71-928-8800).

**ROYAL NATIONAL THEATRE:** Anyone who visits this trio of houses in a handsome, large, Thameside drama complex is sure to have plenty to talk about — even if the fare is not to his taste. That, however, is unlikely, for Maggie Smith, Albert Finney, John Gielgud, Ian McKellen, Ralph Richardson, Peggy Ashcroft, and Paul Scofield all have appeared here. And plenty of breath-stopping acting takes place, in roles ranging from the soul-stretching to the small, in a selection of plays that embrace the classics; translations of works by European dramatists such as Schnitzler, Horvath, Feydeau, and Brecht; revivals of contemporary plays; new pieces by living playwrights such as Pinter, Stoppard, Brenton, Storey, Bolt, and Ayckbourne; and adaptations of such books as *Lark Rise* and *The World Turned Upside Down.*

The building itself is wonderful, with an interior that feels like a walk-through sculpture, a huge foyer with bars that seems to be London's answer to Paris's sidewalk cafés, and all manner of walks, terraces, and restaurants with fine views of Somerset House and the river curving off toward St. Paul's.

Before performances, ensembles and soloists play for free in the foyers, and it's possible to browse through art exhibitions while listening. There are also almost always so-called platform performances — brief plays, readings, poetry, music, and mime — in all three theaters: the 400-seat *Cottesloe,* which is otherwise mainly used for works requiring small-scale staging, the 890-seat proscenium-arch *Lyttelton,* and the 1,160-seat open-stage *Olivier.* The last two feel almost as intimate as the *Cottesloe,* thanks to their excellent design. Details: *Royal National Theatre,* South Bank, London SE1 9PX, England (phone: 71-928-2252).

**ROYAL OPERA HOUSE, COVENT GARDEN:** Worth a look for its grandeur alone, this jewel of a 2,098-seat opera house, the third on the site, is splendidly Victorian, with red plush, shaded lights, scarlet and gold tiers, domed turquoise ceiling, and sweeping horseshoe-shaped balconies. But the play's the thing, and some of the best singers in the world have performed here — among them Dame Nellie Melba, Dame Joan Suther-land, Kirsten Flagstad, Maria Callas, and Kiri Te Kanawa. The tradition of excellence continues unabated, and the hall ranks among the world's half-dozen true greats of its kind. The *Royal Opera* shares the house with the *Royal Ballet,* which, under noted choreographers such as Sir Frederick Ashton and Sir Kenneth MacMillan, with danc-ers such as Antoinette Sibley and Dame Margot Fonteyn, Rudolf Nureyev and Anthony Dowell, has become one of the world's most noted companies. Nearby, on the south wall of St. Paul's Church in *Covent Garden,* a silver casket contains the ashes of Ellen Terry, the famous actress, who died in 1928. Details: *Royal Opera House, Covent Garden,* London WC2E 9DD, England (phone: box office, 71-240-1066).

**SADLER'S WELLS THEATRE:** Built on the site of two mineral springs discovered in 1683 by Richard Sadler, this member of the trio of the capital's oldest more or less continuously operating halls has seen its jugglers and clowns, rope dancers and performing animals, plays and pantomimes, and even roller skaters and boxers. The theater once hosted the world premiere of Benjamin Britten's *Peter Grimes* and, in its time, also has been home to the *Royal Ballet* and the *English National Opera.* Today, it hosts touring opera and dance companies from all over the world — among them *Merce Cunningham, Twyla Tharp, Pilobolus,* the *Central Ballet of China,* and the *Sydney Dance Theatre.* The London seasons of the country's leading dance companies, including the *Rambert Dance Company,* the *London Contemporary Dance Theatre,* and the *National Youth Music Theater,* also take place here. (The *Sadler's Wells Royal Ballet* has moved to the *Birmingham Hippodrome* and changed its name to the *Birmingham Royal Ballet.*) *Sadler's Wells* has a second auditorium, the *Lilian Baylis Theatre,* beside the principal building. This newer space is small (220 seats), but is fully equipped technically; presentations here are divided between small-scale professional work (music, drama, dance) and community and education projects. The theater's exterior, foyer, and performance areas have all been beautifully redecorated. Details: *Sadler's Wells Theatre,* Rosebery Ave., London EC1R 4TN, England (phone: 71-278-6563; box office, 71-278-8916).

**THEATRE ROYAL (DRURY LANE):** The productions here may not be London's most innovative, but this 2,283-seat theater, with its beautiful symmetrical staircase and domed entranceway, is definitely one of London's most historic. The fourth playhouse on the site, it was preceded by a theater where Charles II met Nell Gwyn, who once sold oranges at the entrance; another predecessor was designed by Christopher Wren, with John Dryden as chief playwright, and David Garrick and Richard Sheridan as managers, the latter of whose *School for Scandal* was written in 1777 upstairs while actors rehearsed completed sections below. The present house, designed by Benjamin Wyatt in 1812, has hosted opera and drama, pantomime and film, and even musicals. Edmund Kean, whom many believe to be the greatest tragedian of all time, played here in 1814, as have Sir Henry Irving, Ellen Terry, Sir John Gielgud, and other famous thespians. The theater has its tradition, the cutting of the so-called Baddeley Cake (named after the actor whose will supplied the funds) in the Grand Saloon after the performance every January 6, and its ghost, a gray-cloaked, high-booted, bewigged fellow who haunts the upper circle — in the daytime only, however. For a splurge, theatergoers can hire the Royal Box or the Prince of Wales Box, both of which come complete with seating for six and tiny Regency or Adamesque retiring rooms. Tours of the theater can be arranged through its historian, George Hoare. Details: *Theatre Royal (Drury Lane),* Catherine St., London WC2B 5JF, England (phone: box office, 71-836-8108; tours, 71-836-3352).

**THEATRE ROYAL (HAYMARKET):** Architect John Nash, who designed this small, stylish theater, gave it a wonderful Corinthian portico, which looks all the more grand when floodlit, as it often is at night. Henry Fielding managed a predecessor on the site around 1737, and the present hall, built in 1821, has been the setting for plays by everyone from Ibsen to Wilde, T. S. Eliot and Tennessee Williams to Noël Coward, J. M. Barrie, and Terence Rattigan; Sir Beerbohm Tree played here in the late 19th century. The hall itself, renovated at the beginning of this century, is all white, rich blue, and gold leaf; there's a wonderfully crafted royal arms above the stage. Details: *Theatre Royal,* Haymarket, London SW1Y 4HT, England (phone: 71-930-9832).

**WIGMORE HALL:** One of Europe's most elegant and intimate concert halls, this fine example of the Art Nouveau style — full of alabaster, marble, polished mahogany, and brass — was created in 1901 by Carl Bechstein (of piano fame) and is famous for its nearly perfect acoustics. A delightful hall for recitals and chamber music, it has hosted debuts by Elisabeth Schwarzkopf (in 1948) and Daniel Barenboim (in 1958) and recitals by Julian Bream, Peter Pears, Andrés Segovia, and many others. Arthur Rubinstein made his second appearance in England here (in 1912) and also his last public appearance (in 1976). Nowadays, the hall attracts artists such as Olaf Bär, Shura Cherkassy, and the *Beaux Arts Trio,* and has a regular series of celebrity and early music concerts, as well as a very popular series of *Sunday Morning Coffee Concerts.* Details: *Wigmore Hall,* 36 Wigmore St., London W1H 9DF, England (phone: 71-935-2141).

**YOUNG VIC THEATRE:** This theater, founded more than 15 years ago, is new by London standards, but the spirit of experimentation and the *joie de jouer* that go into the productions are as much a tradition in the British theater as is the Bard himself. David Thacker, the theater's artistic director, is particularly renowned for bringing fresh interpretations and contemporary staging to Shakespeare and modern classics. Among the theater's most recent successes have been *The Price* and *Two-Way Mirror,* both by Arthur Miller, and *The Plough and the Stars* by Sean O'Casey. The works of William Shakespeare, Henrik Ibsen, David Holman, and other modern playwrights are typically presented, along with a comprehensive program of work for younger audiences. It's a lively place and quite different, architecturally, from most theaters. The building includes a café and is easily accessible by public transportation. Details: *Young Vic,* 66 The Cut, London SE1 8LZ, England (phone: 71-928-6363).

# The Best Festivals

 Music is just one inspiration for the variety of festivals that take place in London throughout the year, both in the city center and in the suburbs. Choral, symphonic, chamber, folk, and jazz are only some of the sounds that can be enjoyed in all sorts of venues.

**CITY OF LONDON FESTIVAL:** London's own festival, held for 2½ weeks in July within the Old City's square mile, takes advantage of the area's many fine halls and churches — including the Tower of London, Guildhall, the *Barbican Centre,* and St. Paul's — for concerts of serious music, featuring choirs, orchestras, chamber groups, and leading soloists of international repute. A popular program of jazz, dance, street theater, poetry, and a wide range of exhibitions runs concurrent with the festival. Details: *City of London Festival Box Office,* Bishopsgate Hall, Bishopgate, London EC2M 4QH, England (phone: 71-248-4260).

**DANCE UMBRELLA:** A dance treat, this festival has been an important part of the international contemporary dance scene since it was founded in 1978, and it attracts participants from all over the world. During October and November, festival events are held in various theaters both in London and around the country. Details: *Dance Umbrella, Riverside Studios,* Crisp Rd., Hammersmith, London W6 9RL, England (phone: 81-741-4040).

**EARLY MUSIC CENTRE FESTIVAL:** One of Britain's most important early-music events, this festival mixes orchestral, chamber, and choral music — all played on original instruments by professional groups from here and abroad. The concerts are held in a number of important London halls and churches in the fall. Details: *Festival Secretary, The Early Music Centre,* Charles Clore House, 17 Russell Sq., London WC1B 5DR, England (phone: 71-580-8401).

**FESTIVAL OF BAROQUE MUSIC:** Internationally known for its innovative June programs, when leading players perform on period instruments in Christopher Wren's beautiful St. James's Church in Piccadilly. Details: *Lufthansa Festival of Baroque Music,* 4 Bennet Park, Blackheath, London SE3 9RB, England (phone: 81-852-0823).

**GREENWICH FESTIVAL:** The events of this annual 2-week-long festival in June include mime and dance performances; poetry readings; concerts featuring rock, reggae, jazz, classical, and folk music; as well as many children's events. Internationally known artists such as Janet Baker, Claudio Arrau, James Galway, Alfred Brendel, and others perform alongside amateurs and local groups; the *Greenwich Festival* began as a purely community-oriented affair. Details: *Greenwich Festival Office,* 147 Powis St., London SE18 5SL, England (phone: 81-317-8687).

**HENRY WOOD PROMENADE CONCERTS:** Better known as "the *Proms,*" it has been so named because this annual festival, since its foundation in 1894, has taken place in an auditorium capable of providing a considerable area of "promenade" or standing places to which the mostly youthful audience is admitted at very reasonable prices. Since World War II (when their original home was bombed), the *Proms* have been held at the *Royal Albert Hall* in Kensington, a masterpiece of Victorian architecture which accommodates nearly 8,000 people. The *Proms* have been organized by the BBC since 1942, and each night, from mid-July to mid-September, they attract crowds from all over the world. In addition, several million others listen to live broadcasts of the concerts on radio and television. The *BBC Symphony Orchestra* performs most of the concerts — 60 to 70 in all — but every year appearances are made by most of the other major British orchestras, along with prestigious visits by some of the world's most renowned ensembles, such as the *Vienna Philharmonic,* the *Concertgebouw* from Amsterdam, the *Leipzig Gewandhaus,* and the *New York Philharmonic.* The *Proms* reflect music from all eras. Traditionally, the last night concludes with familiar British music, including Elgar's "Pomp and Circumstance March No. 1," and the active participation of the audience. Details: *Royal Albert Hall,* Kensington Gore, London SW7 2AP, England (phone: box office, 71-589-8212; administration, 71-589-3203).

**LONDON FILM FESTIVAL:** Every November this fête presents the best of British and international movies from the latest international film festivals, with occasional lectures and discussions led by participating film directors after many of the screenings. *The National Film Theatre* on the South Bank is the principal location, but other London houses are used as well. Details: *National Film Theatre,* South Bank, London SE1 8XT, England (phone: 71-928-3232).

**LONDON MARATHON:** Since London held its first marathon in 1981, over 200,000 people have completed the 26-mile course from the Greenwich suburb south of the river to the finishing point at Westminster. The halfway mark comes as the runners cross Tower Bridge. From there they go around the new Docklands area before finishing beside Big Ben on Westminster Bridge. It has become Britain's most popular sporting event, with thousands of spectators lining the route and millions more watching it on television throughout the world. Competitors come from all over the world — as many as 65 different countries have been represented — and the organizers receive around 80,000 applications for 34,000 places. Although some are top runners, including Olympic champions, most are ordinary people, of all ages and occupations, chosen on a random first-come, first-served basis. Many raise money for charity through sponsorship. Held on a Sunday in mid-April. Details: *London Marathon,* Andy Ritchie, PO Box 262, Richmond-upon-Thames, Surrey, TW10 5JB, England (phone: 81-948-7935; fax: 81-948-8633).

**LONDON-TO-BRIGHTON VETERAN CAR RUN:** Until 1896, a British law prohibited the operation of a car unless it was preceded by a man on foot carrying a red flag (so as not to scare horses). Its repeal is the raison d'être for this 50-mile drive full of shiny antique autos, held annually on the first Sunday in November. Details: *RAC*

*Motor Sports Association Ltd.,* Motor Sports House, Riverside Park, Colnbrook, Slough SL3 0HG, England (phone: 753-681736).

**LORD MAYOR'S PROCESSION:** This event, held annually on the second Saturday in November, honors the newly inaugurated Lord Mayor of London and the profession that he is leaving for the duration of his mayoral term. The lord mayor inaugurated in 1991 was the 664th to hold the position since it was established in 1189. During the parade he is transported — in an 18th-century gold state coach drawn by six gray horses — from the Guildhall to the Royal Court of Justice, where the oath of office is administered. A parade follows, made up of floats, which represent each guild (union), and marching bands. The names of the parade groups are quite amusing, such as the *Worshipful Company of Fruiterers* (they've dressed as bunches of grapes in the past) and the *Worshipful Company of Upholders.* The Thames Water float carried men dressed as toilets one year! Other wonderfully colorful characters include buglers and bagpipers and the *Royal Yeomanry.* The wacky parade is especially great fun for kids. Details: *City of London Public Relations Office,* Guildhall, London EC2P 2EJ, England (phone: 71-606-3030).

**PUNCH AND JUDY FESTIVAL:** Every weekend on the steps of St. Paul's (the actors' church in *Covent Garden*), enjoy a traditional Punch and Judy show performed by Percy Press. On the first Sunday of October, however, the 160 members of the Punch and Judy Fellowship gather for a grand day-long festival, at which guest artists from around the world perform. The present festival dates back to 1981, but the Punch and Judy tradition at St. Paul's goes as far back as 1662. A plaque in the portico commemorates the first performance of these combative puppets, watched by Samuel Pepys. Details: *Punch and Judy Festival,* Percy Press II, 16 Templeton, London N15 6RU, England (phone: 81-802-4656).

**ROYAL TOURNAMENT:** For nearly 3 weeks every July, Britain's armed forces stage a spectacular military pageant in the huge indoor Earl's Court arena. All sorts of skills are displayed, from musicians on horseback and acrobatic gymnasts to police dogs and cavalry chargers. Tanks and planes are often on exhibit, too. It's colorful, breathtaking, exciting, and noisy. The queen and all the leading royals are in attendance each year. Details: *Royal Tournament, Earl's Court Exhibition Centre,* London SW5 9TA, England (phone: 71-373-8141).

**SPITALFIELDS FESTIVAL:** The Parish Church of Spitalfields, built in 1729 in the East End, provides a superb setting for this varied program of mostly 18th-century music, ballet, and opera, held during the last 2 weeks in June. Guided walking tours around the area's Georgian buildings are also available. Details: *Spitalfields Festival,* Christ Church, Commercial St., London E1 6LY, England (phone: 71-377-0287).


# Antiques and Auctions

Perhaps no nation takes better care of its past than Britain and, naturally, London is the home of its main auction houses — the place to find the largest selection of antiques — from old coins and jewelry to paintings, toys, and weapons. Inevitably, however, the presence of so many dealers and other experts means that you are unlikely to find a real bargain. But if money is no object, it shouldn't take too long to locate whatever you want.

Many genuine antiques taken out of the country are subject to duty. Also, an export license may be required. It is available from the Export Licensing Division, Department of Trade and Industry, Kingsgate House, 68-74 Victoria Street, London SW1 6EW, England (phone: 71-215-5000).

# A REPERTOIRE OF ANTIQUES SOURCES

There are four distinctly different types of dealers in Britain. At the low end of the scale are the flea markets, where true bargains are often available — to those willing to sift through piles of not always interesting miscellanea. Auction houses frequently yield a find, under the right circumstances, to those able to visit the pre-sale exhibition before bidding. Antiques shops offer convenience. A dealer has made the rounds of the markets and has purchased the pick of the auction houses for resale — and a customer pays the price for the dealer's time and trouble. Fairs often bring many dealers and many wares together in one place. The quality may be high, with prices to match, but the selection can't be beat. In short, the repertoire of sources for antiques is not so different from that in the US, Canada, and many other countries. What is notable is the selection of these fairs, auction houses, shops, and markets. Below we describe a few of the very best.

**SHOPS AND ANTIQUES CENTERS:** Whether the quest be for barometers or bond certificates, tools or toy soldiers, enthusiasts should be able to find a shop in London catering exclusively to their collecting passion. Over the centuries the antiques trade in Britain has become very sophisticated in many specialties.

Ethical standards are generally high, and dealers usually will spontaneously divulge all the defects of an item a customer is considering buying. A number are members of recognized, reputable national guilds, with clear and rigorous codes in matters of authenticity and quality. But if the caveats aren't offered unsolicited, prospective buyers should be sure to question the dealer about what is original, what has been restored or retouched, and what has simply been replaced. If a purchase involves a significant sum, the buyer also should ask to have the qualifications put in writing.

For advice about purchasing and shipping and customs regulations, and for a list of members, antiques lovers can contact one of the following dealers' associations:

> *British Antique Dealers' Association* (20 Rutland Gate, London SW7 1BD, England; phone: 71-589-4128). Members of this organization, to which some of the most reputable shops and dealers belong, display a blue-and-gold plaque engraved with the figure of the Renaissance sculptor and goldsmith Benvenuto Cellini. They also publish a handbook ($20) available from *Joyce Golden Associates,* 551 Fifth Ave., New York, NY 10176.
>
> *London and Provincial Antique Dealers' Association* (*LAPADA;* 535 King's Road, London SW10 0SZ, England; phone: 71-823-3511). Over 750 members are committed to the strict *LAPADA* code; look for the chandelier sign. They also publish a book called *Buying Antiques in Britain* (£3.80 in Great Britain; $10 by surface mail or $20 by airmail in US, from above address).

These organizations can send lists of their members, who adhere to association standards. In addition, a comprehensive list of dealers in Britain is available in the following books — revised annually and for sale at fine bookstores in London:

> *Guide to the Antique Shops of Britain* (£12.95/about $21), published by the *Antique Collectors Club* (5 Church St., Woodbridge, Suffolk IP12 1DS, England; phone: 394-385501), contains more than 6,000 entries that outline the type of stock, size of showrooms, years in business, hours, and much more.
>
> *Miller's Price Guide* (£17.95/about $30) provides an overview of approximate prices for various items.

A recent trend has been the gathering of many small shops into antiques centers — something like tony shopping centers or indoor markets with all the stalls under one roof. These are intriguing places to spend a rainy hour and to get a quick overview of the local market, with no great pressure to buy. There are hundreds of interesting items that rarely make it across the Atlantic.

There are several antiques centers in London:

*Camden Passage Antiques Centre* is an 18th-century, traffic-free pedestrian walk that houses 350 dealers. In Islington, north of the city, in Camden Passage, N1. Antiques market days are Wednesdays and Saturdays; book market day is Thursday.

*Grays Antique Market,* installed in a beautiful terra cotta Victorian structure, houses dozens of stands, and its dealers are more selective than not. There is a fine selection of antique jewelry, as well as antiquarian books, maps, prints, arms and armor, lace, scientific instruments, and thimbles. Around the corner, *Grays In The Mews* (1-7 Davies Mews) has Victorian and Edwardian toys, paintings and prints, and Orientalia. 58 Davies St., W1 (phone: 71-629-7034).

*Chenil Galleries* is increasingly important as a center for Art Deco and Art Nouveau objects. But dealers' specialties range from Gothic furniture, tapestries, and textiles to 18th-century paintings, scientific instruments, and fine porcelain. 181-183 King's Rd., SW3 (phone: 71-351-5353).

*Alfie's Antique Market* is housed in what was once a Victorian department store. This warren of 370 stalls, showrooms, and workshops is the biggest covered antiques market in London — and likely the least expensive, since it is where the dealers come to buy. 13-25 Church St., NW8 (phone: 71-723-6066).

*Dukes Yard Antiques Market* at Richmond-upon-Thames is a newly designed center in the classical style. Seventy leading dealers have stands here, some having moved from central London, while others have opened an extra branch. Vendors specialize in items ranging from the 17th century to the 1950s, including furniture, paintings, silver, jewelry, glass, and china. There are also collections of memorabilia, printed ephemera, and household accessories such as mirrors, lighting, and fireplaces. Open Tuesdays through Saturdays. 1a Duke Street, Richmond-upon-Thames TW9 1HP, England (phone: 81-332-1051).

**FAIRS:** There are dozens of fairs in all sizes and qualities. Whether they last 2 days or 10, they attract dealers from all over the region, the country, and Europe. Many dealers make the rounds of these events, beginning in January and continuing through-out the year. The monthly *Antique Dealer and Collectors' Guide* magazine (PO Box 805, Greenwich, London SE10 8DT, England; phone: 81-691-4820) publishes a comprehensive yearly calendar listing antiques fairs in London and throughout the country.

The most prestigious fairs by far are the *Burlington House Fair,* held in September in odd-numbered years at the *Royal Academy* in London, and the *Grosvenor House Antiques Fair,* held in June at the *Grosvenor House* hotel in Park Lane. But there are others, which include the following:

*City of London Antiques Fair, Barbican Centre,* EC2. Late November.
*Kensington Antiques Fair,* New Town Hall, Kensington, W8. Early November.

**FLEA MARKETS AND OTHER WEEKLY SPECTACLES:** That heady mixture of rubbish and relic known as the flea market is the ultimate paradise for the collector. It offers the chance to find that special, unrecognized rarity, the eye-catching castoff whose true value only a devout aficionado would perceive — say, a yak saddle from the Indian Mutiny, a left-handed pewter monocle, or a chipped 78 rpm recording of Edward VIII's abdication speech.

The buyer's best allies in this odyssey are bad weather and early arrival. A serious collector should get to the market at dawn and pray for torrential rain, or if the spectacle itself is the main attraction, hope for a sunny morning. Fine days provide such good theater — at such moderate cost — that even the most eager treasure seekers won't be too disappointed at trudging home empty-handed. Though the British have managed to get many of their markets under a roof, thereby sacrificing local color to comforts, the bargains are still there. In London, open-air markets flourish all over the city, and for ferreting out the curious, they can't be beat. The interested can try their luck at the following:

*Bermondsey–New Caledonian Market* complex, where several dealers set up every Friday in a good-size open space off Tower Bridge Road, at the end of Long Lane and in an erstwhile factory nearby, is known as a dealers' market. Fresh shipments from the country go on sale here first (and, in fact, many of the goods for sale in Portobello Road were purchased here). Arrival after 9 AM means the best will be long gone; regulars try to arrive not much after 5 AM — with flashlights. Tower Bridge Rd., SE1.

*Greenwich Antiques Market* is a less frenetic place to be on Saturdays (and on Sundays in summer). Greenwich High Rd., SE10.

*Jubilee Flea Market.* Held on Mondays, it's a good bet for small antiques, old jewelry, and crockery. Don't miss the stalls on the south side of the piazza outside the main covered market. *Covent Garden,* WC2.

Portobello Road is famous for antiques shops, junk shops, outdoor pushcarts, and legions of antiques lovers from all over the world trying to buy up bits and pieces of England. The activity is astonishing — but eager hunters shouldn't necessarily expect to turn up a treasure at a good price, except occasionally in winter, when the weather is so blustery that only the most intrepid antiques hounds venture outside. There are flea markets on Fridays and Saturdays; on Saturdays, there are antiques as well. Portobello Road, W11.

**AUCTIONS:** An auction, as any addict knows, is a mixture of stock market, gambling casino, and living theater. It's the perfect answer to rainy-day blues, provided newcomers pay attention to these notes:

*Don't expect to make a killing.* Even Chinese peasant children are hip to the art market today, it seems. But chances of unearthing a real find are better for those who shop at smaller country auctions. Look carefully at mixed lots, and always venture out in inclement weather. Every so often someone picks up a golden goblet for 10p at a Girl Guide (the British version of a Girl Scout) auction and then resells it for £9,000. In any event, there is about a 30% saving on the shop price of a comparable item.

*Buy the catalogue before bidding.* Catalogues often include a list of estimated prices. Those prices are not a contractual commitment, but they do act as a guide for prospective buyers. An elaborate stylistic code hints at the conviction the house may have about the age and authenticity of an item. The use of capital letters, of artists' full names, and of words like "fine," "rare," and "important" all carry positive connotations. The use of a last name only and of words like "style" and "attributed" should serve as warnings.

*Visit the pre-sale exhibition carefully, thoroughly, and even repeatedly.* There is the pleasure of browsing in a store without a hovering clerk. Even more important is the prospective buyer's chance to examine the offerings. *Caution* is the prevailing rule at an auction. Serious buyers should have paintings taken down from the wall and ask to handle objects under lock and key. Those who can't be at the sale can leave a commission bid with the auctioneer or even place a bid by telephone — but if they can't be at the exhibition, they should be wary of buying.

*Decide on a top bid before the auction begins, and don't go beyond it.* The bidding has its own rhythm and tension. The auctioneer becomes a Pied Piper, with the buyers winking, blinking, and nodding in time to his music. This situation arouses unusual behavior in some people. Suddenly their self-worth is at stake, and they'll bid far beyond what the item is worth — or even what they can afford. A bid may be canceled by promptly calling out "Withdrawn." *Note:* In determining their top price, bidders should remember to add the house commission, which is generally 10%, but can be more, and any value added tax.

London is still the auction capital of the world, and the market price of a work of art or an antique generally refers to the price that other items of its genre have fetched in the London salerooms. Fingers rise and hammers fall all over Britain — but the following spots warrant prime attention:

*Christie's* was founded in 1766. The fortunes of England's great families can be read in *Christie's* records, and an object's whole lineage can often be traced through its appearances in 2 centuries of *Christie's* sales. No wonder the mother house is something of a national landmark. There are auctions daily, and the exhibition rooms are a constantly changing museum. The clientele includes furred ladies, pin-striped Rembrandt hunters, bespectacled experts from US museums, and ordinary Londoners who do their *Christmas* shopping here, especially at the South Kensington saleroom, which handles items of recent vintage and some lower value — toys, telescopes, top hats, and the like. Some higher priced sales at *Christie's* in South Kensington (8 King St., St. James's, SW1; phone: 71-839-9060) include tribal art, Oriental and Art Deco items, paintings, furniture, and textiles. The South Kensington branch is at 85 Old Brompton Rd., SW7 (phone: 71-581-7611).

*Sotheby's* is the world's oldest auction house. The little white building in which it is discreetly housed, on the most elegant street in England, is a kind of nerve center of the art world. Its roster of experts in every field rivals the *British Museum*'s. An important sale of Old Masters or Impressionists, with hundreds of thousands of dollars riding on every twitch, beats an evening at the *Royal National Theatre,* as the chandeliers glitter next to a computer board that translates bids into dollars, yen, marks, lire, and Swiss and French francs as it did November 11, 1987, when van Gogh's *Irises* sold for $54 million. In its surprisingly large complex of salerooms, auctions of every kind of work of art, including books, manuscripts, coins, medals, and jewelry, take place regularly throughout the year. 34 New Bond St., W1 (phone: 71-493-8080).

*Phillips* is number three, and it's trying harder and harder. Auctions are held almost daily, and items range from fine works of art to more affordable collectibles. The house also handles a large number of estate sales, held on the owners' premises in fine English country houses. Since they are often sparsely attended by the general public, there's a fair chance of encountering dealer-level prices. The house does a large volume in modestly priced lots, and the staff is extremely helpful to auction novices. Besides the London house (7 Blenheim St., W1; phone: 71-629-6602), there are 20 salerooms throughout the UK. Weekly picture sales are held at *Phillips Marylebone Auction Rooms* (Hayes Pl., NW1; phone: 71-723-2647), and collectibles — including toys and dolls — and textiles can be bid on at *Phillips West Two* (10 Salem Rd., W2; phone: 71-221-5303).

## ANTIQUES PEAKS ON THE LONDON LANDSCAPE

For centuries, the city represented a safe haven for things of value. Consequently, it became the unquestioned center of the world's antiques trade. Anything can be bought here, and everything has a market value and instant liquidity.

There are a handful of places in London that stand out for their selection of shops, antiques centers, flea markets, and auction houses. These are the places that savvy antiques dealers from the Continent visit when they're on the prowl for newly fashionable 19th-century English furniture and objets d'art — and they are a must for any antiques lover.

**Best Antiquing Streets** – Shops are in greatest supply along the Brompton Road, Fulham Road, New Bond Street, Jermyn Street, Kensington Church Street, King's Road, and Mount Street.

**Antiques Centers** – In addition to the enormous variety of flea markets, there are also excellent markets that are open almost any day of the week:

*Antiquarius Antique Market.* 170 vendors with specialties ranging from theatrical items and delft to faïence and items from the 1950s. 135-141 King's Rd., SW3 (phone: 71-351-5353).

*Bond Street Antique Centre.* A source for finely worked antique jewelry, watches, portrait miniatures, silver, porcelain, and other objets d'art. 124 New Bond St., W1 (phone: 71-351-5353).

*Chelsea Antique Market.* The original indoor antiques market, and still one of the best. 253 King's Rd., SW3 (phone: 71-352-1424).

*Grays Antique Market.* Davies Mews and 58 Davies St., W1 (phone: 71-629-7034).

**Street Markets** – London is unique in its great variety of street markets, and each one has its own flavor and appeal.

*Petticoat Lane,* London's largest Sunday market, has a special antiques section in Goulston Street, E1. It is known as the *New Cutler Street Market* and is well known for the sale of scrap gold and silver, as well as coins, stamps, and medals. Open until 2 PM.

*Camden Lock,* not to be confused with Islington's *Camden Passage* (below), is now the trendiest of the city's markets. Though less important for very old antiques, it is chockablock with items from the 1930s and 1940s, along with masses of secondhand furniture, clothing, and crafts. Saturdays and Sundays, Camden Town, NW4.

The *Jubilee* antiques market, in *Covent Garden* (WC2), has a good selection of small items such as silver and glassware.

*Camden Passage* in Islington (N1) is not a market for bargains, but offers good-quality porcelain, clocks, prints, and silver. Some of the 350 dealers and 150 stalls packed into this mere 200-yard passageway are indoors in the *Georgian Village,* others are in the *Mall.* Wednesdays and Saturdays are the days to browse; there's little to see at other times.

*Bermondsey–New Caledonian Market* is open Fridays, and dealing starts briskly at dawn or before. It's a market for the dedicated and the knowledgeable and is frequented primarily by dealers. Flashlights are essential in the wee hours. There is also some activity throughout the week in the area's furniture warehouses. Bermondsey St. at Long La., off Tower Bridge Rd., SE1.

*Portobello Road* often turns up merchandise that you could have had for less at the *Bermondsey–New Caledonian Market* the day before. W11.

**Shops** – London is not only auction action and wearying market mobs. It is also the cushioning courtesy of some of the world's most distinguished antiques shops. Visitors can browse in their carpeted serenity and examine some of the world's best wares:

*Alexander Juran,* a continuation of a business started in Prague during the reign of Emperor Franz Josef II. The showrooms are small and shabby, but the textiles, rugs, and carpets on display here can be exceptional. 74 New Bond St., W1 (phone: 71-493-4484 or 71-629-2550).

*Antique Porcelain Company Ltd.,* for 18th-century English and continental porcelain. 149 New Bond St., W1 (phone: 71-629-1254).

*Asprey & Company.* Much like *Tiffany's* coveted blue box, a purple box from *Asprey* means luxury goods. Antiques, china, glass, silver, jewelry, clocks, and leather goods are available here. The company holds three Royal Warrants. 165 New Bond St., W1 (phone: 71-493-6767).

*Grosvenor Prints* resembles a great aunt's attic with more than 100,000 prints, on all subjects. The shop also holds four annual exhibitions covering portraits (April), mixed subjects (June), London and topographical views (October), and dogs from 1660 to 1940 (December). 28-32 Shelton St., *Covent Garden,* WC2 (phone: 71-836-1979).

*London Silver Vaults,* for silver. An underground warren of dealers of fine china, objets d'art, and silver (new, old, secondhand), in the strongrooms of the original

Chancery Lane Safe Deposit Company, which opened its doors in 1885 and started serving as a secure base for silver vendors during World War II. 53-54 Chancery La., WC2 (phone: 71-242-3844).

*Lucy B. Campbell* features 17th- to 19th-century decorative prints of birds, animals, plants, and architecture, as well as contemporary watercolors. 123 Kensington Church St., W8 (phone: 71-727-2205).

*Mallett and Son* sells almost all things antique, but specializes in the finest English furniture, choosing every item with consummate taste. The shop is a miniature museum displaying wares ranging from the late 17th to the early 19th century. 40 New Bond St., W1 (phone: 71-499-7411). A branch, selling French and continental furniture and a large, eclectic stock of works of art and decorative items, is at Bourdon House, 2 Davies St., W1 (phone: 71-629-2444).

*Milne and Moller* deals in British and continental watercolors by 19th- and 20th-century artists. By appointment only and Saturdays. 35 Colville Terrace, W11 (phone: 71-727-1679).

*Partridge Ltd.,* for the absolutely best 18th-century French and English furniture, paintings, and objets d'art. 144-146 New Bond St., W1 (phone: 71-629-0834).

*Pickering and Chatto,* for antiquarian books in English literature of the 17th and 18th centuries, economics, science, and medicine. 17 Pall Mall, SW1 (phone: 71-930-2515).

*S. J. Phillips,* for silver, jewelry, and objets d'art from the 16th to the early 19th centuries. 139 New Bond St., W1 (phone: 71-629-6261).

*Temple Gallery,* for Byzantine, Greek, and early Russian icons. 6 Clarendon Cross, W11 (phone: 71-727-3809).

*Vigo-Sternberg Galleries,* for tapestries. 37 S. Audley St., W1 (phone: 71-629-8307).

**At Auction** – The great auction houses, *Christie's* (8 King St., SW1; phone: 71-839-9060) and *Sotheby's* (34-35 New Bond St., W1; phone: 71-493-8080), are instrumental in setting market prices; they're superb places to develop a feel for the market.

**At the Fair** – The *Grosvenor House Antiques Fair,* held for 10 days every June at the *Grosvenor House* hotel (Park Lane, W1) is a sun in the antiques dealer's solar system, where everything from Etruscan heads to Victorian bustles are found, and every piece has been authenticated by independent experts. For more information, contact the *British Antiques Dealers' Association* (20 Rutland Gate, Knightsbridge, London SW7 1BD, England; phone: 71-589-4128).

## RULES OF THE ROAD FOR AN ODYSSEY OF THE OLD

*Buy for sheer pleasure and not for investment.* Treasure seekers should forget about the carrot of supposed resale value that dealers habitually dangle in front of amateur clients. If you love an object, you'll never part with it. If you don't love it, let someone else adopt it.

*Don't be timid about haggling.* That's as true at a Bond Street jeweler's as at the most colorful flea market. It's surprising how much is negotiable — and the higher the price, the farther it has to fall.

*Buy the finest affordable example of any item, in as close to mint condition as possible.* Chipped or tarnished "bargains" will haunt their buyers later with their shabbiness.

*Train your eye in museums.* Museums that specialize in items dear to a collector are the best of all, though they may break his or her heart. The furniture and clocks of London's *Wallace Collection,* for instance, help to set impeccable standards against which to measure purchases.

*Peruse British art books and periodicals.* Among the best are the following:

*Antique Collector,* available from the National Magazine Company (72 Broadwick St., London W1V 2BP, England; phone: 71-439-5000), and on newsstands.

*Antique Dealer and Collector's Guide,* available by mail (PO Box 805, Greenwich, London SE10 8DT, England; phone: 81-691-4820), and from *W. H. Smith* (bookstores) and leading newsagents.

*Antiques Trade Gazette,* available by mail (17 Whitcomb St., London WC2H 7PL, England; phone: 71-930-4957, subscriptions department). A weekly newspaper listing and reporting on auctions and shows in Britain and on the Continent. Available at the newsstand adjoining *Sotheby's* on Bond Street (W1) and at other antiques centers.

*Apollo,* an international magazine of arts and antiques, available on newsstands or from 3 St. James's Place, London SW1A 1NP, England (phone: 71-629-3061).

*Burlington Magazine,* available by subscription (6 Bloomsbury Sq., London WC1A 2LP, England; phone: 71-430-0481), and at selected newsagents.

*Buying Antiques in Britain,* published by the *London and Provincial Antique Dealers' Association* (535 King's Rd., London SW10 0SZ, England; phone: 71-823-3511). Lists 770 dealers. Free in return for valid antiques business card; subscription is £3.80/about $6 (surface), £12/about $20 (airmail), purchased by sterling checks only.

*International Herald Tribune* art pages, particularly on Saturdays.

*Get advice from a specialist when contemplating a major acquisition.* The various dealers' guilds can be helpful. Major auction houses like *Sotheby's* and *Christie's* have fleets of resident specialists who can be consulted. So does the *British Museum.* Those who are interested might enroll in a special instructional program to become experts in their own right. *Christie's Education* (63 Old Brompton Rd., London SW7 3JS, England; phone: 71-581-3933) is actually two intensive year-long courses on the fine and decorative arts, one covering Greek and Roman antiquity to AD 1450, and the other covering the period from AD 1450 to the present day. Evening courses are also available in specialized subjects, including wine. *Sotheby's Educational Studies* also offers day-long, weekend, and week-long courses (30 Oxford St., London W1R 1RE, England; phone: 71-408-1100) and holds Works of Art Courses, which include 3- and 9-month studies on fine and decorative arts and styles in art, and study weeks on topics such as "Collecting on a Limited Budget" and "Contemporary Painting and Sculpture." The British Tourist Authority offers a list of special interest holidays that includes several others.

# Ancient Monuments

Britain has been inhabited for thousands of years, and scarcely a single one of the population groups who have settled here has disappeared without leaving a trace. London and the countryside are littered with their remains: stone walls, tombs and burial chambers, barrows and henges, hilltop forts, castles, abbeys, crosses, churches, and towers. Ruined and crumbling, they stand as reminders of a turbulent and fascinating past.

An independent body called the Historic Buildings and Monuments Commission for England (and Scotland), more briefly known as English Heritage, was recently established to record and preserve many of these important sites. Several now ask for admission charges to cover upkeep. The organization's *Guide to English Heritage Properties* can be helpful. It is available for £2.25/about $3.70 from English Heritage, PO Box 43, Ruislip, Middlesex HA4 0XW, England (phone: 81-845-1200).

**TOWER OF LONDON:** The Tower — known in some quarters as the world's most famous castle — is actually a complex of buildings. Begun during the days of William the Conqueror and expanded many times over the centuries, it has figured in British history for nearly a millennium as palace, fortress, treasury, mint, bank, arsenal, munitions factory, garrison, library, museum, observatory, and even zoo. Its most famous function, however, has been that of a prison, and many people came through the so-called Traitor's Gate hoping to be ransomed or pardoned and thereby avoid the fate — endless incarceration or death — of those who had passed that way before them. Many hoped in vain. The stories of the executions, murders, and suicides within these walls are legion. Henry VI, imprisoned during the Wars of the Roses, was stabbed to death during his prayers. The boy King Edward V and his brother disappeared from public view in 1483 while lodged in the Tower; the next trace of them (apparently) was two sets of bones found under a staircase in Charles II's time. Henry VIII hustled wives, dissidents, and possible claimants to the throne into the Tower, the first step in the journey that usually ended at the executioner's block. Among those who made that journey were Anne Boleyn and Catherine Howard, the monarch's second and fifth wives, who were executed on the Tower Green and buried in the chapel of St. Peter ad Vincula; Sir Thomas More ("the king's good servant but God's first"), who met his end after rejecting his sovereign's claim to rule the English church; and Thomas Cromwell, the not-always-so-jolly king's chief administrator.

Later, Lady Jane Grey was beheaded on Tower Green after the Duke of Northumberland, the father of her husband, Lord Guilford Dudley, persuaded her dying cousin Edward VI to pass his crown to the 17-year-old Jane rather than to his Catholic half-sister, Mary, the rightful heir to the throne; she reigned for 9 days, beginning on July 10, 1553, until the English rallied around Mary. In the days of Elizabeth I (who herself had been imprisoned in the Tower on the orders of Mary), the Earl of Essex was executed at the age of 34 after the discovery of a plot to kidnap the aging queen he had courted. James I dispatched Sir Walter Raleigh to the Tower in 1603; Raleigh passed the time writing *A History of the World* until his release in 1616, which was then followed by his death in 1618 when the monarch finally had him beheaded.

In modern times, German spies were executed in the courtyards during the two world wars, and in 1941, Rudolf Hess, Hitler's deputy, was imprisoned here for a few days. Today, such colorful episodes of the Tower's history are hard to imagine amid the multitudes of tourists and guides milling about, as they do most of the year. It's most atmospheric when there are few visitors — on a rainy day, for instance, or at night for the Ceremony of the Keys. (Travelers may book ahead by writing to the Resident Governor, Queen's House, HM Tower of London, London EC3N 4AB, England, and enclosing the appropriate international postage coupons.) Rapiers, clubs, maces and flails, longbows and crossbows, cannon and muskets, shields, daggers, and all manner of other weapons, as well as glittering armor, are displayed in the White Tower, the 92-foot-high structure begun by William the Conqueror in 1078 as his palace and fortress, and renamed in the mid-13th century when Henry III had the structure whitewashed; the collections are among the finest of their kind in the world.

In the Jewel House, a later addition to the complex (closed annually in January), visitors can see the Crown Jewels — the splendid St. Edward's crown, worn only during coronations; the Imperial State, which contains over 3,500 precious stones, including four large pearls that probably belonged to Elizabeth I; the ancient Black Prince's Ruby, which Henry V wore at Agincourt; the Stuart Sapphire; and the 317-carat Second Star of Africa, the second-largest of the nine major stones cut from the 3,106-carat Cullinan. The largest Star, a 530-carat, pear-shaped bit of glitter, which is not only the world's biggest cut diamond but also, according to some experts, its most perfect, embellishes the Royal Sceptre, which is also in the Jewel House, along with countless swords, bracelets, ewers, dishes, and other dazzling items. Details: *HM Tower of London,* Tower Hill, London EC3 4AB, England (phone: 71-709-0765).

# Genealogy Hunts

 For those interested in their British heritage, it's possible to trace British ancestors by mail or to hire a professional genealogist. Stateside, researchers can go to the Church of Latter-day Saints' genealogical library in Salt Lake City, where thousands of reels of microfilmed records are filed. But nothing is quite as satisfying as going to the British Isles, flipping through the records, and actually visiting the area where your ancestor lived. Thanks to an abundance of records kept throughout the ages in Britain, the descendants of yeoman and middle class families can trace their heritage back to the 1400s; but even if your pedigree is not quite so grandiose, there's a good chance that you'll be able to worship in a church where some great-great-great-great-grandfather was married, walk up to the house where his children were born, read a will written in his own hand, or photograph his moss-covered gravestone in some peaceful country churchyard. Doing the research in person, on the spot, rather than by mail, is more efficient, since clues can be followed up immediately.

It goes without saying, however, that it isn't possible to even begin to search in Great Britain until the groundwork has been laid at home. It is necessary to know not only the name of the emigrant ancestor, but also the dates of his or her birth and emigration. It also is important to have a general idea of the area from which he or she came. The names of your ancestors' relatives also can be useful. From there, it will be possible to consult parish registers and the archives of various public record offices and genealogical libraries. *Note:* Don't forget about the realignment of British counties that took place in 1974; many records were relocated at that time.

Birth certificates give the date and place where the event occurred; the child's forenames; the father's name and occupation; the mother's name and maiden surname; her usual residence if the birth took place elsewhere; and the name and address of the person providing the information.

Marriage certificates give the names of the contracting parties; their ages (most of the time, that is — remember that some people stretched the truth a bit); their fathers' names and occupations; the date and place of the marriage; and the names of the witnesses.

A death certificate records the date, place, and cause of death, plus the deceased's name, age, occupation, and usual residence (if different from the place of death), and the name and address of the person furnishing the data.

The details on a birth certificate usually reveal enough so that you can look for the parents' marriage certificate, and the marriage certificate usually will give you the information you need to find the records of the births of the two parties.

## ENGLAND AND WALES

In the 13th century, England united with Wales, so although the Welsh have their own language, the two countries' records are essentially one and the same.

The search is easiest if your ancestor emigrated after 1837, when civil registration of births, marriages, and deaths was introduced in both countries. The General Register Office (St. Catherine's House, 10 Kingsway, London WC2B 6JP, England) houses the records. Like most in Britain, they're indexed, but to get particulars you have to request a certificate, the preparation of which takes a day or two. A certficate costs £10 (about $16) if applied for by mail, £5 (about $8) if in person.

Once you know the addresses, you may get further information from returns of the censuses taken decennially from 1841 and now housed at the Census Room of the Public Record Office (Land Registry Bldg., Portugal St., WC2) as far back as the year 1881. Later returns are held by the General Register Office (address above). Complete data from later returns become available only after a century has passed from the census date, but partial information from the 1891 and 1901 censuses is available in some circumstances.

These and other British records should lead you, if your American research did not already, to the period before 1837. In this era, it's the registers of the 14,000 parish churches in England and Wales that are your most valuable source. Gaps in their listings of baptisms, marriages, and burials do exist, but some volumes date from as early as 1538, when the law requiring the clergy to keep such records went into effect. Copies of many of them are at the *Society of Genealogists,* a private genealogical library open to the public for a fee (14 Charterhouse Buildings, Goswell Rd., London EC1M 7BA, England; phone: 71-251-8799); it has catalogues of the copies that can be found here and elsewhere. Where no copies exist, you can find out the originals' whereabouts from the appropriate County Record Office. (A list of County Record Offices' addresses has been published by Her Majesty's Stationery Office, London.) When you do locate the parish, use *Crockford's Clerical Directory* to find the name and address of the clergyman who currently has custody of the records. Make an appointment as far in advance as possible to be sure that the clergyman will have time to show you his records.

The County Record Offices provide other valuable information. Many well-to-do folk were married by license in the good old days, and records of the proceedings can often be found in the County Record Offices. Others are housed in the Lambeth Palace Library (London SE1 7JU, England; phone: 71-928-6222) and the Guildhall Library (Aldermanbury, London EC2P 2EJ, England; phone: 71-606-3030), which has an extensive collection of the material on London.

Various central indexes of vital records, available in genealogical libraries, also can be useful. *Boyd's Marriage Index,* which covers the period from 1538 to 1837, is only one.

Among the genealogist's best tools are wills, especially in Wales, where, until the mid-19th century, surnames changed with each generation, as in Scandinavian countries. The information in a will can often clarify relationships of people whose names you've found mentioned elsewhere, and the particulars are almost always reliable. Sometimes you can make charts for several generations of a family from just one will. If the document (or a copy) was proved since 1858, you'll find it at the Principal Probate Registry (Somerset House, The Strand, WC2; phone: 71-936-6000). Before 1858, wills were proved in a variety of courts, depending on the deceased's holdings. If these were varied and widespread and the deceased lived in the southern half of England, the will generally was proved in the Prerogative Court of Canterbury (PCC); if he lived in the north, in the Prerogative Court of York. The PCC records, which begin in 1383 and are indexed, are at the Public Record Office (Chancery La., London WC2A 1LR, England; phone: 81-876-3444). The York probate records, which date from 1389, are at the Borthwick Institute (St. Anthony's Hall, Peasholme Green, York YO1 2PW, England; phone: 9046-42315), and are indexed to 1858. (By appointment only, so write well before your visit.)

When, sooner or later, you hit a snag in your research, you can get help at the *Society of Genealogists.* In addition to the parish register transcripts, it houses a vast general index of names, a 7-million-entry marriage index, and a collection of documents relating to some 13,000 families, plus material for Scottish and Welsh families and for English families abroad. When you need professional help, consult the College of Arms (Queen Victoria St., London EC4V 4BT, England; phone: 71-248-2762). The *British Travel Bookshop* carries *Discovering Your Family Tree* ($5.95) and *Discovering Surnames* ($4.95 each); postage depends on the amount ordered; call 212-765-0898 or write to 40 W. 57th St., New York, NY 10019, and ask for its book list. *Genealogical Resources in English Repositories* ($32.95) is available from Ancestry Inc. (PO Box 476, Salt Lake City, Utah 84110; phone: 800-531-1790); add $2.50 per order for shipping and handling.

## SPECIAL PROBLEMS

If your ancestor did not belong to the established church of the land, you may have difficulties at first, but there are special genealogical societies and/or guides for just about any sect you can name. The records of the Society of Friends, for instance, are a dream — superbly indexed and organized. Information about the Huguenots, the French Protestants who came in great waves from the late 16th century and especially around 1685, following the revocation of the Edict of Nantes, can be pursued by writing to the *Huguenot Society of London* (c/o University College, Gower St., London WC1 E6BT, England; phone: 71-387-7050). Research into Jewish ancestry can be slow going because of frequent name changes. The *Jewish Historical Society of England* (33 Seymour Pl., London W1H 5AP, England; phone: 71-723-4404) is a great resource. For help in finding societies concerned with other groups, contact the big genealogical libraries in the country of your ancestors' origin.

Other books worth consulting include the following: *Vital Records Handbook* ($19.95) and *International Vital Records Handbook* ($24.95), both by Thomas Jay Kemp, and *Do's and Don'ts for Ancestor-Hunters* ($10.95) by Angus Baxter; available from the Genealogical Publishing Company (1001 N. Calvert St., Baltimore, MD 21202-3897; phone: 301-837-8217); add $2 postage and handling for the first book, $1 for each additional book.

# A Shutterbug's London

 The historic corners of London, the markets, the majestic Thames, and the regal buildings all make for numerous and choice photo opportunities throughout the city. Even a beginner can achieve remarkable results with a surprisingly basic set of lenses and filters. Equipment is, in fact, only as valuable as the imagination that puts it into use.

Don't be afraid to experiment. Use what knowledge you have to explore new possibilities. Don't limit yourself by preconceived ideas of what's hackneyed or corny. Because a palace guard has been photographed hundreds of times before doesn't make it any less worthy of your attention.

In London as elsewhere, spontaneity is one of the keys to good photography. Whether it's children feeding pigeons in Trafalgar Square or a street performer in *Covent Garden,* don't hesitate to shoot if the moment is right. If photography is indeed capturing a moment and making it timeless, success lies in judging just when a moment worth capturing occurs.

A good picture reveals an eye for detail, whether it's a matter of lighting, of positioning your subject, or of taking time to crop a picture carefully. The better your grasp of the importance of details, the better your results will be photographically.

Patience is often necessary. Don't shoot a view of Westminster Abbey when a big bus passes in front of it. Reframe your image to eliminate the obvious distraction. People walking toward a scene that would benefit from their presence? Wait until they're in position before you shoot. After the fact, many of the flaws will be self-evident. The trick is to be aware of the ideal and have the patience to allow it to happen. If you are part of a group, you may well have to trail behind a bit in order to shoot properly. Not only is group activity distracting, but bunches of people hovering nearby tend to stifle spontaneity and overwhelm potential subjects.

The camera provides an opportunity, not only to capture London's charm, but to interpret it. What it takes is a sensitivity to the surroundings, a knowledge of the capabilities of your equipment, and a willingness to see things in new ways.

**LANDSCAPES:** The London architecture is so varied and picturesque that it is often the photographer's primary focus. Be sure to frame your subject appropriately, however.

Color and form are the obvious ingredients here, and how you frame your pictures can be as important as getting the proper exposure. Study the shapes, angles, and colors that make up the scene and create a composition that uses them to best advantage.

Lighting is a vital component in landscapes. Take advantage of the richer colors of early morning and late afternoon whenever possible. As it often rains, it's necessary to use the weather to your advantage, and thunderous skies can often add to the drama of a scene. Bright sunlight, however, must be handled differently. This is when a polarizer is used to best effect. Most polarizers come with a mark on the rotating ring. If you can aim at your subject and point that marker at the sun, the sun's rays are likely to be right for the polarizer to work for you. If not, stick to your skylight filter, underexposing slightly if the scene is particularly bright. Most light meters respond to an overall light balance, with the result that bright areas may appear burned out.

Although a standard 50mm to 55mm lens may work well in some landscape situations, most will benefit from a 20mm to 28mm wide-angle. St. Paul's Cathedral and Buckingham Palace are just two of the panoramas that fit beautifully into a wide-angle format, allowing not only the overview, but the opportunity to include people or other points of interest in the foreground.

To isolate specific elements of any scene, use your telephoto lens. If you want a close-up shot of a guard or passing royalty, this is the time to use the telephoto lens. The successful use of a telephoto means developing your eye for detail.

**PEOPLE:** As with taking pictures of people anywhere, there are going to be times in London when a camera is an intrusion. Your approach is the key: Consider your own reaction under similar circumstances, and you have an idea as to what would make others comfortable enough to be willing subjects. People are often sensitive to having a camera suddenly pointed at them, and a polite request, while getting you a share of refusals, will also provide a chance to shoot some wonderful portraits that capture the spirit of the city as surely as the scenery does. For candids, an excellent lens is a zoom telephoto in the 70mm to 210mm range; it allows you to remain unobtrusive while the telephoto lens draws the subject closer. And for portraits, a telephoto can be used effectively as close as 2 or 3 feet.

For authenticity and variety, select a place likely to produce interesting subjects. London is an obvious spot for visitors, but if it's local color you're after, visit Chinatown, the West End, or Leicester Square. Aim for shots that tell what's different about London. In portraiture, there are several factors to keep in mind. Morning or afternoon light will add richness to skin tones. To avoid the harsh facial shadows cast by direct sunlight, shoot in the shade or in an area where the light is diffused. The only filter to use is a skylight.

**NIGHT:** If you think that picture possibilities end at sunset, you're presuming that night photography is the exclusive domain of the professional. If you've got a tripod, all you'll need is a cable release to attach to your camera to assure a steady exposure (which is often timed in minutes rather than fractions of a second).

For situations such as evening strolls along the Thames or the Houses of Parliament lit up at night, a flash usually does the trick, but beware: Flash units are often used improperly. You can't take a view of Tower Bridge with a flash. It may reach out as far as 30 feet, but that's it. On the other hand, a flash used too close to your subject may result in overexposure, resulting in a "blown out" effect. With most cameras, strobes will work with a maximum shutter speed of 1/125 or 1/150 of a second. If you set the exposure properly and shoot within range, you should come up with pretty sharp results.

**CLOSE-UPS:** Whether of people or of objects, close-ups can add another dimension to your photography. There are a number of shooting options, one of which is to use a 70mm or a 210mm lens at its closest focusable distance. Unless you're working in bright sunlight, a tripod will be worthwhile. If you are very near your subject and there is a good deal of reflective light, it may pay to underexpose a bit in relation to the meter reading.

If you do not have a telephoto lens, you can still shoot close-ups using a set of magnification filters. Filter packs of one-, two-, and three-time magnification are available, converting your lens into a close-up lens. Even better is a special macro lens designed for close-up photography.

## A SHORT PHOTOGRAPHIC TOUR

Almost everywhere you look in London, there is an interesting photo waiting to be taken, but the following are some of the best opportunities for getting memorable pictures of both places and people:

**Berwick Street Market:** There's nothing like a London market filled with fresh produce and colorful wares. Try to capture the expressions of the vendors, and include shoppers in the photos. Contrast colors and textures, fabrics and wood, fruits and vegetables of different sizes and colors. Also try to show the background of the building in relation to the stalls and tents.

**Buckingham Palace:** The best shot of the royal family's home is either from the Victoria Memorial or with the memorial in the foreground. Another vantage point might be up close to the wrought-iron fence, with the majestic building showing through the bars.

**Brigade of Guards:** Visitors to London are always enthralled by the scarlet-coated guardsmen marching past for the Changing of the Guard at Buckingham Palace. This is a perfect time to try out the telephoto lens, to get a close-up shot of the stone-faced guards as they go on and off duty.

**Camden Lock:** Almost any shot taken of the Thames makes a lovely photo, and with pictures of the colorful narrowboats at the Camden canal lock, you can't go wrong. Try to get the busy market stalls in the background to add to the atmosphere of the locks. It's interesting to get shots of people on the boats as well.

**Harrods:** Nothing compares to the food hall at Harrod's with its mouth-watering displays of meat, poultry, baked goods, spices, and exotic produce from overseas. Be sure to use a flash when shooting indoors, and try including customers as well as store staff in your photo — shots of consumers choosing vegetables and attendants cutting prime slices of beef for Sunday dinner.

**Horse Guards:** The splendidly uniformed mounted troopers standing guard in

Whitehall at the entrance to Horse Guards is about as British as you can get. This is another good spot to use the telephoto lens, as visitors are not allowed too close to the guards. The regal horses make for some striking pictures as well. The guards are there from 10 AM to 4 PM daily.

**Houses of Parliament:** Get a shot from across the Thames between Westminster and Lambeth bridges for the best and most complete shot of the building.

**Oxford Street:** London's shopping area provides ample opportunity for snapshots of locals and tourists alike. And a trip to London wouldn't be complete without a photograph of one of its red double-decker buses. Try to get more than one of them as they line up in front of the clock and columns of *Selfridges* department store.

**Parliament Square:** When tourists think of London they think of Big Ben, and now after years under scaffolding it stands resplendent in its former glory. A shot with one of the now-rare red telephone boxes in the foreground makes a memorable photo. Try shooting at sundown to get the dramatic sky in the background.

**Rush hour:** Like New York City, London is a town of bustling businesspeople, and there's no time like rush hour to capture a picture of some of the trains pulling into Waterloo, the city's biggest station, as impatient commuters open the doors and start jumping out before it stops (not nearly so good if the doors are sliding ones). It's also amusing to see the commuters "queueing" on the platform, *before* the train even arrives. The frequent travelers know exactly where the doors will open.

**St. James's Park:** All the parks in London provide a pleasant reprieve from the hustle and bustle of traffic and people. Go to St. James's Park to get a shot of children and adults alike feeding the ducks on the lake, or office workers enjoying the sun at lunchtime. Occasionally, you'll be able to get an equestrian on his or her daily prance.

**St. Paul's Cathedral:** The spectacular cathedral where Prince Charles and Princess Diana were wed is a popular photo spot for tourists and Brits alike. Here's a place to try out a wide-angle lens in order to get the expanse of the grand front staircase in the shot. Another interesting picture can be taken of the surrounding area viewed from the cathedral's Golden Gallery at the very top (627 steps up). Pictures of the stained glass windows are especially beautiful when taken as the sun — just at the right time — streams through, casting rays on the nave of the church. Interior shots generally require a flash, unless the camera's shutter speed is very slow and the lens is opened wide.

**Statues:** London is a city abounding with statues, and it's possible to snap a photo of one almost anywhere the road turns. An especially good spot is at the bottom end of Lower Regent Street, where the cluster of statues includes Florence Nightingale and Captain Scott. Try to get a red bus going past in the background. The dusk sky also makes for interesting silhouettes of the figures.

**Tower Bridge:** Although the "London Bridge" made famous by the song is no longer even in Great Britain (it's in the US), the Tower Bridge is equally exciting, and is a striking example of English bridge architecture. After taking shots of it from the banks, try taking one from a boat to get a head-on view. Best of all is when the bascules go up about twice a day to let a large boat through. Skippers have to give 24 hours' notice, so check with the Bridge Office (phone: 71-407-0922) to find out when the next boat is due.

**Trafalgar Square:** Nowhere in the world does it seem as if there are more pigeons congregating at one time than in Trafalgar Square. Old men and women can be seen feeding them directly out of their hands, while others stand covered from head to shoulder with the feathered friends. Buy a bag of feed from one of the vendors and tempt the birds yourself. Try making a horrified face and pretend to be a character in Alfred Hitchcock's film *The Birds.* Besides the pigeons, also get some shots of the huge stone lions at the foot of Nelson's Column.

**Westminster Abbey:** The sight of historic coronations and events throughout British history, Westminster Abbey is a definite shot for the photo album. Try shooting the towers and west door from Victoria Street or the top of the towers from Dean's Yard. With a flash, take inside photos of the interior, including Poets' Corner and the stained glass windows.

# DIRECTIONS

# Introduction

Our walks are designed for the thoughtful visitor, someone who wants to penetrate the neighborhoods in which knowledgeable Londoners take the most pride. We have deliberately not said much in this section about the largest, set-piece attractions, such as the Houses of Parliament and Buckingham Palace. They are described in detail elsewhere in this book. Instead, the walks go through historic districts, each of which has a distinctive flavor. That flavor may come from row upon row of 18th-century houses, hidden courtyards, or gaslit alleyways. Spending a couple of hours — the average length of each walk — in an area with a steady character usually leaves it firmly set in a visitor's memory. In contrast, a fine building seen in isolation for a few minutes may leave a snapshot on film but is unlikely to have this lingering effect.

No one ever knows all of London, or even all of its most historic parts. There's a cynical saying among Londoners that most of the city dwellers know only two districts: the area around the hole into which they disappear each morning, and the area around the hole from which they emerge to go to work. The hole is the entrance to the tube — the underground railway. So don't think that, in order to feel you belong in London, it's necessary to know vast areas of the city. Perhaps it's best, therefore, to choose two or three of the walks here and let them teach you more about the pleasantest parts of the city than the average Londoner knows.

How to choose from among the walks listed? Mood, time of day, even the weather may be important. On the first page of each walk we've sketched the character of the area and given hints about the best times to make the particular walk — such as how to find (or avoid) streams of local people, and when road traffic is lightest (not that we spend much time near busy roads; quiet side streets and courtyards are more the style). But here, for convenience, is a brief guide to the character of each of the walks:

**Whitehall:** The grand heart of the old British Empire, with Georgian and Victorian architecture, parks, and a spacious parade ground; magnificent official propaganda-by-building, to banish thoughts of the devious governmental scheming that went on here.

**From St. Paul's:** From the shadow of the cathedral, skirting the traditional business quarter, to scenes of grim social history straight out of Dickens's day.

**The Old City (From the Romans to the Victorians):** From the Roman walls, where London began, through narrow, busy streets laid out after the Great Fire of 1666. Through churchyards and alleys to a Pickwickian tavern and a Roman temple.

**Covent Garden (Dickensian Alleys):** Quiet and historic houses, corners and pathways, leading to a thriving and elegant district of street markets, theaters, restaurants, and pubs.

**Lincoln's Inn and the Law Courts (a Medieval Community), and Fleet Street and the Temple (two walks):** A hidden set of medieval college campuses and gardens, where attorneys practice, next to the traditional home of British journalism — which also means fine pubs!

**Hampstead:** Formerly a Georgian village, still with sleepy 18th-century streets and pubs for a lazy lunchtime; across the countryside of Hampstead Heath to an opulent mansion (and art collection) from George III's day.

**Whitechapel and Spitalfields (the Old Ghetto and Jack the Ripper's Haunts):** A rough diamond — not a place for the unimaginative tourist. Teeming with social history; streets that were magnificent in the 18th century, picturesquely squalid in the 19th and most of the 20th, and are now being carefully restored to glory for the 21st century. See it before it's made *completely* decent!

Finally, two points to note. London takes itself rather seriously, with many large statues of imperial grandees. Our walks include much of legal London, and British lawyers take themselves especially seriously. To offset this, the style of our walks is often irreverent, and we haven't used the common technique of most guidebooks by explaining everything in a mere two sentences. To get the most from the streets and their stories, perhaps it's best to read each walk once beforehand, as well as while on the walk.

# Walk 1: Whitehall

As Whitehall is the center of the British government, the beginning of this route can be quite busy — though the weekend ratio of people to cars tends to be somewhat greater (and more bearable) than it is during the week. Mornings around 11 o'clock (10 on Sundays), a small crowd gathers at Horse Guards for the ritual changing. On most days (except for Sundays and Mondays) visitors can tour the inside of the lovely early-17th-century Banqueting House. Along the route stand some of the most famous buildings from the history of British government — many designed to be pompous. Our approach to viewing this area is intended to be just the opposite.

From the lowest part of Trafalgar Square, look first at the equestrian statue in the middle of the road, which faces the main street of Whitehall. Far older than most of central London's statues, it has a grisly tale to tell. Dating back to the 1630s, this structure portrays the disastrous king of the day, Charles I. The sculptor, Hubert Le Sueur, displayed intricate detail in his work — veins on the horse's flanks and wrinkles on the king's riding boots. King Charles clashed with Parliament over the control of taxes, tried to arrest Parliament's leaders, and when that failed, declared war on Parliament. When he lost, he was imprisoned (but in great comfort). In 1649 he was caught trying to start another war against Parliament, this time with foreign troops; his chief opponent, Oliver Cromwell, had him executed. (The exact site of the beheading is farther along in this route.) Some 11 years later, after Cromwell's death, royalty struck back. In revenge, the leading parliamentary enemies of Charles I were ripped apart — hanged, disemboweled, and quartered — on the spot where the statue now stands. It was arranged that they should die within sight of their "crime" against the late king.

The statue itself was lucky to have survived the civil war. London was a parliamentarian stronghold; the statue, being royalist propaganda, was slated for destruction, but a cunning metals dealer hid it under the church in *Covent Garden.* When royalty returned to the throne, the statue re-emerged triumphantly (and no doubt profitably). It was placed here to celebrate the death of the king's enemies.

Walk in the direction that the statue faces, along Whitehall, on the left-hand sidewalk. Where the second road (Great Scotland Yard) enters from the left, stop for a moment and look right across the road. Through the large stone gateway with fish motifs is a courtyard; beyond it stands the Admiralty, an early-18th-century building, headquarters of the British navy when it was the most powerful in the world. Above its roof is a mass of aerial wire,

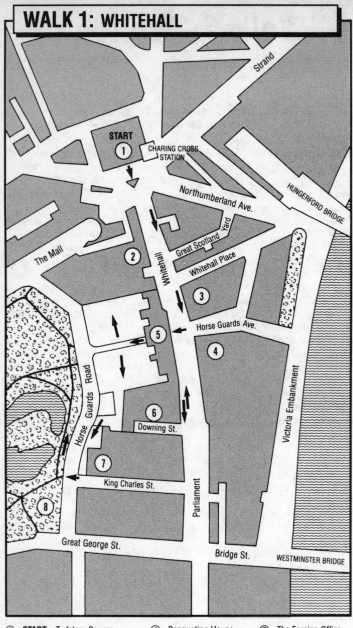

# WALK 1: WHITEHALL

START

CHARING CROSS STATION

Strand

HUNGERFORD BRIDGE

Northumberland Ave.

The Mall

Whitehall

Great Scotland Yard

Whitehall Place

Horse Guards Ave.

Victoria Embankment

Horse Guards Road

Downing St.

King Charles St.

Parliament

Great George St.

Bridge St.

WESTMINSTER BRIDGE

① **START** Trafalgar Square—Charing Cross Station
② The Admiralty
③ War Office
④ Banqueting House
⑤ Horse Guards
⑥ Downing Street
⑦ The Foreign Office
⑧ St. James's Park

apparently still used for signaling the fleet. Recent naval campaigns, however (in the Falklands and the Persian Gulf), have largely been controlled from obscure underground bunkers on the outskirts of London.

Cross the next street on the left, Whitehall Place, and continue for 10 yards along Whitehall. The building on the left is known as the War Office, the headquarters of the British army since just before World War I. Walk farther along Whitehall, cross the next road that enters from the left, Horse Guards Avenue, and stop on the corner. This was the site early last year of a daring and nearly fatal IRA attack. A van carrying mortars shot its shells over buildings toward the back of Downing Street. One of the mortars landed in the garden of No. 10, but was seemingly prevented from making a direct hit by the branches of a cherry tree. The Cabinet, in session, dived under the table, from which position Prime Minister John Major — in office for only a matter of weeks — allegedly uttered words of great coolness.

The yellow stone building at Whitehall and Horse Guards Avenue is the Banqueting House. This is all that remains of a vast, rambling, royal palace built during medieval times, which later became Whitehall. A great part of the palace was accidentally burnt in 1698. The Banqueting House, designed by Inigo Jones, court architect of James I and his son Charles I, was built around 1620. Perhaps more famous are the paintings inside on the ceiling (try to go inside if time allows; admission charge). The story of the paintings — done by Peter Paul Rubens, a subject of the Spanish Netherlands (now Belgium) — is worth telling. Rubens combined his roles: for the King of England he was an artist, but for the King of Spain he acted as a diplomat and spy. Britain was at war with Spain, and Rubens's job was to persuade the British of the advantages of peace. His paintings for the Banqueting House, therefore, displayed monstrous figures, representing the horrors of war, and contrasting images of joyful peace — including the well-fed women for which Rubens is now best known. The central painting in the ceiling shows James I ascending to heaven, his face seeming less than blissful as he is led upward. Because the Banqueting House was the gaudy pride of the Stuart court, Charles I's Puritan opponents chose it for the site of the king's ultimate degradation. His scaffold was erected here to allow as many as possible to witness his death. (Civil war could have been retriggered by a false rumor that the king was still alive.) When Charles stepped out, he pleaded with those on the scaffold not to blunt the ax, which might have caused him extra pain.

Cross Whitehall to see cavalrymen, purely ornamental these days, outside the fine mid-18th-century building called the Horse Guards. But before going into the Horse Guards, catch a glimpse of the traditional view of No. 10 Downing Street, for centuries the official home of British prime ministers. For this, go 150 yards farther along Whitehall and look into the first road on the right, Downing Street (No. 10 is not open to the public). When Mrs. Thatcher was in power, and robustly defied terrorism as she saw it, large security gates were installed to block access. This ended the British tradition of photographing small children by the door of No. 10, next to the carefully chosen British bobby on duty here.

More on Downing Street later, from a quieter and more pleasant position.

Go back now to the Horse Guards. Turn left from the sidewalk and go past the cavalrymen into the courtyard. Look back at the roof of the Banqueting House and note the weather vane. In 1688 King James II, Charles I's younger son, was widely unpopular. He was a Catholic, and at the time Catholicism was linked in British minds to the absolute Catholic monarchies on the Continent, particularly those of France and Spain. One Catholic reign could be tolerated in Britain, but when James II had a son, potentially a Catholic heir, the prospect of a Catholic dynasty seemingly had no end. The loyalty of James's army began to fade. Protestant forces gathered in the Netherlands to invade England. When would the invasion come? How stood the winds from Holland? James had to know. That's why, it is said, he put up the weather vane. (The invasion came and succeeded. James fled in a boat, was caught, but was allowed to go free. The male line of the Stuart dynasty withered away in exile.)

In this courtyard, with its tall and famous horsemen, there are some interesting antiques which often go unnoticed. On the wall beside the tunnel are the brackets of oil lamps. During the 18th century they held glass and small metal reservoirs of oil; each night a lamplighter would climb his ladder, fill, and ignite them. Horse Guards had to blaze with light. Most of the streets were dark and the night belonged to criminals; even in well-populated and prosperous parts of 18th-century London, metal railing fences of houses were cut down at night and stolen — either for personal use or to sell. (No one dared to confront the thieves.) Also on the wall above the tunnel is a plaque showing a soldier on horseback. This marked the territory covered by an 18th-century fire brigade run from the Church of St. Martin-in-the-Fields (the church by Trafalgar Square). The mounted figure on the plaque is St. Martin, in legend a Roman soldier. He took pity one day on a shivering beggar, sharing his cloak by cutting it in half with his sword. The beggar is the figure on foot with the stick.

Go through the tunnel and out into the open space beyond. This is Horse Guards Parade, famous in Britain as the site of a military pageant — the *Trooping of the Colour* — in which the monarch takes part, in June (also when her official birthday is celebrated). The "Colour" was the flag of a regiment. In earlier centuries it was shown to new troops to familiarize them with their flag as the rallying point for battle. The buildings of Horse Guards themselves are best seen from here. The scale is pleasantly modest, and there is a fine clock tower on the roof. The buildings were created in the mid-18th century as the headquarters of the army, and remained so until the early 20th century, when the War Office took over. It was here that the British end of the American War of Independence was organized. George III felt obliged to fight that war because he believed in a domino theory. He said that if America was lost, the West Indies would follow, and then Ireland.

Two ornamental cannon, sitting close to the Horse Guards, look out over the Parade. Stand with your back to Horse Guards; one cannon is about 50 yards to the right, the other about the same distance to the left. Each gun has its own story. Go first to the longer cannon, the one on the right. Its carriage was made in Britain in the early 19th century, but the barrel has Turkish markings from the early 16th century. It was captured by the British in Egypt in 1801 and soon played a part in a radical plot against George III. Enthusiastic supporters of the French Revolution planned to use the cannon to kill the king while he was riding in his carriage along the road between Horse Guards Parade and the park beyond. As with many such plots in Britain, someone informed, and the leader, Colonel Despard, was hanged.

Now walk most of the length of Horse Guards Parade to the other cannon. Notice the Oriental-style dragon on the gun carriage, influenced by the taste of the prince regent, the effective monarch during the lunacy of old George III. The inscription on the cannon in Latin and English records that it was given to the prince regent by Spain in acknowledgment of Britain's help against Napoleon's armies. The barrel of the cannon is squat and fat, which proved to be quite an embarrassment to the authorities. Such a gift could not be slighted. However, the contemporary name for an artillery piece such as this was "bombard" or simply "bomb" — and "bomb" was then pronounced "bum." It happened that the prince regent was known for his extraordinary physical size in that department. Cartoonists had a field day portraying the arrival from Spain of the prince's mighty new "bomb."

Facing the direction the cannon points, look to the left toward the high garden wall, which is the rear of No. 10 Downing Street. No. 10 has witnessed countless historical events. One marked the anticlimax at the end of the British Empire. In 1956, then Prime Minister Anthony Eden was trying in vain — against the opposition of the US — to regain control of the Suez Canal from Egypt. Eden was under a lot of strain and his face was permanently ashen. He commissioned a plan from Basil Liddell-Hart, the strategic genius of the day, to invade Egypt. Liddell-Hart's first plan was rejected by Eden, as were following ones. Finally, he came here to No. 10 to discuss his fifth submission. Eden accepted it; but why, he asked, had Liddell-Hart needed five attempts? Liddell-Hart replied that he hadn't. The fifth submission was the original plan — resubmitted. As the prime minister realized his own humiliation, he reached for an inkwell and threw it at Liddell-Hart. Both men watched as the ink spread slowly across Liddell-Hart's stylish white jacket. Liddell-Hart then picked up a wastepaper basket, upturned it onto the head of the chief executive of the British Empire, and walked out. The eventual invasion of Egypt, though militarily competent, was called off when the US threatened to cause the pound sterling to collapse. Eden resigned the next year.

No. 10 Downing Street itself was built in the late 17th century by George Downing, one of the first graduates of Harvard. The interior was much changed in the 1960s, partly, it was said, because old crevices were full of mice. A governmental cat was retained here, too. Next to the prime minister's house — toward the park — is No. 11 Downing Street, the official home of the chief finance minister, the chancellor of the exchequer. No. 12 is the house of the government's chief whip. The whip's job is to ensure that Members of Parliament (MPs) of the governing party support the official line during voting. When majorities are slim, this is an agonizing task. During the mid-1970s, when the Labour government was reduced to a majority of one, it was said that the dead were voting — or, rather, an invalid MP on his deathbed. At one point opponents claimed that the Labour majority of one was achieved by trickery. In his anger, Michael Heseltine, a leading Conservative, picked up the ceremonial mace in the House of Commons and waved it at the seething Labour benches opposite. A journalist then reported that "fighting broke out all over the House." This episode helped to establish Heseltine's nickname of "Tarzan." It is an important part of the chief whip's job to prevent such jungle scenes from occurring in the Mother of Parliaments. Parliament is in session from December through June. Entry to the prime ministers' Question Time on Tuesdays and Thursdays can be arranged through the American Embassy (for more information, call 71-499-9000). It is possible to attend the less exciting sessions simply by lining up at St. Stephen's Entrance and then walking in. No admission charge.

The area under Horse Guards Parade was once a secret colony. Known as the "Cabinet War Rooms" (see *Quintessential London* in DIVERSIONS), a great network of chambers and passages ran from the New Admiralty Building, near the plotters' cannon, to the Foreign Office, beyond Downing Street. It was here during World War II that the prime minister and his staff could work, safe from bombing, but within reach of the Whitehall officials. (Regular public visits to the Cabinet War Rooms have been allowed only since the 1980s.) Within these rooms Winston Churchill was known to have a private place — his toilet. Naturally, as intended, no one asked about it or went near it. The "toilet" was in reality a telephone room, from which Churchill talked with President Roosevelt.

From the Prince Regent's Cannon, facing as before toward the gun points, walk to the lawn a little to the left. If policemen allow, it is worth trying to maneuver around a sharp left to reach the gate atop a few steps; a look through the gate affords a close view of the famous doorway of No. 10. Otherwise continue to the end of the next great building on the left, the Foreign Office, constructed during the late 19th century. It was supposedly from here, at the start of World War I, that Foreign Secretary Edward Grey, observing the gaslights of Whitehall, commented that "the lights are going out all over Europe. We shall not see them on again in our lifetime."

The Foreign Office is known as the most patrician of government departments. Bright young people from unfashionable schools may find work readily enough in the unglamorous Department of Social Security or even in the intellectually elite Treasury. But to get into the "F.O.," it helps to have "the right background." A well-known danger for the F.O.'s diplomats abroad is that, in the Whitehall phrase, they "go native" and adapt too thoroughly to the countries in which they are stationed. Great is the distaste of the F.O. grandee, acclimatized in exclusive circles abroad, at being required to take responsibility for some delinquent and drunken British tourist.

Skirt the rounded end of the F.O. to the broad steps on the far side of the building. Beyond, and right next to these steps, is the entrance to the Cabinet War Rooms, complete with a tasteful miniature maze of stone to show visitors where to line up. Towering above the steps is a statue of Robert Clive ("Clive of India"), another character more lively and controversial than his staid, imposing statue might suggest. During the 1730s, the young Clive was considered a "bad lad" in his Shropshire home. He reportedly risked his life climbing a church steeple, where he proceded to build his own criminal underground. Thomas Macaulay, a 19th-century biographer of Clive, used stately and ironic words to describe a racket organized by the young Clive:

> ". . . he (Clive) formed all the idle lads of the town into a kind of predatory army, and compelled the shopkeepers to submit to a tribute of apples and halfpence, in consideration of which he guaranteed the security of their windows."

Packed off to India, from which many never returned, Clive rose from civilian clerk to general. In the 1750s, his strategic skill brought victories over the French in India, and largely determined which European power would rule the subcontinent. But when Indian towns surrendered to Clive, temptation appeared. Townspeople often collected an enormous bribe to persuade the British commander not to let his troops pillage. Clive was proud of having turned down most such offers. Parliamentary opponents at home were indignant that he had accepted *any.* In the matter of bribery, Clive protested, "I stand astounded at my own moderation." He settled down, very wealthy, in London, and became the object of much jealousy. He symbolized a class of British people — called "nabobs" — whom India had made suddenly rich. Clive killed himself in London in 1774.

A pleasant way to end this walk is to enter St. James's Park, by the gate opposite Clive's statue. Then turn right immediately and, keeping the lake on the left, follow the paths that run by the lakeside. A café near the lake serves salads and sandwiches: a perfect spot for enjoying views — and resting feet. The park was created during the 17th century at the order of Charles II. For him the area was sacred; his father had walked through it on the way to his execution at the Banqueting House. Exotic birds were kept nearby for Charles II, who appreciated bright plumage on birds as much as he did on courtiers — in reaction against the dull shades of the Puritans. The colors still thrive; many species of pretty ducks are kept on the manmade lake, created in the early 19th century. Walk to the footbridge at the far end of the lake; here for over 150 years sparrows (normally wary birds) have eaten out of people's hands. A few Londoners make this part of their social life, and hand out seed free to visitors. If you wish, wiry little claws will grip your finger as a sparrow feeds from the palm of your hand. The birdmen here know the individual sparrows, and delight in telling visitors how, in the spring, mother birds teach their young to come to hand, passing on the tradition.

# WALK 2: ST. PAUL'S

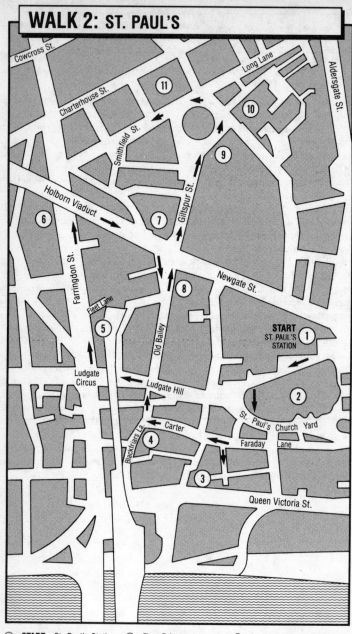

① **START** St. Paul's Station
② St. Paul's Cathedral
③ Wardrobe Place
④ Apothecaries' Hall
⑤ Fleet Prison
⑥ Holborn Viaduct
⑦ St. Sepulchre's Church
⑧ Central Criminal Court ("Old Bailey")
⑨ St. Bartholomew's Hospital
⑩ St. Bartholomew the Great
⑪ Smithfield Market

# Walk 2: From St. Paul's

This walk has a strong Dickensian flavor. It explores historic corners and alleys, some pleasant and some grim, in an area where one might hardly expect anything to survive. This is the western part of the financial quarter, known as the City. Yet skyscrapers and demolition have not done their usual work here, in part because they would interfere with one of London's most cherished views, that of St. Paul's Cathedral, seen from the area of Fleet Street and Ludgate Hill. The view, incidentally, is enjoyed best from the top of a double-decker bus going eastward down Fleet Street. Get any bus from Trafalgar Square or the Strand that displays the word "Bank" (i.e., Bank of England) as part of its destination. Then get off the bus as soon as it has passed St. Paul's Cathedral, and work your way around — or across — the churchyard to the tube station, the start of the walk. From the ticket barrier of the tube station, take the exit that says St. Paul's Cathedral. Once out on the street, take a sharp left and walk 50 yards to the mighty railings of St. Paul's churchyard.

London used to be a city of railings, but now fairly few remain. During World War II the government decreed that all except the most historic should be scrapped to make arms. Turn right to walk along the path that skirts the churchyard. From here it is easy to understand the general design of the cathedral. The nave and choir are long, the transepts very short. The architect, Christopher Wren, didn't want this orthodox design; he wished for four equal arms, which he claimed would give the finest interior in Christendom. But it appears that the Catholic faction at the court of Charles II insisted on a design more suitable for the Romanist cathedral they hoped it would one day be. Another feature that was forced upon Wren's design was the balustrade that can be seen along the top of the cathedral's wall. That, Wren said, was built at the insistence of the women of the court; he claimed they were never content with anything unless it had edging.

About 100 yards along the metal fence, the path leads to a fine old red brick building — the Chapter House of the cathedral. Go immediately beyond the Chapter House to see a rare survivor: a parish pump. Though most pumps of the time were made of wood and have long since rotted away, this one was made of metal — rarely used except in well-to-do neighborhoods. Built with style (look at the taper on the handle), the pump bears the date 1819, a time when the prince regent, comical but elegant, insisted that public buildings be designed with a certain flourish.

Now continue the walk beside the cathedral, turning left where the building ends. Walk halfway along the steps at the cathedral's front, then climb four steps and look up to the right to see the great bell tower which houses the cathedral's clock. Dickens describes some late-night reading near here; at 11 PM, "St. Paul's, and all the many church clocks of the city, some leading, some accompanying, some following, struck that hour." He was writing of the churches Wren created after the Great Fire. There are more churches, perhaps, than the population needed. But it was widely believed that Charles II was not a sound Protestant. This was not just because of his fleet of mistresses. His brother (and heir) was a Catholic. And Charles himself, to gain money for his women, secretly made a treaty with France promising to reconvert England to Catholicism, something that probably would have caused his downfall, if it had become known. The king, however, had reason to assert his Protestantism, and did so by creating in London a plethora of churches. Many have now gone, but from this spot you can see one of the most delightful of Wren's varied steeples. Facing the front of the cathedral, turn 90° to the left; in the distance, over the rooftops, are the miniature columns of the steeple of Christchurch Greyfriars. In fact, it is best viewed from this distance; though unseen from here, on the site where the body of the church should be, there is a bomb site from World War II, where only remnants of a foundation stand.

Now, still on the steps, face away from the cathedral and look to the left, where, at about 50 yards' distance, is the entrance to a little street called Dean's Court. Make a brief detour to the crosswalk on the right. Go 25 yards along Dean's Court on the left-hand sidewalk, then climb the three or four steps on the left to view the fine Old Deanery opposite, built by Wren about 1670 and now housing the sleek offices of a bank. In the 1970s the building, then in poor condition, was given over to licensed squatters — for its preservation. A government study into the effects of squatting — which at the time was widespread in London — showed that squatters usually preserved or repaired the premises in which they "lived." Publication of the study was later suppressed for being politically inconvenient. The Deanery, with great stone ornaments and a former gaslight on its wall, marks the start of the district of the former Doctors' Commons — a rambling ecclesiastical court, which Dickens attacked with great energy in *David Copperfield*. The clerical lawyers here scrambled and cheated, Dickens said, to get marital business. Colorful offenses that could be tried here included "brawling and smiting in vestries" and "calling ladies by unpleasant names" — that is, presumably, irreligious names.

Doctors' Commons was demolished later in the 19th century, but we'll get much of the flavor of the place in a moment. First, go to the far end of Dean's Court. On the left-hand corner is another neglected period piece, in a style that is now coming back into fashion — a humble café from the 1930s. Note the period lettering in the glass of the windows, and the long lines in the glass emphasizing the vertical. Now turn right down the aptly named Carter Lane. It's only wide enough for a single cart at a time; one of the most common sights of Georgian and Victorian London was the quarreling between carters when two horse-drawn vehicles met in a place like this. A horse-drawn cart is far harder to reverse than a car. Fifty yards along Carter Lane, turn left through the covered passage into Wardrobe Place, a delightful hidden backwater that preserves the atmosphere of Doctors' Commons in Dickens's day. The "Wardrobe" that once stood here was a building housing clothes and equipment for the court of Henry VIII. In its place now stands a late-17th-century flat-fronted house with a fine row of little garret windows at its top. Note the separate (mid-Victorian) doorbells for visitors and tradesmen. A boot scraper made of iron outside the door recalls the days of unpaved, muddy streets. On the wall opposite this house are the dull metal brackets of former gas lamps. Go back into Carter Lane and turn left. At the next corner there is a fine display of Georgian and Victorian iron bollards, or posts, put on corners to prevent carts and carriages from taking shortcuts across the sidewalk and breaking the curbstones. Follow Carter Lane for another 120 yards to the intersection with Blackfriars Lane. Turn left and walk 70 yards on its left-hand sidewalk. There is an intricately painted heraldic sign above the antique doorway of Apothecaries' Hall, a set of 17th- and 18th-century buildings. To the right of the door hangs the chain of an ancient bellpull. The Apothecaries' (druggists') organization is one of the Livery Companies, centuries-old London societies created to protect the interests and maintain the standards of particular trades. Nowadays most Livery Companies seem to be a chic form of specialist gentlemen's club. If the Apothecaries' door is open, go through into the delightful courtyard with its battered 18th-century drainpipes.

From the Apothecaries' door retrace your steps up Blackfriars Lane; follow the slightly winding line of this street, which changes its name to Ludgate Broadway and Ludgate Court to the main road, Ludgate Hill. Cross Ludgate Hill, then turn left onto its sidewalk and walk 100 yards downhill to the great crossroads (Ludgate Circus); there, turn right. After another 100 yards, Fleet Lane appears on the right. Ten yards into Fleet Lane there is a small opening on the right, now used to park a few cars. Go in to the grounds of the old Fleet Prison.

One 18th-century inmate called the Fleet a "poor but merry place." It was only for debtors. Many were genteel — unless one had had some appearance of prosperity, he would have been unlikely to have been granted much credit in the first place. Some prisoners even had some money; they might be refusing to pay on principle, or might have debts so large that it seemed pointless to give what money they had to creditors. Dickens despised the process of imprisonment for debt; his own father was jailed twice for this reason, though not in the Fleet. (He was in the Marshalsea, bitterly evoked in *Little Dorrit.*) Mr. Pickwick, however, does come here to the Fleet, sued by the widow Bardell for breach of promise and refusing on principle to pay his damages. Bardell later finds herself here, too. Because Pickwick has paid her nothing, she can't afford to pay her lawyers. So they imprison her along with her adversary. Pickwick then pays — but only her bill. So the sole profit in the case goes to the lawyers. (Some things never change.)

While here, Pickwick enjoys liquor and cigars; Dickens was being realistic in this matter, as he so often was. The debtors who could afford it had considerable comfort, while facing the risk of "gaol-fever" — typhoid. Whist, wrestling, racquetball, and backgammon were some of the charms of the Fleet. Clergymen in jail here, and they were many, made money by marrying people (with no questions asked). Their agents touted outside, "Please, sir, won't you walk in and be married?" Heiresses could thus be secured here by young men in a hurry, before the young lady's father caught up with them — or before *she* changed her mind.

Come back the 10 yards down Fleet Lane, and turn right; walk along the right-hand sidewalk of the main road (Farringdon Street) for 150 yards until approaching the bridge called Holborn Viaduct. Its grim setting, as it crosses the howling traffic of Farringdon Street, usually prevents people from appreciating the elaborate decorations formed by its Victorian ironwork. To create the viaduct and its approach roads, in the late 1860s, the authorities demolished the evil district of Field Lane, which had been the setting of thiefmaster Fagin's den in *Oliver Twist.* Ten yards before the viaduct, go up the stairway on the right. When it opens into the street above, turn right and walk 200 yards along the main road (Holborn Viaduct). Then, on the left, across the street, is St. Sepulchre's Church, and on the right is the street called Old Bailey. Turn into Old Bailey, and go a few yards along its sidewalk to escape the noise of traffic.

Stop and look across the street to the long, gray building, officially called the Central Criminal Court, but better known as the "Old Bailey." Above its dome is a statue of justice, a female figure with scales. (Cynical Londoners note that she faces the more prosperous half of the city, the west.)

The most famous criminal cases come to the Old Bailey. Until the mid-1960s, prisoners were sentenced to death here by judges who put on a black square of material, the "black cap," for the purpose. In murder cases, if the jury voted "guilty," people in court watched the judge's hands, to see if the cap would be produced. A visit here can be much like going to the theater — only free. The accused, sitting in a wooden box known as "the dock," often poses as bemused, and slightly contemptuous of the proceedings. Clearly, he asserts by his manner, the whole case is based on error! In the late 1970s a leading politician, Jeremy Thorpe, stood trial here on a charge of conspiring to murder a former gay companion. Thorpe's chair in the dock was positioned to distance him from the less cultivated men accused with him. The jury now sits out of sight of the public gallery. Too many jurors in the past were identified and "nobbled," in the British phrase (intimidated or bribed).

To watch a case, go to the public entrance across the street. The uniformed men at the door are often rather surly; some believe they are actually under orders not to encourage the use of the place for the amusement of idle curiosity seekers. But be persistently polite. (Americans are fortunate; they're outside the British class system.) If interested, ask whether there is a murder case in progress, and if so, in which courtroom. In highly publicized cases, the gallery soon fills up. For the best choice, come about 9:45 AM or, for the afternoon session, about 1:45 PM. Be aware that officials won't let you in with a camera, and they won't hold it for you. No admission charge.

Most of the Old Bailey was built shortly before World War I. Until 1902 the infamous Newgate Prison stood on this site. In earlier centuries prisoners facing capital charges often refused to stand trial, so that their relatives could inherit their property (the goods of a condemned man were forfeited). To "persuade" prisoners to stand trial, authorities put them on the floor beneath boards on which crushing weights were placed. There the strong-minded chose to die so their families could gain the inheritance. Better known are the public hangings that took place outside the walls of Newgate until the 1860s. They were timed for 8 AM, allowing citizens to take in a hanging on the way to work. Vast crowds gathered; the upper windows of nearby houses were rented to the wealthy for a privileged view. At 8 o'clock, the bells of nearby St. Sepulchre's Church would ring. A door in the prison wall opened and a roar went up in the crowd; the entertainment was beginning. The prisoner was brought out, to yells and abuse. People at the back pleaded for a better view, shouting, "Down in front!" Mock religious cries went up; a favorite was the line from a revivalist hymn: "Oh my! Think I've got to die."

In the 19th century, one familiar hangman here did not know his job. His name was Calcraft ("callous craft"), a character in a Dickens novel. After his victims had dropped, Calcraft could sometimes be seen swinging from their legs, since he hadn't made the drop long enough, and extra weight — in this case his own — was needed to dislocate the vertebrae. This represented humane progress: In the 18th century, victims were left to dangle in agony, unless perhaps a relative came and did the tugging.

Dickens was appalled. After attending a hanging in London, he wrote that "the conduct of the people was so indescribably frightful that I felt for some time afterwards almost as if I were living in a city of devils." Even the children took part. They were sold little model gallows with a doll to hang; the doll was filled with sawdust which "bled" if the head was pulled off. Thomas Hardy, another Victorian novelist, witnessed the hanging of a statuesque young woman for murdering a brutal husband. Rain fell, revealing her body through the clothes. Hardy became obsessed. His heroine "Tess of the D'Urbervilles" is similarly hanged. Hardy subtitled the novel "A Pure Woman."

Go back up the Old Bailey, to the busy junction by St. Sepulchre's Church. Cross, following the line of Old Bailey into Giltspur Street; keep right for about 200 yards, until the road opens into a circle around an insignificant park, Smithfield. Continue right to an arched gateway, bearing the date 1702 and topped by a stone statue of Henry VIII. This is the entrance to St. Bartholomew's Hospital (known locally as "Bart's"). Originally a medieval monastic hospital, it was seized and "refounded" by the king. Go in through the gateway, and go straight ahead past a church on the left (St. Bartholomew the Less). Then pass underneath a second arch, also of an 18th-century building. While underneath it, look to either side. Here are rare survivors: poor boxes, complete with ancient lettering, appealing for the charity by which hospitals, once wretched places, were funded.

Through the arch, enter the main courtyard of Bart's. The buildings here are mostly from the 18th century; note the miniature Georgian-style gables above some of the windows. Now a famous teaching hospital, Bart's was once notorious. Until the mid-19th century, hospitals were mainly for the poor, built to concentrate disease and unsightly suffering away from the general population. The genteel died at home — witness the many deathbed scenes in Victorian novels. Hospital wards were unsanitary places; as one Victorian put it, "when scrubbed, they give off the smell of something quite other than soap and water."

A realistic Dickensian nurse connected with Bart's is the monstrous Sarah Gamp. She was the person whose company you could not enjoy without also appreciating the smell of gin. Early-19th-century nurses fell into two categories. There were the nuns, the original sisters, whose chief skill lay in straightening pillows and smoothing the path to heaven. Then there were the secular nurses: ignorant, friendly women, who, unlike today's nurses, might well sleep with their male patients while they were still on the ward. As one authority wrote, "The nurses are all drunkards, sisters, and all." Their pay was partly in beer. And to be accepted as a nurse in the first place, it helped a woman to have, in another delicate Victorian phrase, "lost her character" — to have had an illegitimate child. Such a woman was unlikely to leave the profession through marriage; she was scarcely seen as marriageable at all.

Before exiting through the tunnel that has the poor boxes, look at the large, ornamental, lead water tanks, bearing the date 1782 — now used as planters. They stretch for a few yards on each side of the entrance to the tunnel. Go back under Henry VIII's statue into Smithfield. Turn right onto the sidewalk, then work your way counterclockwise around the great circle. The handsome black-and-white ("half-timbered") façade on the right is the entrance to the churchyard of St. Bartholomew the Great. Though this Elizabethan exterior is distinctive and valued, no one realized its true worth for many years. Then, in World War I, a bomb from a German zeppelin blew off an outer covering and revealed the ancient workmanship beneath. Walk farther around the circle to a wide stone archway, topped by the shield and red cross of the City of London. Go under it to the center of the building. Then look up and down the length of it.

This is *Smithfield Market* (built in the 1860s), wholesale center of the meat trade, and open daily to the public. Carcasses are heaved around. With recent scares about food poisoning, *Smithfield* is a handsome anachronism, a Victorian institution possibly in its final days — though the building itself will probably survive. Like other 19th-century markets in London, *Smithfield* has the air of a cathedral. Look at the ornamented metal screens that cross the "nave" at intervals. The market is at its busiest in the very early morning, when the surrounding streets and cafés come to life. On the far side of the market, Farringdon tube station is 100 yards away (down Cowcross Street), or during pubs' open hours (usually from 11 AM to 11 PM), try the *Bishop's Finger* pub (Smithfield Circle), back and to the right of the Smithfield travel circle.

# Walk 3: The Old City (from the Romans to the Victorians)

This walk traverses the area from the fringe of the Old City to its center — the heart of modern British finance — around the Bank of England. The area is very busy on weekdays, as people and cars crowd into its narrow streets, laid out in the late 17th century, after the Great Fire. On weekends, the place is still as Dickens described it — "the City of the Absent." Considering the extremely high value of land here, historical sites are surprisingly well preserved, though the battle of conservation versus modernization is ongoing. Many of the city's powerful financiers had a traditional liberal education, and they can often be persuaded — or shamed — into putting a historic site before the bottom line.

The Romans didn't intend to found London. Their plan, when they invaded in AD 43, was to make the capital of the new province at Colchester, a grand Celtic site more than 40 miles to the northeast. But to get there they had to bridge the river Thames, and they did so where it ceased to be tidal — the site of London Bridge. Traffic converged on this, the one and only span over the Thames. Traders followed. By AD 60, when Celtic rebels under Queen Boudicca (also known as Boadicea) swept in, there was a large town in existence — Londinium. Many Roman traces remain — in ruins, in the city plan, and in the living language. When English people say "the City" they don't mean simply London; that's "town." They mean the city defined by the Romans, "The Square Mile," which was once surrounded by Roman walls, the best surviving stretches of which are in evidence here.

On emerging from the tube, take a sharp left. Fifty yards ahead is a high stone wall. Approach it, then go down the steps to the right, to the small lawn. The lower part of the wall is Roman, the upper medieval, distinguishable by looking at the red courses of tiles every few feet. These tiles are a Roman device for running through, and bonding, the rubble-filled center of the walls. The upper, medieval section doesn't have regular tiles. Close to here was found the tombstone of Alpinius Classicianus, a Roman financial official, who successfully pleaded with the bureaucracy of the Emperor Nero to stop the punishment of Britain after the revolt of Boudicca had been suppressed. A facsimile of his gravestone is set a few feet away, in a modern wall overlooking

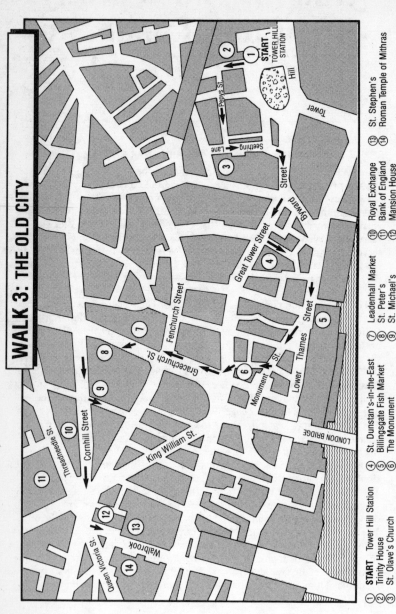

# WALK 3: THE OLD CITY

① START **START** Tower Hill Station
② Trinity House
③ St. Olave's Church
④ St. Dunstan's-in-the-East
⑤ Billingsgate Fish Market
⑥ The Monument
⑦ Leadenhall Market
⑧ St. Peter's
⑨ St. Michael's
⑩ Royal Exchange
⑪ Bank of England
⑫ Mansion House
⑬ St. Stephen's
⑭ Roman Temple of Mithras

the lawn. The wall in this area ran roughly north to south: south to the Thames and the site of the Tower of London, and north a few hundred yards to modern Aldgate, where the wall turned westward. Medieval gates in the Roman wall, like Aldgate, are referred to in surviving place-names. It is a delightful exercise to take the "gate" names on a map — Aldgate, Bishopgate, Newgate, Ludgate, and others — and join them up to reconstruct the line of the Roman wall. Nowhere does the wall itself survive as it does here. It was seemingly built in an emergency around AD 200, when most of the Roman troops went off to Gaul to fight a civil war, and London needed protection against any second Boudicca.

Go back to the tube station entrance. Stop outside it for a moment. The fine building 30 yards away across the road is Trinity House, traditional control center of the lighthouses and lightships around the coast of Britain. Note the model sailing ship on the weather vane. Then walk on, as if turning right on leaving the tube. Walk 50 yards, then turn right, passing through columns under a modern building, and into an unexpected courtyard; a fountain may be flowing. Ahead is the best section of medieval wall, on its Roman foundations. Trace the V-shape remains of a large stone stairway, its line now marked by wild plants. The stairway once carried armed guards up to patrol the walkway on top of the wall. Their aim was to protect the gold of the medieval city. The enemy were bandits out in Essex. (They are still a problem, though nowadays, instead of swords, they use sawed-off shotguns.) Look, too, at the stone windows in the wall. They are narrow at the outside of the wall to reduce the target presented to the enemy. But inside they broaden to let the defending archers swing their bows in a wide angle.

Retrace your steps to the road, turn right for 25 yards, then left into Pepys Street. Walk the whole of its length, about 150 yards, keeping to the left. Stop on the final corner. On the left now is a pleasant ornamental garden, where there are shaded benches for resting. It marks the site of the old Navy Office — the center of naval administration in the 1660s, during the age of Samuel Pepys, who lived here. Pepys is probably more popular today than ever before, because of his racy diary, the first uncensored edition of which wasn't published until the 1970s. (For a story from Pepys's love life, see *Walk 5*, below.) Pepys was relatively uncorrupt — he didn't take *all* the bribes he was offered. One sailor's wife, especially eager for her husband to be promoted, offered payment in kind. Pepys gratefully accepted. He owed his original appointment to nepotism; as he says with his famous candor, "Chance without merit brought me in." But within 6 years he had acquired a fortune, several thousand pounds in gold. When the Great Fire threatened his house here in 1666, he needed a cart and a boat to take all his treasures away. When the fire died down, he returned, afraid to ask about the fate of his home. Only at the last minute did he find out that his house was still there. But a later fire destroyed it, leaving the garden that now remains.

Look across to the strange gateway of St. Olave's (originally Olaf's) church. Dickens described it as one of his favorite City churches, "with a ferocious, strong spiked iron gate like a jail." He called it St. Ghastly Grim — look at the skulls and crossbones in stone above the spiked gate. These were created in the 1650s, the short period when England was a republic, by a Puritan advertising his piety — and his politically correct attitude. In lettering here he boasted *mors mihi lucrum:* "Death to me is gain."

Cross to the gate and look through it to the churchyard path, which unusually goes down steps to reach the church door. The graveyard has risen, due in part to the plague of 1665, which killed about a quarter of the City's population. Pepys recorded that the graves of plague victims here stood "high upon the churchyard." The church is open most of the week. Upon entering, notice high above the communion table the bust of Pepys's wife, Elizabeth, who died at a young age. Pepys himself had it put here — perhaps to keep his mind on family duty when worshiping — since during his wife's lifetime he had preferred to while away sermons by holding hands with young female strangers in the pew, and by staring at other women through his naval telescope. The coffin and bones of this energetic man were found earlier this century under the communion table, in the aftermath of bombing that destroyed the building's upper parts. In the corner to the right of the communion table, look up at the models of fashionable women in hooped skirts, made during Shakespeare's time. Near them, in the same corner, is a small brass plate, engraved with the image of an earlier Elizabethan lady; her dress, caught under the bust, looks medieval in comparison. A poem on the brass plaque advises readers to spend all their money, either on charity or themselves, as everything is lost after death.

There is now a 3-minute walk to the next good site. Facing away from the church gate, turn right and walk the 100 yards along Seething Lane to the main road. There go right again, into busy Byward Street, which becomes Great Tower Street, then take the second turn on the left, St. Dunstan's Hill. Twenty yards down this narrow lane, look at the church of St. Dunstan's-in-the-East, wrecked by bombing in World War II and left deliberately in ruins as a memorial to the Blitz. There is a gate to the church gardens; if it is open, go in. This is one of the more than 50 churches Christopher Wren built after the Great Fire. Each was given a tower of different design in order to give the City a varied skyline. The steeple of St. Dunstan's is Gothic, supported by flying buttresses. In the steeple above the buttresses — a level largely free of people — kestrels (falcons) nest. The birds particularly enjoy soaring in the updrafts created by the skyscrapers nearby, and survive, for the most part, on pigeons.

From the gate of St. Dunstan's, continue downhill to the right, until the little lane hits the grim highway, Lower Thames Street. There, turn right, noting across the road the former *Billingsgate* fish market, with stone fishes above its façade. Exactly level with the end of the fish market, a road forks to the right from Lower Thames Street, going gently uphill. This is Monument Street. Follow it, noting the name of the second road on the right, Pudding Lane. Here the Great Fire started (September 2, 1666) in a baker's oven. The lord mayor of the day, an unfortunate named Bloodworth, visited the fire in its early stages and dismissed it as insignificant. His words, as remembered, were that "a woman could piss it out."

The fire destroyed most of the City, but killed only half a dozen people. During the previous year, the plague had killed some 100,000 in London. The two disasters looked like punishment from heaven. Puritans, recently deposed from power, blamed the lifestyle of the new king, Charles II. "The king spends all his time with his mistresses, kissing and feeling them naked," wrote Samuel Pepys, an expert in such matters. So when London was rebuilt, royal counterpropaganda was needed: the towering Monument. The 200-foot column commemorates the fire, or rather London's resurrection after it. The ball with golden spikes above the column represents the flames. Go to the right of the Monument. The long Latin inscription on the base tells the story of the blaze, and suggests that heaven intervened to stop the wind which was spreading the flames. So God was *helping* the king. Note how the last part of the inscription has been systematically chiseled away; it blamed the fire on a Catholic conspiracy, and was removed in the early 19th century. Go to the far side of the column to see a sculpted scene — Charles II directing the rebuilding of the City. At bottom left, the collapsed female figure represents London; she is being helped up by the bald figure of Time. The king wears a long wig, in contrast to the short hair favored by the Puritans. (The king and his courtiers were the original "Big Wigs.") The royal band is shown next to a bare female bosom.

On weekdays and weekend afternoons (closed Sundays from October through March), visitors can climb the Monument (admission charge). At the top, a strong metal grille stops people from imitating desperados of the 1840s, who marked the recession ("the hungry forties") by jumping off.

From a position facing the sculpture of Charles II, turn 90° left and go up Fish Street Hill (a 4-minute walk), along busy streets, toward *Leadenhall Market,* a superb Victorian market. Walk 70 yards to the junction with several main roads. Go straight ahead, on the right-hand side of Gracechurch Street. Continue to the point where Gracechurch Street is joined on the right by Fenchurch Street, walk another 100 yards, and turn into the entrance, on the right, of *Leadenhall Market.* Hollow and echoing on weekends, bustling during the week, the market is a favorite of City people. Look up at the intricate decoration of the ironwork in the roof. As with other Victorian markets in the City, the design is church-like. At the point where the "nave" meets the "transepts," look up to see dragons and red crosses, heraldic badges of the City of London. At this point there is an atmospheric (and inexpensive) café, and also a pub selling the famous strong beer brewed by the firm of Young's. A large sign with the Young insignia hangs outside.

The best-known commodity of *Leadenhall Market* is exotic meat. A butcher near the Gracechurch Street entrance sells game birds from Scotland, including Capercaillie and grouse. Sea gulls' eggs are another delicacy sold here. They are eaten hard-boiled, to the horror of the uninitiated. (The shells are an off-putting green.) Have gulls' eggs and champagne at the Bank of England, and you know you have arrived socially.

*Leadenhall Market* stands on the site of a basilica, the City Hall of Roman London. Excavations suggest it was over 150 yards long, which would make it the largest known north of the Alps. This has surprised archaeologists, since Britain was a poor province of the Roman empire, captured and kept for reasons of prestige rather than of profit.

Leave the market by retracing your steps to Gracechurch Street. On reaching the street, cross it immediately, turn right, and after 5 yards turn left into narrow St. Peter's Alley. This opens into a churchyard. Tall surrounding buildings keep out light; plants and trees fare poorly here. In this dank spot Dickens, who loved sinister churchyards, set a scene in *Our Mutual Friend*. The virtuous heroine, Lizzie Hexam, is cornered here by a lout named Bradley Headstone ("gravestone"), who threatens to do violent things. Note the former oil lamp above the church gate; unusually, it still has glass in it. Its original purpose was to prevent ambushes in this hidden place.

Follow St. Peter's Alley around to the right, until it joins busy Cornhill Street. Turn left; 50 yards along on the left, by the door of St. Michael's church, turn left into St. Michael's Alley. Go to the *Jamaica Wine House*, just ahead, a popular haunt of London's financial community. A few yards from the *Jamaica* hangs the sign of the *George and Vulture* (Castle Court), an ancient tavern (now a restaurant) that is featured in the *Pickwick Papers*. Below the sign, look at the battered but highly polished brass plates with the name of the inn. Here Mr. Pickwick was arrested after a breach-of-promise suit. Amid its dark, high-backed seats, this Dickensian tavern, hidden in a tangle of alleys, is an excellent place at which to have lunch.

Return to Cornhill Street, walk 50 yards to the left, then look across to the Victorian building. This is the Royal Exchange, formerly a stock exchange which the Elizabethan financier Thomas Gresham helped to create. His name was given to Gresham's Law, the theory that bad money drives good money out of circulation (people pass the dud coins and hoard the good ones). Now look up to the roof of the building to the gold weather vane, a learned reference to Gresham. Heraldry specialized in weak puns on people's names. Gresham's badge, shown in the weather vane, was a grasshopper. Cross Cornhill, then turn left. A few yards along is a superb 18th-century pump, still lined with advertisements of the long-extinct insurance companies that originally subscribed to create it. These pumps were reassuring, with their brightly painted superstructures, but things were less orderly belowground; it was feared that sewage might contaminate the city's drinking water. And in the 1850s, Dr. John Snow, in his study of epidemiology, showed that disease was significantly concentrated around London's pumps.

Continue down Cornhill for about 100 yards to an open triangle of land on the right, just beyond the Royal Exchange. To the right is a towering building, its classical Greek features too high up for viewing. This is the Bank of England. Note the lack of windows accessible from the street; mobs once threatened to ransack the place. Until recently, the central bank of the United Kingdom manipulated the value of the pound sterling by using reserves of gold stored on this site and guarded by troops. The soldiers were removed during the 1970s. Officials were asked to explain why; in traditional British style they gave vague answers. The truth was, the gold had been removed to somewhere less well known. (Gone are the days when a run on sterling on the international exchanges could provoke the urgent transporting of plane-loads of American gold to USAF bases in eastern England, from which the gold was carted to the Bank of England amid heavy military security.) On a more human scale, the bank also kept personal accounts, for a select few. Bank employees tell of an old lady, in the mid-20th century, who would sometimes turn up here and ask to see "the king's money." She would insist that whatever was in her account be counted before her eyes. She had been a mistress of King Edward VII (who died in 1910). The money was her pension — in fact, her hush money — for life.

Walk across the intersection, via the pedestrian underpass (known as a subway) on the left, to the second exit on the left — by the Mansion House. The 18th-century mansion, which fronts the street, is the official residence of Lord Mayors of London, top financiers of unusual integrity. Here, once a year, comes the prime minister of the day, from the other city of London — the governing city of Westminster. The prime minister then makes a speech to reassure the city financiers of the government's monetary soundness. Pass in front of the Mansion House, then turn left into Walbrook. In this district the walk ends, as it began, with a note of ancient history. "Walbrook" is the only place-name in London to reflect the fact that London was once a Welsh city, the Welsh being the descendants of the native population from Roman and pre-Roman times. The Walbrook was a stream — still existing but now underground in a pipe — sacred to a god or goddess of the pagan Welsh. Into the stream they threw valuable metal objects as sacrifices. (There is just one memory of this Celtic practice in more modern fairy tale: the throwing of King Arthur's sword, Excalibur, into a lake.) Archaeologists have recovered many small objects from the stream here. The *Museum of London* (see *Special Places* in THE CITY) shows a selection. "Walbrook" is an English word; the fact that the conquering Anglo-Saxons knew that this stream was sacred to the Welsh indicates that the invaders co-existed here with the Welsh. Immediate genocide probably would not have left a linguistic trace.

Turn left into Walbrook, noting the fine Wren church (St. Stephen's) on the left; take the first right into Bucklersbury, then the first left, and go along the main road for 70 yards. Go up the steps on the left. Here is the jewel of London's archaeology: the foundations and lower walls of the Roman temple of Mithras. The temple is shaped like a miniature Christian church. It is about 20 yards long, with a nave and aisles. On each side of the nave are the stumps of 7 stone columns, which once held up the roof. The number 7 may be symbolic: The worshipers of Mithras were divided into 7 categories. Notice the red tiles that run through the walls, as with the Roman city wall at the start of the walk. See also how the stone at the door has been worn hollow by Romano-British feet.

The Mithraic religion, which came from Iran, reached the Roman Empire before Christianity. Christians, in fact, may have copied some elements from the Mithraists. Both have a ceremonial feast, for example. One early Christian blustered that the Mithraic feast was "a blasphemous imitation of the Last Supper." Historians are not so sure. Mithraism was a rival of Christianity; it offered personal salvation to believers in Mithras, who "saved mankind by shedding the eternal blood." Christians destroyed sacred objects of the Mithraists and vandalized their shrines.

At this *mithraeum,* precautions against Christian attack may have been highly successful. When the temple was found, in 1954, far underground and a few yards from its present site, nearby were discovered sacred treasures that presumably the Mithraists had carefully hidden. In amazingly good condition, they include a small silver infuser, perhaps used for stewing some sacred drug, and statues of pagan divinities made from the finest Italian marble. These London Mithraists clearly had money. The statue of Mithras himself is identified from its headdress, protruding at the front — the badge of the god. The finds are now displayed at the *Museum of London.*

The museum, with its attractive displays, is open every day except Mondays, and is close to here. It is also a good spot to have lunch or tea at the end of the walk. Come back down the steps from the *mithraeum,* turn left onto Queen Victoria Street, then take the first main road to the right, Queen Street. A hundred yards ahead is the junction with Cheapside; there, turn left and walk 250 yards to St. Paul's tube station. At the entrance to the tube, look right — along the wide street called St. Martin's Le Grand — and in the distance, in enormous white letters, is the sign of the *Museum of London.*

# Walk 4: Covent Garden (Dickensian Alleys)

STARTING POINT: EMBANKMENT TUBE STATION

This is a stylish, old-fashioned area with dark passageways still gaslit, a Georgian market, and a row of ancient hovels (now clean, meticulously kept — and extremely valuable). For centuries the society of *Covent Garden* was arranged in layers — quite literally. Aristocrats lived in the grand houses. Below them, in dark and cold tunnels, was an underworld of crime, which Dickens explored. *Covent Garden* is still remembered by most Londoners for its now-departed vegetable trade. "Mud Salad Market" carpeted the streets with decaying vegetables. Nowadays the market area is an expensive Bohemian shopping and business quarter. Traffic is banned from much of the district; the crowds on foot create some of the happiest surroundings in London. For lively atmosphere, go any time between noon and midnight. For a more peaceful look at the history, go before noon on the weekends.

The walk starts in a manicured park, where many of the occupants are rather less tidy than the flower beds. To reach the park, on leaving the ticket barrier at the tube, turn left. Upon leaving the tube building, turn right, go past the fruit and newspaper vendors, who include some kind and patient individuals (by the standards of the hard-boiled city), and head for the park at the end of the passageway.

The park is Victoria Embankment Gardens, created in the 1860s when the river Thames was pushed back to its present banks. But it is still possible to trace from the architecture the line of the old river shore. Once in the park, look left (north) to the line of buildings just beyond the park — some of them Georgian and Victorian — that mark the old waterfront. The large stone gateway, now forming part of the park's boundary, was once a watergate: the flashy entrance to the gardens and palace of George Villiers, Duke of Buckingham. This close — very close — friend of King James I had the gate built in the mid-1620s to impress his noble visitors who came by river, the preferred route. Its role was short-lived. Buckingham, a disastrous naval commander, was stabbed to death by an ex-sailor in 1628. His gambler son inherited, and sold, the palace to cover debts. The palace was demolished, and the fine Buckingham Street, which runs away from behind the watergate, was built in its place. All that survived was the watergate, out of the way at the river's edge, and perhaps too sturdy to demolish.

Many of the parks of central London suffer from Victorian statues; towering, gloomy effigies of forgotten imperial administrators and religious reform-

# WALK 4: COVENT GARDEN

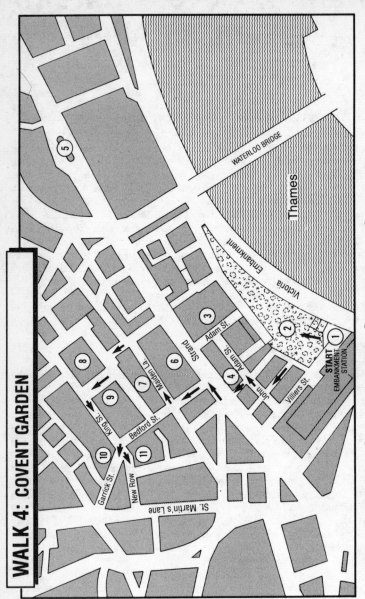

① **START** Embankment Station
② Victoria Embankment Gardens
③ Adam House
④ Royal Society of Arts
⑤ St. Mary-le-Strand
⑥ Adelphi Theatre
⑦ Rules Restaurant
⑧ Covent Garden
⑨ St. Paul's Church
⑩ Lamb and Flag
⑪ Goodwin's Court

ers. But in this park there are some unorthodox treasures. First, 130 yards along the path from the tube station, is a miniature statue — only about 4 feet high — of a camel and rider. This is a memorial to the Imperial Camel Corps, which helped to overthrow the Turkish Empire during the First World War.

Stand by the little camel, and look back. Slightly to the left of the watergate in the distance is a tall, ultramodern building with long lines of vertical glass. It marks the site of Warren's blacking factory, where Charles Dickens worked in the 1820s. Dickens's father had just been imprisoned for debt; the 12-year-old boy was put to work preparing pots of shoe blacking, while from the cellars below the squealing of rats "could be heard at all times." The scene is described in *David Copperfield* — D.C. was C.D. in many ways. When Dickens began to earn a comfortable wage, he returned to this area, perhaps with a sense of triumph, this time to live in a fine apartment in Buckingham Street, with a view over the river. This, too, D.C. is described as doing in the novel.

From the camel, go a few steps and stand on the rising bank of lawn. This was once the site of the Adelphi Stairs, the great steamboat dock when the river reached here, and before the railways captured the market for commuters. The crowds of riverboat passengers expected to be brushed against or jostled, and delicate little hands exploited the fact. Children plundered watches, purses, and silk handkerchiefs here before darting away to hide in a nearby fortress of tunnels, which will be explored in a moment; they now lie underneath the tall, white, 1930s structure, the Adelphi, viewable beyond the lawn and its shrubs. The 1930s building is itself now an architectural landmark; notice its rounded corners, the heavy emphasis on the vertical, and the brutalist statues.

What forced the Victorians to push away the river and to create this park was the dreadful smell of sewage dumped on the river mud at low tide. The year 1856 was so bad that the Victorians named it "the year of the Big Stink." Never again would that smell be tolerated. From a building overlooking this spot Thomas Hardy, the future novelist, watched workmen creating the land you now stand upon.

Walk 200 yards farther along the path to a pleasant statue, commemorating the death of the Victorian composer Arthur Sullivan. (W. S. Gilbert and Arthur Sullivan were the Tim Rice and Andrew Lloyd Webber of their day.) The young woman shown in the statue is supposedly the muse of song in mourning. The tremendous emphasis placed by the sculptor on her semi-clothed bottom reflects the date of the work; when Sullivan died (1900), Victorian morality was crumbling. Retrace your steps for 30 yards, then turn right by the statue of Robert Raikes and go out through the park gate. Beyond the gate, turn left into the road outside the park railings, and walk alongside or under the 1930s colonnade of the Adelphi. About 150 yards along, where the colonnade ends, go into the tunnel on the right and walk for 50 yards. The area doesn't look attractive, but it's quite safe; just watch out for traffic. This is the entrance to the Georgian and Victorian underworld — home of the child thieves.

Somewhere in these tunnels, around 1840, was a derelict prison-wagon. It was under the control of a real-life Fagin, named Larry. Dickens wrote that there were "forty or fifty boys sleeping rough any night in Covent Garden." But here in the prison-wagon was shelter, and a pack of little companions for warmth. There was one proviso: To be in the gang, one had to steal for Larry. Victims of robbery in daylight must have quickly guessed where the thieves had fled, but to follow them into the tunnels was foolhardy, as there were no lights in those days. Walk almost to the far end of the tunnel, then turn left uphill into the daylight, and walk under the massive archways that form the roof of the tunnel. Dickens used to come here in his time off from the blacking factory: "I was fond of wandering about the Adelphi, because it was a mysterious place with those dark arches."

The little hill rising under the arches is called Lower Robert Street — Robert Adam, renowned architect of the 1770s, built the arches and streets of fine houses on top. Turn right where Lower Robert Street ends, then take the first right into John Adam Street, noting in the distance the elegant Adam house with its pilasters; then take the first left into Durham House Street — all three turns in the space of a few yards. Follow Durham House Street to the right, to the foot of some steps. Turn your back to the steps and look up at the building facing you. Note the fine pilasters and, between them, statues of cherubs with harp and artist's easel, symbols of the arts. This building, the Royal Society of Arts, was created by Robert Adam in the 1770s to promote the new industrial revolution by glamorizing inventors. Inside the building were chandeliers, fine carpets, and oil paintings. Directly below the building were tunnels and crime. As one Victorian sociologist categorized Londoners, there were "those who will work, and those who will not work." Here the two groups almost met. Now go up the steps, noting the iron posts at the top. They were meant to prevent stray carriages from careening down. Posts like this, called bollards, were originally formed quite simply from obsolete cannon, placed on end with the mouth blocked by a cannonball to prevent litter from being dumped in the barrel. The design became traditional; the tops of these purpose-built bollards are still shaped like the cannonball.

The main road ahead is The Strand — originally the word meant the "Beach" — in the days when the Thames was far closer. Cross at the lights, 10 yards to the right. On reaching the opposite sidewalk, glance right for a moment toward the church 400 yards away, in the middle of the road. This is St. Mary-le-Strand, where Dickens's parents married in 1809. Turn left at the lights; after 3 yards, turn right into the narrow alley, Exchange Court. This quickly opens into an unexpected miniature courtyard with an Edwardian gaslight hissing away. Continue up the alley, noting the slum landscape on both sides. The tall gas lamp standard in the alley is worth a look; on its base is the date, 1910. This was long after the coming of electric power. Theaterland starts here. The tatty building on the right is the *Adelphi Theatre*. The gaslights of the *Covent Garden* area, which you are now entering, added to the charm of theatrical evenings.

After the theater often came a late supper. For a Georgian restaurant that provided it — and still does — turn right where the alley ends, into Maiden Lane. *Rules* restaurant is 50 yards along, on the left side of the street. At its door are highly polished antique brass plaques, advertising food and cigars. Inside is an authentic Victorian profusion of statues and pictures. This is an excellent place for an atmospheric evening meal. The most famous cigar smoker here was Victoria's son Edward VII. In middle age he visited the restaurant so often, with his mistress Lillie Langtry, that a special private room was created for them on the second floor at the front. Edward's cigars were widely imitated. So was his habit of leaving undone the bottom button of his waistcoat — from overindulgence. This became compulsory for British waistcoat wearers of breeding, and still is. Look for some on the walks around the Law Courts (*Walk 5*) and Fleet Street (*Walk 8*).

Continue past *Rules* to the end of Maiden Lane, then turn left into Southampton Street. Just ahead now is *Covent Garden* market. Walk to it, then turn left, and stand on the flagstones between the market and the pillars of St. Paul's Church. Then look back at the market. Well preserved, in fact embalmed in money, the market lay derelict for years after the vegetable trade moved away in the 1970s. Belowground, in cellars suddenly empty of food, things grew desperate. A story goes that one night, as the lights of a taxi raked the flagstones outside the market, they revealed a surface gently heaving — a carpet of marauding rats deprived of their accustomed food. But from rats to riches. Now in the cellars are pleasant (and numerous) wine bars, a crêperie in the basement called the *Crusting Pipe,* and bookstores.

The square stone pavilions at the corners of the market are Georgian, from 1830. They were new when David Copperfield visited the spot to buy flowers for his first love, Dora Spenlow. (Another character from real life, she was the daughter of a mean banker whom Dickens resented — "Spendlow.") On the right-hand pavilion, some 15 feet up, is a great rarity: early-19th-century painted lettering, surviving on an outdoor advertisement. It mentions lavender water, a favorite perfume of the day. The metal roof of the market is Victorian. The stalls selling antiques and junk underneath the roof are pricey, but well worth exploring. At the far end, accomplished musicians play for coins. This is the opposite end of the market, in both senses. Here the street musicians are more humble, but even they are said to have to pass an audition for the right to perform here. As one visitor put it, "In that case, I'd hate to hear the ones who failed."

Turn to face the portico of St. Paul's Church. Here, between the iron brackets and reflectors of some of the world's largest gas lamps, is the setting of a theatrical classic — the opening scene of George Bernard Shaw's *Pygmalion,* which became *My Fair Lady.* Eliza Doolittle stands under the portico in the rain trying to sell flowers to theatergoers. The details of her working class speech are quietly recorded by a phonologist. He's working out from her speech exactly which street she comes from. He's challenged, and he reveals his academic interest, boasting that he can convert Eliza's accent within months into the speech of a duchess. Accent is still the clearest badge of social class in England. Politicians know the importance of manipulating their voices. In the 1960s, the Labour politician Harold Wilson, after years as a smooth Oxford academic, became prime minister and returned to the proletarian vowels of his Yorkshire childhood. In the 1980s, Margaret Thatcher used the porcelain vowels of the elocution class. But one day, in the excitement of a rowdy House of Commons debate, the mask slipped. "The Right Hon. Gentleman," she crowed at the opposition leader, "is frightened, afraid, *frit"* — a rare and highly distinctive piece of working class dialect from her childhood in the East Midlands. The Commons erupted. Her Ladyship was unmasked as No Better Than the Rest of Us. The press ran with it for months. And long after, at a moment of advantage, the opposition in the House roared back at her, "Who's frit now?"

Beyond the church portico is a grand early-Georgian house, its pilasters crowned by Ionic (ramshorn) volutes. It was built for a lord high admiral in 1717. Later, in Victorian times, it became a music hall and brothel. London then was reckoned to have about 80,000 prostitutes in a population of some 3 million. In the middle class, strict chastity was demanded of women, and both sexes married late. Even the shapely wooden legs of pianos had to be covered for decency's sake. All this created a market, which kept many women alive between more orthodox jobs. Here in the music hall, intending couples hired a box where, at a strategic moment in the show, they ducked out of sight.

Head toward the admiral's house, and then turn left where King Street appears. Walk the length of King Street — about 150 yards — exploring perhaps the gateway and tunnel about halfway along on the left (they lead to a hidden rose garden, St. Paul's churchyard, where you can rest on the benches and have a picnic). At the end of King Street, the last building on the left, now a bank, was from the 1920s to the 1980s the British headquarters of the Communist Party. The windows were of opaque glass and said to be bulletproof. A security guard screened callers through a metal grille. Here British Intelligence, MI5, tried out the new equipment that decoded speech from the vibration of windows. The comrades got wise to this, and began to hold their most secret meetings in an inner, "windowless" room. But the room had a ventilation duct. Peter Wright (*Spycatcher*) and his friends, working from the sidewalk of King Street here, buried a microphone in the wall where the ventilation duct emerged. As *Covent Garden* became more valuable in the 1980s, the Communists saw their chance of a capital gain and sold out to the Midland Bank.

Look high on the wall of the opposite building on King Street. There's a large badge, including the three feathers of the Prince of Wales. This was the emblem of the private fire brigade and insurance company that was based here in the 18th century. Unless its firemen saw a miniature version of this badge on the wall of a house, they wouldn't put out the fire.

Cross to the old fire-insurance building (27 King St.), continue 20 yards to the end of King Street, then turn right, and after 30 yards right again into Rose Street. Here is a much-loved, centuries-old pub, the *Lamb and Flag*. The interior may seem dingy, painted in shades of brown, but it's highly acceptable in terms of Old World fashion. The ceiling of the bar has exposed wooden beams. On them is painted a medieval poem in Latin praising drink, along with the translation. The meals on the ground floor — of English cheese, pâté, and French bread — are good value. The bar is often crowded; there's more space, and hot food, on the next floor. In the street outside, John Dryden, the 17th-century poet, was beaten up, probably for offending an aristocrat.

Retrace your steps down Rose Street. Where it joins Garrick Street, turn left, then take the first right into New Row, and the first left into Bedfordbury. Fifteen yards along Bedfordbury, on the right sidewalk, is a very narrow alley — Goodwin's Court. From the street, people can barely see what's down the alley — that's why it has survived so well. Go in, and find a gem.

Goodwin's Court is a single row of tiny houses built in the late 1600s. The ground floor has small bow windows in 18th-century style. Look discreetly through a window — the last window in the row usually gives the best view — to see a tiny room, perhaps 11 feet deep. The room contains a staircase; it has to, since it is the entire width and depth of the house. These houses, now beautiful, were once part of a great chain of slums well known to Dickens. He included the district in *Bleak House,* calling it "Tom All Alone's." He wrote indignantly of governments that allowed such foul, infested places to exist. Until the 1920s, each little room here might house an entire family. The alley outside acted as a toilet. The inevitable official order to demolish was narrowly defeated by a promise of refurbishment, carried out by the Sympson family, who still own the alley. The row was allowed to survive, on condition that it never again house residents, except for that family. Instead, the houses are now used for businesses, such as public relations firms. In one of the rooms is a couch rumored to have been used by the handsome young Laurence Olivier, as his casting couch, with young actresses.

Nowhere in central London is there such authentic Dickensian flavor as in Goodwin's Court. (If most people knew of it, the place would be drowned in kitsch and "Dickensian tearooms.") Most little courtyards of hovels were demolished around 1900. They were known to the Victorians as "rookeries," the haunt of people who "rooked" (cheated). Often it was only when such alleys were knocked down that the authorities discovered exactly where all the brothels, liquor stills, and coin counterfeiting dens had been. Make a note to return to Goodwin's Court. It's a fine place to visit at night, perhaps after a visit to the theater, and then have a drink at the *Lamb and Flag.* With its 19th-century gaslights gleaming on 18th-century wood set in 17th-century brick, you may feel yourself alone at the heart of the city.

# WALK 5: LINCOLN'S INN AND THE LAW COURTS

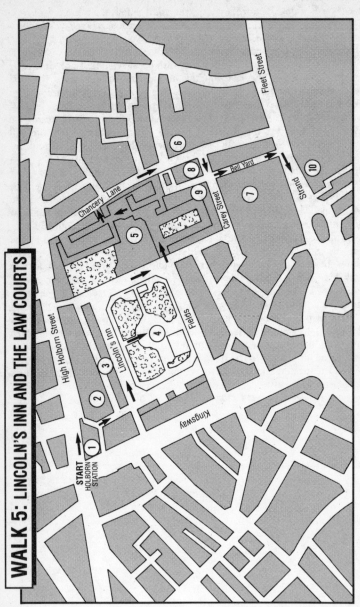

① **START** Holborn Station
② Whetstone Park
③ Soane's Museum
④ Lincoln's Inn Fields
⑤ Lincoln's Inn
⑥ Ede and Ravenscroft
⑦ Royal Courts of Justice
⑧ President of the Law Society Residence
⑨ Seven Stars Pub
⑩ The George

# Walk 5: Lincoln's Inn and the Law Courts (A Medieval Community)

This is a walk for a weekday, as both Lincoln's Inn and the Courts are closed on weekends. During the week they form an extraordinary island of calm, of historic buildings — and of antique behavior. The lawyers' ways are secretive and need interpretation. Much of the legal behavior has managed to survive so long only because the public is unaware of the strange things that go on behind the high walls of the Inns of Court.

Holborn tube has two exits, within feet of each other (at the corner of Kingsway and High Holborn Street). Start from the one in High Holborn; that's the one on the right coming up the escalator from the tube. From that exit, turn right into High Holborn; take the first alley on the right, New Turnstile; where that ends, turn left, then take the first right — where the trees of Lincoln's Inn Fields are visible in the distance. Head toward them, but pause at the first turn on the left, Whetstone Park — in reality a narrow, quiet street behind the backs of tall, old buildings. This was the scene of the sad end to an intense love affair. Samuel Pepys, a fashionable and wealthy young administrator in the Navy, drove his wife Elizabeth mad in matters of love. She was enraged upon discovering one particular affair, remembering the many offers from men she might have accepted if only she had known. Pepys's great love was his servant, Deb Willett. His wife caught them together in a compromising situation and fired the girl. Following this episode, she turned to lovemaking with her husband "more often and with more pleasure to her than in all the time of our marriage before." Jealousy was evidently doing its healing work. But Pepys wasn't finished with Deb, and Elizabeth knew it. She lay awake beside him, examining his sleeping body for signs of an illicit dream about Deb. Pepys wanted to give the unemployed Deb money, but was persuaded instead to write her a letter of renunciation, calling her a whore. He wrote in his diary, "I find that I cannot forget the girl, and vexed I know not where to look for her." Then his wife let it slip. "I away to Holborne about Whetstones Park where I understand by my wife's discourse that Deb is gone; which doth trouble me mightily, that the poor girl should be in a desperate condition forced to go thereabouts. . . ." But he did not find her. The affair did not revive.

Whetstone Park was apparently a squalid place. Lincoln's Inn Fields certainly were. Go on now to the next corner, where the Fields open in front of you. Today, the Fields have a double life. In the daytime, they are serene. Prosperous young office workers, many of them lawyers, stroll under the trees. Academics from the nearby London School of Economics have tea by the tennis courts, relieved to be away from the sweaty corridors of their cramped building nearby, its notice boards overwhelmed by appeals for Third World causes. At midday in Lincoln's Inn Fields, young female office workers play intense games of netball (akin to basketball) under the plane trees. But at night, large, scattered pieces of cardboard seem to grow legs, and converge on the wooden shelter by the netball court; the homeless are gathering for a night in cardboard city. These poor men (and a very few women) unknowingly re-create the squalor of earlier centuries in Lincoln's Inn Fields. In the 18th century, the Fields were officially called a "receptacle of every form of nastiness." Horrific executions took place here, such as those of the Catholic plotters of 1586, publicly disemboweled for seeking to replace Elizabeth with Mary Queen of Scots.

Before crossing the Fields — we suggest doing so in full daylight — turn left on the sidewalk and go along 100 yards to No. 13, the house with statues in its façade. This was the home, from 1812, of John Soane, an architect, a learned magpie who filled his house with antiquities and fine art. It is open Tuesdays through Saturdays; go in and look for *The Rake's Progress,* the series of paintings by the 18th-century moralist William Hogarth. They show the career of a young aristocrat, from mercenary marriage through gambling to debtors' prison. (For more information, see *Marvelous Museums* in DIVERSIONS.)

Leaving *Sir John Soane's Museum,* cross the road to enter the park, Lincoln's Inn Fields, by the path 20 yards beyond Soane's door. Ten yards along the path that leads to the center of the Fields, notice the 10-foot-high iron brackets. These were new in the 18th century, and contained oil lamps. A poet of the day urged travelers not to enter these Fields at night, for fear of "the lurking thief." Instead, they should keep to the strip around the square where, as the poet put it, there were "oily rays, shot from the crystal lamp." (Today, the park is a haven to the homeless, who have built all manner of temporary shelters.) On reaching the netball courts and the wooden shelter, turn left, taking the path that leads from the Fields in the direction of a long wall. It's the wall of Lincoln's Inn. On reaching the road that runs between the Fields and Lincoln's Inn wall, turn right and head for the gatehouse of the Inn, about 80 yards away and across the road. Go through the gateway and into the grounds of the Inn.

The gatehouse, a Victorian building from which strangers trying to enter are challenged on weekends, is the first sign that you are entering a closed, old-fashioned community. The judges and barristers (attorneys) who work here are in love with the past. Perhaps only here in Britain can one sometimes spot a top hat worn informally. Nineteenth-century gaslights burn at night.

The barristers stroll across the courtyards wearing 18th-century wigs, and at the neck, bands — two strips of white linen as a necktie. Why this picturesque conservatism? Partly because barristers receive no regular salary; especially in the early years of a career, family money is almost essential to get by. So barristers tend to come from wealthy, conservative families. Also, age makes traditionalists of most of us, and the law is controlled by unusually aged people. Only recently were judges obliged to retire at all, and even now the age of retirement for many of them is 75. English case law depends heavily on precedent. This encourages a reverence for tradition in non-legal matters, too. (Historians often mutter that lawyers in Britain are people who have never learned to criticize their sources.)

Lincoln's Inn is one of four Inns of Court. (Two others, Middle Temple and Inner Temple, are visited on *Walk 8.*) The name "Inns" probably comes from the medieval origins of these places. When the roads were bad, lawyers normally stayed overnight at inns near the courts. A community of professionals grew up and made formal rules. At first, there was much wildness to be ruled out, among younger lawyers. Go from the gatehouse straight ahead for 50 yards, then turn into the road that opens on the left and walk for 30 yards. In the distance, ahead, is a lawn — once overgrown and alive with rabbits. It's still known by its medieval name, the "Coney Garth" (Rabbit Garden). Medieval lawyers were forbidden to shoot the rabbits with bow and arrow. Events here during the 1400s caused the lawyers to pass a rule forbidding fornication in the rabbit garden by humans.

Look left to the tallest building in sight. It's early Victorian, but is built in the style of ca. 1600. Notice the very tall chimney pots built in different styles, some of them twisting. This was a late-Elizabethan fashion. The building is the dining hall of the Inn. To qualify as barristers, young people must eat at their Inn a specified number of times; they may fly from New Zealand or West Africa to do so. "Eating dinners" is an attempt to keep the Inn alive as a medieval community, though senior lawyers normally go home in the evening to their spouses. There is often cheerful uproar in the hall, as the trainee barristers hold a medieval moot — a mock trial of certain points of law.

Ahead, slightly to the right, is a small brick hut, Victorian again, with pointed, Gothic door and leaded windows. This was the workplace and den of the ostler, the man who looked after the horses that used to clatter into the Inn, pulling the carriages of grandees. Notice the chimney above the little hut; the ostler had his coal fire, though Victorian servants were usually given fireplaces much smaller than their masters'. Beyond the ostler's hut and facing the Coney Garden on the right are the white Stone Buildings, from the 18th century. Especially fine is the painted sundial high on the wall facing the lawn. It bears the initials of William Pitt the Younger, prime minister during the wars against Napoleon and nominally an official of the Inn. It's interesting to explore the pleasant courtyard behind the Stone Buildings; to do so, turn right at the ostler's hut and then take the first left. Otherwise, come back now to the road that leads from the gatehouse, to see some older parts of the Inn.

Once at the road in from the gatehouse, with the gatehouse itself on the right, look left to the low red brick building with battlements and tall, church-like windows. This is the Old Dining Hall, built in 1489, early in the reign of Henry VII, the first Tudor monarch and father of Henry VIII. Around 1800 this building was used to try cases — disputes about property which could last for many years, to the great profit of the lawyers. For Dickens, the court here was the symbolic heart of the legal miasma. (His attitude toward lawyers was one of informed hatred; he had worked as a legal clerk and his father had twice been in prison for debt.) He opens *Bleak House,* his great attack on English law, with the following:

> "London. Michaelmas Term lately over. . . . Implacable November weather. . . . Fog everywhere. Fog up the river. . . . Fog down the river. . . . And hard by Temple Bar, in Lincoln's Inn Hall, at the very heart of the fog, sits the Lord High Chancellor in his High Court of Chancery. . . ."

Here, in the novel, a dispute over a will — Jarndyce vs. Jarndyce — goes on for so long that eventually it involves lawyers not yet born when the case started. People connected with the case cluster around the court, living distorted lives of false hope in the pokey lanes behind Lincoln's Inn. Meanwhile, streets of houses, those whose ownership is disputed in the case, go to ruin, while the lawyers agreeably stroll in and out of the court here, securing their incomes. At last the legal men come streaming out, radiantly happy to have witnessed a historic moment: the ending of Jarndyce against Jarndyce. The case has not been settled. Instead, it has "reached its threshold." In other words, the entire estate has been used up in paying lawyers' fees. Dickens was scarcely exaggerating; he derived his story from an actual case.

Immediately to the left of the Old Hall is a tunnel. Go through it into the delightful little courtyard beyond, called Old Buildings. Look to the corner, and a sharp right, for a multifaceted tower of brick with a winding staircase. Immediately to the left are stone piers supporting a chapel — originally built in the early 1600s. The poet John Donne worked here; it's suggested that he had this chapel's bell in mind when he wrote: "Send not to know for whom the bell tolls, it tolls for thee."

The intense and closed little community here might certainly have inspired Donne's point about the interconnection of human lives. The piers of the chapel are the originals; set into flagstones by the central pier is the gravestone of John Thurlow, spymaster to Oliver Cromwell in the 1650s. Often rows of rickety desks are piled under the chapel — presumably for the writing of exam papers by student barristers. The main chapel building is modern; the original was wrecked by a bomb from a zeppelin in World War I.

On the side of this courtyard opposite the Old Hall is a fine gatehouse, originally 16th-century but mostly rebuilt in the style of a Cambridge college. Its great door stretches from the ground to the top of a 16-foot archway; within the woodwork of the door is set a smaller door, next to the lodge, for evening use. The little door ensured that people entering in darkness went in single file where the porter could see them. This arrangement made it harder to smuggle women in.

From the gatehouse, go around to the corner with the multifaceted tower. Painted at the entrance to the staircases are the names of barristers who practice here (look at No. 22). These, in the jargon, are their "chambers."

Members of chambers don't share incomes; each barrister is always a free-lancer. They have to get along socially, however, since being accepted into chambers is essential for a barrister to practice, and social considerations are very important. Women, and men from state schools (composing about 98% of the population), form a minority among barristers. What barristers strive for are the accents, manners, and sense of humor of the most famous private boarding schools ("schools" in Britain means high schools; they, rather than top universities, give the socially desired qualities). Also at the entrance to every set of chambers is the name of the barrister's clerk (pronounced *clark*), often painted in a different lettering — no doubt to reflect a social difference. Clerks are the barrister's agents, setting prices, distributing work among them, and mediating between the barristers and the solicitors, from whom the barristers' work comes. Clerks are not grand, often of blue-collar background, and many have no legal training. Yet traditionally they get 10% of their barristers' gross fees. If a clerk is lucky enough to have a top barrister (a Q.C., Queen's Counsel), earning half a million a year in the chambers, the clerk automatically gets £50,000. On top of that there will probably be at least 10 other barristers to tithe, each earning on average about £40,000. Clerks, therefore, commonly earn more than the average barrister, certainly far more than the young ones. In the evening the clerk shuffles to his Jaguar, while the penniless young barrister puts newspaper in his leaky shoes and strides proudly toward the tube. Visitors sometimes ask, "In that case, why not become a clerk rather than a barrister?" The answer is that here, as elsewhere in the world, status is more important than income. Become a clerk after such expensive schooling? A mother would never forgive such an action.

Go back 40 yards to the 16th-century gatehouse, then pass through it. Turn right onto Chancery Lane. Here Dickens once stepped out happily to buy a nursing chair after the birth of his first child. He went hand in hand with his wife's sister, Mary Hogarth, with whom he was also in love. (Mary's death shortly afterward is evoked tearfully in *The Old Curiosity Shop;* she was Little Nell. As Dickens put it, "When I think of Little Nell, poor Mary died yesterday.")

In Chancery Lane, pass two alleys on the right, to reach the shop of *Ede and Ravenscroft,* suppliers of finery to the lawyers and the aristocracy. Politicians who move (sometimes against their will) to the House of Lords can get their baronial robes here. Barristers' and judges' wigs are usually displayed in the window — now a distinctive badge of role, but originally simply the mark of a stylish (and politically correct) gentlemen. The wigs are made from horsehair and are designed, above all, never to look new. That would suggest inexperience. Ideally one inherits one's father's wig, or buys one secondhand. The wearing of these wigs goes back to the civil wars of the mid-1600s. Puritans, perhaps as a symbol of honesty and simplicity, wore their hair famously short; they were the Roundheads, "prick-eared Puritans." Royalists, in contrast, had long locks for display. When the royalist side eventually triumphed, in 1660, hair sprouted to show allegiance. Courtiers went to extraordinary lengths with their wigs. The long wigs are now known as "full-bottomed," and are worn only in ceremonies by judges and by Q.C.s. Short wigs, on the 18th-century model, are the rule in court.

Pass *Ede and Ravenscroft* and turn in to the first road on the right, Carey Street. "To be in Carey Street" is British slang for being bankrupt. The huge red-and-white Victorian building on the left, the Royal Courts of Justice (usually simply the "Law Courts"), houses the bankruptcy courts. The grand litigants, in the glare of television lighting, sweep in and out by the front entrance in the Strand. Bankrupted individuals creep out here at the back, on Carey Street. On that street, the first opening on the right is Star Yard. In the days before pubs had toilets, it was normal for customers to relieve themselves in a nearby alley. The pub on Carey Street is called the *Seven Stars;* presumably that's how this alley got its name. This use of alleys created what the Victorians called, in their code, a "nuisance." So they put a stylish cast-iron urinal in the yard, a rarity in Britain. You can see it from the corner here.

On the corner of Star Yard and Carey Street is a magnificent townhouse with wooden shutters outside its windows. Go to its front door to see the great fanlight above. This is the official residence of the President of the Law Society — the organization that represents solicitors. Unlike barristers, solicitors come from all ranks of society; they outnumber barristers by about ten to one. They are the workhorses of the legal industry, dealing directly with clients. Also unlike barristers, solicitors earn a regular salary. But they don't wear wigs, and normally they are prevented from pleading in the higher courts. So in the public eye solicitors don't have the glamour of barristers. Since judges are nearly always drawn from the ranks of barristers rather than solicitors, and barristers themselves are not recruited democratically from society, a constitutional problem arises: Almost all judges are drawn from an oligarchy of wealth. In the late 1980s, the Thatcher administration took some steps to try to begin opening the courts and the judiciary to solicitors.

Go past the president's house. Twenty yards farther on there's an opening on the right, overhung by a fine gas lamp in an ornamented bracket. This entry to *Lincoln's Inn* is flanked by *Wildy's* legal bookshop, a civilized business that has been here since Georgian times. Go for a moment into the alley under the lamp to see copies of ancient cartoons, satirizing the law, for sale. They are very popular, especially in American legal offices. Among British lawyers, self-criticism is less common.

Back in Carey Street, turn right and walk 50 yards to the *Seven Stars* pub. It has a glittering, Victorian interior, while the brickwork of the building is claimed to be late Elizabethan. Many informal legal deals have surely been struck here, just a few yards from the courts. Cross the road now for a view of a nicely painted metal plaque, high on the wall of the pub. This is a fire mark, which proved that the building was insured with a local, private fire brigade before 1833. Fire marks are now treasured as proving the great age of a building. The plaque here shows clasped hands, the badge of the Amicable Contributors Company.

You are now on the sidewalk next to the Law Courts. Almost exactly opposite the sign of the pub, look up on the wall of the courts here to see the Victorian sculptures, which show animals in aggressive confrontation. This was a joke by the architect about the business of the courts, suggesting that the litigants inside fight like cats and dogs. To reach the main entrance to the Law Courts, go back along Carey Street until level with Star Yard, then turn right into Bell Yard. Walk the length of Bell Yard until it hits a main road, Fleet Street–The Strand. Turn right into the Strand; 100 yards along on the right is the grand entrance to the courts. Through the entrance is a soaring, Gothic hall (its function is mainly ornamental, to create awe in this cathedral of justice), the stained glass of its windows shows not biblical scenes but the coats of arms of bygone legal grandees.

Go to the center of the hall, where a wooden cabinet carries lists of cases in progress. If interested, it's possible to sit in on a case. Which courtroom should you choose? Look right for a moment, to the staircase marked "1–10 (up)." This leads to a corridor where appeal cases are heard. Appeals often turn on the interpretation of dusty precedent; even in criminal cases the convicted people often aren't present behind the iron bars that mark their place in court. Here it is common to see a barrister, instructed to appeal against the odds by some dogged litigant, struggling in the face of unsympathetic judges.

More lively cases usually can be found by turning left from the wooden cabinet and going up the staircase marked "11–19 (up)." At the top of the stairs, look immediately left and right for courts 13–15. A group of people in the dark corridor often marks an interesting case. Here, in the late 1980s, the jury in a libel case found that the novelist Jeffrey Archer, although he had paid £2,000 to a prostitute, had never had any improper relationship with her, or even met her. The judge showed a close legal interest in the dignified and ashen Mrs. Archer: "Is she not fragrant?" he asked the jury. In another recent libel case here, an actress sued a gossip columnist for stating that the actress was miscast as a groupie in a TV play because she was too old and had too large a bottom. The actress, when she went into the witness box, wore a dress most carefully chosen. The case was declared a mistrial. But the actress came at it again; clearly, more was involved than money or professional pride. (She won, but less, it was said, than was needed to cover her legal costs.)

Don't be put off by the fact that these courtrooms have no signs advertising a public gallery. The back two benches in each courtroom are for the public. The legal people on the benches immediately in front, with large files, are solicitors and solicitors' clerks. In front of them sit the barristers in wigs and gowns. The solicitors usually can't address the court, but may know the case intimately after days or weeks of work. On the other hand, it's traditional for barristers to learn their brief only the night before. So you can often see the solicitors getting rather frustrated at being unable to control, as they would like, the presentation of the case. They lean forward to whisper to the barristers, who sometimes ignore them. Agitated solicitors can occasionally be seen tugging at the barristers' robes. In the aisle beside the benches, there is a small wooden gate. Any barrister who sits below this is a Q.C.; note that his or her gown is of silk (Q.C.s, as a result, are often known simply as "silks"). The other barristers, on the nearer side of the gate, are called "juniors," no matter what their age. Notice that on the junior barristers' gown, behind the shoulder blade, is a single flap. This once was a pocket. In the days when barristers were technically forbidden to receive a fee from their clients, the pocket was used for the clients to slip golden coins into, supposedly without the barrister's knowledge. To leave the courts, go down almost any one of the stone staircases from the corridor, re-enter the grand hall, and pass once more through the main doors to the Strand. Across the road is the *George,* a pub that serves good lunches. For equally good lunches in a more legal atmosphere, go down the alley beside the *George* to the *Devereux* pub.

# Walk 6: Hampstead

Hampstead is an extremely pretty suburb, where many of its residents will eagerly assure you, "It's really a village, you know." Open countryside is now many miles away, but the former village still has its little streets from the early 18th century, twisting to exploit every corner of land that could be developed. Next to Hampstead is Hampstead Heath, one of the glories of London. Nearly 800 acres of public park, with hills, valleys, and lakes, much of the Heath looks like informal countryside, but it also contains the site of Kenwood, one of the finest of all Georgian mansions. The Heath is surprisingly uncrowded even on public holidays, and is good to visit on almost any day. Bear in mind that there's a long walk across the open Heath to the mansion.

Among literate people, Hampstead has swung violently into fashion and then out of it. During the Middle Ages the place was an obscure settlement, on a hilltop that few wished to climb. In the 1690s, however, spa water was produced from a spring here, and fashionable Londoners gathered to take the waters. However, within 20 years the gentry had largely abandoned Hampstead, appalled by the vulgar people who had followed them here. Hotels had sprung up specializing in "unexpected marriages lasting one night." Some of the women involved were described as loose characters in vamped-up clothes, here to catch the city apprentices. Other spas flourished at Hampstead's expense, such as Bath, far enough from London to be inaccessible to the poor of the big city. By the late 19th century, Hampstead was a prosperous dormitory for the upper middle class, with a Bohemian reputation. And so it remains. The British media present an image of Hampstead as the haunt of gentle and wealthy socialists with a taste for secondhand bookshops. (George Orwell worked in one nearby, when he was far from wealthy.) But the chief impression on the ground today is one of defensive and somewhat assertive money. For every genial old radical, there are dozens of executive spouses paying inflated prices in the local shops and complaining about their *au pairs.* Hampstead is best enjoyed now as a showpiece rather than as a pleasant social setting. But the tenacity of the moneyed folks has saved the area from the arterial roads and slabs of rectangular building that would have broken up the village if it had been situated almost anywhere else.

From the exit of Hampstead tube station, go to the corner a few yards away. There, standing with your back to the tube station, take the second exit working clockwise onto Heath Street. Walk 100 yards along Heath Street, then turn right into Church Row. Here is a magnificent parade of tall, flat-fronted, Georgian houses, mostly built in the mid-18th century, when the village of Hampstead was connected to London by two stagecoaches a day.

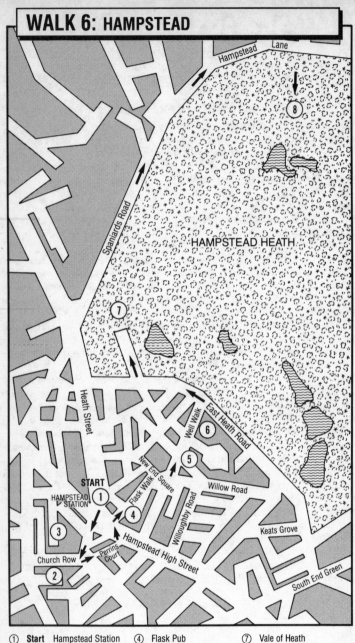

# WALK 6: HAMPSTEAD

HAMPSTEAD HEATH

Hampstead Lane

Spaniards Road

Heath Street

Well Walk

New End Square

East Heath Road

Willoughby Road

Willow Road

Keats Grove

Flask Walk

Perrins Court

Hampstead High Street

Church Row

South End Green

**START**

HAMPSTEAD STATION

① **Start** Hampstead Station
② H.G. Wells's Home
③ St. John's

④ Flask Pub
⑤ Marie Stopes's Home
⑥ Wells Tavern

⑦ Vale of Heath
⑧ Kenwood

Go to the sidewalk on the far side of Church Row. Above the house doors of Nos. 27 through 24, notice the different designs of fanlight in the glass. These are from a time when most streets had no public lighting. On a dark night, the distinctive pattern formed by the light above its door was helpful in identifying a house. Numbers 24 through 22 have iron brackets at their doors that held oil lamps when the houses were new. Look up at the wandering 18th-century drainpipes outside some of the houses. At the top, some of the drain heads have decorative moldings. H. G. Wells, one of Hampstead's literary leftists, lived at No. 17 Church Row in the early 20th century. Wells was intrigued by the progress of science, which he hoped would eventually liberate the poor. He dreaded a chasm opening between rich and poor, as the recession of the 1930s threatened. In his novel *The Time Machine,* Wells imagined the human race divided into virtually two species. Privileged, leisured, human butterflies were aboveground; under the earth, in tunnels, lived pale, enfeebled, resentful creatures called "Morlocks." Wells's inspiration for this vision was almost surely found in London. The human butterflies are still here; visit the restaurants and pubs of upper Heath Street, the other side of the tube station, on a fine summer evening. (For the Morlocks, try a winter afternoon on a Sunday in nearby Camden Town.)

Go downhill to the far end of Church Row. There's an elaborate wrought-iron gate leading into the churchyard of St. John's (a church built in the mid-1740s). Go in through the gateway. The place has kept its character as an English country churchyard. Notice the evergreen yew trees just inside the gates. Yews had been seen as vital to the security of medieval England. Longbows made from their wood were remembered as the crucial weapon that had defeated the French armored cavalry at Agincourt (1415). Archery practice was long compulsory in English villages. The berry of the yew, however, is poisonous to cattle, so the tradition, reflected here, was that yew trees were grown in churchyards, where farm animals did not penetrate.

Face the front of the church and then walk to the left-hand corner of its front. From here, two paths lead down through the bushes. Take the one on the left, which starts about 5 yards from the church wall. Where the path reaches its lowest point, forking left and right, look a couple of feet to the left to see the family tomb of John Constable (who died in 1837). Perhaps the best loved of British painters, Constable specialized in romantic landscapes. People in Constable's pictures tend to be few, picturesque, and distant. Buildings are also scarce; Constable's is a world "where every prospect pleases, and only man is vile." Typical of work by Constable is his dramatic painting of Hadleigh Castle, a ruin shown under a thundery sky. The dark clouds, like the ruin itself, hint at the thought — agreeable to romantics — that the works of man will come to naught. Constable and his customers were reacting against the Industrial Revolution, and the squalor of the towns. Also, he was part of a movement away from the vast, flattering portraits of aristocratic individuals that the artist Thomas Gainsborough and others had done in the 18th century. (There'll be some pre-Constable portraits of fashionable beauties to see later in the walk at Kenwood House.)

Also on the tomb are details of Constable's eldest son. He — unlike his father — had an expensive university education at Cambridge. The effect on a family of one extraordinarily talented individual is clearer on another tombstone in the churchyard. Go to the right from Constable's tomb and, where the churchyard path turns uphill to the right again, take the left-hand fork. Where it reaches the church and turns right, look 10 feet away to the right to the tomb of John Harrison. The inscriptions on English tombs are usually frustratingly brief, but here we have a much longer and more interesting one. John Harrison, we are told, was the "inventor of the timekeeper for ascertaining the longitude at sea." During the Industrial Revolution, it was common for large prizes to be offered for inventors. The inscription here tells of the long struggle Harrison had to convince the relevant authorities that his invention qualified for the £20,000 prize. This was an enormous sum; common soldiers in the 18th century were earning less than £20 a year. The inscription suggests that John Harrison had no great education, and taught himself to build clocks as a young man. His son was a socially grander figure. It's recorded here that he became Lord Lieutenant of Monmouthshire, a post normally reserved for aristocrats and gentry. The father's brains had elevated the son.

Follow the path back to the gate by which you entered the churchyard. On leaving the gate, turn left and 10 yards away, across the road, look at the tomb with an urn on top. The inscription says that here is buried Hugh Gaitskell, leader of the Labour Party, who died in 1963. Gaitskell was from the right of his party, and fought to keep his more socialist colleagues from renouncing Britain's use of nuclear weapons. His chief opponent on the left, Harold Wilson (like Gaitskell, a Hampstead resident), spoke out against the nuclear bomb — but kept it once he became prime minister. Gaitskell's death was untimely, from an extremely rare disease (lupus disseminata). He died shortly after a visit to Russia, and Peter Wright in *Spycatcher* records the suspicions in MI5 that Gaitskell had been poisoned by the KGB, to make way for a more acceptable Labour leader.

Turn right from Gaitskell's grave, to go back up Church Row, keeping to the left-hand sidewalk this time. Outside Nos. 9 and 8 look at the pleasant, homely scale of the 18th-century metalwork. Six feet up, an oil lamp is on the horizontal bar where the lamplighter once rested his ladder each night. Continue, slightly uphill, until Church Row ends. Cross the main road here, then turn right onto its sidewalk and turn into Perrins Court, the second entry on the left. Walk the 100 yards to the far end of this pedestrian alley and turn left into Hampstead High Street. Cross the High Street and turn into the third entry on the right, which is Flask Walk. This is the area where the fashionable growth of Hampstead began 300 years ago — from its spa. Little Georgian cottages and shops are crammed in here. A few yards along the left is one of the secondhand bookshops for which Hampstead is well known. And a little farther on the right is the sign of the *Flask* pub, deservedly a favorite of Hampstead's slightly Bohemian middle class. Notice the long vertical lines of antique floral tiles at the front of the pub. The sign shows a soldier from the 1820s, the age of King George IV, filling a powder flask. This suggests that the origin of the pub's name had to do with the need for one to have a loaded gun when crossing the Heath at the time, to deal with highwaymen. But a likelier derivation of the name is from the flasks of spa water sold here, expensively, during the early 18th century. (Recent research into the water from the spring has suggested it never contained anything more unusual than iron.)

The pub is served by Young's brewery, revered by English connoisseurs of beer. This is "real ale" — served flat (not fizzy), at room temperature, with its yeast still alive. (The normal beer, despised by fashionable folk, comes fizzy, pasteurized, and cold from the metal keg; it's served by turning a tap.) Most British people judge whether "ale" is "real" by watching if it is drawn by use of the long vertical hand pump at the bar, with a handle of wood or china. If you go into the *Flask*, look at the bar for the china handles here. Such is the moral ascendancy of real ale that some brewers have taken to disguising the metal taps with which they dispense the unfashionable keg beer; they attach dummy hand pumps to an electric switch. Such pumps, however, are held still when used; identify the genuine article, here, by the way the bartender's arm has to jerk the pump back and forth while serving. During the 1970s, there was an extraordinary consumer revolt against keg beer and in favor of real ale. It became fashionable to use venomous wit against the "big bad brewers" who marketed the bland keg beer. As a result, several national brews went out of existence. In an attempt to market the weak and unfashionable brew called "Double Diamond," its brewers launched an advertising campaign pushing "DD." The real ale campaign promptly retaliated by renaming the beer 'K9P." It never recovered. In contrast, Young's beer at the *Flask* comes in reassuringly old-fashioned wooden casks. In much of London, Young's deliver their beer on horse-drawn wagons.

Continue along Flask Walk, on the sidewalk to the left. Here are former artisans' cottages, now immaculate and approaching half a million pounds in value. The fashion here is to have front gardens densely grown with flowers. To have flowers spaced out at regular intervals is lower middle class or worse; the gentry prefers a decorous tangle.

Beyond the *Flask* pub, 150 yards on the left, is the façade of a former Victorian bathhouse. Above the door is a fine gable in a Dutch style, with a large inscription on the front that reads "Baths and Washhouses 1888." This delightful building, with its red brick, is no longer used for bathing; there is hardly anyone in the area now poor enough to need a public washhouse. When the building was new, in late-Victorian times, its facilities were divided into first and second class. Complaints soon arose from the first class bathers; their baths were being invaded by second class bathers and beetles. One might wonder which they thought were worse.

Two red phone booths — of the type found everywhere in Britain until the 1980s — survive outside the bathhouse. During the 1980s the state-owned telephone system was sold to a private company, British Telecom. The new company cleared away the traditional, iron red booths and, in an expensive attempt to create a corporate image, replaced them with booths of Perspex and yellow paint. But, in Hampstead, where residents combine a firm aesthetic sense with political clout, some old booths blissfully remain.

A few yards farther, Flask Walk ends. On the left is the street called New End Square, but look right to Willow Road. Don't go down it, but the street has a story to tell. Willow Road leads quickly to Willoughby Road. Here, surely, George Orwell got the inspiration for the monstrous Hampstead landlady and her house, described in *Keep the Aspidistra Flying*. In the novel, she lives in "Willowbed Road." The hero of the novel, her tenant, Gordon Comstock, worked in a secondhand bookshop nearby, as did Orwell himself. (Directions to the real-life original in a moment.) Comstock's landlady believes in rules — above all, no making of tea in the bedrooms. Illicit tea-making, consequently, becomes the tenants' fascination. Letters, when they come for tenants, are handed over grudgingly. After all, the landlady feels, they are addressed to *her* house and so in a sense belong to her.

All this is highly realistic. The Hampstead landlady is a formidable breed. During the 1970s, long after Orwell's time, a Hampstead boardinghouse became notorious. It was a dismal Victorian mansion, run by an old (and extremely lucid) lady who owned several such houses and lived in the basement. A low-voltage light bulb glimmered dismally in the main hall. The gas meters were rigged to profit the management. One honorable thief used to make a living off them by breaking into tenants' rooms. He would leave their valuables untouched, but empty the meters of their coins. Mice fought in the wastepaper baskets at night, and were bold enough to still be there in the morning. To defeat the law, which gave security to tenants, the old lady arranged for eggs to be served every morning, so that technically the place could be called a hotel, and tenants could be put out at will. Each tenant was known by his or her number. So for each there was a stark choice every morning as they entered the egg-reeking cellar: "Fried or boiled, number six?" Tenants found the eggy odor clinging to their clothes at work, so one tenant had special clothes just for breakfast: his Hampstead egg suit.

Go straight ahead into Well Walk, which is the continuation of Flask Walk. Forty yards beyond the end of Flask Walk (on the right, at No. 14 Well Walk) was the home of Marie Stopes. The building is marked with a plaque. Stopes is well remembered today as a campaigner, in the early 20th century, for the sexual education of women; her mission was to teach working class women about birth control. To many, Marie Stopes was an utterly scandalous woman. The fact that she was highly educated and dedicated to her cause may have further incensed the traditionalists, making her harder to despise. Perhaps to show her contempt for traditional attitudes, she had herself publicly photographed semi-nude. Today, one of the most respected of women's clinics in central London bears her name.

Continue along Well Walk to the next junction; on the right is the sign of the *Wells Tavern*. Outside there is an advertisement for traditional pub games, including dominoes and shove halfpenny. Forty yards farther along Well Walk (on the right, at No. 40) is the former home of the painter Constable. From here, it is said, he would go to set up his easel on Hampstead Heath. Ten yards farther, on the left, is a towering Victorian villa, home of socialist leader Henry Hyndman and his wife, Eleanor Marx — Karl Marx's daughter. In spite of an impoverished childhood spent in disease-ridden Soho, while her father attended to his writing, Eleanor became enough of a linguist to produce a translation, which is still famous, of Flaubert's novel *Madame Bovary*. She wrote under financial pressure, while her husband created grave problems. Outside the house is an intricate former drinking fountain bearing the crest of the aristocratic family who gave land to the poor here in 1698. Thirty yards beyond the fountain, on the right, is a late-Victorian house built on the site of the old Hampstead pump room, the heart of the former spa.

Continue along Well Walk for about 100 yards to East Heath Road, which skirts the heath. Before crossing this road, a word about two of the literary shrines to the right. The home of the romantic poet John Keats, and of his beloved Fanny Brawne, is in Keats Grove (the third right turn off East Heath Road). The house is open to visitors daily except Sundays. Half a mile to the right along East Heath Road is South End Green; at the far right-hand corner stands a small shop bearing in its wall a very small bust of the author George Orwell. Orwell himself worked here in the 1930s and, as mentioned above, the place helped to inspire his novel *Keep the Aspidistra Flying*.

But our walk now heads across Hampstead Heath toward the mansion at Kenwood.

For simplicity of navigation, go via the little settlement called the Vale of Heath, where D. H. Lawrence lived during World War I. To reach this, turn left into East Heath Road to Well Road on the left. Here look out to the right for a path that heads across the Heath. Take this path, and after passing through the little lakeside colony of houses, which is the Vale of Heath, continue in approximately the same line up the steep hill ahead where a footpath leads to the main Spaniards Road. Turn right on reaching Spaniards Road, which becomes Hampstead Lane; follow it around the edge of the Heath for about half a mile to the main entrance to Kenwood on the right. More scenic, and more fun to explore (though hardly possible to describe closely in words) is the route by various footpaths across the Heath itself.

Hampstead Heath, the haunt at all times of a few lovers and on summer nights (it's rumored) of would-be witches, is better known for family picnics. During the 19th century, it was plagued by young horsemen letting rip; the technical term for this at the time was "furious riding."

Kenwood House was designed in part by Robert Adam in the 1760s. Its artistically ambitious owner at the time was the Earl of Mansfield, who was lord chief justice of George II, and is remembered today by lawyers for his role in obstructing slavery. In 1780 rioters, protesting against the government's (and Mansfield's) reluctance to persecute Catholics, came to burn Kenwood, but were diverted by the attractions of the Spaniards Inn nearby. Even visiting one room in Kenwood is worth the trip. Be sure to see the library, decorated in Italianate style. In 1925 Kenwood was bought by Lord Iveagh, head of the Guinness brewing family of Ireland. He installed a magnificent collection of paintings, specializing in those of the late 18th century when the building was new. On his death, Lord Iveagh left the building and its art collection to the public. The house is open every day of the year except *Christmas* and *Good Friday*. The paintings include Rembrandt's *Portrait of the Artist* and Vermeer's *The Guitar Player*. See also the vast portraits of fashionable late-Georgian dames, including that by Romney of Emma Hamilton, the statuesque mistress of Admiral Lord Nelson.

The gardens of Kenwood contain much famous artificial landscaping. A great lawn slopes to a lake; a bridge crossing the lake proves (on close inspection) to have only two dimensions. On summer evenings orchestras play by the lake's edge, exploiting the acoustics of the water, which carry the music to the audience sitting on the opposite side of the lake.

Kenwood is a long way from a tube station. To rejoin the tube system without a long walk, go to the main entrance of Kenwood, on Hampstead Lane, and locate the nearest bus stop on each side of the road. Wait for a No. 210 bus, going in either direction. (This means having to be ready to cross the road quickly and carefully if you see a bus coming from the other direction.) If the bus is going back in the direction of Hampstead, ask for Golders Green tube. If it is going the other way, ask for Archway tube.

# Walk 7: Whitechapel and Spitalfields (The Old Ghetto and Jack the Ripper's Haunts)

All the other walks in this section go through handsome and historic areas, sought after for residence or business. They can, however, give a false impression of London. Since a walk through a typical London district might lack sufficient color and history, here, to balance the expensive antique districts, is a walk through picturesque and historic grime. This is an area that may soon pass away; wealthy colonizers from the nearby financial district nibble steadily at its edges. You may be among the last to see old Whitechapel and Spitalfields in a form that Jack the Ripper would easily have recognized.

Best times to walk: in daylight any day for the architecture and at twilight for the atmosphere. Sunday mornings are the time for a packed and touristy street market in *Petticoat Lane* (officially Middlesex Street).

A special note: Since the walk directs you down several crumbling and quiet streets, some reassurance about safety is in order. Safety for the walker is normally taken for granted in public by Londoners, except in a very few areas that are far away from any of our routes. The predominant social group in this district now is Bengali; to other Londoners, Bengalis give the impression of being slightly built, retiring people. The local people are well used to visitors here. Whitechapel and Spitalfields are very much in the eye of the media as they slowly change their character.

This area has for centuries been settled largely by immigrants. Until the 1960s, London's main ports of entry were nearby. (Nowadays the former Docklands are being transformed into areas of expensive housing — for yuppies, say the locals. The vast container ships dock far downriver at Tilbury.) During the 18th century, Huguenots came to the area, seeking refuge from religious persecution in France. Many of them made their livings from silk weaving; traces of this craft survive along Huguenot streets in this area. Early

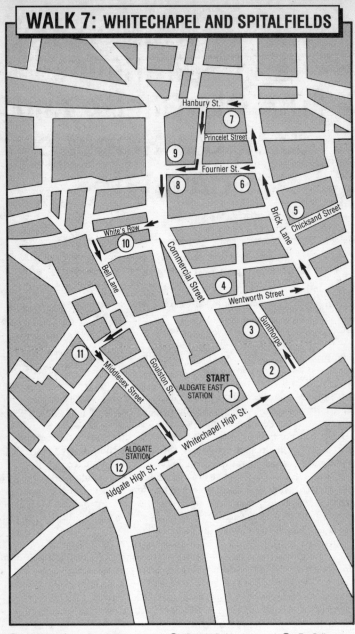

# WALK 7: WHITECHAPEL AND SPITALFIELDS

Hanbury St.

⑦

Princelet Street

⑨

Fournier St.

⑧

⑥

⑤ Chicksand Street

Brick Lane

White's Row

⑩

Commercial Street

Bell Lane

④

Wentworth Street

③ Gunthorpe

⑪

Middlesex Street

Goulston St.

② 

**START**
ALDGATE EAST
STATION ①

Whitechapel High St.

ALDGATE
STATION

⑫

Aldgate High St.

① **START** Aldgate East Station
② Whitechapel Art Gallery
③ Toynbee Hall
④ The 4% Industrial Dwellings Company
⑤ Punjabi Restaurant
⑥ Mosque
⑦ Huguenot Housing
⑧ Christchurch Spitalfields
⑨ Ten Bells
⑩ Miller's Court
⑪ Petticoat Lane
⑫ Aldgate Station

in the 19th century Irish people came, driven into exile by a famine for which British government policy concerning grain was partly responsible. In the late 19th century, Jewish refugees arrived from Poland and western Russia, where they had become a target of official persecution. There are striking signs of Jewish history along the route. Many Jewish people still come to the area to do business, but few live here now. Like other immigrant groups with growing prosperity, they have moved away. The streets of Whitechapel and Spitalfields are still remembered by most Jewish families of London as the places where their great-grandparents arrived owning nothing. In the 1970s, the Bengalis came, from a land horribly fought over as Pakistan tried in vain to prevent the emergence of an independent Bangladesh. By the 1970s there was no great passenger dock nearby to direct immigrants here. Bengalis came to the district because it had some of the least expensive — which also meant poorest — housing in Britain.

From Aldgate East tube station there are two exits, at opposite ends of the platform. If possible, leave by the one marked High Street East/Whitechapel Art Gallery. If that exit is shut, leave by the exit marked High Street/Leman Street, and turn left into Whitechapel High Street. Then, from this second-choice exit, walk 50 yards and cross the horrible main road, Commercial Street, which comes in from the left. Continue along Whitechapel High Street until you come to the first-choice tube exit on the left — beside the White-chapel Library.

Right beside the tube exit is a plaque, recording that Isaac Rosenberg (1890–1918) studied in the building here. He was training as a painter, but is now perhaps better remembered as one of the greatest of the soldier-poets of the First World War (in which he died). This is from his *Break of Day in the Trenches:*

> *Only a live thing leaps my hand —*
> *A queer, sardonic rat —*
> *As I pull the parapet's poppy*
> *To stick behind my ear.*
> *Droll rat, they would shoot you if they knew*
> *Your cosmopolitan sympathies.*
> *Now you have touched this English hand*
> *You will do the same to a German . . .*

Turn your back to the tube exit, then go 20 yards to the right until reaching the *Kentucky Fried Chicken* shop. Behind this bland, modern member of the multi-national chain there is an old den of local subversion hidden. Turn right into tiny Angel Alley, its name crudely painted at the entrance. Thirty yards along the alley, on the left, is *Freedom Books,* a dark, Victorian building which has long been the chief meeting place and bookstore of anarchists in Britain. In the days of Jewish immigration from Eastern Europe, anar-chism — not communism — was the secular faith of many of the poor in this district. Russia was the home of anarchist theory; the Russian aristocrats Bakunin and Kropotkin were its chief thinkers. Shortly after 1900, there was a thriving anarchist club for working men near here; it was this east London tradition (now almost dead) that caused the anarchist headquarters to be sited here. For most of the second half of the 20th century, the organizer of these premises has been Vernon Richards, formerly a good friend of George Orwell. (Orwell's own sympathy with anarchism comes out strongly in his *Homage to Catalonia.*)

Come out of Angel Alley, turn right into Whitechapel High Street, and just before *Bloom's* kosher restaurant, turn right under an arch into the alley called Gunthorpe Street. Once in Gunthorpe Street, the noise of the traffic fades. Sixty yards along on the left is a classic pre–World War I school building for children under 11. Such places are familiar to Britons, but visitors seldom see them, especially in central London, which is largely a child-free zone. The school building is 5 stories high; the height of these schools was deliberately emphasized by tall gables, bell towers, and (inside) by high ceilings. Former pupils, when grown up, often return to marvel at the grandeur in which their early education took place. But as children they were more likely intimidated by the large scale of a school that reached so high into the sky. The ambitious program of Victorian school-building was a reaction to political alarm; it was reported in the late 19th century that competing industrial nations (notably Germany) were running ahead of Britain in their schooling. There is a similar alarm in Britain today, but this time no ambitious program of educational investment is in sight.

Walk 50 yards farther along Gunthorpe Street. Ten yards before the street ends, the back of a modern red brick building appears on the left. This is Toynbee Hall, a charity that has been working in the area since 1884. Charity, here, has long been connected with murder. The deprivation and violence of the district were two reasons Victorian and Edwardian charity workers came here. In August of 1888, the corpse of Martha Turner (or Tabram) was found on a site close to here. This, unfortunately, was not a notable event. Turner's death — her body was covered with stab wounds — is remembered now because she just may have been the first victim of Jack the Ripper, though the ripping that linked the later victims wasn't done to her. As the Ripper's murders, in the autumn of 1888, caused an international sensation, further charities crowded to the area. The playwright George Bernard Shaw rather callously called Jack the Ripper "a social reformer before his time."

On the right in Gunthorpe Street, opposite Toynbee Hall, is the crumbling wall of a building once owned by the local Board of Works — a Victorian department of local government, whose job included the maintenance of roads. Part of the board's name, inscribed proudly above the windows, is still readable. Near the name, wild plants grow in the brickwork. The seemingly mid-Victorian building, in this obscure place, has survived, as rare antiques often do, through neglect. On the wall of the same building, about 5 feet from the ground and 7 yards from the end of the street, is — in faded paint — a large white letter "S." Again, this is now something that can be seen hardly anywhere else in Britain. The lettering is white on black, the reverse of the usual, because this "S" was designed to be read in the blackout, the nighttime curfew of World War II, which was meant to frustrate enemy bombers. "S" stood for air-raid shelter; the word "shelter" is written underneath. East London was particularly hard hit by the Blitz. In the aftermath of a raid, one fireman famously called for all the available equipment, shouting, "The whole bloody world's on fire." East London made an attractive target since it could easily be found on moonlit nights by pilots flying along the line of the river Thames. The strategically important docks were nearby. This densely populated area was the Jewish district; also, this side of London was closest to the German bombers as they approached. The pilots, surrounded by anti-aircraft fire, were anxious to drop their bombs as quickly as possible and head for home. Buildings of Toynbee Hall here, for example, were badly hit.

Where Gunthorpe Street ends, turn left for a moment into Wentworth Street. Walk 20 yards and cross the street. Here a large gateway survives from a recently demolished building. Above the gateway is inscribed the name of the company that created the building — the 4% Industrial Dwellings Company (1886). This was caring capitalism: The company attempted to solve (profitably) the housing problems of the area by building decent apartments that the poor could afford. Come back along Wentworth Street and, after about 100 yards, take the second turn on the left onto Brick Lane.

Brick Lane is now seen by Londoners as the center of this fluid, colorful district, also the heart of the Bengali community. Notice, 50 yards along Brick Lane on the left, the doctors' office with a sign above the door in English and Bengali. Continue for 70 yards along Brick Lane. On the right, at the corner of Chicksand Street, is a Punjabi restaurant, now popular among young Bohemian middle class Londoners. The curries here are fiery, satisfying, and very inexpensive. Most of the clientele are themselves from the same culture as the food, always a good sign in an ethnic restaurant. Opposite the restaurant is a small, approachable-looking police post, an unusual feature in Britain, where police stations normally are large, forbidding buildings. This was put here in response to pressure from Bengali residents, against whom there have been many racist attacks. When groups of visitors come to the area in the evening, they sometimes find a police car cruising to a halt beside them. "What are you people doing?" "Oh, looking for Jack the Ripper." "All right then!" grins the policeman, and off he goes.

On the left of Brick Lane, 50 yards beyond the police post, is the junction with Fournier Street. Here, on the corner, is a famous (but not prosperous-looking) building from the 18th century — a treasure for people with an interest in social history. Go 10 yards into Fournier Street, on the left-hand sidewalk, and look up at the building. Below the roof is a sundial with the building's date: 1743. When first built, this was L'Eglise Neuve, the Huguenots' new church. Then, as the children of the Huguenots became assimilated and ceased to be a distinct community, the building was turned into a chapel. In the late 19th century it became a synagogue. Now it's a mosque for the Bengalis. The building, in other words, is a social barometer of the area.

On the sundial, above its arm (the gnomon), is a Latin phrase, appropriate for the religious context: *umbra sumus* (shadow is what we are). Below the upper windows is a cream-painted horizontal band. Until the late 1970s, when a fresh coat of paint was put on, you could make out the ghosts of Hebrew letters (from the building's previous occupants) through the paint here .

Come back into Brick Lane, turn left, and walk 30 yards to the door of this religious building. Look in — discreetly — and you may see the removed sandals of the Muslim worshipers. On the opposite side of Brick Lane, and in the neighboring streets, there are shops and workshops of the clothing trade: the "rag trade," as it's known in Britain. The clothing trade is traditionally one for immigrant people; the necessary machinery is inexpensive, small, and quiet enough to be contained in a home. The work is labor-intensive, and labor is one thing that the poor immigrant can offer in abundance. Also, in the clothing trade there is no great economy of scale; so the little workshop can compete with the big factory. This means that the immigrants can employ their own people, and are not at the mercy of the alien large employer. Before the Bengalis, it was Jewish people who dominated the local clothing trade. This has preserved one of the very few Yiddish words to have entered the English language in Britain: If a man in London wears a striking new jacket or coat, he's quite likely to be cheerfully confronted by a friend who seizes his lapel, feels the cloth, and exclaims — in what's meant to be an imitation of the accent of a Yiddish speaker — "Nice piece of *schmutter* (cloth) you've got there, my boy." It was from this little area that the expression reached the rest of London.

Continue along Brick Lane, then take the second turn on the left, which is Hanbury Street. On the right is a modern brewery. But on the left are 18th-century houses built for Huguenots. It is said that the windows of these were made especially large, to let in light for silk weaving. Stop for a moment at 30 Hanbury Street, on the left. Roughly opposite here, in a passageway beside the former No. 29 (on the site now covered by the brewery), the body of Jack the Ripper's second known victim, Annie Chapman, was found. She, like the preceding victim, had been widowed and was dismally poor. Turned away from an inexpensive lodging house because she didn't have the 2 pence required, she seemingly tried to raise the money in the common way. The job was usually done quickly, and the sense of intrusion minimized; the women were skilled, apparently, at using their legs. The regular fee was sixpence. Until the 1960s a very old man in this area entertained others with the tale of how, as a child laborer, he had made himself late for work by viewing Annie Chapman's warm corpse.

Walk another 50 yards along Hanbury Street, then turn left into Wilkes Street. Here elegance is being taken over by dereliction. Compare the doorways of Nos. 13 and 19 on the right. Above them are battered fanlights and decayed, intricate woodcarvings. These mark the great prosperity that was here in the mid-18th century. Some houses of this type nearby have simply collapsed from neglect. Some now contain clothing workshops. Others have been taken over and restored by speculative middle class people, attracted by the ghosts of Georgian splendor and the nearness of the business quarter. To walk to work in the financial district is a rare luxury; it's normal for the commuter to travel for well over an hour in a series of packed trains. For restored houses, look here at Nos. 17 and 25. But the gentrification of an area is a long and nerve-wracking process for newcomers. Will enough like-minded people follow? Or will the newcomer be left with a magnificently restored house, standing out in a crumbling street like a sound tooth in a geriatric jaw? What often happens is that the area does "come up," but painfully slowly. Meanwhile the newcomer has become intolerably sensitized to the negative side of the district and leaves, before the investment bears full fruit.

Continue along Wilkes Street. On the left, Princelet Street has some faded 18th-century splendors worth exploring. Walk the full length of Wilkes Street, and turn right where it ends, into Fournier Street. You're now alongside a church of the 1720s, Christchurch Spitalfields. Designed by Nicholas Hawksmoor, a pupil of Christopher Wren, its mighty scale — and presumably the expense of employing this top architect — suggests how wealthy the area once was. But there are few Anglicans (Episcopalians) in the district now. The church's main role at present is to give shelter to derelict people, for whom there's a refuge in the crypt. On the right-hand side of Fournier Street, where it meets the busy Commercial Street, is a pub from the Ripper's day, the *Ten Bells*. For much of its life it has been known as the "Jack the Ripper"; in the late 1980s local feminists protested to the brewery that owns it, and the place reverted to its former name. The "Ripper" sign is still here, inside over the bar. It shows the famous gaslight and fog, the atmospheric setting that helps to explain why the Ripper killings became so famous in the first place. The elusive figure of Jack is portrayed as a gentleman in a fine coat and top hat. The theory that the killer was a gentleman, or an aristocrat, is long-established. As one old lady in the area said recently, "My mother always used to say, 'Royalty done it.'" If the pub is open, go in, and while having a drink, look at the Victorian tiles inside. They show a scene of the Huguenot weavers selling their silk.

On leaving the pub, walk in front of the church, on the left-hand sidewalk of Commercial Street. The park on the left has supported various life-forms. Long ago a survey of the poorest people in the park uncovered body lice; as a result, the place became known as Itchy Park. Fifty yards beyond the park use the pedestrian crossing, then double back a few yards along Commercial Street, and turn left into White's Row. Eighty yards along White's Row on the left is a well-repaired Huguenot house with weavers' windows. Stop a moment. The opposite sidewalk runs alongside a multi-story car park. This stands on the site of Dorset Street, an infamous Victorian slum, off which there was an alley named Miller's Court. In Miller's Court lived, until November 1888, a young Irish widow named Mary Kelly, who owed her landlord some 35 shillings in rent. To get that sum in the familiar way would involve dealing with about 70 customers. She picked up a man described as a gentleman in appearance, wearing a coat with an astrakhan collar. Next morning the police found her, in several parts of her room. This was the last of the killings attributed to Jack the Ripper: the only one, seemingly, where he had the luxury of carving up his victim in private. His other women were dealt with in streets and alleys. The police, desperate for a lead, photographed Kelly's eyes in the hope of detecting there an image of the killer. (The idea is not wholly ridiculous; modern experimenters on the eyes of dead rabbits have claimed to reconstruct from them the outline of the last thing seen by the animal.)

Within 2 months of the death of Mary Kelly, an obscure young barrister named Montague Druitt killed himself by loading his pockets with stones and jumping into the Thames. The killings ceased. A senior figure from Scotland Yard later wrote that Druitt was, after his death, the police's chief suspect, though it was never made clear why. If the killer was indeed a gentleman, it would help explain why he was able to gain the confidence of his victims, and perhaps also why he could afford the privacy to wash himself near here. The natural suspects for the killing, the poorest and roughest men of the area, would have found it very difficult to find a place to clean themselves and their clothes of the copious amounts of blood.

In 1970, an elderly physician named Thomas Stowell published the suggestion that the killer had been Prince Albert Victor — Queen Victoria's grandson who, had he lived, would have become king in 1910. Stowell claimed as his source the private memoirs of Sir William Gull, Victoria's physician, though exactly what the memoirs said has never been made clear. Stowell is now dead and Gull's papers have disappeared. Even the Scotland Yard file on the case now contains little. The urge to protect the royal family is extremely powerful in Britain. (It was only recently revealed, for example, that Albert Victor's brother, King George V, refused sanctuary to the Czar of Russia, when the Bolsheviks offered to release the imperial family after the Revolution.)

Continue along White's Row to the first left, Tenter Ground, and take the first left again onto Brune Street. Here, 40 yards along on the left, is a rare and colorful institution from the post-Ripper era. The building bears the inscription "Soup Kitchen for the Jewish Poor." The date of the building is recorded on its front, 1902 in Christian terms, 5662 in Judaic years. It seems that the charity was set up by wealthy Jews, who feared the effect of a particular Christian charity that aimed at converting the poor Jews of the area. The Christians were offering substantial inducements for converts. (In fact they got few; for Jews to abandon religion was commonplace, but to convert to Christianity was to put themselves outside the Jewish community.) Nowadays, with the great immigration 100 years in the past, few local Jewish people, if any, qualify for the charity. But help is still given to the poor in this building. Inside, the walls are stained at shoulder level where people in dirty clothes have leaned while waiting for their handouts of bread and baked beans. Today, the charity is open to non-Jews as well. Retrace your steps along Brune Street, then turn at the first left onto Bell Lane. Stop at the first crossroads; directly ahead, the continuation of Bell Lane is Goulston Street. It's aptly named; a public washbasin that once stood a few yards along the street on the left was found running with blood a few minutes after a Ripper killing nearby. Turn right at the crossroads into Wentworth Street, now the site of a thriving street market. There are many shops and stalls still owned by the Jewish families who once populated this area. A "pitch" (a place for selling) here is highly valued and is usually passed down through families. Take the first left onto *Petticoat Lane,* a great Sunday-morning street market (especially for clothes). The official name, Middlesex Street, may derive from the Victorians, to whom "Petticoat Lane" sounded as rude as "Bra-and-Undies Avenue" would to us. Continue along *Petticoat Lane* to the third right, which is Aldgate High Street; 100 yards along to the right, in Aldgate High Street, is the Aldgate tube.

# Walk 8: Fleet Street and the Temple

STARTING POINT: THE JUNCTION
OF THE STRAND AND FLEET STREET

Thoughtful Londoners are intensely proud of this area where 4 centuries of colorful, modest buildings can be found squeezed along busy Fleet Street, and where traffic is all but defeated by crowds of pedestrians. Although alive with history, there's only one really popular, overcrowded spot along all of Fleet Street (a fine pub called *Ye Olde Cheshire Cheese*). Almost all the orthodox beauties of the area are hidden in the dozens of courtyards and alleyways that branch from Fleet Street. The mood of this district changes with the time of day. Come at lunchtime or early evening (4 to 7 PM) on a weekday and the place is filled with lawyers. Home to many members of London's legal community, Fleet Street grows quiet on weekends; traffic is far lighter as the lawyers' courtyards are almost deserted. The neighborhood wasn't always a legal center. In fact, until the late 1980s Fleet Street was the home of the British newspaper industry. All the big newspapers have now moved away, scattering to a sterile collection of high-tech buildings in desolate and inexpensive parts of London, but the journalists still come back here, hankering for the sidewalks where they knew people, the cool antique pubs, and the distant view of St. Paul's Cathedral.

To reach the starting point of the walk — the sidewalk at the western end of Fleet Street by Temple Bar — take any red bus heading east from Trafalgar Square that goes along the Strand and bears the word "Bank" (i.e., Bank of England) on its front. Go to the upper deck of the bus, for the view and for ease of navigation. On its three-quarter-mile journey along the Strand the bus passes two churches, each in the middle of the road. Immediately after the second church, St. Clement Danes, get off the bus and, walking in the same direction as the bus was traveling, stay on the left-hand sidewalk until you reach a large statue of a dragon in the middle of the road. This is Temple Bar.

Temple Bar marks the beginning of the ancient City of London, as defined by the Romans and slightly extended in medieval times. "Temple," because the medieval Knights Templars had their English headquarters nearby, as we'll see; "Bar," because until Victoria's time various fortifications, real or symbolic, barred the entrance to the city of London at this point. If traffic allows, go right up to the dragon, although its base hardly accommodates pedestrians. On the base, notice the miniature sculptures, about a foot high. Those on the far side show Queen Victoria passing this spot in splendor at

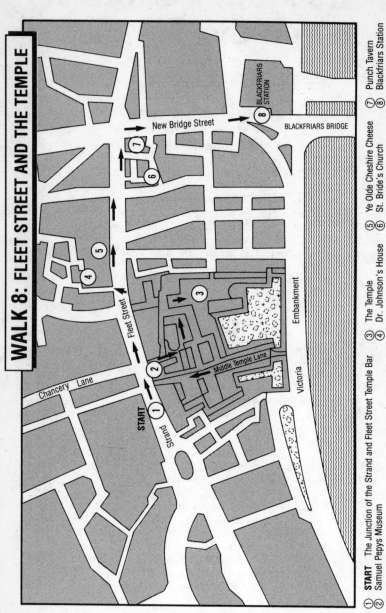

# WALK 8: FLEET STREET AND THE TEMPLE

Chancery Lane

Strand

START

Fleet Street

Middle Temple Lane

Victoria

Embankment

New Bridge Street

BLACKFRIARS STATION

BLACKFRIARS BRIDGE

① START  The Junction of the Strand and Fleet Street Temple Bar
② Samuel Pepys Museum
③ The Temple
④ Dr. Johnson's House
⑤ Ye Olde Cheshire Cheese
⑥ St. Bride's Church
⑦ Punch Tavern
⑧ Blackfriars Station

the start of her reign, in 1837. The Lord Mayor of London rides to greet her, offering his sword. On the east side of the base — the side that looks into the City — there is a model of the old Temple Bar as it appeared until Dickens's day (he called it a "leaden-headed old obstruction").

Until the mid-18th century, the heads of executed politicians and rebels were displayed at Temple Bar, just out of reach of trophy hunters. Traders here rented out telescopes for a ghoulish close-up. Modern ghouls sometimes look up here at the great clock, which towers 100 feet above the spot on the wall of the late Victorian Royal Courts of Justice. A few years ago a man attending to the clock got his tie caught in the mechanism and was pulled to his death.

Now for a rare link with the London of Shakespeare. Most of the city he knew was destroyed in the fire of 1666, but the deadly east wind dropped just before the flames reached here. From Temple Bar cross the street and walk 70 yards into the City until Chancery Lane comes in from the left. You are now on Fleet Street. Look at the black-and-white (half-timbered) house that overhangs Fleet Street on the right. It dates from 1610, some 6 years before Shakespeare's death. On a weekday afternoon, when it's open, there's a delightful museum on the first floor of this building. The museum is a single wood-paneled room, filled with mementos of the racy diarist Samuel Pepys. Pepys never lived here, but must have known the building well. In 1665, when Pepys lived nearby, the building was a pub that sold quack remedies for the Great Plague.

Directly underneath the Shakespearean house is an archway, with the date 1748 in its keystone. On weekends the arch is blocked by a large wooden gate. This is where Londoners and most visitors stop, unsure whether the public is allowed any farther (it is). Go under the archway, opening the gate if it's in place. Once inside, enter the world of the lawyers — the Temple.

The Knights Templars, who lived here until the early 1300s, were monks who trained to fight for the Holy Land. They also acted as bankers who could be trusted with people's gold (and they knew how to fight in its defense). The monks' secretive ways created suspicions. The scheming King Philippe IV of France, followed by the feeble Edward II of England, exploited public doubts, abolished the Templar order, and seized its wealth. For the sake of appearances, the authorities accused the Templars of sexual deviation and worshiping the devil in the form of a black cat. Soon after the Templars moved out, lawyers moved in. Since the Middle Ages, the Temple has been the site of two legally separate Inns of Court (for more information, see *Walk 5*). Passing around the Temple, notice the many versions of two badges. One, showing a lamb (the symbol of Christ) and a crusader flag, marks the property of the Middle Temple. The other badge, showing Pegasus the winged horse, belongs to the Inner Temple. The sign bearing Pegasus is thought to derive from the seal of the Templar order, which showed a horse bearing two men: a Knight Templar in the Holy Land and a pilgrim whom he was rescuing.

The lawyers who control the Inns are barristers, advocates, and judges, and they cluster in "chambers." Walk down the passage from the gateway, called Inner Temple Lane, and the first doorway on the right is No. 1. It bears the names of the judges and barristers who work here, among them Mr. John

Mortimer, a successful defense attorney specializing in cases affecting freedom of speech. Mortimer also writes novels and plays about his profession. He is the creator of the eccentric and honorable barrister Horace Rumpole, "Rumpole of the Bailey." In one novel Rumpole finds himself on a luxury vacation in the Florida sunshine — "poolside," as he self-consciously puts it. But he finds it impossible to relax. He dreams instead of setting off from his chambers here, of walking down Fleet Street in the rain to defend some seedy criminal at the Old Bailey, and of the moment when there comes to him the glimmer of a defense that may thwart the overwhelming prosecution case.

Immediately outside Mortimer's door is the first of many gaslights. Notice the small blue cylinder inside the glass, which contains a clock. Until the mid-1980s there were no modern accoutrements in these Victorian lamps; in fact, each one was lit by hand. The lamplighter who hurried from one lamp to another with a long copper-topped pole was perhaps the last such professional in Europe. He was a bearded, gaunt character, with a face like a Byzantine mosaic of Christ.

Ten yards beyond Mortimer's door, turn left for a moment. Forty-five yards along the path (which turns to the left) is an 18th-century statue of a judge reclining above a tomb. He wears the long, "full-bottomed" wig, knee breeches, and bands at the neck. After viewing this, return to Inner Temple Lane. Turn left for 20 yards to look at the elaborate Norman doorway of the Temple church. The doorway is a rarity for having a rounded arch in the Norman style; in the later Middle Ages this fashion was overwhelmingly replaced by the pointed Gothic arch. Open the iron gateway below the stoic canopy to get a close look at the doorway. The church is often open, but not at this door. Go 20 yards farther around the church to try the modern door. If you go inside, look on the floor at the medieval effigies in stone of aristocrats who patronized the order. From outside look up to see the rounded outline of the main body of the church. It was built in this shape in the 1180s in imitation of the round Church of the Holy Sepulcher in Jerusalem. Notice that the stone in the upper courses of the building is of a different color than that below; the higher stones were replaced after bombing in World War II.

From a position facing the modern door of the church, turn right and walk the length of the courtyard. Go through the short tunnel where the courtyard ends. As you emerge from the tunnel, ahead and to the right is a glorious run of tall buildings dating from the 1670s, the age of Charles II, to the mid-1700s. The row stretches for perhaps 200 yards and heads downhill to the Thames. It is known as King's Bench Walk; the King's (or Queen's) Bench was, and is, a set of courts nearby. At No. 9 King's Bench Walk were, in 1888, the chambers shared by one Montague Druitt, for long the chief suspect in the Jack the Ripper murders. (For more on these, see *Walk 7.*) The area of the killings was within walking distance of here, and it was suspected at the time that the killer must have had a private room nearby, to wash off the blood from his clothes.

Above the steps that lead up to several of the doorways of King's Bench Walk are metal arches; at the center of each metal arch is a square bracket, which held an oil lamp in the 18th century. Upon emerging from the tunnel that leads from the Temple Church, turn right and walk 30 yards slightly downhill to see the early-19th-century Paper Buildings. An earlier version of the buildings was burnt down when a drunken judge took out his chamber pot from under a bed, used it, and then in his confusion put a lighted candle back in its place (or so barristers here will tell you). Go almost to the door marked No. 1 (Paper Buildings), where there is a white Pegasus on a blue background. Then turn right and pass, on the left, the Temple Gardens with their intricate wrought-iron gates of 1730. Look through the gates or over the railings of the garden, and if it's summer, the garden will be filled with red and white roses. These commemorate the 15th-century Wars of the Roses, fought by royalist factions and triumphantly ended by Henry VII — the father of Henry VIII. The red rose stood for the House of Lancaster, to which he belonged; the white rose symbolized the rival House of York. Shakespeare in *Henry VI* imagined the start of the war occurring in this garden. To prevent deaths on the battlefield from the medieval equivalent of "friendly fire," before going to war soldiers commonly picked plants to put in their clothing for identification. In this garden, in Shakespeare's imagination, the factions of Lancaster and York picked roses.

Walk on, with the garden on the left, and go through an arch into Middle Temple Lane. Turn right, uphill, for 40 yards and then go left into the first opening, a courtyard with tall trees. Here is the Dining Hall of the Middle Temple, refurbished outside but having an interior dating from the 1560s and 1570s. In this Elizabethan building entertainment was provided for the riotous young lawyers who ate here. In 1602 a barrister of this Inn wrote in his diary: "February 2nd. At our feast we had a play called *Twelfth Night* or *What You Will*. Much like the *Comedy of Errors* . . ." In all probability Shakespeare himself took part in the production in this hall. All the famous theaters of the Elizabethan age have long gone, including the *Globe,* making the Middle Temple Hall a rare treasure.

This courtyard of the Middle Temple is a good place to observe some of the subtle snobberies of the English law. Large numbers of barristers cross the courtyard each day on their way to and from the Royal Courts of Justice in the Strand. Nearly all of them are involved in civil law; the criminal lawyers go instead to the Old Bailey. Barristers at the criminal law are seen by many lawyers as a coarser breed — their successes come from impressing juries of mere laypeople. The finer minds, it's claimed, prefer the civil law, where judges rather than juries need to be persuaded. There is also more money to be made at civil law. The barristers of the Temple, unlike those of Lincoln's Inn, are forbidden to wear wigs and gowns when walking through their Inns to the courts. How to spot barristers here? Experienced observers can usually tell them by the length of their stride, reflecting the barristers' feeling that they own the place. Look also at the necks of the besuited characters crossing this courtyard: Those with two long flaps of linen in place of a necktie are barristers. Look also for the large shoulder bags with initials embroidered, which barristers carry here. These are known as "wig bags" and again reflect an informal hierarchy. Ordinary barristers have a wig bag of blue material. Those barristers reckoned to have shown rare qualities while acting as juniors to eminent Queen's Counsel (the leading advocates), are presented by their Q.C.s with red wig bags. Red bags are cherished and flaunted. Most barristers, it should be understood, spent their formative years at traditional boarding schools for boys, where the pupils wore numerous badges of rank on their jackets. A metal badge, half an inch square, carried on the lapel denoted a prefect, a boy of 17 or so with the power effectively to arrest, to imprison for half an hour, and sometimes to beat younger boys. Not even the rarest distinctions of adult life can match the intimate power of the school prefect. Such intensity is never forgotten, and ex–boarding school boys re-create hierarchies wherever they can.

Back to Middle Temple Lane. If it's a weekday, turn left and go uphill for 100 yards to the gateway on to Fleet Street. If it's a weekend when the gateway is closed, retrace the roundabout route past the gardens and along Mortimer's Alley. By either route, when reaching Fleet Street again, turn right and go some 200 yards along the street and downhill, crossing to the opposite sidewalk. Look for Hind Court, an alley on the left with signposts to Dr. Johnson's house. Follow these by twists and turns for 100 yards or so into Gough Square. Johnson's house is a Georgian building of delightful faded brick. The structure has buckled over the centuries and large metal discs are in the wall, attached to rods (wall ties) binding the house together. The building is open as a museum. Open May through September, daily from 11 AM to 5:30 AM; October through April, Mondays through Saturdays from 11 AM to 5 PM. In this well-placed backwater of Fleet Street, Johnson wrote his dictionary, with its famous fighting definitions. For example, he defined oats as a form of grain eaten in England by horses and in Scotland by people. In the 18th century many Englishmen found Scots oppressively well educated compared to themselves. One definition in his dictionary that returned to haunt Johnson concerned the word "pension," which at the time meant a retainer paid by the government to useful or deserving people. Johnson wrote that a pension was "generally understood to mean pay given to a state hireling for treason to his country."

Shortly after writing this, Johnson was himself offered a pension by George III's government. Should he refuse the money, or take it and be impaled on his own epigram? He took it. As a loyal pensioner he helped the government (before the American Revolution) by writing a pamphlet entitled *Taxation No Tyranny.*

On leaving Johnson's house go back via Hind Court to Fleet Street. Turn left into Fleet Street, then, 10 yards along the street, go left into another little alley, Wine Office Court. A few yards up this alley on the right is *Ye Olde Cheshire Cheese* pub. The decor inside is stark enough to impose its character in spite of the crowds of visitors and locals. There are dark wooden panels on the walls, and exposed beams in the ceilings. In the 1890s, the Rymers' Club met in its upper room. Its most famous member was the Irish poet W. B. Yeats, who was not only a dreamy-eyed romantic but also a driving organizer. He later mentioned his "Companions of the Cheshire Cheese" in a famous poem. Yeats was inspired, negatively, by this gray and crowded part of London. He said that he was inspired here to write his idyllic poem about the remote west of Ireland, *The Lake Isle of Innisfree:*

*I will arise and go now, and go to Innisfree,*
*And a small cabin build there, of clay and wattles made . . .*

Yeats recorded that he had this delicious vision of quiet water after seeing an artificial fountain playing in a shop window near here in the Strand. He and friends seriously toyed with the idea of founding an ideal community on Innisfree. Part of Yeats's purpose, it seems, was to lure and detain there his unresponsive love, the actress Maud Gonne.

On leaving *Ye Olde Cheshire Cheese* go back into Fleet Street, turn left, and walk downhill for 100 yards before crossing to the opposite sidewalk. There turn right into St. Bride's Avenue. The church, which is seen from the sidewalk of Fleet Street, is famous for its lovely spire, designed by Christopher Wren, and its tiers that rise like a wedding cake. The story goes that William Rich, a local baker in the 18th century, had the wonderful gimmick of producing wedding cakes in the shape of St. Bride's spire. The fashion spread to the United States. Go into the church and, immediately inside its door, go down the steps on the right to the museum in the crypt. On display is a party dress that belonged to Rich's wife. Also in the crypt, at the opposite, dusty end of the corridor from the dress, is a grisly exhibit, the lid of an iron coffin discovered in the churchyard and originally designed for special security. It dates from the early 19th century, a time when it was illegal to anatomize any corpse except those of executed prisoners. The legal system of the time supplied a fairly generous number of the latter, but not enough to satisfy the anatomists, whose research was making important progress. There was a market, therefore, for fresh corpses supplied to the medical men with no questions asked. Those who dug up and sold the newly dead were known dryly as "resurrectionists." Dickens has one in *A Tale of Two Cities:* Jerry Cruncher, he calls him — with a wicked choice of initials for a resurrectionist. To defeat these gentlemen on their moonlit visits to the churchyard, fortified iron coffins were sold. Next to the coffin lid here is displayed a copy of a contemporary advertisement: "Safety for the Dead!" it screams alluringly.

To end, there is a fine journalists' pub. Go back down St. Bride's Avenue into Fleet Street, turn right, and go a few yards to the *Punch Tavern*. Whether or not you mean to have a drink, go into the lobby of the pub to see its antique mirrors and tiles. Inside are served exotic forms of real ale (see *Walk 6*), trucked for great distances and served by a hand pump. In 1989, when drunkenness from lager was a favorite scandal of the press, some journalists were overheard planning a story here: "It's got everything," one journalist gloated, "sex, royalty, and lager." "Shh," said a more sober colleague, "pubs have ears!" He was right.

Coming out of the *Punch,* turn right into Fleet Street and head for the massive road junction a few yards ahead. Turn right and walk about 300 yards along the main New Bridge Street to the Blackfriars tube station.

# INDEX

# Index

# BIRNBAUM TRAVEL GUIDES

Order by phone, toll-free: 1-800-331-3761

Name_____ Phone_____

Address_____

City_____State_____Zip_____

*Discover the Birnbaum Difference*
*More Details and Discounts Than Any Other Travel Guide*

Get the best advice on what to see and do and where to stay while benefiting from money-saving information from America's foremost Birnbaum Travel Guides.

## Country Guides—$17.00 Each

☐ Canada                ☐ Great Britain              ☐ Portugal
☐ Caribbean             ☐ Hawaii                     ☐ South America
☐ Eastern Europe        ☐ Ireland                    ☐ Spain
☐ Europe                ☐ Italy                      ☐ United States
☐ France                ☐ Mexico                     ☐ Western Europe

## *New* Warm Weather Destination Guides 1992—$10.00 Each

☐ Acapulco              ☐ Bermuda                    ☐ Ixtapa &
☐ Bahamas               ☐ Cancun/Cozumel/Isla            Zihuatanejo
  (including Turks         Mujeres (including Playa
  & Caicos)               Del Carmen

## *New* City Guides 1992—$10.00 Each

☐ Barcelona             ☐ London                     ☐ Paris
☐ Boston                ☐ Los Angeles                ☐ Rome
☐ Chicago               ☐ Miami                      ☐ San Francisco
☐ Florence              ☐ New York                   ☐ Venice

## Business Guides 1992—$17.00 Each

☐ Europe 1992 for the Business Traveler
☐ USA 1992 for the Business Traveler

| | |
|---|---|
| Total for Birnbaum Travel Guides | $ |
| For PA delivery, please include sales tax | |
| Add $4.00 for first Book S&H, $1.00 each additional book | |
| Total | $ |

☐ Check or Money order enclosed. Plase make payable to HarperCollins Publishers.
☐ Charge my credit card  ☐ American Express  ☐ Visa  ☐ Mastercard

Card no.                                                    Exp. date
_____

Signature
_____

Send orders to:
HarperCollins Publishers, P.O. Box 588, Dunmore, PA 18512-0588